What's in a Name?

WHAT'S IN A NAME?

...Everything You Wanted to Know

By Leonard R. N. Ashley

Genealogical Publishing Co., Inc.

For
MARGARET

She might be Pearl since she comes from the Greek word for that jewel. She has been a lady of sanctity in one aspect and of regal status in another and of assorted roles in secular and family life in the home. In the garden she has named a flower, Marguerite, the ox-eye daisy. She has been the patron and protecting saint of women in child-birth. Also the name has been a prolific parent of alternatives. . . . I prefer Margaret in its proper length and pleasant quality. Good friends have justified the liking. Why forget the pearly origin?

—Ivor Brown, "Margaret," *A Charm of Names*

. . . sous la consideration des noms,
je m'en voys faire icy une galimaufree
de diverse articles . . . .

—Montaigne, *Essais*

READ THIS FIRST

his is a book that answers the perennial question, "What's in a name?" It also addresses many specific questions. Where do names come from? Why do some carry positive or negative connotations or go in and out of fashion? Which have been the most popular from generation to generation? What are the most common American or Italian surnames? The most striking or amusing? What's in a nickname? And what about the names of places and pets and products and all other sorts of names?

I have put in a quarter century of study and published widely in the field of onomastics, that branch of linguistics that deals with the nature of proper names. I have been twice president of the American Name Society, been president of the American Society of Geolinguistics, and held other offices in scholarly organizations connected with linguistics. I have delivered papers at some 100 professional meetings and conferences, nationally and internationally, and I have listened to many more. I believe I can safely claim to speak with authority about names. My purpose in writing *What's in a Name?* is to distill the knowledge gained from my longstanding interest into a practical, compact and yet chock-full book that will, I hope, entertain as well as inform. Above all, while not ignoring the complexities of the subject, I want to bring to the general reader the delights to be enjoyed from a keener understanding of where names come from, how we use them, and how they affect us all.

What's in a Name?, then, is meant for the ordinary reader, for anyone who has a name or knows someone who has, for everyone who has ever thought about his or her own names or those of others, or of the impact of the names of places, of names in advertizing, of names in literature, of names in all their applications. This book deals not only with the forenames and surnames of persons but also with town names and street names, the names of dogs and detergents, the names in fiction (and real names stranger than fiction), even the occult relationship some people see between names and numerology. At the end of the book I discuss fundamental principles and pitfalls in the most important naming the average person ever has to do: the naming of babies, which is a crucial matter for the lucky or hapless child involved.

In preparing this survey I have borrowed freely from a vast number of specialized scholars. I cannot overwhelm the text with footnotes in order to recognize so many individually. I do mention some scholars in the text when I am convinced that interested readers can and will be able to consult their works, which is all the bibliography a book of this sort requires, in my opinion. Of course I realize that some scholars who have contributed a great deal to the field will be sorry their names do not appear. I want in particular to name just a few colleagues who will stand for many. I am especially indebted to Margaret M. Bryant, professor *emerita* of Brooklyn College and the Graduate School of the City University of New York; she introduced me to the study of names, as she has so many others. Moreover, through her, I have had the pleasure of knowing personally such scholars as Allen Walker Read (D. Litt., Oxon.) and other distinguished academics such as W. F. H. Nicolaisen and Kelsie B. Harder, such government experts as Donald J. Orth and Roger L. Payne, and more. Wayne H. Finke and other members of the American Name Society have been of unfailing assistance: Virgil J. Vogel helped me with Amerindian names, Alan Rayburn with Canadian names, and so on.

To them and to all the others who have tilled this sometimes esoteric field, which is at the same time of great interest to the general public and has been the subject of thousands of studies both specialized and popular, I give thanks. I thank them for giving me information I needed to write this book. I thank them, also, for not having written such a book before I got around to doing so.

The philosopher Francis Bacon, no stranger to a curious surname himself, once observed that there is "much impression and enchantment" in names. I agree. Without employing the fearsome technical vocabulary of onomastic science, I hope to convey that in an authoritative way. This book cannot be complete but I trust it is replete with useful facts. I am grateful to patient and demanding editors who have helped me to cram in a lot of detail—never as much as an author would wish, and with no room for the massive indexing this work would require—without missing the forest for the trees.

L. R. N. A.

CONTENTS

What's in a Name?

PART ONE

PERSONS

Father calls me William,
Sister calls me Will,
Mother calls me Willie,
But the fellers call me Bill!

—Eugene Field, "Just 'fore Christmas"

1. Forenames: First Names First

From the beginning people had to have names to identify themselves. At first, one was enough. There are cultures in which one is still enough, but generally, with increases in population and refinements in civilization, there arose a need for additional designations to identify the members of a society. To a given name like *John* or *Mary* was appended a second name, usually an inherited family name. With the advent of this "last name," which came to be known as a surname (from the French *surnom*), given names came to be called "first names," or, because we can have more than one, "forenames."

Since the coming of Christianity, the most popular forenames in western societies have been those of saints or biblical figures. Even today Christians are supposed to get saints' names at baptism and in some denominations get a second saint's name at confirmation. We still refer to given names as "Christian names." To *John, Mary, Peter, Matthew,* and *Christopher,* the Puritans added, for girls, *Prudence, Constance,* and *Charity,* and for boys, *Increase, Preserved,* and *Learned,* reflecting virtues they esteemed and hoped, literally, to transmit to their children. They also liked *Zeal-of-the-Land* and such.

Although the more extreme Puritan names soon went out of fashion, the religious tradition in forename selection remained strong in western culture. This tradition was rooted in both the Old and New Testaments, and we sometimes forget that many of our most familiar "Christian" names, such as *John* and *Michael,* in fact came from the Hebrews' Old Testament. The Dare family named the first white baby born in Virginia *Virginia,* not a conventional name in the late sixteenth century but hardly daring considering the religious association. Indeed, along with a slew of native British names that the English colonists transported to America, the traditional biblical names would dominate US birth registers well into the twentieth century.

In early America, much as in Elizabethan England, boys were called, typically, *John, William, James, George, Charles, Robert,* or *Thomas;* girls, *Mary, Elizabeth, Barbara, Dorothy, Ann(e), Margaret,* and *Helen.* Names that appear

3

in records from Virginia's Lost Colony of 1587 include, among the men, *John, Thomas, William, Henry, Richard, George, Robert, Hugh, Michael, James,* and *Roger;* among the women, *Jane, Elizabeth, Agnes, Alice, Audrey, Elyoner (Eleanor), Emma, Joan, Joyce, Margaret,* and *Marjorie.* The Jamestown Colony 20 years later listed the names *David, Daniel, Abraham, Jonas, Nathaniel,* and *Samuel.* Charles Parish in York County, Virginia, has our oldest surviving parish records. From them we learn that of 442 boys baptized there between 1648 and 1699, 105 were named *John,* 55 *William,* 45 *Thomas,* 32 *James,* and 20 *Robert;* among the 384 girls, 90 were named *Elizabeth,* 79 *Mary,* 47 *Ann(e),* and 29 *Sara(h).*

Attesting to the enduring popularity of these early names is a list of the most common US male and female names in the 1870s, as compiled by the British scholar Leslie A. Dunkling *(First Names First,* 1977):

Men	Women
William	Mary
John	Anna
Charles	Elizabeth
Harry	Emma
James	Alice
George	Edith, Florence
Frank	May
Robert	Helen
Joseph	Katherine
Thomas	Grace

The late nineteenth century, of course, was the heyday of Darwinism. The obsession with evolution and apprehensiveness over its implications that certain racial and national lineages were superior to others spurred many Americans to celebrate their Anglo-Saxon heritage and reaffirm it in the christening of off-spring. *Arthur, Alfred, Harold (Harry),* and *Mildred* joined the old standbys, so that the Top 10 names among American university students (mainly middle-class whites) born in the year 1900, according to Dunkling's survey, included the following:

Men	Women
John	Mary
William	Ruth
Charles	Helen
Robert	Margaret
Joseph	Elizabeth
James	Dorothy
George	Catherine
Samuel, Thomas	Mildred
Arthur	Frances
Harry	Alice

By 1925, with the passing of the evolution mania, *Arthur, Harry,* and *Mildred,* although still in vogue, had relinquished their select places to the more mainstream names *Richard, Edward,* and *Ann(e).*

In the 1940s, the American expert Elsdon C. Smith undertook to rank the most popular 100 boys' and girls' names in the United States. As the lists below indicate, the stock of American forenames had expanded to include new variations and new names altogether, the product of the ongoing ethnic and cultural diversification of America that saw Scottish immigrants introduce *Alan* and *Kenneth,* Germans *Herman* and *Carl,* and the French *Norman* and *Guy.* Again, however, what was remarkable about the Smith rankings was the continuing dominance of the standard English and biblical names even after three centuries of sweeping cultural and social change and by now the pervasive secularization and modernization of the society. I'll quote the rankings of the male forenames, which, though less susceptible to change than female forenames, have undergone (as you can readily see) drastic shifts in popularity lately. The lowest-ranking on the list have more or less disappeared in the eighties. Even the most popular then have been shifted around now.

Top 100 Boys' and Girls' Names (1940s)

BOYS

Name (Variations)	Rank	Language Origin* and Meaning
Abraham (Abram, Bram)	68	(H) father of the multitude
Albert	20	(Ger) noble and bright
Alexander	22	(G) helper of mankind
Alfred	30	(OE) wise (elf) counselor
Alan (Allan, Allen)	76	(S) handsome, cheerful
Andrew	29	(G) strong, manly
Anthony	61	(L) priceless
Archibald	92	(Ger) genuinely bold
Arthur	19	(OE or W) bear-hero, noble
Augustus	59	(L) majestic
Benjamin	21	(H) right-hand son
Bernard	83	(Ger) brave bear
Carl (Karl)	37	(Ger) man, farmer
Charles	3	(Ger) strong, manly
Chester	77	(L) fortified camp (castra)
Christopher	85	(L) bearer of Christ
Clarence	39	(L) bright, famous
Claude	84	(L) lame
Daniel	23	(H) "God is my judge"
David	18	(H) beloved

* (H) Hebrew, (G) Greek, (L) Latin, (Ger) Germanic, (OE) Old English, (F) French, (W) Welsh, (N) Norse, (S) Spanish, (Ar) Aramaic, (Sc) Scottish.

Name (Variations)	Rank	Language Origin and Meaning
Donald	51	*(Sc)* dark stranger
Earl	53	*(OE)* nobleman
Edgar	60	*(OE)* successful spearman
Edmond (Edmund)	50	*(OE)* prosperous protector
Edward	10	*(OE)* happy protector
Edwin	28	*(OE)* rich friend
Elmer	64	*(OE)* famous, noble
Ernest (Earnest)	40	*(OE)* earnest
Eugene	43	*(G)* well-born
Francis	15	*(L)* Frenchman
Frank	12	*(Ger)* free landholder
Franklin	67	*(OE)* free landholder
Fred	27	see *Frederic(k)*
Frederic(k)	16	*(Ger)* ruler in peace
George	5	*(G)* farmer
Gilbert	91	*(OE)* trusted
Guy	79	*(F)* guide
Harold	25	*(N)* army leader
Harry	14	see *Harold*
Harvey	87	*(Ger)* army warrior
Henry	8	*(Ger)* ruler of an estate
Herbert	34	*(Ger)* glorious warrior
Herman(n)	66	*(Ger)* nobleman
Horace	54	*(L)* keeper of the hours
Howard	45	*(OE)* watchman
Hugh	44	*(OE)* mind
Isaac	46	*(H)* laughter
Jacob	36	*(H)* supplanter
James	4	see *Jacob*
Jeremiah	93	*(H)* appointed by Jehovah
Jesse	56	*(H)* "God is"
John	1	*(H)* "God is gracious"
Jonathan	63	*(H)* "Jehovah gave"
Joseph	9	*(H)* "he shall add"
Joshua	96	*(H)* "Jehovah saves"
Josiah	82	*(H)* "Jehovah sustains"
Julius	74	*(G)* youthful
Kenneth	80	*(Sc)* handsome
Laurence (Lawrence)	52	*(L)* crowned with laurel
Leo	78	*(L)* lion
Leon	95	see *Leo*
Leonard	69	*(Ger)* heart of a lion
Lewis	42	see *Louis*
Lloyd (Floyd)	98	*(W)* gray-haired
Louis	24	*(G)* famous in war
Martin	55	*(L)* bellicose

Name (Variations)	Rank	Language Origin and Meaning
Matthew	73	*(H)* gift of God
Maurice (Morris)	90	*(L)* dark as a Moor
Max(imillian)	97	*(L)* most excellent
Michael	41	*(H)* "who is like God?"
Moses	88	*(H)* saved
Nathan	70	*(H)* gift
Nathaniel	47	*(H)* gift of God
Nicholas	75	*(G)* victory of the people
Norman	71	*(F)* Norseman
Oliver	57	*(L)* olive tree
Oscar	58	*(N)* spear god
Otto	81	*(Ger)* rich
Patrick	62	*(L)* patrician
Paul	26	*(L)* small
Peter	31	*(G)* rock
Phil(l)ip	33	*(G)* lover of horses
Ralph	32	*(OE)* wolf counselor
Ray(mond)	49	*(OE)* wise protection
Richard	13	*(Ger)* powerful ruler
Robert	6	*(OE)* bright fame
Roger	100	*(Ger)* famous spearman
Roy (Leroy)	48	*(F)* king
Rufus	94	*(L)* redhaired
Russell	72	*(F)* fox [red]-haired
Samuel	11	*(H)* "name of God"
Sidney (Sydney)	86	*(F)* St.-Denis
Stanley	65	*(OE)* rocky meadow
Stephen (Steven)	35	*(G)* crown
Theodore (Ted)	38	*(G)* gift of God
Thomas	7	*(Ar)* twin
Tim(othy)	89	*(G)* honoring God
Walter	17	*(Ger)* powerful warrior
Warren	99	*(Ger)* defender
William	2	*(Ger)* determined guardian

GIRLS

Girls' names are often (a sign of sexism?) given diminutives, nicknames, odd spellings, but these are the major names and variations of traditional use. This time I omit the rankings. In the generation or two since Smith ranked them (from *Mary* and *Elizabeth* down to *Vivian* and *Lucy*) the fashions in these names have changed beyond all recognition.

Name (Variations)	Language Origin and Meaning
Adelaide (Adele, Adeline)	*(Ger)* kind, noble
Agnes	*(G)* pure
Alice (Alison, Alyson)	*(Ger)* noble *(F* diminutive)

Name (Variations)	Language Origin and Meaning
Ann (many variations)	*(H)* graceful
Anna (with combinations)	see *Ann*
Anne	see *Ann*
Barbara (Babette, Babs, Barbie)	*(G)* stranger
Bea(trice)	*(L)* bringer of happiness
Bernice	*(G)* bringer of victory
Betty (Bette, Beth)	see *Elizabeth*
Beverl(e)y	*(OE)* beaver meadow
Carmel(la)	*(H)* biblical Mt. Carmel
Carol(e)	feminine of *(Ger) Carl*
Caroline (Carrie)	*(F)* feminine of *Charles*
Carolyn	see *Caroline*
Catherine	*(G)* innocent
Cecilia (Cecile, Cissy, Sissy)	*(L)* blind
Charlotte (Carlotta, Lottie)	feminine of *Carlos* or *Charles*
Clara (Claire, Clarissa)	*(L)* clear, bright
Constance (Connie)	*(L)* constancy
Dolores	*(S)* sorrows (of The Blessed Virgin)
Doris (Dory, Doreen)	*(G)* from the sea
Dorothy (Dot, Dotty, Dolly)	*(G)* gift of God
Edith (Eydie)	*(OE)* rich gift
Edna	unknown *(The Apocrypha)*
Eileen (Ailene, Ilene)	*(G)* light, is wrong (Irish *Eibhilin*)
Elaine (Elena)	see *Helen*
Eleanor (Elinor, Eleanora)	see *Helen*
Elizabeth (many variations)	*(H)* oath of God
Ellen	see *Helen*
Elsie (Elsa, Ilsa, Lisa)	see *Elizabeth*
Emily (Amelia)	*(L)* family name *Aemilius*
Emma (Emmaline)	*(Ger)* universal, whole
Esther (Hester)	*(H)* star
Evelyn (Evalina, Eve)	*(Ger)* surname, origin obscure
Florence (Florrie, Flo)	*(L)* blooming, or from Florence, Italy
Frances (Francesca, Franny)	*(F)* French
Genevieve (Jenny, Jinny)	*(F)* from Celtic "wave" originally
Geraldine (Gerry, Geri)	*(Ger)* spear rule
Gertrude (Gertie)	*(Ger)* spear strength
Gladys	*(W)* of uncertain meaning
Gloria	*(L)* glory
Grace	*(L)* grace
Harriet (Hattie)	*(F)* from *Henri*
Hazel	botanical name (like *Rose, Ivy, Iris, Violet, Heather*)
Helen (Helena, Helene, Lena)	*(G)* bright one?
Irene	*(G)* peace
Jacqueline (Jaclyn)	*(F)* from *Jacques*
Jane (Jayne)	*(H)* from *John*

Name (Variations)	*Language Origin and Meaning*
Janet (Jeanette)	see *Jane*
Jean	*(F)* from *Jean* (French *John*)
Jeanne	see *Jean*
Joan	see *Jean*
Joanne	see *Jean*
Josephine (Jo, Josie)	*(F)* from *Joseph*
Joyce	*(L)* joyous (or of Celtic origin)
Judith (Judy, Judi)	*(H)* of Judah
Julia (Juliet, Juliana)	*(L)* surname *Julius*
June	month (like *April, May*)
Katharine (Kate, Kathy)	see *Catherine*
Katherine (with variations)	see *Catherine*
Kathryn (Katrina)	see *Catherine*
Laura (Laurel, Laurette)	another botanical name (like *Lily, Rhoda, Rosemary*)
Lillian	see *Elizabeth*
Lois	uncertain *(2 Timothy)*
Loretta (Etta, Lorrie)	see *Laurence* and *Laura,* also religious
Lorraine	*(F)* from a placename
Louise (Louisa)	*(Ger)* woman warrior
Lucille (Cilla)	*(F)* from Latin "light"
Lucy (Lucia, Luci)	*(L)* light
Margaret (Margot, Marguerite)	*(G)* pearl
Marian (Marianne)	see *Mary* and *Ann*
Marie (Maria, Mariah, Merry)	see *Mary*
Marilyn	see *Mary* (with *Lynn*)
Marion	see *Marian*
Margery (Marjorie, Madge)	see *Margaret*
Martha	*(Ar)* lady
Mary (Miriam, Marie, etc.)	*(H)* wished for
Mildred (Millie)	*(OE)* mild power
Nancy (Nan, Nanette)	see *Ann*
Norma	coined for a Bellini opera?
Patricia (Trisha, Patty, Pat)	*(L)* patrician
Pauline (Paula)	see *Paul*
Phyllis	*(G)* leaf
Priscilla (Prissy)	*(L)* strict
Rita (Margarita)	see *Margaret*
Rosalie (Rosalinda)	see *Rose*
Rose (Rosa, Rosamund)	botanical name
Rosemary	*Rose* plus *Mary,* or the herb
Ruth	Moabite name from the Bible
Sally	see *Sara(h)*
Sara(h)	*(H)* princess
Shirley (Shelley, Sherry)	*(OE)* placename (shire meadow) used first for boys and then for the heroine of Charlotte Brontë's novel of 1849

Name (Variations)	Language Origin and Meaning
Stella	*(L)* star
Susan(ne) (Suzanne, Suzy)	*(H)* lily
Sylvia	*(L)* of the woods
Theresa (Therese, Terry)	chiefly from Empress Maria Theresa
Violet (Viola, Vy)	botanical name
Virginia (Ginny, Gina)	*(L)* virgin, or placename
Vivian (Vivien, Vyvyan)	*Vivian* or *Vyvyan* should be male, *Vivien(ne)* female, from surname ultimately *(L)* lively

The rankings of feminine forenames would only have given you historical information, documenting details (for example) of how *Ruth* and *Dorothy,* once common, have plummeted in popularity. What the average person needs to know is what forenames are currently in or out of fashion, that *Alvin* is a chipmunk and *Dennis* is a menace, that there are too many Jennifers.

More recently, we see more adventurousness in name choices. Boys' names now include *Addison* (OE son of Adam), *Ahmed* (Arabic, highly praised), *Alastair* (Scottish version of *Alexander*), *Ashley* (OE ash [grove] in a field), *Blair* (Celtic, boy from the plains), *Bryce* (Celtic, alert or ambitious), *Clay* (of the earth), *Damian* (G, tamer [of the people]), *Drew* (from *Andrew*), and other nonconformist names (the essence of which may be Danish *Einar,* "he thinks for himself"). Girls are now often given boys' names (*Tracy, Kelly, Shaun, Ashley*), which are then soon dropped as male names. Girls are even called *Michael, Glenn, Stacy,* and so on. *Mary* is no longer the "top name" for girls nor *John* for boys, and everyone has noticed the *J* craze: *Jessica* has ousted *Jennifer* from the top place and boys may be called *Jason, Jeffrey, Jared,* but infrequently *James.*

Fashions always had an influence. They took on greater importance about 1950 when the traditional family and conventional names altered.

By 1950 one could finally discern in US name rolls and registers a shifting pattern away from conventionality. That was clearly evidenced by the updating of Dunkling's university men's list for that year, in which *Charles, George, Donald, Joseph,* and *Edward* lost their Top 10 spots to *Michael, David, Steven, Thomas,* and *Mark.* The latter were hardly unorthodox names, but (with the exception of the perennial *Thomas*) they had somehow a fresher feel and their ascendancy foreshadowed the more pronounced transformation that would follow in the decades ahead.

As long-established standards and precepts were undermined by young and old alike through the turbulent sixties and seventies, it was inevitable that the grip of tradition, in naming as in values and mores, would be loosened. The irreverent "Now" and "Me" generations graduated into pseudo-sophisticated yuppies (young, upwardly mobile professionals). Conservative in some ways, the yuppies did not balk at rewriting the rules along the way so that once venerable names became frowned upon as dull or stodgy. Yuppies were especially conscious of the "image," in names as in name brands and everything else. *John* and *Mary* became quaint if not anachronistic; a movie featuring those names in the title suggested the ordinariness and dreariness of the characters, played by actors unprepossessing except in their own forenames, Dustin Hoffman and Mia Farrow. Novelty and originality became the order of the day, cued by television soap operas that offered up monikers like *Monica, Lance, Storm, Tiffany,* and *Heather;* meanwhile, the contrived misspellings of Hollywood press agents spawned *Barbra, Lynda, Luci, Shaun, Elisabeth,* and an alphabet soup of imitations. We saw *Mikel, Jan'et, Jacque-Lynn,* etc.

By the 1970s, traditional favorites like *Robert* and *James* were still holding down places on Top 10 charts, and some antediluvians like *Christopher* and *Matthew* were unaccountably enjoying a revival, but, particularly in the more progressive northeastern and western states, those cute *J* names—add *Justin, Jeremy, Jheri, Ja-Net*—and a swarm of sexually ambiguous names (*Blake, Robin, Cary, Kim, Randy*) were dislodging the old standards. Parents named *Henry* and *Catherine* were incongruously introducing toddlers named *Nicole, Krystle, Samantha,* and *Bever-Leigh*. In 1972 in New York State the shuffled popularity lists looked like this:

Michael	Jennifer
David	Michelle
Christopher	Lisa
John	Elizabeth
James	Christine
Joseph	Maria
Robert	Nicole
Anthony	Kimberly
Richard	Denise
Brian	Amy

By 1984 *John* had dropped to ninth in New York, and elsewhere, too, it was being supplanted by another of the captivating *J*s, *Jonathan. Elizabeth* tied for last place in the girls' Top 10 in New York in 1986. It sank out of sight by 1987. The chart below, compiled by Valerie Monroe for a May 1988 article in *7 Days,* shows the contemporary trend in New York State naming over roughly the past decade. (Note how the girls' lists depart from tradition much more conspicuously than the corresponding boys' lists, an intriguing fact I shall elaborate on shortly.)

1976	1980	1984	1986	1987
Jennifer	Jennifer	Jennifer	Jessica	Jessica
Jessica	Jessica	Jessica	Jennifer	Jennifer
Nicole	Melissa	Melissa	Stephanie	Stephanie
Melissa	Nicole	Stephanie	Nicole	Melissa

Michelle	Michelle	Nicole	Christina	Christina
Maria	Elizabeth	Christina	Amanda	Nicole
Lisa	Lisa	Tiffany	Melissa	Amanda
Elizabeth	Christina	Danielle	Tiffany	Ashley
Danielle	Tiffany	Elizabeth	Danielle	Tiffany
Christine	Maria	Lauren	Elizabeth	Samantha
Michael	Michael	Michael	Michael	Michael
David	David	Christopher	Christopher	Christopher
John	Jason	Daniel	Jonathan	Jonathan
Christopher	Joseph	David	Anthony	Daniel
Joseph	Christopher	Joseph	David	David
Anthony	Anthony	Anthony	Daniel	Anthony
Robert	John	Jason	Joseph	Joseph
Jason	Daniel	Jonathan	John	Matthew
James	Robert	John	Jason	John
Daniel	James	Robert	Andrew	Andrew

Traditional names had more staying power in the conservative heartland and in the hinterlands. In 1982, Robert Hertzberg of the Fort Wayne *Journal-Gazette,* during an interview with me on name trends, observed that in Indiana people seemed to prefer to name children after family members (i.e., "Jr.") rather than bestow new names. Still, by the 1980s one could find clearcut evidence even in the Midwest of a forename revolution. The most common given names in Washtenaw County, Michigan, in 1981, according to a study of birth records there by Cleveland Evans, were as follows:

Boys (2,974 births)	Girls (2,851 births)
Michael (113)	Sarah (118)
Matthew (100)	Jennifer (98)
Christopher (83)	Jessica (72)
Ryan (80)	Kristen (60)
Jason (79)	Amanda (58)
David (75)	Elizabeth (50)
Andrew (67)	Katherine (49)
Brian (67)	Emily (43)
John (64)	Rebecca (43)
Daniel (61)	Melissa (42)

Nationwide in 1980, based on a "popularity" poll in *Parents Magazine,* the results looked like this:

Boys	Girls
Michael	Jennifer
David	Jessica
John	Nicole
Christopher	Melissa

Joseph	Michelle
Anthony	Maria
Robert	Lisa
Jason	Elizabeth
James	Danielle

Granted the magazine's readership reflected primarily urban, middle-class tastes, nonetheless, with far-reaching communications and transportation advances rapidly erasing regional boundaries and styles, *Melissas* and *Michelles* were coming to the most provincial corners of rural America as surely as McDonald's and Burger King.

Perhaps the most striking development of all in recent years, beyond the changing fashions in popular names, has been the sheer proliferation of names. At the beginning of this century the Top 10 names in each gender category sufficed for half of all boys and girls. Today the Top 10 accounts for only 25 percent of all American forenames. In Pennsylvania in 1972, 78,071 new-born boys took 4,012 different names and (not to be outdone) 74,499 girls took 7,114 different names. Why the name explosion? Partly it was the product of the continuing search for originality and individuality. New spellings alone— *Teri, Toni, Debi, Jan'et, Shere*—created multiple versions of the same name. To a large extent, however, the phenomenon could be attributed to blacks and other ethnic groups seeking stronger cultural identities. Minorities felt the need to go outside the WASP mainstream to invent new names or resurrect ancestral ones. Thus Jews, perhaps in reaction to the steady drift away from orthodoxy in modern times, have of late increasingly resorted to Old Testament names like *Joshua, Leah,* and *Hannah,* as well as turned to literal Hebrew names—this while more Reform elements, to be nonconformist, were calling their kids *Christopher* and *Ryan.* What better evidence of the current chaos in the name domain?

Regarding blacks, it is wrong to assume that only recently have *Hatties* and *Jemimas* given way to *LaToyas* and *Genelles.* Although during the slave era blacks typically took their names from white masters (hence the prevalence of *Toms, Sams,* and *Johns*), there have always been unusual and distinctive black forenames. Think of early black men in US history such as *Denmark* Vesey and *Crispus* Attucks. The three blacks who accompanied the Mormons to Utah in 1847 were *Oscar* Crosby, *Hark* Lay, and *Green* Flake. Heavyweight champion Joe Louis' sisters, long before Cassius Clay (a.k.a. Muhammad Ali) named his children *Maryum, Jamillh* and *Reeshemah,* were called *Eammarell, Eulalia,* and *Vunies.* The Black Power and Black Muslim movements gave tremendous impetus to a new generation of black forenames, which included *Jamal, Tomica, Delonte,* African names such as *Keisha* (favorite) and even Celtic names such as *Donnell* (brave dark man). They banished *Leroy, Clarence, Ruby,* etc. They were a great departure from the slave names of 1619 to 1799 that Newbell Niles Puckett collected. He found 972 slave names and these were the most popular:

Male		Female	
Jack	Dick	Bet	Sara(h) or Sary
Tom	John	Mary	Phillis *(sic)*
Harry	Robin	Jane	Nan
Sam	Frank	Hanna(h)	Peg
Will, Caesar		Betty	

Note the nicknames (affectionate? degrading?), but the slaves' names were not radically different from those of their owners, while selected names from "Letters to the Editor" in *Ebony* for August 1988 are unusual: *Myrlie, Divia, Kecia, Parthenia, Tracie, Willie, Aryan* (male), *Booker, Genelle, Kwame, Lenna,* and *Diedra.* In a Liberty City (Miami) black day-care center in 1989 were *Bioneva, Deyphan, Ladarius, Larquasha, Levod, Shunteria, Tykema, Tyshika,* and *Vavakia.* In North Miami Beach the mostly-Haitian day-care kids were *Apple, Cindy, Farrah, Gregory, Natasha, Rodney, Shirley, Stephanie,* and *Watson.*

Permit me to conclude this first part with some general observations about forename tendencies. Then we can move on to forenaming traditions around the world.

First of all, names have fashions. You will have noticed that boys' names have historically been more stable than girls'. Why? I should say that boys have traditionally been regarded as heirs and breadwinners. Therefore they have been given sober, strong, mature, dependable names. Their names represent continuity and seriousness. Parents have perhaps allowed themselves more freedom of expression and whimsy in naming daughters. This longstanding pattern may be nearing an end, however, with the blurring of sex roles and the increasing popularity of unisex names like *Jamie* and *Jody* (two more of those ubiquitous *J*s). Cuban-Americans may use *William José,* etc.

In terms of name origins, on the whole boys' names have tended to denote occupations, leadership, and strength. Girls' names have stood for beauty, softness, and passive personality traits, the same qualities feminist critics have identified as being encouraged in the way women speak and write. While 35% of girls' names today have roots in words referring to appearance and personality, the 25% of boys' names that are in this category are mostly out of fashion (*Augustus, Albert, Claude*). Names referring to God (*Daniel, Nathaniel, Theodore*) and objects of substance (*Peter*="rock," *Stephen*="crown") tend to be masculine. Of course there are a raft of female names that derive directly from male names, such as *Roberta, Geraldine, Bernadette, Victoria,* and, women's liberation aside, current charmers *Stephanie* and *Danielle.* These feminized male forenames do not tend to masculinize the bearers; rather, they tend to underline the preference in the society for men over women. They are, in their way, sexist. It is also sexist to speak of the "fair sex." Women often are named after pretty things, as in the case of the so-called "botanical" names (*Olive, Blossom, Myrtle, Daisy, Ivy, Violet, Rose*) and "gem" names (*Opal,*

Coral, Pearl). Curiously, just when it seemed that the "botanicals" and "gems" had become obsolete, *Holly* and *Laurel* have gained currency, as has *Crystal,* thanks to Linda Evans of the TV series "Dynasty," where it's *Krystle.*

Indeed, another generalization that may be made with regard to forenames is that, as with any fashion item, certain styles have passed in and out of favor. Thus—and again this has been more the case with girls' names—*Jennifer* has finally begun to fade somewhat after catapulting into prominence as the heroine's name in Erich Segal's 1970 novel and subsequent film *Love Story* and topping the distaff lists for nearly two decades. Although other pop leaders like *Jessica, Ashley,* and latecomer *Lindsay(sey)* show no signs of flagging, the pendulum may be swinging back in the direction of the more traditional names, given the revival in the last few years of old standards like *Sara(h), Emma,* and *Jane.* On the male side the old-fashioned *Max* is suddenly making a comeback.

What causes names to slip in and out of favor? I've noted certain sociological trends such as Darwinism, which gave a boost to the early Anglo-Saxon names, and the convulsive changes of the 1960s and 1970s that played havoc with all conventions, including names. Sometimes more capricious, faddish forces have been at work: hence the *Jennifer* vogue; the current popularity of "Dynasty" 's *Krystle* and *Fallon;* the short-lived enthusiasm for the male name *Clark* before World War II, possibly influenced by the *macho* celebrity of Clark Gable and Superman's Clark Kent; and the *Rowena* craze that followed publication of Sir Walter Scott's novels in America in the early nineteenth century. It should come as no surprise that the name *Fritz* and German-sounding names generally were anathema during World War I, or that many boys born on the night of a presidential election some years back were christened *Franklin Delano. Jennifer's* counterpart *Oliver* made no significant dent in the men's list as a result of *Love Story* (again suggesting that masculine names are less susceptible to the winds of fashion), but newsworthy names have their impact on the name parade.

Names that have seemed elegant to one generation—*Archibald, Percy,* and *Reginald* come to mind—have been rejected as too prim or prissy by another. An attractive, high-profile individual like *Warren* Beatty or *Mel* Gibson or *Ollie* North may give instant respectability to a previously undesirable name. Then there are those names that seem beyond redemption because of long negative associations: *Bertha* (fat), *Gertrude* (plain), *Ethel* and *Edith* (stupid), *Earl* and *Wayne* (hayseed), *Bruce* (effeminate), and *Harvey* (nerdy). I shall return to subjective name impressions later. Some names that endure do so because of special circumstances: a child born at daybreak may be *Dawn* or *Lucy,* and at Christmas we get *Noël* (*Noëlle*), at Easter *Pasquale.*

Finally, there are those forenames that defy all convention, trends, and indeed categorization itself. I am referring here to those offbeat, eccentric, or merely odd names that we all have encountered at one time or another, usually the inspiration of a flaky or free-spirited parent seeking to make a "personal statement" (such as the feminist's *Sarachild*), to be clever, or simply to be different. As often as not, such free-lancing turns out to be a form of child abuse. Thus, among show-biz folk, Sylvester Stallone and his then wife *Saha* (formerly just Joyce) called their baby, for whatever reason, *Sage Moonblood*. Other entertainers have saddled their kids with *Libra, Free, god, Amerika, Zowie, Moon Unit,* and *Chastity* (Cher, ironically, giving her daughter a name that would have made the Puritans proud). Less goofy but just as perverse, Ernest Hemingway named his daughter *Margaux* for the bottle that got him drunk enough to father her. Oscar Wilde, spurning both the male *Vivian* and female *Vivien,* mischievously named one son *Vyvyan.*

Rudyard Kipling got his unusual forename from the lake where his parents courted. Similarly, baseball commissioner *Kenesaw Mountain* Landis was named for the vista his mother saw outside the window as he came into the world. Less sentimentally, the American painter Charles Willson Peale (1741-1827) must have been intent on demonstrating that one's name as much as biology is the key to destiny: the single-minded Peale may have been on to something, because, of his 11 children, *Rembrandt* Peale, *Rubens* Peale, *Rafaelle* Peale, and *Titian* Peale all attained some fame as artists.

On the cute side, Stanford and Loyola Bardwell, happening to have "college" names themselves, decided to name their brood after universities. Comedy writer *Alpha-Betty* Olsen had parents named Alf and Betty. After a dozen daughters a boy called *Welcome* John Weaver is understandable. Less defensible, aviation genius Bill Lear is reported to have inflicted *Chanda* and *Lava* on his daughters. Joke names handicap children; avoid them.

We all know parents who out of cuteness or compulsiveness insist on giving each of their children the same first initial: Roger and Rose Schultz did okay with *Roger, Jr., Rodney, Ricki, Ryan, Reid,* and the like, but then there was the case of the Maynards of Louisiana who selected, with more determination than discretion, *Odile, Odelia, Olive, Oliver, Olivia, Ophelia, Odelin, Octave, Octavia, Ovide, Onesia, Olite, Otto, Ormes,* and *Opta.* Branded in the same manner was *Ambrose* Bierce, the son of cranks Marcus Aurelius Bierce and Laura Sherwood Bierce, who began all their children's names with the letter "A." Little Ambrose grew up to become the most famous American humorist of his day, but, like so many other casualties of their parents' perversity, he turned out to be as strange as his name—a crotchety misfit, misanthrope, and lifelong neurotic.

The identical-first-initial idiosyncrasy such as claimed Bierce is fairly commonplace. There have been numerous other, more imaginative forenaming systems, the more bizarre of which the average person may not even notice: Harry C. Thompson, for example, called his first child *Jean* and his next three *Nancy, Eleanor,* and *Mary Louise* (hint: count the syllables). Few couples can procreate enough offspring to cover each letter of the alphabet, but some have given one child 26 forenames or 13 children two each, producing some real

Lulus (pardon the pun) and worse, *Audie Bryant, Curtis Drew,* on down to *Yon Zircle.* A charming if rather silly system had a Green family naming their sprouts *Holly, Kelly, Forest,* and *Leif.* Two-time Pulitzer Prize winner Vermont Connecticut Royster was named for his grandfather, the father of that man having given all his children the names of states. The silliest system I have ever heard of? I'll tell you just so someone will write to me to top it. The Ernest Russells of Vinton, Ohio, had 11 kids, each given two names of which one was the reverse of the other: *Lledo Odell, Loneva Avenol, Lebanna Annabel,* and so forth. And that wasn't even an original idea, as Mrs. Laur Rual Gee disclosed in 1972 ("Mother did it but I don't know why!") when she got on the UPI wires.

I have barely scratched the surface here. In later sections I explore many more varieties and combinations of odd and amusing names. I have sought in these opening pages merely to whet your appetite—and your understanding— as to the fascinating (sometimes cruel) quirks, the vagaries and vicissitudes, as well as the prevailing conventions and trends, that have all been a part of our forenaming tradition.

2. Forenames from the Four Corners of the Earth

Pascal remarked that truth might be different on either side of the Pyrenees. Similarly, customs regarding forenames differ from place to place as well as from time to time. This section takes a look at forename practices and patterns around the world, demonstrating the diversity.

Let's use as a starting point Alfa-Betty Olsen; you recall that her unusual forename was made from those of her parents, Alf and Betty. Though *Alfa-Betty* departed from the American practice, the ancient Britons often composed names that way. You could find the occasional *Stuf* or *Ine,* but many people had compound names put together from parts of their parents' names. Likewise, the practice of sticking one's offspring with names all beginning with the same initial, now viewed as peculiar, was well established in British custom once upon a time. These were ways in which children's names related them intimately to their parents and their siblings.

Take the Saxon chieftain who became first King of Wessex in Britain. He was called *Cerdic* (though Sir Walter Scott reported him as *Cedric* and started a fad for that name). Cerdic was followed by Cynric. Other royal personages then were Ceawlin, Cuthwulf, Cutha, Cuthwine, Cwichelm, Cenferth, Ceolric, Ceowulf, Chad, Cynebald, Cenfud, Cenbert, Ceolward, and Cedwalla (who was baptized Peter). You get the idea. Of those names from more than 1,000 years ago only *Chad* is still around.

In A.D. 802 Egberth became King of Wessex. Stay with this genealogy business a little longer and you'll see some names which are more modern. Egberth's sons (by Redburh, whose father may have been King of the Franks) included Ethelwulf and Aethelstan (both underkings of Kent). Ethelwulf succeeded his father, married Osburh (daughter of Oslac of the Isle of Wight), and had a son whom he named Aethelstan, the same as his brother. There followed Ethelbald, Ethelbert, Ethelred I, Ethelswith (a woman who married Buhred, King of Mercia), and the first of Ethelswith and Buhred's lot whom you are likely to recognize: Alfred (called the Great, first King of all Eng-

18

land). The English royal house later intermarried with that of Denmark and so to the Edwards and Edgars were added Harolds and Canute, and his son Hardicanute. A few of these names became popular in English-speaking countries (*Alfred* and *Harold,* for instance) and some still are popular (such as *Edward*).

Other popular names can be traced back to A.D. 1066, when William the Bastard of Normandy became William the Conqueror of England. Names such as *Edward* continued in use but were joined by names of the Normans, which in their English forms were *William, Richard, Henry, Matilda, Margaret, Geoffrey,* etc.

Here are 20 common names each for men and women from Anglo-Saxon England (tenth century) and 20 common names each from Norman England (eleventh century):

Common Names in Anglo-Saxon England		Common Names in Norman England	
Men	**Women**	**Men**	**Women**
Alfred	Alditha	Alan	Adela
Alwin	Alveva	Archibald	Alice
Coleman	Edild	Arnold	Avis
Edgar	Edith	Bernard	Bertha
Edmund	Ediva	Denis	Constance
Edward	Estrilda	Eustace	Emma
Gladwin	Ethelfreda	Geoffrey	Jocelyn
Godric	Ethelreda	Gerald	Joyce
Godwin	Goda	Gerard	Laura
Harding	Godiva	Gilbert	Margery
Herbert	Godrun	Henry	Matilda
Osbert	Golda	Hugh	Maud
Osmund	Goldburga	Humphrey	Millicent
Seward	Goldcorna	Leonard	Muriel
Sperling	Goldhen	Louis	Olive
Theodgar	Goldyva	Raymond	Oriel
Theodoric	Leofrun	Richard	Rosamond
Wat	Leveva	Roger	Rose
Wulfred	Milda	Walter	Sybil
Wulfric	Wakerida	William	Yvonne

By 1605, William Camden was able to "set down alphabetically the names which we call Christian names, most usual to the English nation":

Aaron	Aelward	Alfred	Ananais	Arnold
Abel	Alan	Alphonse	Andrew	Arthur
Adam	Albah	Alwin	Angel	Augustine
Adelard	Albert	Ambrose	Anselm	Avery
Adolph	Aldred	Amery	Anthony	Baldwin
Adrian	Alexander	Amias	Archibald	Balthazar

Baptist	Elmer	Hamon	Lewlin	Raphael
Bardulph	E[m]manuel	Hannibal	Lionel	Raymond
Barnabas	Englebert	Harold	Ludovic	Reinfred
Bartholomew	Enion	Hector	Luke	Reinhold
Baruch	Erasmus	Hengest	Madoc	Reuben
Basil	Ernest	Henry	Malachaias	Richard
Beavis	Esau	Herbert	Mannasses	Robert
Bede	Ethelbert	Hercules	Marcel	Roger
Bennet	Ethelred	Herman	Mark	Roland
Benjamin	Ethelstan	Herwin	Marmaduke	Roman[e]
Bernard	Ethelwold	Hierome	Martin	Samson
Betrand	Ethelwolph	Hilary	Matthew	Samuel
Bla[i]se	Eusebius	Hildebert	Maugre	Saul
Bonaventure	Eustac[h]e	Horatio	Maurice	Sebastian
Boniface	Eutropius	Howel[l]	Maximilian	Sigismund
Botolph	Evan	Hubert	Mercury	Silvester
Brian	Everard	Hugh	Meredith	Simon
Cadwallader	Ezechias	Humphrey	Michael	Solomon
Caesar	Ezechiel	Ingram	Miles	Stephen
Caius	Fabian	Isaac	Morgan	Swithin
Caleb	Felix	Israel	Moses	Sylvanus
Calisthenes	Ferdinand	Jacob	Nathaniel	Theobald
Caradoc	Florence	James	Neal	Theodore
Charles	Francis	Jasper	Nicholas	Theodoric
Christopher	Frederic	Jeremy	Noel	Theophilus
Chrysostom	Fremund	Joab	Norman	Thomas
Clemens	Fulbert	Joachim	Odo	Timothy
Constantine	Fulcher	Job	Oliver	Tobias
Conrad	Fulke	Jocelin	Original	Tristram
Cornelius	Gabriel	John	Osbern	Turstan
Crescens	Gamaliel	Jonathan	Osbert	Uchtred
Cuthbert	Garret	Jordan	Osmund	Urban
Cyprian	Gawain	Joseph	Oswald	Urian
Daniel	George	Jos[h]ua[h]	Owen	Valens
David	Geoffrey	Josias	Pascal	Valentine
Demetrius	Germa[i]n	Julius	Patrick	Vincent
Denis	Gervase	Kenard	Paul	Vital[e]
Drogo	Gideon	Kenhelm	Payn	Vivian
Dunstan	Gilbert	Lambert	Percival	Waldwin
Eadulph	Giles	La[u]ncelot	Peregrine	Walter
Ealdred	Godard	Laurence	Peter	Wilfred
Ealred	Godfrey	Lazarus	Philbert	William
Edgar	Godrich	Leger	Philip	Wimund
Edmund	Godwin	Leofstan	Posthumus	Wischard
Edward	Gregory	Leofwin	Quintin	Wolstan
Edwin	Griffith	Leonard	Ralph	Wulpher
Egbert	Grimbald	Leopold	Randal[l]	Zachary
Ellis	Guy	Lewis		

Camden added: "Lest women, the most kind sex, should conceive unkindness if they were omitted, somewhat of necessity must be said of their names:"

Abigail	Christian	Gertrude	Lydia	Prudence
Adeline	Cicely	Gillian	Mabel	Rachel
Agatha	Clara	Gladuse	Magdalen	Radegunde
Agnes	Denise	Goodeth	Margaret	Rebecca
Alethia	Diana	Grace	Margery	Rosamund
Alice	Dido	Griselda	Mary	Rose
Amabel	Dorcas	Helena	Matilda	Sabina
Amy	Dorothy	Ida	Maud[e]	Sanchia
Anastasia	Douglas	Isabel	Meraud	Sarah
Anchoret	Dousable	Jacquetta	Millicent	Scholastica
Anna	Douze	Jana	Muriel	Sibyl
Arabella	Dulcia	Jane	Nest	Sophia
Audrey	Eleanor	Je[a]net	Nicia	Sophronia
Aureole	Eliza	Joan	Nicola	Susan
Avice	Elizabeth	Joanna	Olympias	Tabitha
Barbara	Emma	Joyce	Orabilis	Tace
Beatrice	Emmet	Judith	Penelope	Tamsin
Benedicta	Eva	Julianne	Pernel	Temperance
Benigna	Faith	Katherine	Petronilla	Theodosia
Bertha	Felice	Kingburgh	Philadelphia	Thomasin
Blanche	Florence	Laura	Philippa	Ursula
Bona	Fortitude	Laurentia	Phyllis	Venus
Bridget	Fortune	Lettice	Polyxena	Warburg
Cassandra	Frances	Lora	Prisca	Wilmetta
Catherine	Francesca	Lucia	Priscilla	Winifred
Cecilia	Frediswid	Lucretia		

By 1605 the Stuarts from Scotland had risen from tending pigsties (whence *Stuart*) to royalty and had taken over the English throne as well. The Stuarts popularized *James* and *Charles*. The Hanoverians from Germany later introduced *George, Frederick, Augustus* and *Augusta* and (although Sir Walter Scott said it was "too Germanic" and would never be popular in Britain) *Victoria*. Queen Victoria's consort made popular his own Germanic name, used by many of their descendants: *Albert*.

All these British royal names were in time transplanted to America; they dominated American forenaming, along with such saints' names as the Puritans still liked, their own Puritan fancies (such as *Hope* and *Purity*), and the surnames of ancient aristocrats (*Howard, Sidney, Seymour, Percy, Stanley, Russell*), which came to be fancy forenames for the socially ambitious.

British aristocrats tended to add to their fancy last names rather simple first names (*John, James, Jane*). Later, when they picked up *Sarah, Diana, Simon, Emma* and the like, so did we, though we seldom used as many forenames as they did. We still don't. The criminal in John Banville's *The Book of Evidence* (1989) offers evidence of that: this British nogoodnik is *Frederick Charles St. John Vanderveld Montgomery*.

The British middle class copied aristocratic names and added some distinctly their own. The lower class in Britain adopted names like *Brenda, Nicola, Tracy* and some the True-Born Englishman thinks of as "too American": *Earl, Scott, Wayne,* and such. The quintessential low-class English girl's name was *Doreen* (with the accent on the first syllable) and now may be *Tracy*. A typical "loser" name is *Clyde,* though the British slang for a loser is *Charlie* (from Charlie Chaplin).

If a name gets too closely linked with a certain class, other classes may avoid it. However, some names fit all classes (*Mary, Elizabeth, William*) and the Royals' having names such as *Charles, Diana, Andrew,* even *Henry,* has boosted their adoption everywhere in the English-speaking world.

As in America, forenames in Britain have their fashions. Today some Norman warrior names (*Robert, Hugh, Walter*) have some life left in them; however, others from that class and time (*Algernon, Mortimer, Montmorency*) are rejected as too pompous by most people, who also think names like *Arabella* and *Elspeth* are "a bit much."

Now some popular British forenames come from American television. *Darren* was picked up from "telly" reruns of "Bewitched," *Alexis* from "Dynasty," along with some of the odder forenames of actors. In the old days popular names sometimes came from novels (*Shirley, Lorna*) or plays (*Wendy, Gloria*) and some of these are still used, though Victorian favorites (*Alma, Edith, Fanny*) are not now likely to appeal. If Americans want to pick up new or revived British forenames, they can choose from *Anthony, Ian, Simon, Colin, Clive,* etc.

The British do like eccentrics, so there has always been a smattering of extraordinary names among them, but more representative of the prevailing attitude today is the letter a Mr. Bond wrote to *The Times* urging a "Christian Name Discrimination Act which would make it illegal for parents to give their children any name not on a democratically approved list."

In point of fact (as the British like to say), British parents police themselves pretty well and it would be quite unusual for any baby now to be baptized with any name as odd as that given at the font in 1547 to a child of the Goldhams that lived only one day. He was called *Creature*.

The Irish in Britain tend to use English names but occasionally you see one from the Gaelic past such as *Caitlin* or *Bridget* or *Deirdre*. The non-Irish use these too. Patriotic motives lie behind the translation of forenames back into Gaelic: *Séan* for *John, Séamus* for *James, Padráic* for *Patrick*. In America we have created *Shaun, Shawn, Shane, Deshawn*.

Welsh forenames include *Evan, Ivor, Llewellyn,* and *Lloyd* (which we sometimes spell as pronounced, *Floyd*). Some of the Welsh names have been used outside Wales, but *Floyd* Americans would now regard as just as "corny" as *Gladys* or *Enid,* and names like *Blodwyn* are too strange even for a country with a college named Bryn Mawr (Welsh for "big hill"). However, *Megan* is now enjoying something of a vogue in the US and a few other Welsh names may come along.

The Cornish language is extinct, except among a few scholars and in Cornish placenames (where it is often distorted). The last native speaker of Cornish died in the eighteenth century. The old Cornish forenames are all but forgotten, despite the fact that some few Cornish surnames (*Tremayne, Trevellyan, Bowen, Anderton*) are occasionally given as deliberately unusual first names or for family reasons.

The Scots, on the other hand, have had a large and lasting impact on British naming and indeed on the names of English-speakers (and a few others) the world over. The Scottish forename legacy includes *Craig, Gordon, Cameron, Bruce, Donald, Gary, Bonnie, Angus, Douglas* (mostly originally clan or sept names or surnames), even *Fiona.* In America we have adopted some of these to the extent that they sound 100% American to us. When you hear *Craig* you don't think "Scottish 'rock' " any more than you think "English 'wagon' " when you hear *Wayne.*

British and American names have both influenced Australia. Besides the British names they imported—and the Irish *Sheila* is the Down Under equivalent of "female"—the Aussies have picked up names from US television and films and fads (*Robyn, Kerry*) and have exported to us in return names like *Kylie* (Maori for "boomerang"). The Maoris (except for *Kylie*) have the longest forenames in the world, too strange for any other people to adopt. The Australians have their own fashions, holding onto *Rachel* and some others, for instance, after these names have pretty much disappeared elsewhere. Australians also like British "debutante" names like *Belinda* (the current equivalent of *Felicity,* popular 15 or 20 years ago).

The Canadians also have their own favorites (*Alison* and *Lindsay* are two of them, along with forenames that go equally well in both French and English, such as *Robert* and *Richard*). However, like Australia and most other former colonies, Canada is much affected by the former British Empire. It is also involved in a love/hate relationship with the current American imperium. American products like *Dustin, Tara, Brooke,* and *Cheryl* are seen in all name markets of the world where American (or English) is everyone's second language if not their first. We are even getting the Scots to adopt *Scott.*

Australia and Canada are free in their name choices, in the English tradition. France is one of the countries that like to regulate names. As early as 1539 François I decreed that names for babies had to be approved by a priest and officially registered. That did a great deal to limit them, in the Roman Catholic system, to the names of saints. Napoleon had an Italian forename and was born Italian (though he forged a birth certificate to assert he was born in Corsica when it was under French control and thus was French). He somewhat increased the kinds of allowable French forenames but basically limited them by imperial decree (1803) to names in the church calendar. Another dictator, Charles de Gaulle, regularized French names (1966), banning *De Gaulle* and some others as forenames and eliminating *noms ridicules* or laughable names, among which he unfortunately included "Jewish names," so as to "avoid a repetition of the events" of World War II. Jews and Basques and others in France are angry that they cannot legally bestow their traditional forenames. An occasional *Henry,* which officially must be *Henri,* slips by, but a friend of mine could not get her first name *Clairève* on her French passport. Officials insisted only *Claire Ève* would do. One woman had trouble calling her son *Samuel,* though it's biblical.

On the other side of the Pyrenees, the Spanish have saints' names and a special devotion to the Blessed Virgin and her attributes. They create names such as *Dolores* (sorrows), *Mercedes* (mercies), *Angustias* (anguishes), and *Carmén* (red = color of the lining of the Blessed Virgin's cloak, symbolizing the Passion of Christ). Names are regulated: a Spanish court told one Victor Sanchez he could not take the liberty of calling his child *Libertád.* In far-off Bulgaria, you can go to jail if you won't change your Islamic name; it's an attempt to put down the Turkish minority.

In Germany, predictably, Hitler decreed (1933) that "children of German nationality be given German names." German Jews, much earlier forced to take surnames (some of them the equivalent of French *noms ridicules*), were then forced to give up traditional Hebrew forenames. Now *Adolf* is abandoned and with that the Nazi name laws, but German officials still look askance at *Oscar, Vanessa, Alexandra,* and other names of foreign origin. I notice a number of my German friends are giving pre-Christian, Teutonic forenames to their children these days. Kinder for the *Kinder,* or not? The practice appears to be motivated by aesthetic rather than by religious or political considerations.

In the Soviet Union politics has had an extensive and predictable influence. Ancient forenames still survive: *Svetlana* (light) is not uncommon and *Ivan* (John) is so common it means "guy." However, the Revolution changed much, including names. Vladimir Ulanov called himself Lenin. That inspired the forenames *Vladlen, Ninel* (*Lenin* backwards), and *Villior* (bits of Russian for "Vladimir Lenin, Initiator of the October Revolution"). Later, until he fell into disrepute, the man called Stalin inspired *Stalina.* There was *Myuda* (initials of the Russian for "International Youth Day"). When *Stalin* (steel) became a dirty word, one fellow named *Melsor* changed his forename to drop the *S* for *Stalin* in the acronym for "Marx, Engels, Lenin, Stalin, October Revolution." As political changes wiped away the names of "non-persons" and replaced old placenames with new ones all over Russia, so also they produced personal name changes. The old names of saints (*Yelena, Georgi, Sergei*) have persisted, whatever the government's attitude toward religion as "the opiate of the people," but the non-religious crop of new Soviet names includes *Radii* (radium), *Rubin* (ruby), *Gimilai* (Himalaya), *Traktor* (tractor), *Turbina* (turbine), *Dizel'* (diesel), *Kombain* (harvesting combine), and *Dekabr'* (December, with its political significance there). *Pravda* (truth) once reported two girls named (out of Kropotkin's *Memoirs of a Revolutionary*) for the Russian for "utopia" and "anarchy." Hidden in some of the new Soviet names are political slogans: *Roblen* is from *rodilsya byt' lenintsem* (he was born to be a Leninist) and *Remizan* is from *revolutsiya mirovaya zanyalac* (she participated in world revolution).

The Soviet Union, with its many culturally diverse constituent republics, is even harder than most countries to generalize about, because it contains many races and ethnic groups, Ukrainian and Orthodox Catholics, Muslims and atheists, and most kinds of people in between. Pretty soon half the population of the Soviet Union will be Muslim, but at least the most notable feature of Soviet forenames is the product of the Communist revolution, a watershed between the old days of names equivalent to *Nicholas* and *Alexander* and what the *New York Times* once reported from Moscow as "a new generation burdened with such names as Avangard or Utopiya."

Lately there have been some signs of change in the Soviet Union and one of the minor changes has been in forename control. The head of the USSR Institute for Ethnography (Prof. Nikonov) hailed this trend, conceding that it was hard on kids to be dubbed *Embrion* (embryo), *Telephon* (telephone) and *Alo* (hello), *Diazanteriya* (actually *dizenteryia* in Russian, "dissentery"), *Vinagret* (as in salad dressing) or even *Genii* (genius). He asked for "restraint and good taste" in names. The papers reported that a man in Soviet Armenia who had been named the equivalent of "Five-Year-Plan-in-Four" found the name embarrassing.

Politics have a lot to do with translating forenames into Gaelic or making sure they are French or German or insisting that they indicate a break with the old order. In Israel, the struggle to found the nation, and now to keep it from being wiped away, has produced a nationalist feeling seen in the names as in everything else. It is now popular to avoid the old biblical names and to come up with an unmistakably Israeli name, if (preferably) it is one that English-speakers can easily pronounce. Of course English-speakers might find the names funny, if they could translate the Hebrew: *Abital* is given to both boys and girls and means "my father is dew," *Adman* (peony) is male, and there are *Asisa* (juicy), *Almon* (forsaken), *Arnon* (rushing stream—perhaps suitable for a baby that wets excessively).

Israeli naming patterns are clear. As Jews arriving in America undertook to "Americanize" their names and many Greenbaums dropped the *baum,* so on going to Israel a Mr. Green became Mr. Ben Gurion. An American *Stuart* or *Sondra* or *Scott* (popular with Jews, like *Bruce*) or *Stacy* might on arrival in Israel take an Israeli forename. This has had an effect on American Jews, many of whom are returning to their original surnames (the son of Irving Wallace is David Wallachinsky) and, more germane to this part of the discussion, are increasingly taking Hebrew forenames as a badge of identity, not a yellow Star of David forced upon them but a chosen badge of those who consider they are Chosen. Many of these new Hebrew names go against older Jewish practices.

Orthodox Jews are required to (and Conservative and even some Reformed Jews like to) name a baby for a dead relative. Naming a baby for a living relative, they think, might reduce the older person's lifespan, there being only so much life in any name. With assimilation, however, all but the most Orthodox Jews might have dead relatives who had found "American" equivalents for their traditional biblical forenames. Uncle *Max* might have been a *Moise,* while others whose "real" or "Jewish" name was *Moise* were called *Mortimer, Morton, Murray,* etc. A Hebrew name beginning with an *S* produced first *Stanley, Sidney, Seymour* and later *Stuart, Scott,* and so on. Once the non-Jews noticed that the Jews were fond of *Norman, Irving,* etc., these became "Jewish names" almost exclusively unless there was strong family tradition dictating the use of these surnames as forenames. Jews also more or less took over *Neil* and some other Irish, Scottish, and English forenames. Now there are Jews named *Kevin* and even *Christopher,* while *Jason* (which a generation or two ago was suitable for an assimilated or non-religious Jew whose name might otherwise be, say, *Jesse* or *Joshua*) has moved from "American Jewish" to "American Standard."

That names like *Kevin Klein* and *Neil Simon* are common is a sign that America is a melting pot (or a tossed salad). Many non-Jews will now not adopt *Neil* or *Stuart.* That's prejudice. So, perhaps, was the taking of these names by Jews in the first place; that may have been a sign of self-dislike. The adoption of "ethnic" names by Jews and all other ethnic groups is a sign of a willingness to accept and proclaim identity, to seek roots and seek to honor roots, and to defy bigots and both have and demand respect for self. On the other hand, to have both a "real" ethnic or religious name and another one for daily use is a sign of attempting to keep a foot in both camps and a warning that Hyphenated-Americans of any sort will always be open to the charge that they are not fully Americans, even African-Americans.

Still some Jews have both a religious (Hebrew) and a secular (maybe even WASP) forename, and so, for example, a Japanese-American or even a Japanese doing business with Americans may have an "American" as well as a "Japanese" name. Tradition assigns numbers to boys in Japan (*Taro, Jiro, Sabiro*), even *Man* (ten thousand). If you want a Japanese boy to grow up quiet, you call him *Kiyoshi;* if wealthy, *Tomi* (rich). The Japanese still are much affected by ancient gods: the late Hirohito, who reigned as the *Mikado* (but the term was largely laughed out of existence by Gilbert & Sullivan and he was "the Emperor"), was the Son of the Rice God, whatever we Americans imagined the Japanese thought about his divinity or lack of it. You can dedicate your son to the thunder god (*Reiden*) or to some other deity by name (as we use saints' names), or you can attach virtues to him by creating names for him with such elements as *zen* (just), *yu* (brave), *masa* (good), or simply *toku* (virtuous). Some Japanese references to gods and virtues may be very obscure to us: *Akako* (red girl) stresses a lucky color.

Japanese boys' names may be magical; girls' names are usually pretty. You can name Japanese girls for the seasons: *Haru* (spring), *Natsu* (summer), *Aki* (autumn), *Fuyu* (winter). You can name them for special qualities desired (as we used to name *Prudence* and *Constance*), especially those traditionally associated with women, such as *Sumi* (refinement) and *Setsu* (fidelity). Or you can name them for objects thought to be feminine: *Anzu* (apricot), *Suzu* (little bell), *Kiku* (chrysanthemum), *Umeko* (plum blossom). Americans are confused when such names do not end in *a,* just as they are by *Toshiko* (year child) and other very Japanese given names.

Dealing with the Japanese in business, the Americans may give them western nicknames. Or the Japanese may learn our ways (as they tend to do when we will not or cannot learn theirs) and adopt American forenames. So you meet *Tommy Tanaka,* just as a Chinese in the West might be *Frederick Fu Liu* or *Barry Wong.* The Japanese businessman is quick to press his business card on you (and to ask for yours), knowing that names are important and wanting to get them right. But he also may be wanting to make his name "easy," too, and the name on his business card may or may not be the name he uses at home. He can wear at one time a western business suit and at another the traditional kimono.

Kelly Kamika may be known as *Umaki* (cheerful) by her family. My Chinese student who says he is *Andy* may be *Ak Kum* (good as gold) to his parents. You will notice that all oriental forenames have a clear meaning (if you know the language), even if the Vietnamese *Chai,* for instance, translates simply "female."

The Chinese, with comparatively few surnames, like to be especially creative with first names. Those, of course, come second with them: *Huang Wei-wei* is *Mr. Huang,* formerly *Wang.* The Chinese believe that the family connection (and all people named *Wong,* for example, are considered to be relatives) is the most important thing. That comes first. Then comes the given name. Traditionally, given names were made up by the head of the family and lists were provided from which descendants must choose. In that way, the ancestor in Heaven would know the names of the descendants on earth for whom he should intervene and to whom he would bring luck and prosperity.

Oriental naming practices seem strange to us. The Japanese systems, both the early one and the later one (1868), baffle foreigners with *uji* and *myogi* (surnames), *zokumyo* (given) and *tshusho* (common) and *nanori* or *jitsumo* (true) names. The Japanese system has a possible *yomo* (temporary name for a boy up to age 15), *azana* (pseudonym), *go* (professional name, as of a Kabuki actor), *gago* (professional name of a poet or painter), *goimyo* (professional name of a geisha), even a name granted only after death: Hirohito will receive an *okuri-na* by which he will now be known to Japanese history. Most westerners know that the suffix *-san* is added to show respect (as in *Mama-san*) but such details are beyond us, as are the *homyo* or *kaiymo* (funerary tablet) names given to dead Buddhist priests, let alone the complexities of addressing the living. With the latter even the Japanese have difficulty and, in fact, the mere equivalents of "I" or "you" are hedged with so many restrictions and polite conventions that the Japanese avoid them whenever they can.

Of course there are many orientals in countries other than China and Japan. They have ancient name traditions, too, but sometimes have adapted them to new circumstances, just as a *Vladimir* coming from the USSR might call himself *Victor* in the US or a Pole or Hungarian change the spelling or the placement of his family name. In Hawaii a girl may be given an occasion name (*Ilwalani* if a gull was seen at the time of her birth) the way we name a girl *Dawn* or the Amerindians named *Rain-in-the-Face* or *Sitting Bull*. A Hawaiian girl may still be called *Pualani* (pretty flower) but increasingly one finds she has a Stateside name like *Tiffany*. The old Hawaiian names, more mellifluous than the Teutonic names we inherited from Europe, are unfortunately disappearing in the islands, replaced by *Todd* and *Matthew* and *Cheryl* and *Brittany*.

A key factor in the vanishing of traditional Hawaiian names was the demise of the old Hawaiian religion. Elsewhere, though times have changed, if the traditional religion has remained a vital force, forenames that derived from that religion, whether Spanish (*María, Dolores, Conceptión*) or Sikh, have retained their essential character.

Take the Sikhs, for example. Their religion arose when Guru Nanak (*c.* 1469 – *c.* 1539), sought to reconcile Muslims with Hindus. The tenth and last guru, Guru Govind Singh (d. 1708), made all his co-religionists into warriors and gave every man the surname *Singh* (lion) and every woman *Kaur* (princess). All Sikh forenames came from Guru Arjun (the fifth guru). Followers still open his writings at random when they need a name, just as some of our Puritan forefathers used to get *Fight-Sin* and *If-Christ-Had-Not-Died-For-Ye-Ye-Had-Been-Damned* out of the Bible. The Sikhs choose not a word from the text but a forename that begins with the first letter of the first word on the left-hand page of the randomly-opened *Guru Granth Sahib,* or *Adigranth.* Thus one finds Sikh forenames such as *Zail* (district) and *Zorowar* (strong). As is the case with some other peoples, all names are unisex, given indiscriminately to males and females. To that name suggested by the *Adigranth* one can add a caste name (*Sharmin* for *Brahmins*) or a nickname (*Mota* is "Fatso") or a pseudonym (one poet used *Diwana*, "crazy"). In America the name of the fourth guru (*Ram Das*) was taken by a Jewish fellow who wanted to set up as a California pundit.

A more widespread religion is that of Islam. Its members do not like to be called Mohammedans (they worship Allah, not the Prophet, but they got very incensed recently when Salman Rushdie called him by the disrespectful name

Mahound in the novel *The Satanic Verses*). All the males are called *Moham-med*. They also have 99 names of Allah to choose from and some 500 ways of referring to the Prophet. In the US we have "Black Muslims," but their naming system as well as their religion differs much from conventional Islam.

Surrendering to the will of Allah, followers of Islam say Allah hates boastful titles (*Malik-al-Malik* is "King of Kings") and that humble names (*Abdullah* is "slave of Allah") are good. But tradition emphasizes that "if you have a hundred sons, name them all Mohammed." One honors God and His prophet, not oneself in Islamic naming. Their naming system may be complicated but it is not superstitious: a follower of Islam may not wish to have his or her photograph taken but will reveal his or her name, while some Amerindians, African and Malay tribesmen, etc., will refuse to do so out of fear of magic being worked against them. In India there are some customs which prevent people from reporting (say) the names of their husbands, etc., which makes taking the census difficult.

If the naming customs of foreign peoples look odd to us, so do our customs look strange to much of the rest of the world, despite the fact that the spread of English as a language worldwide has brought with it familiarity with our naming system. We sometimes name a child before it is born. Some Africans will not name a baby until they are certain it will live. Roman fathers did not take up the baby from the hearth (thus accepting it) for a number of days; then they gave boys one of a handful of available names (or a number, such as *Tertius, Quintus, Octavius*) and all the daughters the same (family) name with a distinguishing number: *Julia Major, Julia Minor, Julia Tertia*. The Ibos of Nigeria call on Chi (a spirit) to protect newborn babes and work his name into given names. Hispanics use *Jesús* and some men in Europe have *María* as one of their given names. Some idiots in America give their children nasty names (*Odor, Venal, Vagina*), but some Africans cannily give children nasty names so that the angel of death will leave them alone. Orthodox Jews have ways of confounding the angel of death: change the name of a sick child so the angel cannot locate it, or call the youngster *Alter* (old) to confuse. The Yoruba use *Fayola* (good luck) as the Romans, who believed that *nomen est omen*, used *Felix*. We might call a girl *Linda* or *Bonita* to boast of beauty (as a Turk might use *Cemal* or a Muslim *Kamil*, though that "perfect" refers to Allah, for no one else is perfect). Some Muslims say we ought to translate *Allah* and always say *God* in English. An African child might be protected from jealous spirits by a name translating "worthless" or "unenviable." Such derogatory names make sense. An Arab who has lost many children at birth may name the next one *Kalb* (dog) in the hope that fate will not take it from him. How touching is the Ghanaian *Kaya* ("don't go back") and how much it tells us of the terrible infant mortality rate in some societies.

In Ghana the Akan-speakers use a naming system known elsewhere in Africa. Children are named for the day of their birth: *Kudjo, Kwabina, Kwaku, Kuau, Koffi, Kwamin, Kwashi*. Recall how Robinson Crusoe named his man

Friday. Or the Akans may note birth order (*Anum* is "fifth") or birth circum-stances (*Kontor* is "only boy") or opt for *Donkor* (humble) or *Gyasi* (wonderful).

In other parts of Ghana children may be named for rivers (*Afram, Kroto, Prah*) or they may be called *Odom* (oak), *Bour* (flour), or *Sono* (elephant). First sons often receive celebratory names; second sons are called *Manu*, third sons *Menash*. One of the most striking Ghanan given names is *Nmadi* ("my father still lives"), given where the Romans used to bestow *Posthumus* but also suggesting reincarnation (as we do with *René, Renée, Renata*). *Nmadi* is regarded as the reincarnation of his dead father. Ghanan names of praise include *Arko* and *Bekoe* for born fighters, for every society reveals its values in its names.

Yoruba-speakers call boys *Adigun* (righteous), *Ajani* (victor), *Akin* (hero), and so on down the alphabet. A long-awaited son is greeted with the name *Kayin* (celebrated). The blessing of a fourth son in a row gets *Anane*. The war god (Ogun) is invoked in such names as *Ogunkeye* ("Ogun has earned honor") and his blessing sought in *Ogunsanwo* ("Ogun helps"). This deity also appears as Okun and there are compounds incorporating that name, as with the Ibo spirit Chi already mentioned, source of *Ciese* ("Chi guards") and *Chileogu* ("Chi defends") and *Cinua* ("Chi blesses"). We seek the same protection, intercession, and blessing from the saints for whom we name Christian children, but these African names startle when they are like *Atuanya* ("we throw eyes," meaning that the parents who were expecting or reconciled to a girl baby were startled to receive a boy child) or *Ilkomerika* ("has many enemies") or *Dumaka* ("lend a hand," meaning that the child will grow up to be welcome assistance with the family's struggle to find food and shelter for themselves).

We used to have special names for twins: *Thomas* was one. The Benin people of Nigeria call the first boy of twins *Odion*. The Hausa call him *Hassan* or *Hussein*. The Hausa also use day-of-the-week names: *Danladi* was born on a Sunday. The Tivs use *Gowon* (rainmaker) for a boy born in a storm, although we use *Storm* and *Tempest* (sometimes illiterately *Tempestt*) and of course *Gail* or *Gale* with no such purpose. (I do know a *Thor* in Minnesota, however, named because his birth was accompanied by a thunder storm.) We note birth at night or at morning but Ashanti *Kesse* is "born fat," which some Americans who have adopted some form of this name may be unhappy to learn is worse than *Bertha*. Wataware *Carai* (settled) and *Kemali* (praise for a deity) are interesting but more so is *Kaseko*, which "ridicules" those who said the mother would produce no sons.

Getting tired of all these examples of foreign forenames? Stay for a page or two more and I'll try to make the examples as entertaining as possible. The Ovimbundo of Angola may name a baby *Cilombo* (roadside camp) and mean to compare the pleasure brought by it. Or *Musende* (nightmare) may be the name if a bad dream follows the birth. Or *Matope* may indicate the baby is the last one wanted, just as I know of Americans named *Finis* and *Finale*. Where infant mortality is very high, as among the Ochi or Ga people, small blessings are counted and nothing is as wonderful or welcomed as *Odinum* (fifteenth son).

In Tanzania, Swahili-speakers have *Nassor* (Muslims use *Nasser*) for "victorious" and *Mosi* for the firstborn son (Muslims use *Omar*). Swahili names include *Ashur* (a month, as we might use *April* or *May* or *June*), *Dandi* ("beloved," as we might use *Amy*), *Masud* ("fortunate," our *Felix*), *Jahi* ("dignified," our *Augustus* or *Augusta*), and *Nuru* ("light," our *Lucius* or *Lucy*), so you see that in some name techniques the whole world is kin. Where the Ibo has *Agu* (leopard) we have Latin *Leo* (lion). Where the Urhoto notice physical appearance (*Ottah* is "skinny"), we have *Rufus* and *Russell* (originally for redheads). Where the Japanese have *Jiro* and the Swahili *Pili* we have used Roman number names such as *Septimus*. Where the Arabic has *Abd al-Rahman* (servant of the Merciful One) we have *Amadeus* and *Theophilus* for those beloved of God. But we do not have a special name for a fifteenth son or any equivalent for the Chinese deprecating name *Tidzio* (pig piss) or the plaintive Yoruba *Kosoko* ("we have no hoe," meaning "don't die because we cannot bury you").

From the British Isles to the South Pacific to the Middle East and the Far East and Africa, forenames, because they are basically chosen rather than inherited, are excellent indicators of the mindset of the namers and, by extension, the ethos of societies. We call them "Christian names" very often, but that is inaccurate in many cases even within our own society. Better to call them forenames, though even that term suggests that people have to have more than one name, which is not the case in all societies, and in fact in some groups our concepts of individual names are severely challenged. Where people have names, however, they are both bound to their cultural inheritance and given a certain individual identity. They receive with their names scripts for their lives, expressions of the beliefs and expectations of their parents, clues to where they fit into society and what their duties are. Names are human artifacts that can tell us much of the namers' beliefs about religion and magic, social order, what parents want from children, how they seem often to value males over females, and how the members of the society regard the world in which they live. In short, names are full of historical, cultural, and sociological information.

Further, the very manner in which forenames are used (or avoided) in speech reveals much about the society. Sometimes people interact on a "first-name basis." Sometimes they are not permitted by custom to use personal names at all. "If your lordship pleases." "Would the captain step this way?" Formality increases from nickname *Tim* to forename *Leonard* to *Mr. Ashley, Dr. Ashley, Prof. Ashley* to no-name "What was my grade on the exam, Professor?" Sometimes we use "Sir" or "Madame" in place of names we know. We can even use conventional names that we know are not those of the person addressed. You are familiar with the phrase, "Home, James," but probably are not aware why *James* is in it. British convention dictated once that all footmen were *James* (which saved having to learn the names of insignificant, inter-changeable people). When, about the turn of this century, automobiles came into use, footmen were given the new job of warming up (and driving) the car: a new word came from France, *chauffeur.* But the master riding in the car was used to regarding the "warmer-upper" as a footman—and he continued to call him *James.* Butlers were called by their surnames, some of the more intimate servants by their forenames and the rest by their surnames, and the cook was always *Mrs.,* whether she was married or not.

Knowing how to address whom is to know one's culture. Calling a Pullman porter *George* was *de rigeur,* but to call a butler *George* was a *faux pas.* English Public School boys for generations were not likely to call each other *George;* it might be *Bunny* or some other nickname, or a surname (or a nickname from that, maybe *Aero* from the candy bar and the surname *Ayre*), and a boy might not even know the meaning of the first initials of his best friends. The subtlety of superior/inferior address that we encounter in Japanese life or in reading Russian novels or Scandinavian plays is by no means unparalleled in our own lives. If you ponder a moment, you'll realize that knowing when and where to use forenames in America is not such a simple matter, and that even very informal modes of address—"Beat it, Buster" and "Yo, Dude" and "Thanks, Sport" and "Listen, Mac"—have their own unwritten but clearly understood rules, distinct connotations, specific applications. To know when to say *Mr. Brown, Boss, Chief, J.R., Jimmy, Chip,* etc., is to be acutely aware of subtle degrees of intimacy. We may like to think that Americans comfortably get right to a "first-name basis." Actually we don't. Some few people may even respond to "You can call me Jack" with "And you can call me Mr. Smith." Names can be used as a form of control.

In ancient times, Herodotus said, there were some nameless people. He was wrong. People have to have names; they have always had them. Those names may sound as strange to you as *Yourene, Toileta, Rearis,* and *Especulia* (col-lected by Jay Ames of Toronto), or *Lemaza, Zilpher,* or the moniker of the first baby delivered with chloroform (she was called *Anaesthesia*), and some people may spell *Richard* as *Ryszard* but, as Papa Smurf once said, "there are things of great value in all cultures," even in Florida, where twins have been called *Bigamy* and *Larceny,* and *Pete* and *Repeat.*

There was a time (1898) when *Ida* was in the US Top 10. Today in the Cayman Islands popular names include *Berrick, Erdley, Leebert, Torry, Day-lene, Joyette, Rese, Thora, Uldene, Verta,* and *Wyria,* none of which would sound very odd in some parts of Detroit. There was a time when Puritans per-petrated mouthfuls like *Through-Much-Tribulation-We-Enter-Into-The King-dom-Of-Heaven Crabb*—"her friends called her Tribby," writer Gary Jennings wryly observed—and a time when H. L. Mencken delightedly collected right here in the US—I'll just cite one for most letters of the alphabet—*Armadilla, Bleba, Coita, Dullere, El Louise, Flowanna, Glanda, Hygiene, Iceyphobia, Kiwanis, Ladye, Madame, Navelle, Ova, Phalla, Quay, Roseola, Sing, Twitty, Ureatha, Vanajulia, Wroberta,* and *Zzelle.* In those days there was no really outrageous *J*-name. Today there are plenty, from *Jermaine* (for boys) to *Johjoe* (for girls).

Ultimately, weirdness lies in the ear of the listener, which is to say *Towanna* or *Trayci* are strange or not depending upon one's cultural frame of reference. Many Europeans still cannot credit top American officials having such informal names as *Jimmy* or *Bobby.* Foreigners wonder if the large number of US college presidents with forenames as unusual as *Kingman* and *Delyte* prove that one has to be peculiar to attain such a position. If we have trouble with foreign names such as *Ding Ling* (the novelist), *Yo-Yo Ma* (the musician), and *Kiri Te Kanawa* (the singer), and prefer both Polish *Grzegorz* and Hungarian *Hryhory* to become not "Gregory" but *Harry,* it is hardly surprising. But we cope with both *Oral* and *Orel* and are getting used to names new to us, from Cambodia or Columbia or California. Differences of place and time and taste make for new perspectives and add yet another beguiling dimension to the study of names. *Sistine Madonna McClung* and *Jesús O'Brien* and *Elihu Yale* and *Meryl Streep* and *Oprah Winfrey* and *Darryl Strawberry* are all American names. In San Joaquin County (California) in 1989 so are *Librado, Zarai, Lacy Leeann, Chantel Denea, Pimpaphone, Briana Dence, Willyn,* and *Ilia Nik.*

3. Surnames: Last But Not Least

There are even more surnames and surname systems in the world than fore-names and forename systems. In this section we take a necessarily cursory but wide-ranging look at some of the names people inherit from their families rather than names that are chosen by their parents.

It was the Romans who, in western culture, established the family name. Those *cognomina* (family or clan names), however, did not catch on in Britain during the centuries of Roman occupation; it was not really until the Middle Ages that the average Briton began to acquire an extra name to distinguish him or her from all the other *John*s and *Mary*s and others who had received Christian names at the baptismal font. There were just too many people with the same saints' names, and surnames (the French nobility having introduced the practice into Britain, as the term indicates) were adopted not just by the great but by almost everyone.

From very ancient times, a man was properly identified by his given name and that of his father. The Jews used names consisting of X *ben* (son of) Y, and indeed continued this system until German bureaucrats, to facilitate their record-keeping, insisted that Jews adopt distinctive and inherited surnames. At first, and in general, surnames were individual, but later the system became more formal. Then people took their father's surname for the family name. The first John son of Richard was truly *John Richardson*, but thereafter in that family you might have sons and daughters whose fathers were not named Richard; just some ancestor was a Richard. Among patronymics (names from fathers) not immediately obvious like *Johnson* and *Watson* and *Wilson* are names such as *Adams, Bartlett, Dawkins, Dixon, Empson, Hobart, Jeeves, Jarvis, Hammond, Lucas, Maryat, Opie, Payne* and *Price* (from the Welsh *ap Rhys*, the *ap* meaning "son of"). The Irish *O'* or *Mc* or *Mac* clearly mark descent. The prefix *Fitz-* goes back to French *fils* (son) but was used to indicate bastardy, for in those days it was better to be the bastard son of a Somebody than the legitimate son of a Nobody. One might boast *FitzGerald* even if born,

34

as they used to say, "on the wrong side of the blanket" and adopt the coat of arms of a famous Gerald even with the sign of bastardy, the bar sinister.

Or a surname could originate in a placename. This began with nobles with estates but later anyone might be *John of Lincoln* and later *John Lincoln,* though usually the family had moved. There was no use being *Lincoln* in a town where everyone else claimed the same identification. Hence also appeared *John Lake, John Rivers, John Atwater, John Mill(s), John Dale.* Also, places created surnames such as *Craig, Douglas, Forbes, Innes, Munro* and *Penrose, Trease, Trevor.* My own surname (*Ashley*) derives from an ash tree (or a grove of ash trees, the Sacred Grove of the Druids) in a field. The original Ashleys may have taken their surname from any one of a number of British places of that name; they may have given the name to some of those places.

Or a surname could originate from an occupation—one which the descendants did not necessarily follow—and thus were created *John Smith, John Baker* and *John Barker* (a tanner), *John Cartwright* and *John Wainwright, John Wright* and *John Clark(e)* (a cleric or someone who could write), and *John Franklin* and *John Reeve(s)* (town officials). The original *Lorimer* made things for horses; the original *Arrowsmith* made the arrows on which the original *Fletcher* put the feathers; *Stringer* made the bowstrings and the original *Archer* or *Bowman* fired the arrows. The original *Redman* may have dealt in reeds (for thatched roofs). Many surnames derived from occupations now go unidentified as such because we no longer have (say) chandlers or tenants of hoovers (about 120 acres, a "hide"). Others are misinterpreted: today a *Mailman* delivers letters and is not named because he is a tenant paying rent. *Farmer* used to collect rents; later came farmers.

The favored kind of surname came from being the descendant of someone notable. The Irish *O'* (originally *au*) marked a grandson; the Irish *Mc* or *Mac* was the "son of." We have noted the Welsh *ap;* it produced names like *Pritchard* (*ap Richard*). The son of a Norman noble inherited *de* (from), boasting estates, and hence we find some strange forms like *Danvers, D'Arcy, Doyle,* and *D'Eath.*

Short of being a legitimate prince, named from your place of birth like *Richard of Bordeaux,* you could hardly beat being the illegitimate son of the king, *Fitzroy.* One king of England took *FitzEmpress.*

Your average person, if not named from his father, or his place of origin, or his occupation, got a nickname, as a king might be *Charles the Bold, Charles the Handsome, Charles the Idiot, Edward Longshanks, Richard Crookshanks, Sancho the Cruel, Ivan the Terrible,* or *Erik Pinchpenny.* Thus we got *John Long, John Short, John Black, John Read* and names derived from a person's manner (*John Wise, John Proudfoot, John Makespeace, John Strangeways*) or something else associated with him (*John Shakespeare, John Ford, John Tremaine* [the man who lived in a stone homestead]). Then his descendants, whatever their appearance, etc., inherited the surname, which (as the linguists say) became lexically opaque: you never bothered that your baker was *John Tyler* or your tiler *John Baker*. (You usually only notice such things when your dentist is *Payne* or your surgeon *Slaughter* or your ophthalmologist *I. Doctor*.) You forgot *McPherson* came from a son of the parson, that *Figueroa* made figurines, that *Eastman* was not from the east but was associated with either "protection" or maybe "grace."

Americans picked up all these names, including those from industries perhaps not established here (though we did have the textile industry, which gave us *Walker, Tucker, Fuller,* and more). We did not bother to notice that *Russell* was no longer redheaded or that *Belcher* did not have a pretty face (the French got corrupted, you see) or worry where *Ellington* or *Churchill* may have been. We threw open our country to the peoples of the world and with them we received surnames from everywhere, so that the US Social Security files, for instance, now contain millions of surnames from all sorts of systems.

Let us begin our brief look at some of those systems with old Russia, where *Ivanov* was the son of *Ivan*. The Russians came to use three names: *Ivan Ivanovich Pavlov* was the name of John the son of John of the family derived from Paul. His sister might be *Nastia Ivanovna Pavlova,* Nastia the daughter of John of the family derived from Paul. When she married, her new surname would likewise be feminized. Some Russians had foreign surnames (Scottish, German, etc.) but Russianized them. However, when you addressed these persons you did not call them the equivalent of "Mr. Rock"; you usually said "John son of John." So far so good. It is only when the Russian penchant for nicknames comes into play that we English readers have big trouble sorting out the characters in Tolstoy (fat), Gorky (bitter), and other Russian writers.

The Scandinavians had a patronymic system that was relatively simple and yet could produce plenty of confusion. Anders the son of Lars would be *Anders Larsen* in Denmark or *Anders Larsson* in Sweden, but his son (let's say he's named Peder) would be *Peder Andersen* or *Peder Andersson* and his grandson (little Lars) would be *Lars Pedersen* or *Lars Pedersson*. The great-grandson of our original Anders would, almost by accident, have the same surname as the great-grandfather, *Larsen* or *Larsson*. A daughter could, of course, not be a *-sen* or *-son*. Lavran's daughter was *Lavransdatter* and, in Iceland, Thorstein's daughter was *Thorsteinsdottír*. Brothers and sisters did not have the same surnames, like the Russian *Pavlov* and *Pavlova*. What increased the problem was the fact that there was a comparatively small number of forenames (and thus surnames, too) in use. By 1976, for example, 40% of all Swedes were getting by with a mere 20 surnames. There were 380,000 *Johansson*s (many forenamed like their father), 370,000 *Andersson*s (many forenamed *Anders*), 239,000 *Nilsson*s (many of whose fathers had thought that *Erik* would be a nice change), and so on. Looking up Mr. Eriksson in the telephone book was a challenge! In Denmark there were so many *Jensen* and *Hansen* families that the government encouraged, even paid, people to change their surnames. And some people, trying a bit too hard, became *Dilemma* or *Hundever* (dog lover).

After Scandinavia, with few names, let's look at the world of Islam and its more elaborate system which confers as many as five classes of names. First comes a forename (*Mohammed, Ali*). Then comes a reference to a parent or sometimes a metaphorical relationship: *Abu Musa Ali* (Ali, father of Moses), *Uum Ali* (mother of Ali), *Abu al-Dawaniq* ("father of pennies," nickname of a wealthy caliph). In the third slot might come ancestors listed with *ibn* (son of) or *bint* (daughter of) or the appropriate suffix on a name. Persians add *-i* in the way that other peoples make patronymics with *-son, sen, -ski, -ovich, -poulos, -czyk, -ov, -wicz, -chuk, -ian, -enko, -ez,* or just plain *-s*. Fourth may come a title like *Sayf al-Islam* (Sword of Islam), or a nickname. Nicknames can refer to appearance like *al-Tawil* (the tall), an occupation like *al-Khayyam* (the tentmaker), or a virtue like *al-Rashid* (the upright). Fifth, and finally, there could be one or more references to place(s) of origin, residence, trade, profession, or even clan; here is where we might see something like *al-Misri* (the Egyptian). Additionally, there can be official titles (*sultan, caliph, sheriff, emir, pasha, bey*) which foreigners may mistake for personal names. These come after rather than before the actual names, even in the case of foreigners such as Glubb *Pasha*.

For intricacy there are few surname systems as formidable to foreigners as the Hispanic. Where, for instance, does the "last name" begin in *Pablo Diego José Francisco de Paula Juan Nepomuceno María de los Remédios Cipriano de la Santissima Trinidád Ruíz Picasso?* Why call him Picasso instead of Ruíz? Why is Federico García Lorca called Lorca and not García but José Pamias Alonso is Sr. Pamias? What about Carlos Restrepo Restrepo Restrepo de Restrepo, of Colombia? What about the secretary-general of the Organization of American States who said in 1979:

> Galo is my Christian name; Plaza is my [father's] family name; Lasso is my mother's family name. Some call me Mr. Plaza, others Mr. Lasso. In fact, while I was ambassador for Ecuador in the United Nations, I was called Ambassador Plaza, and people thought I was a hotel.

Hispanics take both father and mother into account. So do the British with surnames such as *Ashley-Cooper,* though the average person is probably unsure who was the mother and who was the father. (In that case, it was an *Ashley* mother and a *Cooper* father and it all took place at the turn of the sixteenth century, since which time *Ashley-Cooper* is the father's name and each mother's name is not in the surname of further generations.) In British practice the mother's "maiden name" became part of the surname just once; in the case of *Ashley-Cooper* because Sir Anthony Ashley had no male heirs and the Cooper bridegroom, though rich, had the name of a "barrel-maker." In time *Ashley-Cooper* began to sound too fancy for all but the branch of the family with the earldom, so everyone else was just *Ashley*. The male-line name,

Cooper, was the one that disappeared. Now people whose real last name is *Cooper* often like to give *Ashley* as a forename; the names somehow "go together," though very few people know exactly why. Hyphenated names are generally considered too stuffy these days, though one can sympathize with *Harley Barker* becoming *Harley Granville Barker* (no hyphen) and people named plain *Hill* escalating to *Goodjer-Hill.* I went to school with *Goodjer-Hill* and even *Parnell-Parnell* and *Knatchbull-Hugessen,* but I don't recommend hyphens.

But back to Spanish surnames of children who honor both their fathers and their mothers. *Juan Fernández Gomez y Torres* means that Juan Fernández's father was a Gomez, his mother a Torres. (*Fernández* came from an "adventurer"; *Gomez* was the son of someone forenamed Gomo.) Now let's have Juan marry María del Carmén García Lorca, who then becomes María del Carmén García Lorca de Gomez (y Torres, if she wishes). Their son Francisco Javier would be Francisco Javier Gomez (y Torres) García (Lorca) and would have either two or four surnames or, a better way of looking at it, a long surname and a shorter one. If Francisco Javier married into the prestigious Ortega (y Gasset) Borbón (y Borbón) family, his child might be María del Dolores Gomez y Torres García Lorca Ortega y Gasset Borbón y Borbón.

You can appreciate how this sort of thing can get out of hand very quickly. In fact, when the *hidalgos* of Spain reached the point of quartered coats of arms that looked like aerial views of the AIDS quilt, and were boasting 50 surnames in a row, the king put a stop to it. One *grandee* in our century, assisted by 89 forenames, set a modern record for a virtually interminable name, but I do not have space to give it to you now.

Hispanics in the US, like most people here, have adapted their ways to general American ones. Juan Álvarez Lopez is likely to be called Mr. Lopez by other Americans, so if he wants to stress his father's name he may call himself *Juan Álvarez* or even *Juan Álvarez L.* If there are too many people named *Álvarez* around, he may call himself *Juan Á. Lopez.* In Mesoamerica and farther south, however, the old customs, however cumbersome, endure. In Loreto (Mexico) a third of the population is descended from one Davis, so there's *Davis Davis Davis* and *Davis Davis Davis Davis.* (Neither lives on the main street which is—you guessed it—Davis.) Similarly, there's a town called Levitch (Yugoslavia) where everyone has the same last name. But that's alright, for in very small societies everyone is more or less on a first-name basis anyway; surnames are not all that important. In an Irish village one might be simply *Pegeen Mike* (little Margaret, Michael's daughter) and on a Swedish farm there might be the equivalent of "Big Erik," "Little Erik," "Big Little Erik," "Little Big Erik," and so on, with no confusion among the locals, though when I visited they thought the nicknames would confuse me so each and every one said, when asked, "My name is Erik."

We've mentioned the Irish, and their surnames are an interesting study. A sampler of derivations would usefully include *Moriarty* (*muircheartach,* navigator), *Murphy* (from the Gaelic for "sea warrior"), *MacNamara* (from the Gaelic for "son of the hound of the sea"), *Coyne* (well-born), and *Feargannon* (without a name). *Docherty* was "stern," *Kennedy* had an "ugly head," *O'Connor* was descended from someone with a "high will" and *O'Reilly* from a "prosperous or valiant one." King Brian Boru and Niall of the Nine Hostages were heroes boasted by *O'Brien* and *O'Neill*.

Surnames like *Coyne* (equivalent to *Eugene* from the Greek) and *Finnegan* (handsome) are adjectival. *Donohue* (brown warrior) is an adjective modifying a noun. Some Irish surnames, also used as forenames now, are so ancient there is a dispute about their origins: *Neill* and *Ryan* are two examples. But *Kelly* clearly means "strife."

Irish surnames have not only been used as forenames by English speakers but have also been translated into English. Others look English but are really of Gaelic origin (*Butler, Palmer, More*). Some are from Norman French—remember *D'Arcy?*—or gussied up to appear so (*Des Moulins* may once have been plain *Mullins*). Some derive from nicknames: *MacAvaddy* is not to be confused with T. S. Eliot's name for a villainous cat (*McCavity*) but is properly *Mac an Mdadaidh* (cognate with *Ó Madáin,* which we usually see as *Madden*) and derives from the word for "dog." Some Irish surnames have as many as 30 or 40 English spellings. There's a famous case of a tombstone on which a father, mother, and their four children are listed as *McEneaney, McAneany, McAneny, McEnaney, McEneany,* and *Bird* (the last based on the mistaken notion that the surname has something to do with Gaelic *éan,* "bird").

So many Irish people came to America that Irish surnames in English form (*Murphy, Sullivan, Walsh, Nolan, O'Brien, Byrne, Ryan, Connor,* etc.) constitute a large part of our surname stock and are even borne by blacks (whose ancestors belonged to slaveholders of the name). The Irish surnames here have outlasted such English names in the first US census (1790) as *Spitsnoggle, Madsavage, Crampeasy, Rottenberry, Laughinghouse, Wentup, Grabtale, Bump, Gouge, Beersticker,* and *Tart*. The fact that Irish names with unwanted meanings have those meanings buried in the Gaelic has kept some from being dropped at the same time that lack of knowledge of Gaelic has disguised the fact that the *O'Sullivan* clan claims descent from the "one-eyed," the Cyclops.

Every humble Pat and Mike has at least a chance of being a descendant of one of the High Kings of Erin. Every *Brennan* descends from someone who was branded as a criminal or, more charitably, let us say from someone whose job it was to brand criminals.

My maternal grandfather was a *Nelligan* (*Ó Niallagáin*) and claimed connection with the chieftain Niall of the Nine Hostages (perhaps in an attempt to keep up with his wife, who was descended from Howard of Effingham, not the Howards, dukes of Norfolk, but pretty prestigious). The Nelligan arms feature the severed right hand of that Niall and refer to a gruesome episode of the past still recalled on the arms of Ulster and the barons of Nova Scotia.

It's obvious that common names such as *Long* or non-specific ones such as *Gallagher* (foreign assistance) were borne by unrelated families and that ancestors of those named *Crump* may all have been bent over but not necessarily all of one family, any more than all people named *Kutzetsov* (the Russian for *Smith*) are related or all people named *Sunderland* (southern land) are from the same ancestors. Anyone with curly hair could be *Crippen* or *Crispin*. People sometimes like to forget that though genealogy requires long memories (and has been unjustly called "the science of fools with long memories"), shared surnames do not always indicate blood relationships. There are tens of thousands of Nelligans in the US (more than in Ireland, I think), but there is no guarantee that your Nelligans or mine all came from Ballynelligan. Genealogy demands careful research to determine whether you Nelligans and I are cousins, all descended from that Patrick Nelligan who went to Canada in 1832, or from some immigrants who landed in New York after fleeing the Potato Famine (1848). Similarly, there are more than 30,000 Ashleys in the US, but some derive from one who went to Springfield (Massachusetts) in 1638, some are from one who went to Virginia, some are from a New York farmer, and so on, and these US family founders may not all have been related back in England. Genealogy can give one a sense of tradition (perhaps even connection with the glories of the High Kings of Erin or the British royal house, with whom former President Jimmy Carter, for instance, is connected) but must also remind us that all families are "old" and that we are all, in fact, members of one human family. The family tree of the entire human race could, at least in theory, be constructed and the prodigious efforts of the Mormons, with their vast data banks in Salt Lake City, are moving in the direction of constructing it. The project is immense but underway.

We must move on here, if our little project is to be realized. We turn next to Italy. Emilio de Felice, working with Italian telephone records, determined that just 226 Italian surnames (which he reduced to 182 basic forms) account for over 18% of all Italian surnames. At the same time, nearly one third of all the surnames listed in Italian telephone books are represented by one subscriber each. Collectors of unique names will have a field day there.

Like all other surnames, Italian surnames reveal much about history and customs. For instance, Italian society treated unwed mothers rather badly; so often the births were concealed and the children left on the church steps to be taken in and raised by orphanages. That's why *Esposito* (exposed) is the sixth most popular name in Italy. That's also why many Italians are descended from "orphans" who were called by the priests or nuns *della Chiese, de Angelo, della Croce, Benedetti*, etc. The most common Italian surname is *Rossi*, suggesting that at one time or another Italians found redheaded people remarkable.

Indicative of how regional differences can affect surnaming within a country is the fact that in northern Italy names tend to stress occupations (equivalents of *Smith* are numerous: *Ferrari, Fabbri, Forgione, Magnani*, etc.) and in some very prominent cases the professions (the great *Medici* family were originally doctors, with three gilded pills on their coat of arms). In the bustling northern Italian cities forenames were much used and so there are a lot of surnames there derived from forenames. In the more rural south, Italian surnames more often derived from nicknames and from physical appearance. Some of these names are hilarious, but English speakers miss the point in *Parlaparla* (talk back), *Boccaccio* (bad mouth), and *Sodoma*. For that matter, elsewhere, too, we miss the "crooked" in *Campbell,* the "flour" in *Lizst,* the "sour cream" in *Smetana,* and the insult in *Trognon* (apple core, French slang for "anus").

Especially in America, where we have so many foreign origins for our surnames, we don't realize that announcer Don Pardo's last name first came from some swearing Norman (*par Dieu!,* "by God!") or that actress Lillian Gish's name is from the French *guiche* (spit curl). Mr. Katz is a Hebrew "righteous priest" (*kohentzadik*) and therefore closer to Mr. Cohen (which also turns up as *Cone, Cohn,* etc.) and Mr. Levi (whose names show their ancestors served in the Temple) than you might think. There's a lot of playing with spellings (*Kahn, Le Vine, Le Frak*) and many a *Haddad* has translated to *Smith* in America. When the Italians turn *Antonio* into the surname *Tonelli,* or *Francisco* into *Ciccone,* or *Giacomo* into *Mazzucci,* no wonder we are baffled, and when the surname translates "salad bowl mixup" we miss the joke in our "tossed salad" society.

The commonest Italian-American surnames are probably *Russo* or *Rossi, Lombardo* or *Lombardi, Romano, Marino, Lorenzo* and *Costa* (either of which may also be Spanish or Portuguese), *Luna, Rossini, Esposito,* and *Gallo.* Do you know what they mean? If not, for these and all other American surnames look at a book such as Elsdon C. Smith's *New Dictionary of American Family Names* (1973). There are specialized dictionaries of the surnames of France (Dauzat) or any other foreign country you may think is the birthplace of the name in which you are interested. Always remember that (as I said) in the US names have been translated, mangled, or dropped altogether for "American" ones. *Wilson, Macy, Bloomingdale, Hershey, Pershing* and such were once names in German, and *Steinway* went half way, from *Steinweg* (stone street). Many a US *Marlowe* once had a Finnish surname, many a *Miller* was once a *Müller, Møller,* etc. *Mondale* was a Scandinavian name, *Hart* was shortened from *Hartpence, Fox* may have been *Fuchs,* and I recently noted a *La Pidus.*

Surname changing has always gone on. The British turned Norman surnames into their own versions: *Beauchamp* into *Beecham, Beauclerc* into *Buckley, Beauvoir* into *Beaver* and *Pibaudière* into *Peabody,* in the same spirit that here in the West we made the French explorers' *Purgatoire* into very American *Picketwire.*

Not only out in the Wild West but here on the East Coast, at Ellis Island, we played fast and loose with surnames. *Judah ben Hur* might become *Jude de Benner.* Someone who said in Yiddish, when asked his name (and not wanting to reveal it, distrustful of authority), "I've forgotten," entered the country as *Séan Ferguson.* Relatives of actress Anne Bancroft, asked their name, didn't understand the question, gave their nationality instead, and were written down as surnamed *Italiano*. I knew a Sicilian baron's son whose father arrived here insisting on his title and reeled off an imposing name only to be recorded as *Barone* (here pronounced Ba-rohn). There's a Swedish family called *Ness* whose forebears thought they were being given a name when the official called "Next!" Some foreign names that did get past customs got phonetic spellings. *Featherstonehaugh* is now spelled by many as said: *Fanshaw. Weiss* became *Wise* and no one the wiser. Middle European names took quite a beating. I know of a Polish family with a Dutch name, *De Witt,* confected from a long surname in Polish beginning with a *D* and ending in the Polish for "son of." They might have been mere *Dee.* Arriving on the East Coast, many immigrants lost their European names, deliberately or by accident. Later some changed their names again on arriving in the new West. "What Was Your Name in the States?" was the title of a pioneer song that recognized that people often cut even name ties when heading out for "the Territories." American genealogy is not an easy study!

This can be somewhat aided by Social Security records. Nevertheless, this incredible store of US surnames gives only a very rough idea of our names. For one thing, some records take note only of the first six letters of the surname, so *Robert, Roberts,* and *Robertson* are regarded as one. Now even little babies are getting Social Security numbers and entering the records, but there are millions of "illegals" who do neither. At best, Social Security records (like telephone books) offer a convenient but far from complete guide to surnames from era to era. In 1984 Social Security name files (with some dead names) had 346,417,726 surnames.

Take the year 1974 (before names like *Ng* began to figure prominently in US records). Of 1,287,000 different surnames then in Social Security files, a whopping 649,000 were used by fewer than 10 persons each. There were 2,200 surnames that year used by more than 10,000 persons each (among them *Ashley,* used by some 33,000, including some California Jews who had adopted it and made it somewhat prominent in the film industry). In 1974 the 100 most common US surnames, according to Social Security statistics, were these:

1. Smith	13. Moore	25. Allen
2. Johnso(n)	14. Thomas	26. Young
3. Willia(ms) (mson)	15. White	27. Morris(on)
4. Brown	16. Thomps(on)	28. King
5. Jones	17. Jackso(n)	29. Wright
6. Miller	18. Clark(e)	30. Nelson
7. Davis	19. Robert(s) (son)	31. Rodríg(uez)
8. Martin(ez) (son)	20. Lewis	32. Hill
9. Anders(en) (on)	21. Walker	33. Baker
10. Wilson	22. Robins(on)	34. Richar(d) (ds) (dson)
11. Harrison	23. Peters(on)	35. Lee
12. Taylor	24. Hall	36. Scott

37. Green
38. Adams
39. Mitche(l) (ll)
40. Philli(ps)
41. Campbe(ll)
42. Gonzál(es) (ez)
43. Carter
44. García
45. Evans
46. Turner
47. Stewar(t) (d) (dson)
48. Collin(s)
49. Parker
50. Edward(es) (s)
51. Murphy
52. Cook
53. Rogers
54. Griffi(n) (th) (ths)
55. Christ(ian) (ianson) (enson) (opher)
56. Morgan
57. Cooper
58. Reed
59. Bell
60. Bailey
61. Kelly
62. Wood
63. Ward
64. Cox
65. López
66. Steven(s) (son)
67. Howard
68. Sander(s) (son)
69. Bennet(t)
70. Brooks
71. Watson
72. Gray
73. Rivera
74. Nichol(s) (son)
75. Hernán(des) (dez)
76. Hughes
77. Ross
78. Myers
79. Sulliv(an)
80. Long
81. Price
82. Russel(l)
83. Foster
84. Daniel(s) (son)
85. Hender(son)
86. Pérez
87. Fisher
88. Powell
89. James
90. Perry
91. Butler
92. Jenkin(s)
93. Barnes
94. Reynolds
95. Patter(son)
96. Colema(n)
97. Simmon(s)
98. Graham
99. Wallac(e)
100. Stephe(ns) (nson)

Telephone directories are often used by name hobbyists who look for odd names, not always giving due attention to the fact that fake names occur in the books for various reasons, the chief reason being that that is a way to get an "unlisted number" without paying for the privilege. These directories can be used, of course, for more serious studies (such as determining the general ethnic composition of a geographical area or, in smaller locales, extended clans). As you realize, you will find lots of *Cohen*s in New York City, lots of *Murphy*s in Boston, lots of *Rodríguez*s in Miami and Los Angeles. Here is a cross section compiled from local directories of the most common surnames in half a dozen US cities in the 1980s:

New York	Boston	Indianapolis	Denver	Los Angeles	Miami
Smith	Smith	Smith	Smith	Williams	Rodríguez
Brown	Brown	Johnson	Johnson	Johnson	González
Miller	Johnson	Miller	Miller	Smith	García
Johnson	Williams	Jones	Brown	Jones	López
Cohen	Miller	Williams	Williams	Brown	Hernández
Williams	Cohen	Brown	Jones	Lee	Fernández
Lee	White	Davis	Anderson	García	Smith
Jones	Jones	Wilson	Davis	Rodríguez	Martínez
Davis	Murphy	Thompson	Wilson	Hernández	Pérez
Rodríguez	Davis	Taylor	Martínez	Martínez	Díaz

This emphasizes the fact that when one asks, "What are the most common US names?," in surnames as in forenames, the answer depends on *where*.

It is true that Hispanic and Asian names have broken into the Top 10 in some areas, but nationwide the commonest names have not changed much over the years, although the demographics of ethnic groups have to be taken into account and in Los Angeles, for instance, half the children born these days have Spanish surnames. *Smith,* seventh in popularity in Miami in the early 1980s, will surely be lower in that list in the early 1990s. About a decade ago, when Elsdon C. Smith published his book on the *Smith* clan (1978), one American in 100 bore that surname. In 1989 there are over 3.37 million *Smiths* in the US (with about 50,000 "extras," spelling variants) and over 2 million *Johnsons.* The great number of kinds of smiths who were around when surnames came into use and the centuries in which *John* was by far the most common male forename in the English-speaking world account for these statistics now. The commonest surnames in the world? A short list would include, besides *Smith* and *Johnson* and *Jones* (another "son of John"), *Chang, Ivanov, Anderson* or some variation, *Jensen, Susuki, Murphy, Papadopoulos, Dupont, Rossi, García,* and the Polish for "smith," *Kowalski.* In the US in 1984, 8,414 surnames each had more than 5,000 entries in Social Security files.

In America we have about as basic a surname system as exists anywhere. The same last name is inherited by both males and females and taken by wives and children. The surname is very often accompanied by a single forename. But, as we have seen, there are many more complex systems in use and some of them to us may seem perverse. In Iceland, for example, where there are comparatively few surnames in use, people are listed by first names in the telephone book. The Hungarians, and the Chinese (as we have noted), put the "last name" first. We have our own surname peculiarities, though we may not usually notice them. Many blacks in America—previously "black" was considered a derogatory term, now it is preferred, and "African-American" is coming along—are here named *Brown* or *White* or *Green* but seldom do we find *Black.* (One actor has adopted *Taurean Blacque.*) Ellis Island changed a lot of immigrant names and yet Americans still go on changing their surnames at a surprising rate, some of the changes attempting greater assimilation and some seeking to restore roots or just increase visibility.

The subject of name changing deserves more attention and will get it here later on, but at this point we might mention actress Barbara Hershey (originally *Hertstein*); she changed *Hershey* to *Seagull* (not *Siegal*) in the flighty sixties, and now is back to *Hershey* (not *Hertstein*). Today, *Hertstein* would do.

To the world's roster of minimal surnames, such as the Korean *O* and the Burmese *U,* Americans have contributed *X,* Black Muslims rejecting their "ex-slave" surnames, like *Malcolm X.* Social Security has one surname for each letter of the alphabet and records of 633 two-letter names.

It should come as no surprise that surnames, like forenames, can express and influence personality. They are considered carefully for their commonness or lack of it, appropriateness or lack of it, good connotations or lack of them. But, a minor matter, have you ever wondered how they might affect one's choice of a career, apart from the fact that prejudice toward certain ethnic groups and toward "ugly" names in general might be a social handicap? We notice surnames especially when we encounter a pastor named *Shepherd* or an artist named *Drew* or *I. Pullem,* the dentist. Thanks to Emery P. Walker, Jr., of Claremont (California), I can give you a list in which the field of expertise is on the left and the name of the expert on the right. You decide if the correlation is significant or coincidental and if what we have here is science or trivia:

> *Self-Actualization* — Better
> *Neurophysiology* — Brain
> *Sex Education* — Breasted
> *Child Psychology* — Child
> *Dream Deprivation* — Dement
> *Fish* — Fish
> *Aggression* — Fite
> *Interuterine Devices to Prevent Conception* — Gamble
> *Photosynthesis* — Green & Wilder
> *Birds* — Hatch
> *Dutch Publishing* — Junk
> *Geology* — La Rocque
> *Elementary Schoolchildren* — Little
> *Juvenile Delinquency* — Lively & Reckless
> *Effects of Parental Pressure on School Performance* — Mumpower
> *Aggressive Behavior* — D. Sade
> *Rabelaisian Laughter* — Screech
> *Theory of Taxation* — Snowball
> *Responses to Authoritarian Discipline* — Stern & Cope
> *Abnormal Psychology* — Strange
> *Animal Behavior* — Tiger & Fox
> *Behavior Modification* — Tough
> *Movement in Denervated Limbs* — Twitchell
> *Satiation Effects* — Wallace H. Wallace

Surnames can be highly approved or not, thought imposing, thought "funny." Having "the right name" does help, and what "right" may be differs from place to place. Surnames can help or hinder, and they cannot be as easily altered as forenames. If you should want to change your surname, it will be best if you "look the part" your new name suggests, or you may be asked, "What was your name before it was ————?" Avoid picking a new name that "doesn't suit you," and don't choose one beginning with *S*. That's the most common surname initial in the US (once again the *Smith* clan is significant) and it can cause what researcher Trevor Watson called "alphabetical neurosis." He argued that surnames coming in the alphabet between *S* and *Z* can adversely affect health and pointed out that people in the *S-Z* group suffer three times as many heart attacks as those in the *A-R* group. Of course figures don't lie but liars can figure, and it was Disraeli who said there are three kinds of lies: "lies, damn lies, and statistics." However, the tension that builds while the *S-Z* people are waiting for their names to be called may, just may, be dangerous. As an *A,* I suggest that some sober scientific study needs to be done on the effect on us first-in-the-alphabet people to determine how being ranked (and called upon) first has affected our lives. I do know that a lot of tension must be felt by those who for one reason or another would like to ditch their surnames but are worried about abandoning their given identities, their heritage, their roots.

A little parting advice before we leave the subject of surnames. Your surname is in a very real sense *you.* Keep in mind that you will be judged by it even before people meet you, probably much more than by your forename or forenames. Other people will want you to know and remember their surnames. Roman emperors used to have a *nomenclator* stand beside them to remind them of, or tell them, the names of people permitted to approach and address the imperial majesty. Whenever Hadrian's *nomenclator* made an error, the emperor loudly corrected him. The people loved that; they were delighted that Hadrian knew their names. I have known college presidents and commanding officers who endeared themselves to everyone (and were thought to be especially nice and intelligent) because they had excellent memories for names and made a point of showing they *knew who you were,* even if the name was just about the total extent of their familiarity. If you think that's silly, just ask yourself if you have ever been annoyed because someone had forgotten your name or mangled it. Actress Tallulah Bankhead used to cover herself by calling everyone "darling." That worked. Consider this: have you ever failed to thrill just a little bit at seeing your own name? You'll like this book better, I'll bet, if I happen to mention one of your names. If there were an index, you'd have looked your name(s) up there by now! We all like our names—if we do not, we ought to change them—and we like to have them remembered, if only by a headwaiter we have tipped so he will do just that (preferably when we are with someone we want to impress).

Surnames in Social Security files in 1957 began with *Aaaaa* and included *Vlk, Srp* and others with no vowels as well as many other oddities. Patricia Hanks and Flavia Hodges give the "meanings" of more than 100,000 common surnames in *A Dictionary of Surnames* (1988), but the US has millions.

What does *your* surname mean and where did it come from? *Moreno, Schwartz, Doyle* ancestors were dark, but *Boyd* had yellow hair like *Blunden,* and *Weiss* and *Wynn* were fair. *Vaughan, Klein, Petit* were small. *Hoare*'s hair was grey and *Whitbread*'s beard was white.

4. Nicknames

A minor but interesting aspect of personal names, nicknames, follows here courtesy of your friend, Tim.

We noted that the Romans gave us the concept of inherited family names. They also introduced nicknames (*agnomina*). Marcus Tullius Cicero's given name (*Marcus*) was one of a very few male first names the Romans used. *Tullius* told you of his family and the added name *Cicero* (chickpea) was inherited from some ancestor who had warts; it was originally an individual appellation. Today our nicknames are *eke* (extra) names given in derision (*Dumbo, Stinky, Curly* for a bald man) or out of affection (*Duke* Wayne, *Babe* Ruth, *Boomer* Eliason, *Whizzer* White, *Toots* Shor). Sometimes they are simply informal versions of forenames (*Tom, Dick, Harry, Charlie* for both *Charles* and *Charlotte*) or of surnames (*Smitty*) and they can replace either forenames or surnames (*Fritz* Mondale, Jimmy *the Greek*). We also use initials (*FDR, JFK, LBJ,* beloved of headline writers) or maybe *Egg* (for Eric Garrett Grae, who happens to be a student at Boston University).

American history abounds in nicknames. *Machine Gun* Kelly, *Lucky* Luciano, and *Scarface* Al Capone (whose associates did not call him that) were gangsters. *Bat* Masterson, *Doc* Holliday, *Wild Bill* Hickok, and *Buffalo Bill* Cody were legends of the West, along with *Billy the Kid. Old Silver Nails* Stuyvesant, *Boss* Tweed, *Gentleman Jimmy* Walker, *The Little Flower* Fiorello Laguardia, *Off the* Beame, and *Ed* Koch have all been prominent in New York City. You probably don't even know the surnames of these very famous Americans: *Molly Pitcher, Calamity Jane, Black Bart, Johnny Appleseed, Gorgeous George.* You may know that *Brady* follows *Diamond Jim,* but did you know that *Bonney* was the name of *Billy the Kid?* You probably don't know that the hermit Charles Ferge was called *Seldom Seen Slim* or that the chorines of the Roaring Twenties (itself a nickname) had names like *Onions* Healy and *Poopsie* Cunningham. Little remembered now, they were as celebrated in their day as were *His Rotundity, Fishbait, Stonewall, Honest Abe, Lighthorse Harry,*

Old Fuss and Feathers, Vinegar Joe, Honey Fitz, The Little Giant, Old Rough and Ready, Them Bums, The Four Horsemen, America's Sweetheart, Bogie, Refrigerator, Kitten, and so on. Incidentally, how many of these people can you identify? Who were football's *Four Horsemen of the Apocalypse* and who was *His Accidence* and who was *Lady Day?* In sports, who were *Y.A.* and *O.J.?*

Many of those nicknames were bestowed in later life when the bearers leaped to prominence, but most nicknames probably can be traced to childhood. We may grow up with and keep *Bubba, Bud, Junior, Sonny, Sis,* etc. Cruel school-yard names (which it would be nice to ban the way ethnic slurs have been banned on Los Angeles playgrounds) like *Pee Wee* and *Fatso* are usually dis-carded as soon as possible (but think of *Pee Wee* Herman). Bob Hope was named for a famous English footballer (Leslie Hope) but school enrolled him as *Hope, Leslie* and the kids called him *Hopelessly.* No wonder he's wanted to be called Bob! Gerald Ford (another Leslie, born Leslie King, but adopting his stepmother's name as an infant) was glad to leave behind *Junie* (from *Junior*) but *Dutch* Reagan never quite gave up his first nickname, even when called *Ron.* The British upper classes are full of distinguished old gents still called *Boy, Plum, Pinky, Boots* and such by their cronies, otherwise addressed by impres-sive titles which substitute for all their names. Some American preppies (*Skip, Tad, Dink, Buck*) and society ladies (*C.Z.,* to name but one lest I get many letters complaining of exclusion here) retain childish nicknames of various sorts. Three characters from the fifties TV show *Leave It To Beaver* can illustrate the basic kinds of American nicknames: *Beaver* Cleaver (rhyme, or alliteration, is often used), *Eddie* Haskell, and *Lumpy* Rutherford. Kids are prime targets for nicknames.

People can also pick up nicknames later in life. A Samantha may say she wants to be *Sam,* a Maureen *Mo,* a Harold may prefer *Harry* or (in Britain more than here) *Hal.* A Roosevelt Green becomes *Rosie* and others may acquire *Slim, Baldy, Butch, Moose, Beau,* etc. Many lovers give each other little tags, often secretly. A Marine general got *Godfather* from a movie. Allen Koenigsberg, when better known for his clarinet than his comedy, became *Woody* Allen. Fans dubbed Elvis Presley the *King* and Bruce Springsteen the *Boss.* In New York, both a late cardinal archbishop and a former director of the state opera have been known as *Bubbles.* Any sports fan can reel off for you the nicknames of all the players, and players who do not have nicknames are somehow lacking something. Remember *Stan the Man* and *The Babe?*

Orthopsychiatrists tell us that nicknames serve five distinct functions: approval, punishment, deprecation, revenge, therapy. They note that nick-names, while found everywhere, flourish in hierarchical institutions such as armies, schools, and prisons. Within those subcultures nicknames challenge authority, confer peer acceptance or rejection, push the eccentric into line or punish them for not conforming, and take the snooty down a peg. Like slang words, nicknames are much more than elegant variations on the lexicon; they promote a sense of identity among the users, create an "in" group and an "out" group, informalize relationships, establish a common and exclusive language which (as the sociologists would say) externalize normative attitudes.

In some societies nicknames are in more common use than "real" names and are, in fact, the real names. In Beaux Bridge (Louisiana), the local Creoles are listed in the telephone book with nicknames, because that is how they generally are known: Moise (*Tee Frère*) Castille, Royal (*Pou-Pou*) Castille, Rebellion (*Boo-Boo*) Durio, and so on. James K "Skip" Skipper, Jr., is the expert on nicknames of professional sports players, blues singers, and jazz.

Those nicknames are readily accepted, but no one is safe from nicknaming, and the more public the person, the more susceptible and inviting is the target. In the US hardly anyone is above being given a nickname, unless they are too dull to be noticed. In Britain, the Princess of Wales is *Di* and the Dutchess of York is *Fergie* (and worse). Princess Margaret is *Yvonne,* the *Royal Dwarf* and her ex-husband (now an earl) has been called *Snowbum* (in lieu of *Snowden*). The former Mr. Anthony Armstrong-Jones was often pilloried other ways, too. He was the victim of a rumor that "he didn't know if May the Sixth was to be the wedding date or his new title." When the malicious were done with him they started telling horsey-set jokes about Princess Anne and named her husband (Mark Phillips) *Foggy,* suggesting he is "dim," slow on the uptake. The Prince of Wales has been called the *Ears Apparent* (for his most prominent features), and before she was married his wife was *Lady Di.* An American joke went: "If he's *Prince* and she's *Lady,* what do they call the dog?" The Queen and Prince Philip are *Brenda* and *Bruce* (very naff or "down-market" names), the dowager queen is known affectionately as *The Queen Mum.*

The lesson here? Even the great have to endure over-familiarity, perhaps attack, from those who want to keep them from having swelled heads, who want to boast equality with them, who are envious of their prominence or privilege. He may be "Mr. President" if you get to speak to him, but anyone can call him *Harry* or *Ike,* and when he gets out of line they'll call him *Tricky Dicky.* If you're too tall the US may call you *Beanpole* (or *Too Tall*), the UK *Snap,* the Japanese the equivalent of *Grasshopper,* for with such names society enforces its norms. As pollster Daniel Yankelovitch said in a 1982 article in *Psychology Today,* in America nicknames "at least in symbolic terms" are part of the leveling process. They may call him the *Great Communicator* for P.R. purposes, but we like to call him *Ronnie.* That neither George Bush nor Michael Dukakis had any real nickname—*Mike* was as unsuccessful as anything else in the campaign—spoke of less colorful characters than *Old Hickory,* more distant people than *Jimmy* and *Jack* and *Jackie O.*

We like to claim familiarity with celebrities, as if we knew them personally. When we call the boss by a nickname, we are saying "you may be the boss, but this is a democratic society and we are all fundamentally equal."

The power of the politicians and the stupendous salaries of sports and other entertainment stars don't prevent us from nicknaming them. Among politicians, besides those already mentioned, there have been *Tip, Scoop,* the *Happy Warrior,* the *Kingfish, Soapy, Sockless,* and more. If you know US sports you should be able to identify most of these: *Yogi,* the *Ice Man,* the *Yankee Clipper, Shoeless Joe,* the *Bambino, Dizzy, Slats, Scooter, Magic, Ma, Night Train, Mean Joe, Broadway Joe, Crazy Legs, Pistol Pete, Rocket, Gump, Sugar Ray, Johnny U.,* and maybe even coaches and managers such as *Sparky, Birdie,* the *Professor, Papa Bear, Duffy, Digger,* the *Lip,* and the *Brat,* all of whom urged players to do the equivalent of winning one for the *Gipper.*

There are nicknames (less famous) in pool: *Tuscaloosa Squirrel, Cornbread Red, Weanie Beanie,* and you know *Minnesota Fats.* Make lists of golf nicknames, or gamblers' nicknames, or nicknames of college and professional teams. An article in *Harper's* for March 1989 has Léon Bing (odd name for a female journalist) interviewing some Los Angeles *Bloods* and *Crips* (or *crabs, e-rickets, cuzzes,* and other teenage terrorists and gangsters into *wilding*) on LA crime. Her informants are identified as *L'il Monster* (of the *Eight-Trey Gangsters*), *Rat-Neck* (of the *107-Hoovers,* another *Crips* aggregation), *Tee Rodgers* (of the *Blackstone Rangers*), and *B-Dog* (of the *Van Ness Gangsters,* these last two *Bloods* groups). There are nicknames among street hoods and nicknames on *The Street* (*Ginnie Mae, Fanny Mae, Sally Mae* on Wall Street), and bums on the street speak of *Sally's Joint* (the Salvation Army) and *Vinny's Joint* (the St. Vincent de Paul Society). Who hasn't heard of *Ma Bell?* Remember *Monkey Ward?* Consolidated Edison wants to sound more friendly as *Con Ed* (which jokers say means "fool the mayor of New York"). We nickname places (*L.A., Beantown,* the *Big Easy,* the *Big Apple*). *Hymie Town, Skid Row, Hell's Kitchen* (more recently "Clinton") are disparaging, like *Fort Apache* in The Bronx. Even churches get nicknames. In New York clouds of incense make St. Mary the Virgin into *Smoky Mary's.* In Stamford (Connecticut) the First Presbyterian Church's architecture looked so much like a fish that people ridiculed it as *Holy Mackerel.* Years ago in Montréal (Québec) we used to call the Church of St. Andrew and St. Paul the *A&P,* that term itself a nickname for the *Great Atlantic and Pacific Tea Company.*

Older readers may know some railroad nicknames. In our history we have had the *Miserable & Useless* (Middletown & Unionville); *Delay, Linger & Wait* (Delaware, Lackawanna & Western); *God Forgot* (Georgia & Florida); and *Old Pokey* (Pocohontas). I used to ride the *PJ&B,* a short trip—Princeton Junction and Back. Compliments have not been common in railroad nicknames but there were a few: Southeastern & Chatham RR was *Soft, Easy & Comfortable Rail Riding.* More likely are complaints: *TWA* is said to be *The Worst Airline.* Fly it to some *Sin City.*

Why mention nicknames that are not of persons? Merely to show that all nicknames arise from similar circumstances and perform similar functions, whether attached to persons, places, or things. Moreover, *Philly* and *Barf & Choke* and *San Berdoo* prove our point that nicknames are all-pervasive in our irreverent society, even *Filthydelphia, Taxachusetts* and *Big D*.

Until we stop to think, we do not appreciate all the properties and nuances of nicknames. They can denote titles but deflate them somewhat (*Doc, Sarge, Teach, Padre, Prof, Prez*). They can be ironic, as when an obese person is called *Tiny*, a slowpoke *Speedy (Gonzalez)*, a chump *Champ*. They can express society's disapproval of anything from your physical appearance (*Two Ton, Four Eyes, Shorty*) to your ideas. Like forenames, nicknames have their fashions: *Butch* and *Buster* are no longer as popular as they once were. Nicknames ending in -*o* are usually putdowns, those ending in -*y* or -*ie* generally affectionate diminutives, those ending in -*nik* or -*sky* denigrating (*Beatnik, Peacenik, Butinsky*). In some cases an ordinarily pejorative nickname can become a kind of compliment: *Pee Wee* for a shortstop, *Twiggy* for a fashion model and actress. The *Greek* or the *Mad Stork* are OK, too.

If you are given a nickname, at least you are noticed. If you accept it, psychologists say, you are "socialized." If people just shorten one of your names, it's basically friendly. Research has shown that people known by nicknames are usually more popular for having been singled out, not just another *Jane Doe* or *Joe Doakes*. If they call you *Mighty Mouth* or *Motor Mouth*, talk them out of it. If they call you *Miss Piggy*, examine your behavior. If you are a parent, don't give a child a name that invites a derisive nickname. *Dennis* will invariably become *Dennis the Menace* and *Dora* will be *Dumb Dora*. But no naming can stop nicknaming. Eisenhower's mother tried to avoid any possibility of nicknames with *Dwight*, and we got *Ike* and learned to like it.

There's plenty of literature about nicknames. On the social implications see Jane Morgan *et al.* in *Nicknames: Their Origins and Social Consequences* (1979). Consult Carl Sifakis' *Dictionary of Historic Nicknames* (1984) for the *Iron Chancellor* and the *Swamp Fox* and over 7,000 more tidbits. James K. Skipper is the expert on baseball nicknames, from the common ones (*Lefty, Red, Babe*) to the zaniest (*Mudcat, Scrap Iron, Oil Can*). Laurence Urdang edited (several others compiled) *Twentieth Century American Nicknames* (1979), and Paul Beale edited the eighth edition of Eric Partridge's classic *Dictionary of Slang and Unconventional English* (1984), among whose treasures are all the conventional (sometimes, as with *Pincher Martin* and *Blanco White*, inevitable) nicknames of Britain, Australia, and other English-speaking countries. All the nicknames of the *Yanks, Brits, Aussies, Canucks*, etc., can be loads of fun for any *Joe Sixpack* to play with.

Many surnames, by the way, derive from nicknames. From *Richard* we derived not only *Richards, Richardson, Pritchard*, but also *Dickens, Dickinson, Dickson, Dix, Dixon* (like *Nixon* from *Nicholas*), *Hickey, Hickie, Hicks, Hickson, Higgins, Higgs, Hitchens, Prickett, Ricketts*, and *Rix*.

5. Titles

Titles (honorifics) are related to nicknames in that they substitute for personal names and can express disapproval or approval, the degree of flattery usually dependent upon whether they are self-centered or bestowed. There have been Alexander the *Great* and Magnus the *Very Good* (of Denmark) and Ethelred the *Unready* (meaning that he would not take advice, not that he was unprepared) and Vlad *Tepès* (which means "Impaler," because he liked to execute people on sharpened poles, but you know him better by his other name "Little Dragon," *Dracula*). Unlike aliases and pseudonyms, which we shall discuss later as means of courting anonymity, titles boast, say "see me." They seek to command not just attention but respect, even *Hizzoner*.

In our republic we permit no official titles of nobility and Americans who have (say) honorary foreign knighthoods are not addressed as *Sir* with the forename. But we do use *Sir* to accord deference, along with *Mr. President, Mr. Secretary, Senator,* the *Honorable, Your Honor,* and *Esquire* (for lawyers here, oddly even women lawyers sometimes). We have elaborate rules about when to say *Mister, Mrs., Ms.* and *Miss,* though *Master* (for male children) has gone out of fashion. Various kinds of persons are addressed as *Doctor* (including surgeons, who in Britain are always plain *Mr.* to remind them that surgeons were once mere barbers) and as *Reverend* or *Professor.* Many people refer to *Rev. Jackson* and *Rev. Sharpton* but the article is required formally: *The Rev. Jesse Jackson* or *The Rev. Mr. Jackson,* and in writing it must be *Reverend,* not abbreviated, just as in letters it must be *Governor Cuomo,* not *Gov. Cuomo.* It's *Dear Colonel,* not *Dear Col.* In conversation one says *Father* to Roman Catholic and Episcopalian priests, *Mister* (or *Doctor* if he or she holds that degree) to Protestant ministers, never *Reverend.* We prefer to say *Bishop* and *Mr. Ambassador* instead of *Your Excellency,* but some know it's *John, Cardinal O'Connor* (not *Cardinal John O'Connor,* but *Archbishop O'Connor*) and say *Your Eminence.* (For a British archbishop, as for a duke, it's *Your Grace.*) For British bishops and nobles lower than dukes, *My Lord* or

Your Lordship are prescribed but actually only servants need to use those forms; you can say *Sir.* That will do for a king (*Sire* is out) after an initial polite *Your Majesty* in conversation. Queen Elizabeth II is *Her Britannic Majesty* but you can call her *Ma'am,* if she happens to speak to you; you are not permitted to strike up a conversation with her. Americans are likely to wave back and say, "Hi, Queen!" and are often unsure about *Your Highness* and such. Our commonest error is that we can't bring ourselves to call a knight by his forename: it's *Sir Walter,* not *Sir Raleigh,* and the same goes for baronetcies (hereditary knighthoods) should you happen to encounter the holder of one. At least baronets warn you with their signatures: *Thomas Beecham, Bart.* A knight doesn't sign *Sir* and just hopes you know enough to realize it goes with (say) *John Gielgud,* called *Sir John.* A baron and higher peers just sign their titles: *Boothby.* Only British judges are invariably addressed as *My Lord* by all ranks (and it's pronounced in this case "me Lud"). Some awkward titles (*Mr. Vice President, Mr. Chief Justice*) can be sidestepped with a simple *Sir.* A rabbi is addressed as *Rabbi* and a nun as *Sister* and a judge or mayor and some other politicos as *Your Honor.* If in doubt, use the surname: *Senator Smith, Congressman Jones, Monsignor Brown, Pastor Swenson* (for a Lutheran minister), *Judge Green, Madame Justice O'Connor* (for a member of the Supreme Court). Lieutenant-Anythings like to be upped a step: *Colonel* is the way to speak to a *Lt. Col.* and *General* to a *Lt. Gen.* A British brigadier told me he always liked Americans because they called him *General;* the British call him *Brigadier.*

Americans have a strange habit of addressing office-holders by their titles after they have left office, so there are several people around called *Mr. President* and plenty of former governors, senators, etc. In France, too, if you've ever been president of anything you are *M. le Président* for life. The French also use titles of nobility, though they are illegal and often phoney, but at the top of the pile the titles simplify. The pretender to the non-existent throne of France is a mere count (not a prince, duke, marquis, etc.) and once at a party I wondered why a young girl was addressed as *Madame:* she turned out to be the daughter of the *Comte de Paris.* If you want a French title, get someone who has one (check credentials carefully) to adopt you; when he dies, you are (let's say) the *Baron de Mont-Rouge.* Helps a lot in "republican" American social circles! Worth the money. But don't buy the lordship of a British manor. True, you get to be "lord of the manor," but you get no power or estate, really, and can only put that on your British passport, and you don't have one of those, right? There are many huge reference books which list the European nobility and others which tell you how to address them, but *Sir* and *Ma'am* are basically all you need.

Sir and *Ma'am* (or *Madame*) are basically all you need in the US and that's been true ever since George Washington was talked out of calling himself *His Majesty, the President of the United States.* But when to say *Sir* and *Ma'am* differs from one part of the country to another, as does when to call a university

professor *Mister* or *Doctor* or *Professor*. At Princeton, my teachers had doctorates but were never *Doctor* (of course not *Teach*), always *Mister*. Everyone at
Mr. Jefferson's university in Virginia is *Mister* or *Ms*. *Mister* comes from
Master and yet now is used to blur relationships, as in sentences such as this I
heard at Princeton: "The President is in Washington today talking with Mr.
Eisenhower." A Southerner will say *Sir* more often but also use it as a putdown,
while in the Navy *Mister* is a way to keep junior officers in their place. *Mister* is
also derogatory in sentences such as "Will you shut up, Mister?" as is *Sir* in a
Southerner's "You are no gentleman, Sir!"

We can be odd in our manners of address in America, sometimes presumptuous. We tend to jump too quickly to the use of first names and we often neglect
titles (except those of pompous foreigners). By tradition and in principle we
tend to avoid hifalutin' titles (except in the ludicrous designations of officials of
fraternal organizations and such). Not for us something like *Haile Selassie*
(Power of the Trinity), *Emperor of Ethiopia, King of Kings,* the *Conquering
Lion of Judah,* the *Light of the World*. (Now he's dead, but Rastafarians think
he's God.) Roman emperor Domitian was *Dominus et Deo* (Lord God) and
one Frederick was *Stupor Mundi,* one Lorenzo *Il Magnifico*. Popes, and high
officials of other religions, are *Holiness*. Innocent III promoted himself from
Vicar of St. Peter to *Vicar of Christ* and his successors use that title and one
from the old bishopric of Rome, *Pontifex Maximus,* not to mention the redundant and ridiculous *Rector of the World upon Earth*. People get used to these
terms as they have to the contradictory *Roman Catholic* and *Universalist
Church of Boston*. These high titles do not look as silly as (say) *Serene Highness* in Monaco (which François the Cunning grabbed for the Grimaldis centuries ago). They seem to fit better than the British Protestant monarchs'
Defenders of the Faith (a title a pope gave Henry VIII and then took back,
but the British won't admit that). Who cares if a familiar name fits? We are
blind to many pretensions and may notice nothing odd or inflated in *National
Bank of New Jersey* or every former *Normal School* becoming first a *College*
and lately a *University*. So *World Series* may hardly describe our little local
baseball playoffs and the Japanese teams can't participate, but so what? It
sounds great.

Great is used for big winners (Alexander), some kings (such as Alfred),
some popes (such as one Gregory), some lesser fry (the *Great Condé,* the
Great Dauphin), and our own heroes (the *Great Emancipator*), and it's
thrown around loosely (the *Great Society*) and used as a synonym for "good"
("This movie is great!"). But the powerful have also been called the *Bad,* the
Bald, Bluetooth, the *Simple,* the *Fat,* the *Penniless,* the *Apostate*. We have
our own musical nobility, too: *Duke* Ellington, *Count* Basie, *Prince*, etc., and
some rather unquotable titles for politicians of the sort once described in
Congress as having "all the qualities of a dog, except loyalty."

For longwinded titles, Indian potentates take the prize. Sir Yavindra Singh
Mahenndra Badahur, the Rajpramukh (we'd say *High Muck-a-Muck*) of

Patalia and the East Punjab States Union, went by *His Highness Shri 108* (which means that officially you had to repeat *Shri* 108 times) *Maharajadhira Raj Rajeshwar Shri Maharajah-i-Rajgan Maharajah,* the *raj* (king) and *maharajah* (great king) getting a little too insistent, for my taste. That made even the British (who thought they had elevated him with that *Sir*) look restrained with *Her Most Gracious Majesty Elizabeth II, by the Grace of God of the United Kingdom of Great Britain and Northern Ireland and of her other Realms and Territories, Queen, Head of the Commonwealth, Defender of the Faith.* Her father was *Emperor of India* and reigned over much more, but times change. Then Ozymandias' *King of Kings* rings hollow.

For the full titles of Queen Elizabeth II and for a survey of all the titles, soubriquets, etc., of British monarchs, see my article on "Pomp and Its Circumstances" in *Names* 15, pp. 85-110, the journal (incidentally, with two fine indexes prepared by Clarence Barnhart and Kelsie B. Harder) in which to find information on this and every other aspect of onomastics and in whose bibliographies you will find the names of all the other journals and books which I do not have space or desire to cite in the present informal survey. Just about every country has some journal more or less equivalent to the long-established *Names,* founded in the fifties, and every aspect of name study has its bibliographer: Elizabeth Rajec for literary onomastics, Edwin D. Lawson for *Personal Names and Naming,* Kelsie B. Harder and others for placenames, etc. Even minor matters such as honorifics have been the subject of more studies than you can imagine.

Now back to titles of persons rather than titles of scholarly works. As I said earlier, the Queen, like the present British Prime Minister, is *Ma'am* for most purposes, but Burma until recent times was ruled by a *King of Kings, whom all other Princes Obey, Regulator of the Seasons, Almighty Master of the Ebb and Flow, Younger Brother of the Sun, Proprietor of the Twenty-Four Umbrellas.* . . . Egyptian pharoahs were thought to be sons of the Sun, the Japanese emperor son of the rice god, and any German with two doctorates is still *Herr Doktor Doktor* (and maybe *Herr Doktor Doktor Professor*).

In our own hemisphere's backyard we've had some very striking titles, too. In 1849 the Emperor Faustin I of Haiti created a new nobility and they took their titles, as nobles traditionally did, from their estates. However, these estates were plantations seized by the government and bestowed on the fledgling Faustin's friends. Unfortunately, those plantations bore some fanciful names. This produced such bizarre titles as *Duc de Dondon* (Duke Redcheeked), *Duc de l'Avancée* (Duke Outpost), *Comte d'Avalasse* (Count Torrent), *Comte de Terrier-Rouge* (Count Red Terrier), *Baron de la Seringe* (Baron Syringe), *Baron de Sale-Trou* (Baron Dirty Hole), and *Comte de Numero-Deux* (Count Number Two). There was also a *Duc de Marmalade,* who outranked the *Comte de Limonade.* Compared to that, our *Imperial Grand Wizard* and the *kleagles* of the Klan, or exalted high potentates of fraternal lodges, are sober and self-effacing. We once, unofficially, had an *Emperor of California,* a San Franciscan character, and of course there was an emperor in Mexico. That was Maximilian. The Aztecs did not really have an emperor. He was a *Speaker.* And Peru had a real emperor, an *Inca.*

For all our professed American disdain for titles, we have invented one. About a third of American women like to be called *Ms.* The opposition declares that this is the silliest title since *Citizeness* in the French Revolution, but, like that (and *Comrade*), it does affirm egalitarianism, blurring the distinction between married women (who in speech are often the equivalent of *Miz* in some parts of the country) and unmarried women. Like *Mr., Ms.* can be construed as a leveling device. Yet titles in their very essence seek to recognize rank (and, ideally, achievement); they contribute to politeness as well as to power. Americans use them for superiors and for strangers perceived as equals, but we prefer first names for friends (except in certain circles where surnames without titles are regarded as familiar) and we can address subordinates either by forenames or surnames. We say *Monsignor* without awkwardness but balk at the equivalent *My Lord.* We are not nearly as "respectful" as the Chinese and Japanese but also not nearly as egalitarian as the Icelanders. For the most part we never have occasion to deal with marquesses or marchionesses, earls or countesses, viscounts and viscountesses, barons and their wives (*Lady* ———— with the surname if the wife of a baron, *Baroness* if in her own right), or the elder sons of peers with courtesy titles (but no seat in the House of Lords until they succeed to the principal title) or the younger sons (the *Honorable*). All the children of dukes and marquesses are *Lord Peter, Lady Jane,* etc., even if they marry commoners. You can't tell by *Lady Jones* the rank of her husband. However, the absence of the Christian name means you are not dealing with the child of a major peer.

We notice the French titles, though France banned them in 1792, brought them back with the First Empire, and now officially ignores them. A useful one to know is not of the nobility but *Maître* (Master) for lawyers and notaries.

The republican constitution of Italy left intact the old Italian titles of the kingdom: *principe, marquessa, conte, barone.* To a marquess you'd write *Gentillissimo Marquessa.* A servant addresses him as *Signor Marquessa.* Writing to a celebrity, in the south you'd begin *Illustre;* in the north *Egregio* would suffice. Call Italians *Signor* and *Signora* and everyone but the former royal family (*Altezza Reale,* Royal Highness) will find that enough.

Spain is a monarchy with *Su Majestád* and *grandees* (*Excelentíssimo Señor*) and regular nobility (*Illustríssimo Señor*). *Señor* and *Señora* will get you by, except for *Vuestra Eminencia* for a cardinal, ambassador, bishop, etc., and you probably will not be signing letters you will wish to end *g.e.s.m.* (for "who shakes your hand") or *q.b.s.p.* ("who kisses your feet").

The two German republics still have the old nobility but regard noble titles as mere names. Nevertheless, the equivalents of *Imperial Highness, Royal*

Highness, and *Serene Highness* are still around, at least in theory. Today the ordinary problems of life involve the citing of *Hochverehter* (honorable) plus titles and surname on envelopes and a crucial decision at the end of the missive: are you *Hochachtung* (respectfully yours) or more informally *Ihr ganz* (or *sehr* or *stets*) *ergebener*—completely or very or always devotedly yours? Be generous with *Doktor, Professor, Gnädige Frau* (dear madame), etc., and note that *von* and *zu* are indicators of noble origins when used with surnames.

You may think high-sounding titles undemocratic and archaic, but some people (not Shakespeare, Newton, Einstein) need them and believe they assist social interaction. They also can reward achievement, though when Sir Anthony Eden became Earl of Avon he changed a famous name for a rather obscure one. Our American belief that hereditary titles reward undeserving descendants is shared now by the British, many of whose titles have gone to life peers since the first of them, Lord Parker of Wassington and Baroness Swanborough, took their seats in the House of Lords in 1958. The titles of life peers die with them, but they are not distinguished by their names from others in the Lords. In 1966, Lord Brooke of Cumnor joined his wife (who had become a life peeress) in the Lords. They are Lord and Lady Brooke, each in their own right.

Americans have their own equivalents of hereditary titles, in *John F. Kennedy, Jr.* and even in *Benjamin Franklin V.* We use II and III in the US and the British think this is foolish even as they create new Labour peers or hail the twenty-somethingth Lord Dunsany. The highnesses remain in India and Pakistan. The Hindu rulers were *Maharaja Bahudur* (Great King Warrior), *Maharaja, Raja Bahadur, Raja, Raj Bahadur, Rai Sahib,* or *Rai.* The Muslim rulers were *Nizam, Nawab Bahadur, Nawab, Khan Bahadur, Khan Sahib,* or *Khan.* (The wife of a *maharajah* was a *maharani,* the wife of a *nawab* a *begum.*) As early as 1612 Coverte's *Voyages* told the British "an Earle is called a Nawbob." The British fortune hunters who came back rich from India came to be called *nabobs* in slang and *nobby* came to be used for "smart, elegant, fashionable" and for the kind of rich pepole you'd find on Nob Hill.

People like that always like high-sounding names and titles.

6. Name Changes

A Harris poll once revealed that half of all Americans dislike their surnames. If your surname is not considered short enough, or is too "ethnic" or not of an approved ethnic origin for your area and station, or if people make fun of it or can't pronounce or spell it, maybe you will want to change your last name. This is not quite as simple as changing your forename. For that you can suppress the truth under an initial or just tell your friends you are now *Cyndi* instead of *Cynthia* (like Ms. Lauper). To change your surname can be a little more difficult. However, you can still do it. If you really want to do it, you should. Changing your surname, wrote Ted Morgan (also known by another name) in the *New York Post* in March 1978, is "as American as a basketball hoop over the garage door, as green money, as sliced bread, as competitive overeating." If you don't like your surname, why stick with it? Why be stuck with it? Change it.

There is ample precedent for name changing, from Paul Revere (who came from a French family named *Rivoire*) to Ronald Reagan (just a change in pronunciation from "Reegan" to "Raygun" when he went into politics, which caused LBJ to say his "beagles may turn into bagels"). Some famous names in US history were the result of change: Charles Lindberg's family was called *Mansson*, Irving Berlin's *Baline*, and Louis Adamic (who "Americanized" his own name) wrote of *Kobotchnik* becoming *Cabot*, *Rabinovitch* becoming *Drinkwater*, and *Romzmyslaws* becoming *Roosevelt*. Not the Roosevelts you were thinking of, but the fact that those were once accused of being Jews in disguise reminds us of the rabid anti-Semitism that had a lot to do with the changing of many Jewish surnames. *Bernard Schwartz* became *Tony Curtis*, *Michael Igor Peshowsky* changed to *Mike Nichols*, etc. The Warner Brothers of the movies were all *Eichelbaum*. One Jewish lad took two very Nazi-sounding names, *Werner Helsenberg* and *Ludwig Erhard:* he emerged as *Werner Erhard* of *est* fame. *Peter Twatt* was changed to *Peter T. Watt*—just one more example of name improvement.

Because of the way surnames originated (in nicknames, for instance) and because of the many foreign languages from which they come, some surnames may sound strange to us and invite ridicule. In France there are laws governing which "funny" names you can change. They permit you to drop *Fromage* (cheese) but not *Chèvre* (goat), for example. In Britain name changing has a long history and the list of name changes from 1760 to 1901 records the jettisoning of names such as *Pricke, Maydenhead, Piddle, Rumpe,* and *Shittel.* It was anti-German sentiment, not "meaning," that caused the name shift of the royal house from Saxe-Coburg-und-Gotha to Windsor—the Kaiser immediately had a command performance of Shakespeare's *The Merry Wives of Saxe-Coburg-und-Gotha* in derision—and the "meaning" did not change when Prince Philip's branch of the family (he and the Queen both being descendants of Queen Victoria) went from *Battenberg* to *Mountbatten.* It was just an attempt to disguise what my Anglophile mother used to call "the Teutonic Plague" in England.

"Meaning" is not really altered by such shifts as *Hogg, Pigge, Smythe* but they attempt to avoid criticism. Shifts to *Levay, Halévy,* and *Offenbach,* all to get away from *Levi,* may be regarded as defensive or offensive. Are they reactions to anti-Semitism or anti-Semitism on the part of Jews themselves? In any case, these changes are not prompted by childish attention-grabbing or kookiness (like Ms. Seagull, mentioned earlier) of the sort we see so frequently in California. For example, Judy Bosworth sent off for *JUDY* vanity license plates, too dumb to realize that in California somebody else would surely have thought of that earlier. The state gave her *JUDY 13.* So she changed her name to *Judy Thirteen,* admitting that "you have to have a little bit of nuttiness to do a thing like this." Well, maybe not nuttiness; just desperate desire for distinction of some sort. That's what drove Englishman *Francis Pit = Taylor,* not satisfied with the Pitt-iful attempt at class in the hyphenated name, to insist on an equals sign (=) instead of a hyphen (-) in his name. I think this is not only amusing but also useful. It is convenient when nuts have nutty names, now that you think about it. The people I feel sorry for are those who are stuck with names some people think are "funny," because people can indeed be cruel. I admire the man called A. Crook. When he got his name in the papers—by accident, because he found and returned a large sum of money—he told the press that with a name like *A. Crook* "you have to be honest." With some names, you have to be crazy to hang onto them. With others, you have to be crazy to adopt them—or simply a person who would rather be notorious than anonymous.

Name changes can be motivated from a desire to be anonymous (let's say to escape child support or to keep from embarrassing your parents by your lifestyle) to a desire for a whole new lease on life. For the Nobodies yearning for the 15 minutes of fame that Andy Warhol said we all can have, name change may be a way to get their pictures in the paper. A cocktail waitress named Cheryl Boone (which is funny enough, or at least fun to say) changed her name to *Sparkle Plenty* (a name from the *Dick Tracy* comic strip) and ran for the

state legislature with slogans like "Put a Little Sparkle in It" and "We All Need
Plenty." I recall California bumper stickers that made a vulgar suggestion about
the then governor: "If It's Brown, Flush It." Names can be a help or a hin-
drance in politics as well as in the real world, but name changing there, if
noticed (*Hart* from *Hartpence*), can give the sort of newsmen who will write
about anything but the issues a stick to beat the candidate with. In politics you
can fix your teeth or dye your hair or even have a hair transplant, but it's better
to have a cancer operation than a surname operation.

Simon became *Peter*. *St. Wilgisforce* changed her name (and also grew a
beard, to protect her chastity) and is now *St. Uncumber*. Naomi turned bitter
and said "Call me Mara" in the *Book of Ruth*. Kings select a name on mount-
ing the throne. So do popes, ever since one came along whose surname meant
"pig's snout." Persons altering their lives spiritually may change their names:
nuns and monks entering the religious life, witches entering a coven, etc. New
names appropriately mark new departures. Members of the Order of the
Golden Dawn (a magical organization which included the great poet William
Butler Yeats and such dangerous perverts as Aleister "the Beast" Crowley)
took Latin tags not so much for identification but, as American jargon today
might put it, "to send a signal." Hippies often changed their names to annoy or
abandon their families, to celebrate a freer lifestyle (how this was done with
Blue and *Wavy Gravy*, I am not quite certain), to break society's rules. Some
are converted to new constraints. Comedian Steve Allen's son wrote to him:
"I have given up my old name and all that went with it. My new name is Logic
Israel. This will be my last letter." *Saul*, a.k.a. *Paul*, could have written a similar
letter.

Logic. What a name! Why not? There's a logic to all the show-biz name
changes. *Henry John Deutschendorf* to *John Denver*, more mainstream and
easier. *Gary Dorsey* to *Englebert Humperdinck*, more attention-getting and not
so "hard," because known already as a real name (of the composer of *Hansel
and Gretel*). Want to erase your background? Change *Ramón Estevez* to
Martin Sheen. Want to boast it? Undo what your father did (take back
Estevez). Play down Jewishness: *Lauren Bacall* (Betty Perske), *Joel Grey*
(Joel Katz), *Michael Landon* (Eugene Orowitz), *George Burns* (Nathan
Birnbaum), or play on Jewishness but simplify *Melvin Kaminsky* to *Mel
Brooks*. Did you ever think what *Tony Bennett, Kaye Ballard, Bernadette
Peters, Jerry Vale,* and *Penny* and *Gary Marshall* have in common besides show
business? Italian ancestry, like *Rudolph Valentino*. If you don't want to play an
ethnic stereotype, a more neutral name gives you more scope. The main reason
behind most show-biz monikers, though, is getting attention (*Barbra, Liza,
Madonna, Sting*) and, better, acquiring a more memorable moniker, one that
"looks good in lights," one that creates the Image you want: Latin lover, pop
idol, exotic beauty, clean-cut American boy, or (as the kids say today) *whatever*. The public will generally take you at face value. They were able to do
that more easily in the days of silent films and *John Gilbert, Theda Bara,* and

the rest, but they still can do it. Moreover, if they find out you have a made-up name (*Tab Hunter, Rock Hudson, Kirk Douglas*) they won't get angry. They are more likely to regard discovering "real names" as a Trivial Pursuit.

In a long article in *Names* blithely called "Flix, Flacks, and Flux" I examined the sociological trends reflected in the publicity-conscious name changes of the Industry (as Hollywood likes to call the movie business); there you will find hundreds of name changes and the motives and patterns behind them. In another *Names* article I explained "Changing Names and Changing Times" and outlined all the implications and legal procedures for name changing. There are many other studies of all aspects of name changing, which you can find in the bibliographies. Here I need only repeat: if you don't like your name, change it, remembering that a change of name will change the way other people regard you and even the way you look at yourself. As in magic, names have the power of metamorphosis.

One guy arraigned as *Archie Outlaw,* charged with selling heroin, petitioned the court to allow a name change before trial lest *Outlaw* influence the outcome. The assistant D.A. objected that *Bimbo, Oddman,* and another person named *Outlaw* had not had their cases prejudiced by their surnames. Nonetheless, the judge agreed that people are, in fact, judged on their surnames every day by the public at large. So *Archie Outlaw* became *Archie Simmons.* Only then did he plead guilty to pushing illegal drugs or, if you like, *non-decriminalized substances.*

In Orange County (California) they have hundreds of name changes in the court, usually without lawyers, each year. Isabelle C. Benson didn't want to keep *Benson* after a divorce or to return to *Caestecker;* she chose *Belle Star.* Alexander J. Reyes became *Sir James Bond.* Andrew Sterna took his stepfather's name, *Zaborowski,* and now wants to go back to *Sterna.* Patricia Leanne Watanabe took a surname from soap opera and a new forename; she's now *Natasha Lavery.* Tiffany Kern became *Djuna Woods* and considered sending her parents the change-your-name ad from the newspaper. Sunita was all the name she had or needed in her native India, but in Costa Mesa (California) she needed a surname: *Sunita Kumer.* In Laguna Beach, Robin Hood won't change his name.

7. A.K.A.: Aliases and Pseudonyms

Name changing to conceal actual identity produces those "also known as" names, aliases and pseudonyms, usually limited to one's profession or to some other particular aspect of one's life. They may sound like nicknames (gangsters are *Pretty Boy, Legs, Bugs, Lucky,* etc., which Steve Allen made fun of with *"Clams" Marinara* and Eric Overmyer with *"Shrimp" Bucket*). They may have the same effect as complete and official, legal, name changes, but they form a separate category of alternate names.

Aliases, though associated in the popular mind with criminals, may be used for perfectly legal activities as well. Strippers and exotic dancers may adopt working names to protect their private lives or save their families embarrassment, but their "professional" names are seldom random (*Sally Rand* came from an atlas). They are more likely to be transparently theatrical names (*Lily St. Cyr, Blaze Starr, Gypsy Rose Lee*) or even humorous (*Candi Barr, Teri Cloth, Rachel Prejudice, Sybil Rights, Fanne Fox,* the *Gaza Stripper*). The names adopted for X-rated movie "stars" are frequently themselves "explicit." The ideal alias in most cases, however, is one that gives no hint of the real name; punning, joking, eyebrow-raising names are no more useful in keeping the fact that a name is being concealed than is *John Smith.* "Fun" aliases are more to be compared with the image-packaging of movie star and rock star names. Interestingly, one's name is so much a part of oneself that even when criminal aliases are chosen they often retain the person's initials or other elements of his or her real name. A *Louis* may hide under *Mr. Lewis* or an *Art Parker* under *Al Porter. William Carroll* became *William Makeit,* declaring he wanted to make illegal money. A successful alias, however, fully departs from the real name without giving any suggestion of fraud.

When writers hide under assumed names we call the names pseudonyms or *noms de plume* (pen names). In some cases they successfully replace the real name (*Molière, Voltaire, Stendhal, Bryher, Clemence Dane*) and even become so entrenched (and sound so natural) that we do not realize that *George*

Orwell, Frank O'Connor, Anatole France, Anthony Burgess are pseudonyms at all. Why some of these were adopted in the first place may puzzle us: why would a man named Eric Blair choose *George Orwell*, or a short-story writer like O'Connor take his mother's Irish name instead of his father's Irish name, or why would a woman take a pen name from a London church (St. Clement's Dane, in The Strand)? We can see why in the last century women got into print as *Action Bell* or *George Eliot* or *George Sand* to counter prejudice or why a married woman might write under her "maiden name" now or why, having established herself under a married name (*Christie*), a woman might keep using it even after divorce and remarriage. So did *Antonia Fraser* (now *Lady Antonia Pinter*). But why *Sarah Grand* or *Anna Kavan* or the initials of *H.D.* or of *P.D. James?*

One clear reason for a pseudonym is a desire for privacy (*O. Henry, B. Traven, Trevanian*). Another arises when an author is very prolific. Under 60 or so different names Frank Stratemeyer disguised his output as *Franklin W. Dixon* (for the Hardy Boys series), *Laura Lee Hope* (for the Bobbsey Twins books), *Carolyn Keene* (for all the Nancy Drew mysteries), and *Victor Appleton* (for the Tom Swift books), and he used other names for other projects. *Ellery Queen* was two Jewish cousins writing together. *Erle Stanley Gardner* and *A. A. Fair* appeared on detective fiction the author thought good or only fair. Stephen King, once famous, admitted the use of an earlier name and republished those books.

Voltaire used some 70 pseudonyms. Daniel Defoe (originally plain Foe) had 100. The modern record is probably held by John Creasey; under numerous names he has written well over 500 books.

Sometimes a pen name can lend a false sense of authenticity to a work, as when a woman breaks into a male-dominated literary field, a man writes romances, or a Ms. Schwartz puts together a cookbook, pretends to a command of French cuisine, and publishes it as by *Colette Black*. Other reasons lie behind such famous pen names as *Mark Twain* and *John Le Carré* and *David Conway*, and they may be very deliberately selected or picked as casually as Ian Fleming took the name of a famous ornithologist (James Bond) for a character. Anagrams produced *ACEEEFFGHHIILLMMNNOORRRSSSTUV* (Christoffel von Grimmelshauser) and Edward Gorey's *Dreary Wodge, Waredo Dirge, Dogear Wryde,* and *G. E. Deadworthy.*

Secretly, I suppose, the vanity of most authors drives them not only to write but also to have the public know who has written. In any case, industrious librarians find out most identities for us and publish them in vast reference books, put them in library catalogues, etc. Nobody's sure who *Junius* or *Martin Marprelate* were, but most mysteries have been solved, if anyone cares. We realize that *Cornetto di Basso* is a fake name and now we know that under this name Bernard Shaw wrote music criticism, even that, as *Gwendolyn,* Arnold Bennett penned advice to the lovelorn as a sort of *Miss Lonelyhearts* or *Dear*

Abby. We know Cicily Isabel Fairfield took *Rebecca West* from an Ibsen play, and so on.

You can drop your given names (like *Stevie Smith*) or use your initials (Roman de Tirtoff turned French *R.T.* into *Erté*). Hilda Doolittle was given *H.D.* by Ezra Pound and you can hardly blame her for hanging onto that. One odd pen name is *Æ.* It was an accident. George Russell signed something *Æon,* a classical reference, and the printer chopped it short, so Russell stayed with that thereafter. Other brief pseudonyms include those of Dickens and one of his illustrators, *Boz* and *Phiz* (for "physiognomy," I think). From a nickname in a Dickens novel (the boy is *Pip*) mime Marcel Marceau got the name for his clown character, *Bip,* which is a sort of pseudonym.

Pseudonyms may serve much the same purposes as formal name changes. For simplicity *Pierre-Augustin Caron* was replaced by *Beaumarchais* and *Louis-Ferdinand Destouches* by *Céline.* Who hasn't heard of *Colette?* Ethnic or religious origin can be hidden: *Dikran Kouyoumdjian* gave way to *Michael Arlen* and Émile Herzog suppressed his Jewishness under *André Maurois.* Or one can just make an improvement: *Henry Vincent Yorke* to *Henry Green, Louis Farigoule* to *Jules Romains, Gérard Labrunie* to *Gérard de Nerval, Solomon J. Rabinowitz* to *Sholem Aleichem,* and of course Samuel Langhorn Clemens' adoption of the Mississippi boatman's cry for "two fathoms deep," which was *Mark Twain.* Some minor alterations can hardly be called pseudonyms: *Ringold Wilmer Lardner* to *Ring Lardner, Harry Sinclair Lewis* to *Sinclair Lewis, Mary Nesta Skrine Keane* to *Molly Keane* (though she also wrote under *M. J. Farrell*), *William Cuthbert Falkner* to *William Faulkner,* our first American playwright *William Clark Tyler* to *Royall Tyler* and perhaps our best one *Thomas Lanier Williams* to *Tennessee Williams,* are borderline cases. But *Margaret Rumer Godden* to *Rumer Godden* is a kind of sex change operation (and she also wrote under *P. Davis*).

Writers tend to avoid the transparently false names adopted by some pop artists (placenames served *Paul America, Judy Chicago, Buster Cleveland, Robert Indiana*) and the outrageousness of punk musicians (*Johnny Rotten* is one quotable example).

If you want to devise an alias, or alter ego, for yourself, learn from the short, crisp, "All-American" (read: Anglo-Saxon), often alliterative, punchy names in this list of superstars from an unlikely place, Marvel Comics. There you will encounter Stanley Lieber as *Stan Lee* and other creators as well as *Peter Parker* (Spider Man), *Reed Richards* (Mr. Fantastic), *Steve Rogers* (Captain America), *Tony Stark* (Iron Man), *Luke Cage* (Power Man), *Clint Barton* (Hawkeye), *Matthew Murdock* (Dare Devil), *Simon Williams* (Wonder Man), and *Rick Jones* (Captain Marvel). D.C. Comics has its own stable of superheroes but the same formula and clean-cut stalwarts named *Clark Kent* (Superman), *Bruce Wayne* (Batman) and *Dick Grayson* (Robin), *Adam Black* (Captain Comet), and *Diana Prince* (Wonder Woman). It's remarkable that the two classic categories of aliases should be those of the Good Guys and the Bad Guys (make your own list of the latter starting with the *Joker*). Frederick M. Burelbach deserves thanks for his analysis of comic-book aliases in his entrancing article entitled "Look! Up in the Sky. It's What's-His-Name!" It's one of many fascinating pieces in the anthology *Names in Literature* (1988), a book you ought not to miss if you are attracted by the names in fiction of all sorts.

For aliases and pseudonyms of real people, you cannot do better than Jennifer Mossman's *Pseudonyms and Nicknames Dictionary,* which reached a third edition in 1987. There you will find all the evidence that substitute names, like name changes, reveal a great deal about individuals and about cultural norms. Consider *Stan Lee*'s Anglicized name and the WASPy aliases of the superheroes. What's *in* the names? Former FBI chief J. Edgar Hoover and his close friend and associate Clyde Tolson were rumored to have a possibly homosexual relationship because they used the aliases *Hazel* and *Fifi* respectively. Drag queens not only dress up in rather outmoded fashions (and use outmoded terms such as *girl* instead of *woman*) but also adopt rather old-fashioned female names. What does that tell you? As always, when we delve into psychology, we must be careful not to reach hasty conclusions, but when the spies call their master *Mother* or when they take code names themselves, the possibility of the mindset dictating the naming is there. Nothing in naming, however frivolous or seemingly accidental, is meaningless or unmotivated.

In a family, a surname and even a forename may be inescapable. In Dickens' *Dombey and Son* the lad was christened Paul, his father's forename and his grandfather's. When it comes to making up a pen name or a criminal alias or some other such substitute name, however, a great deal more freedom and therefore a great deal more self-expression is involved.

8. Married Names

Remember when you were going to summer camp and your mother sewed name tapes on your clothes? Or when you boldly wrote your name in a book you owned? Putting a name on anything claims it, makes it more your own. So the Roman put his name on his wife and all their children. They were his legal property. Your surname claims you for the family.

Women, regarded first as the property of their fathers and then of their husbands, have long endured sexist traditions in our culture, in naming as in other departments of life. There is no male counterpart to the quaint term "maiden name." Women taking their husband's surname declare they are joining his family. It used to be tantamount to becoming his property. Many people argue this is accepting an inferior status from the start of the marriage, a marriage which traditionally begins with him promising to cherish but her promising to obey. Many assert that women thus contribute to society's underestimation of their worth by accepting a dependent and inferior status. Because women's surnames change at marriage, their only "real" names are their forenames, and people who are known chiefly by forenames, as you know, are those who are taken less seriously, on the whole.

Lucy Stone, an early feminist, did not seem to mind carrying her father's surname. That, she maintained, was her name and her name was "the symbol of [her] identity and must not be lost," so she advocated women rejecting the tradition of taking their husband's surnames. Since 1921 the Lucy Stone League has encouraged women to retain those "maiden names" and to use their husbands' surnames only when there is some special need to indicate pairing.

Women have made progress in recent years in naming as well as on other feminist battlefronts, progress that Lucy Stone could not have imagined. Just as women have their "own" names in some other societies, now in ours females may keep their "maiden names" after marriage, which is increasingly a practical idea in a society in which so many marriages end in divorce and such a high percentage of children are now produced by people living together "without benefit of clergy." Women are more and more asserting their right not to get married and to retain their independent names regardless of marital status. The adoption of *Ms.* as a form of address is said to prevent the married woman from being consigned to a lesser status than the single professional woman and at the same time removes from the woman traditionally called *Miss* the stigma of being unattached (maybe unwanted).

It makes considerable sense for a woman who has made something of a name in the world before marriage to retain that name after marriage, to be *Ms. Something* in the business world and *Mrs. Somethingelse* in private life. A woman does not have to make a cause out of this but there is a Center for a Woman's Own Name in Barrington (Illinois) which advises women on their legal rights. "You don't have to be Mrs. Him," they'll tell you, though traditionalists squirm.

So some women no longer take their husband's name when they marry. They still haven't found a way to escape from bearing their father's (not their mother's) name, not conveniently. Some women take their husband's name only when they are required to do so for legal purposes or want to for practical purposes. Some make limited use of their own names during marriage. Some keep their husband's name even after divorce, which doesn't make a lot of sense to me. Some women who want equal billing with their husbands (which makes sense if they pay half of the bills) like hyphenated names. That was (as I mentioned earlier) one way an heiress could seek to perpetuate her family name. James Orchard Halliwell married the Phillips heiress and became James Orchard Halliwell-Phillips, his wife Mrs. Halliwell-Phillips. (The husband's name came first in that case.)

Hyphenated names might be one way of settling the question over whose name the children should bear, especially if the parents are unmarried, but if hyphenated names become too clearly a sign of bastardy they probably will not be very popular. Maybe the boys could take the father's surnames, the girl's the mother's, but that would cause some problems, too. In Britain the law says that "neither father nor mother, when awarded custody, has the right to change a child's surname," but this (like many laws) is less equitable and more paternalistic than might at first appear. After all, the child generally starts off with the father's surname, doesn't it? When a divorced and remarried mother has custody of the kids from the previous marriage and she wants to give the children the surname of their "new father," she is up against the law. But she is also, frankly, up against logic, for the children are *not* the children of the new husband and, convenient as it may be to do so, to pretend that they are, or name them as if they were, is a sort of fraud. The problem is different but no easier if the divorced woman takes back her "maiden name" and wants the children to share that. The kids, after all, are only half hers and tradition, and sometimes the law that supports it, says that children bear their father's surname.

It is nice, however, for all the children in the family to share a surname.

Maybe the "new father" could change his to that of the father of the children!

Anyone can change his own name.

Occasionally a marrying couple will both take her surname, not his. Or they can hyphenate, having negotiated whose surname comes first, giving the children a double heritage. Alan H. Borden and his teenage bride asked a judge in Reno for a totally new surname, *Unum* (Latin for "one"), "which would symbolize [their] relationship." The approach taken by John Ono Lennon and Yoko Ono Lennon was perhaps a better idea, though Mrs. Lennon wound up with the traditional result anyway. Jeffrey and Marsha Goodman wanted a "less Jewish" name they could share. They chose *Forest.* Roy Warren got into trouble in Massachusetts when he took his wife's surname, reasoning that he had half a dozen brothers to carry on his name and his wife had no brothers. The Motor Vehicle Board in Worcester tried to tell him that using his wife's surname was "illegal."

The Spanish, as we have seen, give children the surnames of both father and mother. In Norway a woman may keep her original name and children have a legal right to either their father's or their mother's surname. In East Germany spouses must by law have "a common surname" but it can be "either that of the husband or the wife," and whatever the parents decide on the children get. In Baton Rouge (Louisiana) the *State-Times* reported a problem in 1974: Randy Steven Pigg couldn't get married at all until he changed his surname, but it was the prospective bride who laid down that law.

Men must consider what name their wives will acquire and women what name marriage will bring to them. Not only might a woman not want to be *Mrs. Pigg* but a woman forenamed *Shirley* marrying a man surnamed *Shirley* might think twice. A woman named *Shirley Shirley* gave birth to twins in 1971, so maybe love conquers all. Still, it's not easy to become *Rhonda Fonda* or for a *Lynda Byrd* to become *Lynda Byrd Cage.* There used to be a popular word game that imaginatively paired *Minnie Maddern Fiske* and *Chauncey de Pugh* to create *Minnie de Pugh, Alla Nazimova* and *Elia Kazan* to create *Alla Kazan,* etc. But these problems are usually easily avoided. I know a woman called *Vi* who, if she used her real forename, in marriage would be *Viveca Tenanda* and sound like a guru from India. If you're *Rose Smith* and marry *Mr. Garden,* try a nickname instead of being *Rose Garden.*

My counsel to women is to follow custom and take your husband's surname unless you are really established in your career under your "maiden name." If you are, go on as usual at work and in private be *Mrs. John Jones* or whatever. If both of you getting married hate your surnames, take the occasion to adopt a new surname for both of you and any children who might come along.

If it were not for custom, each person, male or female, whatever their marital status, ought best to go through life with one name of their own, producing a better sense of identity, independence, and an easier time with credit, banks, and all record-keeping generally. Right now, some banks and similar institutions regard a married woman as having no name or credit of her own, which is unfortunate. Even genealogy seems to forget sometimes that we all have as many female ancestors as male ones. (Why is there no commonly used word meaning "female ancestor"?—*ancestress* is almost obsolete.)

As for divorcées, it seems to me that if you can't stand him any more you ought not to hold on to his surname. Go back to your original surname. Or take a brand new one if you like. If you marry often, always keeping your "own" name seems like the best policy. It's silly to keep all the names of former husbands. Keep the kids, be a "good housekeeper" and keep the houses after the breakups, but ditch the names.

Ignore superstitions that insist you must never use a husband's name before the wedding, even to practice your new signature; or that marrying a man with the same surname as yours will give you healing powers (as well as keep you from having to hassle with "married names" at all); or that keeping the same initials is unlucky:

> *Change the name and not the letter,*
> *Change for the worse and not the better.*

These are (to use an old sexist phrase) "old wives' tales" and have no place in the serious business of choosing a Significant Other. That's not to say that women contemplating marriage ought not to give thought to names. Married names, like all other names, have significant psychological and sociological implications. They bear thinking about, not superstitiously but intelligently.

9. What a Name!

Martin F. Tupper's *Proverbial Philosophy* (1858) warned that "few men have grown into greatness whose names are allied to ridicule." Nonetheless, some men (and women) have done well despite *Anaïs Nin, Vida Blue, "Pudge" Heffelfinger, Kyle Rote, Shere Hite, Phyllis Bottome,* and some curiosities so familiar they do not seem remarkable any more, such as *Gore Vidal* and *Loretta Switt.* Now it takes a name like *Egypt Allen* (Texas athlete) or *Medbh McGuckian* (British poet) to give us pause. To stop traffic one has to make the kind of effort displayed in *Great Scott, July A. September* (yes, the *A* is for *August*), and the name of a billionaire's grandson, *Tara Gabriel Galaxy Gramaphone Getty* (who may have a cousin *Spagg* for all I know).

To be noticed some people will resort to funny clothes or eccentric mannerisms, and some cling to "funny" names to be "different," conspicuous. These names may be deliberately odd: *Safety First,* whose only distinction is that whenever he has a traffic accident he gets his name in the paper, is one example. Or the name may accidentally have become so: *Scott Towle* was okay until advertizing made that a household name. *Glen Glenn* and *Ima Hogg* should not have been perpetrated by parents, but the bearers bravely carried on with them. *Cardinal Sin,* the Filipino prelate, could hardly have been expected to refuse elevation from bishop just because people may laugh at him. *Sergeant Sergeant* and such are also due to the bearer's occupation and generally not ridiculous unless the title and the surname rhyme, as in *Col. Turnell* or make a statement like *Cpl. Punishment.* You get a laugh when *Dr. Dotti* is a psychiatrist, *Dr. Katz* a veterinarian, or *Larry Speakes* a mouthpiece. You get a laugh when you get into the news like *Mrs. S. Gardiner Green* of Laurel (Mississippi), elected president of the Garden Club of America, or *Armand Hammer,* who finally bought the baking soda company (though his mother named him for the hero in *Camille*); or *Jack Schwindler* (indicted in a Bank of Sark scandal).

Anyone who has ever been a substitute teacher will tell you the kids make up names for the occasion like *Anne Chovy, Ben Dover* and his sister *Eileen,* and *Ben Gay, Chuck Dupp, Tanya Hyde, Sonja Plate.* Authors like to create *Haggis McBaggis, Ron E. Raygun, Tony Baloney.* An airline magazine's contest inviting passengers to invent such names yielded *Elsie Gundo* (female beach bum) and *Walter Wall* (carpet salesman). Nicknames can sometimes yield *Liz Onya* and *Chuck Waggon.* Some novelists who specialize in hilarious monikers, like trivia buffs, research "real" names in telephone books. However, *Cheval Merde* there was fake. This kind of "research" is perhaps the simplest delight of name study and resembles small boys poking sticks into rotten logs to see what strange creatures may emerge. If you want to engage in this amusing but hardly serious occupation of collecting "funny" names, read Barbara "Rainbow" Fletcher's *Don't Blame the Stork* for a start.

Emphasis on mere "funny" names has not done onomastic science a lot of good despite the fact that the eminent author of *The American Language,* H. L. Mencken, gave it a boost with his lists of show-stopping forenames. Thomas Pyle hit a rich vein of kookiness in Oklahoma nearly half a century ago, discovering *France Paris* (highway commissioner) and, in Agra (Oklahoma), a *Gunga Dean.* Elsewhere among the Okies he located *Harness Upp, Pearl Button,* and *A. Noble Ladd.* Everyone has his or her own favorites which they swear are real names: *Art Gallery, Al Fresca, Fertif Grope.* Here are some of mine, guaranteed to be real names of real people:

Memory D. Orange	*Hardley Davidson*	*Peculiar Smith*
Fice Mork	*E. Pluribus Ewbanks*	*Ima June Bugg*
Lovely Worlds	*Rose Leaf*	*Tony Fiasco*
Mousa K. Mousa	*Solomon Gemorah*	*Friendly Ley*
Hans Off	*Syffren Cats*	*F. Peavey Heffelfinger*
Dazzle Bowsky	*Tempus Fugit*	*Pete Moss*
Oofty Goofty Bowman	*Juanita May Messmore*	*Earl Filter*
Aage Glue	*Original Bug*	*Koo Stark*
Fritiof Q. Fryxel	*Zita Ann Apathy*	*A. Toxin Worm*
Gory Hogg	*Olney Nicewonger*	*Wanton Bump*
Omer Poos	*Ima Hogg*	*Blissful Butts*
Ethel Fay Oink	*Loquacious Devon Odum*	*Hogan Bogan*
April Zipes	*Oscar Asparagus*	*Pearl Ruby Diamond*
Marvin Oonk	*Fritzi Snickle*	*Sunday Somefun*
Heidi Yum-Yum Glick	*Clarence O. Bedient*	*N. M. Ma*
Egon Kornmehl	*Aphrodite Chuckass*	*Another Smith*
Penny Nichols	*Otto Flotto*	*Tufton V. Beamish*
Pink Brown	*Jack Bienstock*	*Frank N. Stein*
Rick O'Shea	*Bent Korner*	*LaRue Walker*
Curzon Whey	*Susan Eatwell Burpitt*	*Buncha Love*
Blanche Almond	*Dallas Geese*	*Katz Meow*

You can add *Butch Fagot* (Cleveland Amory vouched for that one in *Saturday Review*), *A. Morron* (expert on strange names John Train says that

Morron was commissioner of education for the Virgin Islands), *Dr. C. B. Foot-lick* (Kansas City podiatrist), *Donald Duck* (Maryland commissioner of motor vehicles), *DeCoursy Fales* (Emerson College history professor), *Nylic Lewis* (whose father worked for the New York Life Insurance Company), and *Crapsius Pounder* (one of the many gems unearthed by the indefatigable Margaret Whitesides of Chicago). Everett Williams found *Kekapalauliionapali-hauuuliuiokeloolau David Kaapuawakokameha, Jr.* in the Florida Bureau of Vital Statistics and handed it on to Barbara "Rainbow" Fletcher. It is by no means the longest name in her collection, but I love it for the *Jr.* fllip at the end. I have seen Maori names two or three times this long, but my lengthy sample will be *Paula St. John Lawrence Lawler Byrne Strong Yeats Stevenson Callaghan Hunt Milne Smith Thompson Shankley Bennett Paisley O'Sullivan,* a commoner who beats out most of the British aristocracy, lovers of multiple monikers, by being named for the entire Liverpool soccer team of 1962.

George F. Hubbard of New York City collected other wonders right here in the USA:

Loveless Eary	*Ireland England*	*Wanda Farr*
Yetta Gang	*Inez Innes*	*Lizzie Izabichie*
Watermelon Johnson	*Zeno Klinker*	*Logwell Lurvey*
Savage Nettles	*Fluid Nunn*	*Zoltan Ovary*
Freeze Quick	*Little Green Russian*	*Daily Swindle*
Britus Twitty	*Viola Unstrung*	*Pleasant Vice*

Other collectors have specialized in satirical-sounding company names such as *Begg, Barro & Steele* (California) or just motley linkages as that of the Montreal architectural firm of *Affleck, Desbarats, Dimakopoulos, Lebensold & Sise.* One is always hearing of firms such as *Assault & Battery,* and *Dewey, Cheatham and Howe* are real, not invented for a comedian's monologue. John Train (*Remarkable Names of Real People*) is a reliable source because he tracks down the rumors that there is a Chinese waiter named *T. Hee* and confirms them, while admitting he cannot locate *Wun Hung Lo* and *U. Fukov.*

You can see that as *Thomas Hee* our *T. Hee* is unremarkable, just as *Richard Holder* will not be called *Jock* unless he usually uses the nickname *Dick.* Many minor changes or initials or substitutions can avoid the howls that greet *Roald Oates, Anne Droyd, Donny Brooks, Starr Worz.* I once had a student who signed himself *W. Peace* to hide *Warren Peace.* It's pretty silly to be *Willie Nilly,* instead of *Bill,* or *Patty Cake* instead of *Patricia.* I don't know what to advise in connection with these I found in a Dallas telephone book: *Virgin Mary Smith, Vera Necessary, Egidius Swinkels van Puyenbroek, Pastel Black* (who is white) and *Lily White* (who is black). I especially deplore the tin-eared parents who were guilty of *Hazel Angel* (Canadian MP) and the near-misses *Peter Abbott, Alberta Beach* (instead of *Alberta Peach*) and the name of a Brooklyn College colleague of mine—you have to be a Joan Crawford fan for this one—*Milfred Fierce.*

There is convincing evidence that a "funny" name hurts. (What's "funny" depends on the people around you, who may not mind *Twitty* or *Einar Miner* or *Dolores Torres* or surnames like *Raspberry* or *Krapp,* and won't mock *Dukakis* as *Dukaka* or *Dumb-kaka,* etc.) When regarded as "funny" a name can produce a maladjusted child (see Krapelin's study, 1909) or a neurotic adult (Stekel, 1911) or make it likely you will get into or flunk out of Harvard (Savage & Wells, 1948). Ford (1956) proved that people with strange names are more prone to amnesia and may not be able to remember their names at all. Nicolay & Hurley (1968), elaborating the work of Ellis & Beechley (1956), found a high percentage of unusual names among the emotionally disturbed. Nicolay discovered that juveniles with odd names were four times more likely to become delinquents. Charles E. Joubert (1983) found that weird names don't seem to prevent men from graduating with honors but seem to militate against women doing so. Schonberg and others (1974) showed that low-frequency names (as you may politely call strange ones, whether weird or merely infrequently given) went along with low self-esteem, timidity, and feelings of guilt. How would you feel if you felt you were saddled for life with *Hugh Pugh* or *Betty Burp* or *Odor* or *Venal?*

I think that a weird name, a form of child abuse, is a sign of unstable or hostile parents, a hint that the child was off on a hard road from the start and subjected to bad parenting. Parents, after all, do not have to have credentials or experience; a baby is one of the few complex products that can be produced by completely unskilled labor. Unprepared or resentful parents can give a child a bad name and a bad upbringing with it. Of course not to ditch a bad name as soon as one can is itself a sign of big problems.

Fundamentally, it depends upon how you regard your strange name. Do you think you are peculiar, or singular? Do you enjoy standing out from the crowd, or shrink from the limelight? Do you mind having to defend (or maybe just spell) your name over and over again? You can get ahead with a name as stupid as *Oral Roberts,* with all the jokes about "your brother Anal" and "What do you call two gay boys named Bob?," if you will stick to your guns. Such a name can even sound down-to-earth, like *Swaggart,* and is better than misspellings like *Bakker.* If you look in *Who's Who,* you can see which professions are more welcoming of odd names than others and also how the modern equivalents of *Ima Hogg* are battling their way ahead in society, how today's equivalents of *Learned Hand* are making us accept the unusual. Economist Beryl Sprinkel or baseballer Amos Otis are not in fields where odd names are so unusual and college presidents (as previously mentioned) seem to thrive on them. *Merry Christmas,* says its bearer, is "in a way a lot of fun." *Gonzilla Monster,* says its owner, "breaks the ice with boys."

"Funny" name collectors do no harm with their trivial pursuit unless they convince the general public that that's about all there is to the subject of names. Trivia often leads them into more serious name study, to looking for patterns of naming, for keys to the culture. To reward the many "funny"-name buffs who contributed to this section, I want to reciprocate with a few fun facts. *Lieutenant C. Weddington* got only as far as sergeant in the US Army. *Carole Redhead* won the title of Miss Britain as a brunette. *John Angel* lived in Paradise (Kansas). A man named *Bland* colorfully hijacked a Piedmont Airlines 737 and turned out to be from Shanghai (Virginia). In Sweden, Emile Blixty of Katrineholm fathered a dozen children after age 60. (*Blixty* is Swedish for "lightning.") Every day there's some story in the papers tied to a notable name. One more: *Robin Hood* (age 17, and "too young") was refused entry into the "100-year-old Midland Counties and South Wales Archery Championships."

Aptronyms are names that are striking because of the bearer's occupation: *James Bugg* (exterminator), *C. Sharpe Minor* (organist), *U. S. Navey* (of the US Marine Corps), doctors such as *Sir Ronald Brain* (neurophysiology) and *Zoltan Ovary* (gynecology) and *Inquest Coffin, Dick Tracy* of Corning (California) and *B. D. Crook* of Maryland (both police chiefs), and *I. Q. Smart* who had to live in Braintree (Massachusetts), of course.

Can't get enough? *Holland Tunnell, Christian Bible, Uneeda Bias, Benoni J. Bippus, Xenerious Cherkinbower,* and *Faramarz Faramarpour* all appear, with more of the same, in Paul Dickson's lighthearted *A Collector's Compendium of Rare and Unusual, Bold and Beautiful, Odd and Whimsical Names* (1986).

In this league it's hard to say you've found *the* winner, but I'll try. The name is *William C. Fownes, Jr.* His father was Henry C. Fownes, the Pittsburgh iron and steel magnate and noted golfer and Bill was "named after one of his father's brothers," says *The New Yorker* for 25 July 1983, page 47. Beat that!

10. Middle Names, Jr., and Other Ends and Odds

A s you now know, in our culture people at first had single names only and later added hereditary surnames. In the sixteenth century people in England, and later their descendants in America, began to acquire more than one given name at baptism. (They traditionally received an additional Christian name at Confirmation.) In time some name combinations became traditional in families or even generally. Think of *Mary Anne, Mary Louise, Mary Lynn.*

In those instances, however, *Anne, Louise,* and *Lynn* are not regarded as middle names. In America especially, middle names often resulted from boys being given the mother's "maiden name" as well as the father's surname: *Thomas Woodrow Wilson.* Growing up, the boy might become *T. Woodrow Wilson* or *Woodrow Wilson,* known as *Tom* only by his family and close friends. There was a time when it seemed as if promotion to full professor in an American university almost demanded a name such as *Nicholas Murray Butler, George Lyman Kittredge,* or *Allen Walker Read,* and it was no bad thing for a person (almost always a male) to acknowledge both his parents in this way. It was especially useful if the father's name was less distinguished than the mother's (*Peyton, Randolph, Byrd* in Virginia) or one's name was something like *Joseph Wood Krutch.* On marriage a woman often incorporated her "maiden name" into a name like *Alice Roosevelt Longstreet,* but there the "maiden name" was not exactly what we usually mean by "middle name."

So middle names honored a maternal line, gave an alternative to a common or disliked "first name," or could perk up a plain name (*William French Smith, William Tecumseh Sherman,* or *Harry S Truman,* where the *S* was not short for anything). I believe girls ought to be given middle names, too, but I don't mean the combinations like *Betty Sue* or *Carol Lee,* which are as out of fashion as *Jim Bob* and *Billy Joe.* I mean names which connect them to maternal as well as paternal relatives.

It is particularly American to reduce middle names to initials (*Salmon P. Chase, George M. Cohan, William F. Buckley, Jr.*). If it is to be the first name

75

that is to be de-emphasized, I suggest dropping it altogether rather than creating names like *E. Howard Hunt, G. Gordon Liddy,* and the one that T. S. Eliot infused with such pomposity, *J. Alfred Prufrock.* S. Gary Garwood (who hates his *S* name) claims names like his own connote power (*F. Lee Bailey, J. Paul Getty, C. Everett Koop*) but I think they look wimpy or "would-be." *Gary Garwood* or *Gordon Liddy* are stronger, and *W. Somerset Maugham* is not as effective as *Somerset Maugham. William S. Maugham* would sound more American, though I suppose no one ever called the British writer Bill, as we might—unless we could not find out what the *W* stood for.

Many famous Americans have suppressed details, as it were, under initials, like *T. S. Eliot.* Or the poet who preferred the humbler lower case: *e. e. cummings.* We have already encountered H. L. (Henry Louis) Mencken and you've heard of *W. C.* (William Claude) *Fields* (who likewise suppressed some of his surname). In *The Book of Lists #2* (1980), Irving Wallace and his clan of collaborators cite a couple of dozen celebrities known by their initials rather than by given names, including P. T. (Phineas Taylor) Barnum, H. R. (Henry Robert) Haldeman, H. L. (Haroldson Lafayette) Hunt, J. P. (John Pierpont) Morgan, J. C. (James Cash) Penney, J. D. (Jerome David) Salinger, and O. J. (Orenthal James) Simpson. Actor E. G. Marshall, according to the Wallaces, refuses to divulge what *E. G.* stands for; it's "Everybody's Guess."

Whatever happens with our names later in life, today it is pretty much standard in the US for us to get more than one name to go with our surname. The US armed forces expect you to have three names: a first name, a middle name, and a last name. If you have no middle name you'll go down in the records as *NMI* (No Middle Initial).

When choosing a middle name, one first has to see how the mother's "maiden name" sounds with the father's. Keep in mind the initials when you contemplate *Christopher Isherwood Anderson.* Consider that the first name may be dropped as in *George Bernard Shaw* (he detested *George*) even if all three initials are used (he was famous as *GBS*). *Hiram Ulysses Grant* first dropped the *Hiram* and then went for *U.S. Grant,* but that came to pass by accident. When an Ohio congressman nominated young Ulysses (as he was called by his parents) for the US Military Academy, the appointment was made out to *Ulysses S. Grant,* assuming that *Ulysses* was the first name and that he had his mother's name *Simpson* for a middle name. Grant, fearful that his classmates might tease him about his real initials (*HUG*), let that stand and under that name he eventually was president.

Most Americans don't approve of a lot of names in a row; *Oscar Fingal O'Flahertie Wills Wilde* looks pretentious to them. But if you have some treasured family names to bestow, give them. A "laundry list" (as today we call any longish list) of merely fad or favorite names is another matter. Some of the names can always be concealed later, if desired, and *Arthur Annesley*

Ronald Firbank gave the tot at least three different scripts to follow in life. Unfortunately, he chose *Ronald.*

An important and much neglected use for the middle name is to avoid the dreaded *Jr.,* which some psychiatrists assert gives the child a sense of being a carbon copy, not an original, and a name to live up to (or to live down) that is not truly his. For what they are worth, studies have shown that a child named after one of its parents stands a greater chance of being abused and that in a Veterans' Administration mental hospital *Junior* turned up three times more often than in the general population. That study of 1971 is disputed. Undoubtedly, it gives one a jump start in life to be the *Jr.* of a famous person, almost to the extent that it seems that some political offices in America are hereditary.

Junior is also a detestable name for a growing boy. But *Jr.* is easily avoided. If you bear *George Jones* and insist on naming the child after yourself (a matter in which psychiatrists take disquieting interest) give him a break and give him *George Something Jones.* Then he will not be a *Jr.,* for even *George P.* (for *Patrick*) *Jones* is not *Jr.* if his father is (say) *George P.* (for *Preston*) *Jones.* You are not a *Jr.* unless your name is precisely the same as your father's—and he is still alive. When he dies, you drop the *Jr.,* and if Sammy Davis, Jr.'s father is dead, Sammy is ignorant.

There's also the problem of the son (such as *Martin Luther King, Jr.*) becoming more famous than his dad while dad is still alive. This produced the dumb designation *Martin Luther King, Sr.,* which was all the more unjustified because the son was not really a *Jr.* at all, that being just an afterthought some years after he was christened. The informed would have referred to *Martin Luther King* and to *Martin Luther King, Jr.* all the life of the latter, whose father outlived him, as most people know. There is never a reason for *Sr.* because the *Jr.* makes all the distinction necessary to avoid confusion, which is what it's supposed to be all about. Problems do arise with *John F. Kennedy, Jr.,* whose father is well known to be deceased, but who can expect the son now to be *John F. Kennedy?* Or, to be candid, anything like it; so the name is both a help in politics and at the same time courts the charge, "You're no John F. Kennedy," which even non-relatives have had flung at them lately. I believe *Morton Downey* is long gone, but *Morton Downey, Jr.* tenaciously holds on to the extra bit.

Ideally we should abandon the *Sr.* and *Jr.* business just as the British have given up the *Elder* and the *Younger,* only really useful in the case of two famous men named *William Pitt* or the Roman *Cato* pair.

Nor is there much excuse for *II* and *III,* etc., except for monarchs, popes, and German *Euer Durchlauchten* like Heinrich XXXIII of Reuss (in whose family each and every male was *Heinrich*). Remember, you cannot be *W. F. Brown III* unless the initials stand for the same names in each generation (which they seldom do). Calling yourself (say) *Benjamin Franklin V* is quite unnecessary; no one is going to imagine you are *the* Benjamin Franklin now.

The numbers are supposed to avoid confusion, so when there is no possibility of confusion they are pompous, vain, useless. If you insist on the name initials so that you won't have to alter monograms on things, let them stand for different forenames.

In my own case, I bear the same forename (*Leonard*) as my father, but his middle name (*Seville*) I did not get, though some people insisted on calling me *Junior* when I was too young to protest effectively. With too many *Leonard*s around, my mother found it convenient to refer to me, as tradition dictated my schoolmates would, by my surname (*Ashley*). As soon as I was old enough to make my voice heard I went by my schoolyard nickname (*Tim*) with friends and wrote *L. R. N. Ashley* to keep people from calling me *Leonard*. Leonard means "lion-hearted" but to me always seemed to be a prissy, wimpy name, suitable for a *Tony Randall* character, whose real forename happens to be *Leonard*. I use two middle initials. I have a lot more, but none of the relatives after whom I was named left me enough inheritance, in my view, to oblige me to commemorate them now. Three initials, or a forename and two initials, looks more British than American, but that's OK with me.

Pardon that personal paragraph. I contend that it's instructive and I want to stress that you should bear names you like. If anyone calls you anything as odious as *Lennie,* deal with them sharply. Be as considerate with the names of others, including your own children, as you want people to be with you. Names exert great power. Gilbert Highet called them "lifetime labels." George Orwell dropped *Eric Blair* early and confessed in a letter: "People always grow up like their names. It took me thirty years to work off the effects of being called Eric." Orwell added, with as much whimsy as wisdom (our naming decisions almost always involve something of both): "If I wanted a girl to grow up beautiful I'd call her Elizabeth, and if I wanted her to be a good cook I'd choose something like Mary or Jane."

Our names make us as much as we make our names. One American legally made ! part of *Derrick Bang!* One *Grizel Thompson* changed her name but not for the reason that probably occurs to you—she inherited $3,640,000 on the condition that her surname become *Inge*. Ellen Donna Cooperman tried to become *Cooperperson;* the New York Supreme Court refused this feminist move. The court said that this would lead to changes such as *Manson* to *Peoplechild* and hold women's liberation up to ridicule. I once dedicated a book to a late friend who had rejected his father and his father's name (*Williams*) and taken an awkward version of his mother's (*Melbas'son*). These extreme efforts to control names demonstrate awareness, at least, that names have effect upon our identities, our deepest selves.

At the end of the book, as you know, we shall return to personal names and the important matter of "what to name the baby." What follows in closing this part of the book now is some bibliographical references that will get you started in the library on such aspects of personal naming as may hold further interest for you. Ralph Slovenko (1983) has studied aptronyms, surnames that seem occupationally connected (*Prettyman* for a plastic surgeon). A. Arthur Hartman (1951) has shown that 97% of repeaters and 55% of first offenders at Joliet Prison used an alias. Robert M. Rennick (1970) explained name changes (including how immigration officials got *Kelly* out of *Yankele*). Zacharias P. Thundy (1985) proves that people with odd names often get into the study of names, and also that the fad for naming kids after television stars instead of saints is an indicator of the decline in religious belief in the US, whatever televangelists may say. Charles Winick in *The New People* (1968) began the serious discussion of the desexualization of the US and the rise of unisex names and androgynous nicknames. Wayland D. Hand (1981) and others tell us all about how in folklore listing people's names is supposed to be an infallible cure for hiccups. John Money (1974) writes of how sex-changers go from *Desmond* to *Desmarie,* etc. Winifred L. Holman and Donald L. Jacobus (1958) give the hypocristic (diminutive) versions of 70 US names in use between 1700 and 1800 (such as *Nettie* for *Antoinette*). Edwin D. Lawson's *Personal Names and Naming* (1987), already noted as a standard reference, can lead you to all these and more. The works of Elsdon C. Smith (in the US) and Leslie A. Dunkling (author of *The Guinness Book of Names,* a popular and charming introduction to the subject from the UK point of view) are excellent places to start investigating personal names in depth. I may mention that I have published widely on name changing, names in literature, names in the movies, French surnames and the English, names of the American Revolution, names in sexual slang, and (with Michael Hanifin) a huge article on the whole Roman system of naming and all its implications, all of which you can find in the library by yourself or with the assistance of those polite polymaths, the librarians in the Reference section. For an insider's perspective on names, see some of the many scholars who may have turned to the subject because their own names were *Bean, Busse, Chao, Clyne, Dabbs, Delinquant, Emeneau, Fast, Freud,* and so on down the alphabet.

Now we leave personal names and take up toponyms (placenames), from *Aabnye* (Minnesota) to *Zzyzx Springs* (California). The commonest placenames in the US are these: *Fairview, Midway, Centerville, Oak Grove, Riverside, Five Points, Mount Pleasant, Oakland, Pleasant Hill,* and *Georgetown.* Thirty-one states have a *Washington County.* Guess which states are involved in these "borderline cases": *Kenova, Penmar, Sylmar, Kenvir, Kensee, Texahoma, Tennga,* and *Delmar.* California alone has *Calneva, Calada, Calor, Calzona,* and *Calexico* (across from *Mexicali*). There are palindromes (*Harrah*) and "backward" street names (*Initram* and *Tunlaw Road,* in both Washington, DC, and Baltimore, MD), and amusing street names across the country, of which my favorites are *No Way, Primrose Path, Another Street, Sex Drive, Ski Run, Double Parkway, Lois Lane, Della Street, Maria Ave., Tennis Court, Lotta Boulevard, Superconductor Drive, Back Row,* and *Cow Hollow.*

There are *Dobbs Ferry, Sutters Mill,* but *Martha's Vineyard.* There are

Wilkes-Barre, Philsmith Peak, Emmaville, and *Blood and Slaughter Gap.* Every single placename is redolent of history and is the result of some conscious decision. Right now the computers have produced *The Gazetteer of the United States* and we have identified more than three million of the names on US maps. Now myself and the other members of the Place Name Commission of the United States, the scholars in the colleges and universities and in private life (Lewis McArthur, like his father before him, is the expert on Oregon placenames), and the experts in the US Geological Survey and the United States Board on Geographical Names, all have decades of work to complete before we have all the names, all the facts, all the stories behind the names settlers have successively laid down here "in the presence of this continent," not to mention the great problems involved in such Native American names (in hundreds of Amerindian languages) as have survived the white settler claiming America, renaming America, moving across the land and scattering placenames wherever he—and she—went. Recently *Old Lyme* gave us new *Lyme disease.*

PART TWO

PLACES

Where can you match the mighty music of their names?—The Monongahela, the Colorado, the Rio Grande, the Columbia, the Tennessee, the Hudson (sweet Thames!); the Kenebec, the Rappahannock, the Delaware, the Penobscot, the Wabash, the Chesapeake, the Swannanoa, the Indian River, the Niagara (sweet Afton!); the Saint Lawrence, the Susquehanna, the Tombigbee, the Nantahala, the French Broad, the Chattahoochee, the Arizona, and the Potomac (Father Tiber!)— these are a few of their princely names, these are a few of their great, proud, glittering names, fit for the immense and lonely land that they inhabit.

—Thomas Wolfe, *Of Time and the River*

11. Studying American Placenames

The scientific study of placenames is called toponymy. It involves gathering clues not only about linguistic labels for geographical features but additionally details about namers, about exploration and settlement and other aspects of psychology and history. Some placenames date back farther than the beginnings of written language and at the start were studied from the philological point of view for insights into language development. Today placenames are likewise studied for information about other kinds of human behavior; they concern geographers, anthropologists, and many more investigators than etymologists.

When white men reached the Americas they found colorful but confounding aboriginal placenames in use. They were intrigued by these American Indian—linguists say Amerindian—designations but they basically valued neither them nor the culture they contained. The white man swept aside most of the Amerindian placenames; his purpose was to establish here a New France, a New Spain, a New England.

Typically, the British replaced the difficult Amerindian placenames with nods to patrons (*Charlestown, Jamestown, Baltimore, Delaware, Virginia*) and memories of home (*Boston, Cambridge, New York*). They also showed in their renaming of places the impulse to reform (*New London, New Canaan, New Hampshire*) that had prompted many of them to try a new life on a new continent, and in substituting their new names for the old Amerindian ones here they declared their intention of taking over from the aborigines. What one names, one claims. Here was a land in which they could build the New Jerusalem of their religious hopes, the freer New England of their political dreams. The new names often made clear their hopes (*Amityville, Providence, Hope*). Later were to come *Calamity, Hell Hole, Death Valley*.

Early writers commented on the vigor and vitality, sonorousness and mystery of Amerindian placenames but ignorance of the hundreds upon hundreds of Amerindian languages (though derived, it is thought, from only three principal roots) kept colonists from developing any true understanding of the namers of native America until the nineteenth century, by which time many of the speakers of these languages had vanished. The expanding new nation, driven by the Jacksonian notion of "manifest destiny," seemed to spell the end of the red man and whatever vestiges of his culture that remained. However, the celebration of the triumph of the Revolution, followed by increased nationalism after the War of 1812, had the effect of enobling the "savage" and holding in higher esteem the aboriginal, the wilderness, the frontier, anything which was quintessentially American and could be sharply contrasted with the Old World of Europe.

W. F. H. Nicolaisen, in "The Official Treatment of Non-English Placenames in the United States," in *Amtlicher Gebrauch des Geographischen Namengutes* (1986), reminds us that "it is essential to remember that, for almost four centuries, immigrants from all parts of the globe, but particularly from Europe, have transferred to the United States, as part of their intellectual and linguistic baggage, tens of thousands of names or name types with which they were familiar in the homeland and which they reapplied for nostalgic, sentimental or personal reasons, reflecting their own cultural and linguistic heritage."

These Old World names were often as mangled here as the native American ones: we translated *Nouvelle Orléans* and *Montaignes Rocheuses;* we pronounced *Terre Haute, Detroit,* and *Notre Dame* our own way; and we turned *L'Eau Froid* into *Low Freight.* In the *Vieux Carré,* it's *BurGUNDy.* With languages even stranger than French we did worse. With Amerindian names we did perhaps the worst of all.

First we tried to "Americanize." Then we got nostalgic and favored the Noble Savage and *New Sweden* and foreign heroes and hometowns. Explorers, surveyors, cartographers, pioneers, settlers, railroad men, postal officials— many were the agents to carry the naming trends right across the continent. The mapmakers made mistakes: *Nome* (Alaska) came from the uncertain *Name?* on a map. The people from one *Princeton* founded another farther west; we can trace settlement patterns sometimes in this way. At the local level they copied a trend for numbering streets. Now *Second* is the most common street name, *First* having often been renamed (*Market, Main, Front, River,* etc.); and *Park* is followed by *Third, Fourth, Fifth,* while many streets are named for trees (*Pine, Oak, Elm*) or presidents or just letters of the alphabet. Once in a while there will be an Amerindian name at state, county, or local level, generally one picked up and filtered through the language of the earliest explorers and missionaries, many of the latter having become the lexicographers of Amerindian languages, translators of the Bible into native languages, obituary writers of the very civilization they were helping to eradicate.

The early adventurers among the red men noted something of their names. About a century ago the US Board on Geographical Names was established to control all US placenames, old and new. Housed in the US Department of the

Interior, it was connected with the US Geological Survey, and it has recently published *The Gazetteer of the United States.* Over the years, names scholars in both government and the private sector have studied US placenames. A seminal study was Henry Gannett's *The Origin of Certain Place Names in the United States* (1902, reprinted 1971) and much more was collected by WPA workers in the Depression, by dedicated local historians, by individual state organizations, and so on. Thus it was possible as World War II was ending for George R. Stewart to publish the first of several editions of his classic book, *Names on the Land,* a survey of US placenames that was quite authoritative, certainly unequalled for its time, and very readable. Prof. Stewart was a linguist at the University of California but his interest extended from the names of the mining camps of the Gold Rush to just about everything else about names; moreover, he was a popular novelist (*Storm, Fire,* etc.) and he knew how to write a survey of national placenaming history and patterns that the average person would find entrancing reading.

In the early fifties, Stewart and some colleagues in the American Dialect Society (ADS) created the American Name Society (ANS) to study all aspects of names, including placenames. They started the quarterly journal *Names.* Under the tireless bibliographer E. C. Ehrensperger they published an annual report on the progress of placename scholarship, and rejoiced in the appearance of major works on the names in various states, books by Warren Upham (Minnesota), Abraham Howry Espenshade (Pennsylvania), Lewis A. McArthur (Oregon), Frederic G. Cassidy and Allen Walker Read on county placenames, etc. There was both extremely scholarly work (notably that of Robert L. Ramsay in Missouri) and energetic but not always reliable work by more or less untried researchers sent out into the field by the New Deal's Writers' Project. But at all levels placename research advanced. A placename committee set up in ADS in the forties by Prof. Ehrensperger led to guidelines for scholars such as Prof. Cassidy's model study of Dane County (Wisconsin), Allen Walker Read's meticulous documentation of name usages, and other benchmark studies. Pathbreaking works such as Erwin Gudde's big work on the placenames of California may have tended to discourage university presses such as Princeton from doing a placename survey with a volume for each and every state, but then one by one the states were "done." Hammil Kenny's book on West Virginia was just one fine example. By the time Stewart's *Names on the Land* first appeared in 1945, placename study was progressing, spottily, all around the nation, at a level far beyond the ordinary local historian's investigations. A considerable number of new projects and periodicals were well underway before the next decade was over.

Studies ranged from amateur card files and trivial pamphlets or only partial (and only partly reliable) larger studies to such masterworks as the dictionary of Alaska placenames compiled in 1967 by Donald J. Orth of the US Board on Geographical Names, who was later president of ANS. Independent scholars such as Lewis L. McArthur, whose father had blazed the trail for placename

study in Oregon, set higher standards for academic researchers and writers.
Margaret M. Bryant, long-time guiding spirit of ANS (of which she wrote a
brief history in *Names* 24, pages 30 to 55), and other presidents of ANS
encouraged a placename survey, set up and supported names institutes to supplement the annual ANS meeting, and interested names scholars in researching
and publishing throughout the country and abroad. Placename study, from the
start under the prestigious aegis of German philological study, was considered
to be the most "scientific" of all onomastic pursuits. It tended to get more government and foundation support for research. It was closely connected with
national, state, and local patriotism. Its achievements were annually hailed in
The Ehrensperger Report of ANS, now under the supervision of Kelsie B.
Harder, one of ANS's most stalwart supporters, one of *Names'* busiest editors,
and himself the author of numerous articles on placenames and of standard dictionaries and bibliographies of toponymy. Donald J. Orth and Roger L. Payne
of the US Board on Geographic Names (USBGN), and Alan Rayburn, long
in charge of the Secretariat for placenames in the government of Canada,
assisted Prof. Harder and others, such as Wilhelm F. H. Nicolaisen (who had
come to America after directing the Place Name Survey of Scotland) and
Thomas Markey (who called for more rigor in placename study), in placing
toponymy among the most important studies in linguistic science in this country.

Placename study was carried on by all sorts of investigators. Guy Read
Ramsay, a retired forester, was typical of a new breed of hardworking hobby-
ists: he prepared detailed histories of the post offices in all of the 39 counties of
his native Washington State. Ruth Shaw Worthing's *History of Fond du Lac
County as Told by its Place Names* came out in the same year (1976) as Vivian
Zinkin's more academic study of Ocean County (New Jersey) for the New
Jersey State Historical Society. The same year Lloyd R. Moses "did" Clay
County (South Dakota) for the Clay County Historical Society. Larger and
smaller studies of all sorts of toponymic topics appeared.

In 1981 René Coulet du Gard and Dominique Coulet Western together produced a handbook of *American Counties, Parishes, and Independent Cities*,
building on specific county-names studies from such places as Gloucester (Virginia) and Carbon (Utah) to Brown (Wisconsin) and Lane (Oregon). In
time, every county, parish (which is what counties are called in Louisiana), and
independent city will have its historian and have its placenames explained. By
1988, the long-awaited *Gazetteer of the United States* was complete, with all
the names from all the maps, some 3.5 million of them. But (as I said earlier)
to some extent that merely cuts out the work that will have to be directed by
the Place Name Survey of the United States and the Place Name Commission
of the United States operating under ANS in conjunction with government
bureaux. It will be a very long time before the rows of massive volumes on the
shelves or (more likely) the databanks in the computers contain the immense
Place Name Survey of the United States along the lines of the English Place
Name Survey, etc. That will be the work of generations.

Though American placename scholars have earned the respect of their worldwide colleagues who gather triennially at the International Congress of Onomastic Sciences, they have a long way to go indeed before they match the Europeans, who have been at such studies for centuries. Studies on individual states show some gaps. Some frankly will have to be done over.

When I was president of ANS in 1979, I launched a project to produce a book to put on the reference shelf until the great national placename survey is available. *Place Names, USA* will be a collection of toponymic essays, one for each state or territory, with brief bibliographies to get the student started. When I became president of ANS again (1987) the work was still in the works, and so it remains as I write. But it will be done and it will be published, and it will serve its purpose until the national survey is available to the public.

In 1987, I regarded as a very special goal of my second administration as ANS president the reviving of the Place Name Commission of the United States. I put Kelsie B. Harder in charge of an ANS placename survey which had struggled along in ANS for some time and, despite the energies of Byrd Grainger and others, had languished, pretty much collapsed, as 50 state directors found it impossible to co-ordinate and keep at their tasks. The revived Place Name Commission was put together in San Francisco in December 1987. In April 1988 it met in Reston (Virginia) for a couple of days, with Kelsie B. Harder as national director, W. F. H. Nicolaisen elected chairman, and myself and about a dozen other names scholars as members. The work of enhancing the bare US gazetteer with historical, folklore, linguistic and other facts was discussed and put on track. If European experience is any guide, none of us will live to see the millions of US placenames all gathered up, tracked to one of the many languages involved (some of them more obscure than any European tongue), and fully explained. Nonetheless, as we prepare to celebrate the centennial of the US Board on Geographical Names, it's a good time to make new departures and to take long views.

Still, this is a big country, with a lot of talent. We boast scholars such as Robert M. Rennick (doing a superb job in Kentucky, with the state enthusiastically behind him) and Gerald L. Cohen (an academic distinguished in the great tradition of Robert Ramsay, in Missouri) working well with less support. We can point to the achievements of Gudde in California, Claude Neuffer in South Carolina, Lee S. Motteler in Hawaii, Stewart Kingsbury in the Michigan Peninsula, and many others whom space prevents me from giving due notice; they are inspirations and guides. Wallace McMullen has retired after running the Names Institute (where placenames always have had an important part) after a quarter of a century; the institute lives on thanks to Wayne H. Finke and others. It has inspired other regional institutes in which local placenames have been studied: Murray Heller's in the northeast (now sadly but perhaps only temporarily out of business), Fred Tarpley's successful and long-lived institute in Texas, the north central institute now thriving under Larry Seits and Ed

Callary, and more. From all of these, new publications on placenames and new students have come forth. We have "crackerbarrel chronicles" of Texas towns and everything from studies of classical names adopted across America (*Syracuse, Ithaca, Athens*) to French names and Spanish names. We have books, articles in the periodicals, papers at conventions (here and abroad), even courses on onomastics in a few colleges (more will follow when a good textbook is prepared). The subject is attracting linguists, geolinguists, geographers, sociologists, psychologists, historians, folklorists, leading lights of the Academy and amateur collectors of placename trivia. There is a burgeoning interest in American culture as seen in the names on the land, whether they be the oldest Spanish names (*Florida, Canaveral*) or the newest confections for streets in subdivisions (Howard Channing points up Columbia, Maryland's, subdivision with street names like *Deep Calm Street, Sealed Message Street, Sleeping Dog Lane*). Whether you are interested in *Monongahela* or *Shinhopple* or the latest craze in mall names, American placenames hold great fascination.

What have we learned? What are we discovering? An impressive amount about the history of our nation and the outlook of its peoples, about the places where we came from and the places where we live, the places we visit or just hear about in the news of our media-shrunk national village. We have learned to ask questions. Why was *Bubsey Lane* (Stamford, Connecticut) or *Angel's Roost* (California) so named? How many counties are named for presidents or other heroes, and which ones have been the most honored? Why 662 *Moose* names in Canada, or so many for *Laurier*? Should we change the name of *Atomic City* (Indiana) to *Nuclear*? What American names are to be found in Canada, or Canadian names in the US, and why? What about neighborhood names (*SoHo, NoHo, LoHo, Tribeca*, and such in New York City) and street names (lovely ones, as well as *Brown Material Road*) and nicknames of places (*Skid Row, Hell's Kitchen, Cabbage Town, Hooverville, Chinatown*) and the names of fields and farms (in New Jersey I found *Sheep Thrills*)? There's something behind each one, something interesting, informative, even those of barachois and bogans.

How many names are double (*Walla Walla, Pow Pow, Sing Sing*)? Or hyphenated (*Opa-Locka, Winston-Salem, Cal-Ida*) or *by-the-Sea, by-the-Bay, on-the-Hudson,* etc.? Where are the "crossing names" like *Six-Bit* and *P-38*? Why did the town John D. Bell founded in Iowa keep changing its name? Why was *Hum Street* named? (*Ho Street* nearby gives you the clue.) Why *Wateree River* or *Toms River* or *Desolation*? Where are all the places named *Miami*, and why are they so scattered? (There's a Miami Bar near Dakar in Sénégal, too.) What's the meaning of *Coonamesset* (river and pond in Massachusetts)? Why *Rindge* (New Hampshire) or *Sierra Nevada*? Why *Coalinga* (California); can it really be "Coaling A," a railroad name? What was the correct spelling of the chief who sold his name to Seattle? Is *Buffalo* (New York) from an animal or an Indian named Buffalo? Why do people in the French Quarter say "Charters" for *Chartres*? Who was *De Kalb*? Why the *Thunders* or *Bastion Peak*?

Getting the right answers is for some a hobby. For others it is serious business. For everyone involved, placename study is rewarding. It gives us a useful prism through which to view the nature and development of American civilization. It provides us with invaluable insights into the hopes and hardships and humor of our forefathers (and foremothers, too). Placenames preserve, like a fly in amber, our history and our heritage.

To get you started on your own investigations, I shall supply you with at least one placename reference for each state, plus Puerto Rico and the Pacific territories:

ALABAMA
> Virginia O. Foscue, *Place Names of Alabama* (1989)

ALASKA
> Donald J. Orth, *Dictionary of Alaska Place Names* (1967, 1971)

ARIZONA
> Byrd H. Granger, *Arizona's Names* . . . (1983)

ARKANSAS
> Ernie Deane, *Arkansas Place Names* (1986)

CALIFORNIA
> Erwin G. Gudde, *California Place Names* (1949, revised 1960, 1969)

COLORADO
> J. Frank Dawson, *Place Names in Colorado* (1954)

CONNECTICUT
> Arthur H. Hughes and Morse S. Allen, *Connecticut Place Names* (1976)

DELAWARE
> L. W. Hecky *et al., Delaware Place Names* (1966)

FLORIDA
> Bertha E. Bloodworth and Alton C. Morris, *Places in the Sun* (1978)

GEORGIA
> Kenneth Krakow, *Georgia Place-Names* (1975)

HAWAII
> Mary Kawena Pukui *et al., Place Names of Hawaii* (1974)

IDAHO
> Lalia Boone, *Idaho Place Names* . . . (1988)

ILLINOIS
> James N. Adams, *Illinois Place Names* (1969)

INDIANA
> Ronald L. Baker and Marvin Carmony, *Indiana Place Names* (1975)

IOWA

David C. Mott, *Abandoned Towns, Villages, and Post Offices of Iowa* (1973, reprinted from *Annals of Iowa 16 & 18,* 1930, 1932)

Allen Walker Read, "A Comparison of Place Name Patterns in Iowa with Those in the Surrounding States," *Papers of the North Central Names Institute* 3 (1982), 68-78

———, "Observations of Iowa Place Place Names," *American Speech* 5 (1929), 27-44

KENTUCKY

Robert M. Rennick, *Kentucky Place Names* (1984)

LOUISIANA

Clare D'Artois Leeper, *Louisiana Places: A Collection of the Columns from the BATON ROUGE ADVOCATE, 1960-1974* (1976)

MAINE

Philip R. Rutherford, *The Dictionary of Maine Place-Names* (1970)

MARYLAND

Hamill Kenny, *The Placenames of Maryland: Their Origin and Meaning* (1984)

MASSACHUSETTS

The Writers' Program of the Works Project Administration (WPA) in Massachusetts, *The Origin of Massachusetts Place Names* ... (1941)

MICHIGAN

Walter Romig, *Michigan Place Names* (c. 1952)

MINNESOTA

Warren Upham, *Minnesota Geographic Names* (1920. 1969)

MISSISSIPPI

Rebecca M. Carter, "Some Facts and Fancies about Mississippi Indian Place-Names" (unpublished master's thesis, University of Mississippi, 1963)

MISSOURI

Robert L. Ramsay, *Our Storehouse of Missouri Place Names* (1952)

MONTANA

Robert C. Cheney, *Names on the Face of Montana* (1971, 1983)

NEBRASKA

Lillian L. Fitzpatrick (G. Thomas Fairclough, ed.), *Nebraska Place-Names* (1960)

NEVADA

Helen S. Carlson, *Nevada Place Names: A Geographical Dictionary* (1974)

NEW HAMPSHIRE

Elmer M. Hunt, *New Hampshire Town Names and Whence They Came* (1970)

NEW JERSEY
The Writers' Project of the WPA in New Jersey, *The Origin of New Jersey Place Names* (1930)

NEW YORK
W. M. Beauchamp, *Indian Names in New York* (1893)

Murray Heller, *Call Me Adirondack: Names and Their Stories* (1989)

William W. Tooker, *The Indian Place-Names on Long Island and Islands Adjacent* (1962)

NORTH CAROLINA
William S. Powell, *The North Carolina Gazetteer* (1968)

NORTH DAKOTA
Mary Anne Barnes Williams, *Origins of North Dakota Place Names* (1966, 1977)

OHIO
William D. Overman, *Ohio Town Names* (1959)

OKLAHOMA
George H. Shirk, *Oklahoma Place Names* (1965, 1973)

OREGON
Lewis A. McArthur, *Oregon Geographic Names* (1928, 1944, later editions revised and enlarged by Lewis L. McArthur 1952, 1974, 1982)

PACIFIC TERRITORIES
E. H. Bryan, *Guide to Place Names . . . Territory of the Pacific Islands* (1971)

PENNSYLVANIA
Abraham Howry Espenshade, *Pennsylvania Place Names* (1969)

PUERTO RICO
Luis Hernández Aquino, *Diccionario de voces indígenes de Puerto Rico* (2nd edn. 1977)

RHODE ISLAND
Marion I. Wright and Robert J. Sullivan, "Places and Names," *The Rhode Island Atlas* (1982), 35-62

SOUTH CAROLINA
Claude H. Neuffer, ed., *Names in South Carolina, 1954-1977* (collected and published in 3 vols., 1983)

SOUTH DAKOTA
Edward C. Ehrensperger, *South Dakota Place Names* (1973)

TENNESSEE
Ralph O. Fullerton, *Place Names of Tennessee* (1974)

TEXAS
Fred L. Massingill, *Texas Towns* (1936)

Olga C. Murley, "Texas Place Names: Voices from the Historic Past in a Goodly Land" (unpublished master's thesis, East Texas State University 1966)

Fred Tarpley, *Place Names of Northeast Texas* (1969)

UTAH

Rufus Wood Leigh, *Five Hundred Utah Place Names: Their Origin and Significance* (1961)

VERMONT

Esther Monroe Swift, *Vermont Place-Names* (1977)

VIRGINIA

Thomas H. Biggs, *Geographical and Cultural Names in Virginia* (1974)

R. McD. Hanson, *Virginia Place Names: Derivations, Historical Uses* (1969)

Mary Rita Miller, *Place-Names of the Northern Neck of Virginia: From John Smith's 1606 Map to the Present* (1983)

WASHINGTON

Edmond S. Meany, *Origin of Washington Geographic Names* (1923, 1968)

James W. Phillips, *Washington State Place Names* (1971, 1972)

WEST VIRGINIA

Hamill Kenny, *West Virginia Place Names: Their Origin and Meaning* (1945)

West Virginia Geological and Economic Survey, *West Virginia Gazetteer* (1988)

WISCONSIN

Robert E. Gard and L. G. Sorden, *The Romance of Wisconsin Place Names* (1968)

WYOMING

Peter Browning, *Yosemite Place Names* (1988)

Mae Urbank, *Wyoming Place Names* (1969, 1974)

These works vary considerably in length and depth. Some have been reprinted without necessary corrections and editions and state printouts from USBGN are recommended. There is no consistency in quality in these reference books or in methodology and, you will have noticed, none in the spelling of what I call a *placename*. (That is the way I should like to see both noun and adjective standardized; I hope my usage is followed.) The need for brevity has compelled me to make subjective selections, though I have consulted Kelsie B. Harder on the matter and therefore feel that these recommendations are sound. Certainly no such list exists in print anywhere else. Some states (such as Connecticut) can be more or less considered "done"; with some others, the work needs to be done, or re-done. In addition, there are many good studies of street names (such as John McNamara's *History in Asphalt: The Origins of Bronx Street and Place Names,* 1978, and Henry Moscow's *The Street Book: An Encyclopedia of Manhattan's Street Names and Their Origins,* also 1978) and town names (such as Helen Earle Seller's *Connecticut Town Origins,* 1973) and county names (such as Walter M. Brasch's *Columbia County Place Names of Pennsylvania,* 1982), with amusing investigations of the more colorful names (Gerald L. Cohen for Missouri, Robert M. Rennick for Kentucky, Thomas P. Brown for California). The books with popular appeal have done well: Brown's *Colorful California Names* reached a fifth edition by the mid-fifties. Books about the names of New Orleans (John Chase's *Frenchmen, Desire, Good Children: And Other New Orleans Streets*) and Texas towns, etc., have delighted tourists and locals alike. State and county historical societies have issued important specialized studies; a complete and preferably annotated bibliography of all of these needs to be prepared. There must be 100,000 items in the Library of Congress with some relevance to American placenames. Bibliographies and reference librarians will start you on the trail to what interests you. Happy trails!

This much is enough to suggest the nature and extent of US placename studies in print. The following pages will familiarize you with some features of the literature and the major avenues as well as some of the byways of toponymy (the new word you have learned), here and abroad. You do not need a vast vocabulary of words such as *hydronym* (water name). You do not need a geographer's expertise and the ability to define *bluff, butte, branch,* etc. You do not need a psychologist's insights or to be able to explain why people notice some natural features and not others or what patterns of naming reveal about patterns of perception and human personality. You can learn about and learn to love placenames.

Let's turn to the so-called romance of Amerindian names now. It was with a fascination for these "high astounding terms" of Marlovian incantatory power that many people first fell in love with the powerfully evocative and musical names on the land of America.

12. Amerindian Names

Scholars argue over "Minnesota Man," actually the remains of a young woman, which may prove that human beings were in North America about the time that agriculture and pottery were being invented in Europe, before metalworking was ever heard of. But hominids and humans may have been here twice that long, or longer. Certainly they were here when the earliest European explorers arrived, before Scandinavians set up colonies here a thousand years ago. The great Amerindian enthusiast Catlin believed that at the time Columbus got around to "discovering" America the aboriginal population was some 12 million. According to the US Commission on Civil Rights, the Amerindian population of the US in 1961 was just over half a million (551,669 in the census of 1960). In 1492, the Commission says, the population of the same area was only 800,000. However long people have been in North America, crossing by a land bridge from Asia or arriving here by ship, whatever their numbers, the Inuit, the Amerindians, and such have left their names to a considerable extent on the map of what is now the continental United States. Like the red man himself, sometimes more than the red man himself, Amerindian names have survived the white man's genocide, oppression, and "benign neglect" of the people who, as one placename scholar put it, "were here first."

James Kirk Paulding wrote these verses once well-known in America:

Currituck, Cummashawo,
Chikamoggaw, Cussewago,
Canawaloholem Karatunck,
Lastly great Kathippakakmunck.

However clumsily he presented them, poet Paulding thought Amerindian names sonorous, whereas a critic found them "highly humorous, and only to be paralleled by a catalogue of Russian generals." Actually, what you think of the

94

red man's names has a lot to do with how you regard Amerindians themselves, sympathetically or disparagingly. E. M. Ruttenber regarded the Amerindian placenames as valuable "footprints of the red man." William Penn noted that "Oktorokon, Rancocas, Shakamacon, Poquerin [had] a Grandeur in them." Stephen Vincent Benét said he had "fallen in love with American names," among those the aboriginal ones that reverberated down through the centuries:

> *The sharp names that never get fat,*
> *The snake-skin titles of mining-claims,*
> *The plumed war-bonnet of Medicine Hat....*

They sound strange (which can lead to mystery or mockery) but in at least some respects Amerindian names are not as exotic as at first they may seem. At times the white man has created longwinded descriptive names and he has also followed the Amerindian custom of giving occasion names to newborns (though we seldom think of our names as being similar to the Amerindian). Just as a brave might name his son *Big Cloud* for a storm brewing at his birth, a white parent may call a baby *Dawn,* or even (for one that howled in the maternity room) *Diva.* Another Amerindian naming practice is reflected in the British habit of conferring titles that mark significant events in later life (*Nelson of the Nile, Alexander of Tunis, Montgomery of Alamein,* less officially *Lawrence of Arabia*). These function as names, and occasionally titles obliterate previous names. Similarly, in the Amerindian fashion, in the fiction of James Fenimore Cooper, Natty Bumpo became the *Deerslayer, Hawkeye,* the *Pathfinder.* Amerindian names, both personal and otherwise, were basically, however, very different from ours. Today Amerindians may use hereditary surnames like their fellow Americans. In the distant past they had no such fixed names. Sitting Bull (better "Standing Bull," for the name was meant to stress his implacability) had a son named Charles Little Soldier. Other Amerindians had names such as *Pocohontas, Black Hawk, Crazy Horse, Running Bear, Joseph Brant,* many of them given by English-speakers or Spanish-speakers, etc. For example, *Geronimo* (Jerome) was what the Mexicans called the chief of the Apaches (a tribe the French named, as they did the *Nez Percé, Sioux, Illinois, Iroquois, Huron,* etc.).

We in English did not pay much attention to the fact that the French had regarded the Hurons as having wild hair or another tribe as distinguished by pierced noses, and the locals in *Nez Percé* (Iowa) pronounce it "Ness Purse." We named the *Black Feet,* the *Delawares* (Lenni Lenape), the *Creeks,* the *Foxes,* just as we called Metacom *King Philip* and Kintpuash *Captain Jack.* We could not distinguish their names from their titles (*Uncas,* Last of the Mohicans, is "chief," not a name, though treated as one in the fiction). We seldom realized that to themselves these tribes and nations were the *People.* That is what *Tsanish, Numakaki,* and other such "names" translate. We gave them names used by other peoples, not themselves: *Dakota* means "allies," *Seminole* "fires over there." We turned *Pani* into *Pawnee*. We pronounced *Objibwa* as *Chippewa*. It was all (to use the early American equivalent of "it was Greek to me") *Choctaw* to us. We could not see that the *Shawnee* were "southerners" or the *Hopi* were "well-behaved." We for ourselves decided who were the *Civilized Tribes* and who were not. Even if we learned a name we usually pronounced it wrong: *Powhatan* requires the stress on the final syllable, as also do many Mexican names, some say. In Virginia they put the stress on the first syllable of *Powhatan*. What is correct now? I'd say "the local pronunciation," in this and in any other such case.

Today few people can tell you that the *Iroquois* (whose five-nation confederacy had much influence on the government our republic set up) consisted of the Mohawk, Oneida, Cayuga, Onandaga, and Seneca peoples. To us the first is a punk haircut, the second a failed commune, the third what Cornell University overlooks, and the rest unintelligible, like *Ottawa* (a branch of the Algonquian Indians who even in pre-colonial times were famous traders: *Ottawa* means "we buy"). We cannot generally hazard a guess at *Arapaho, Zuñi, Shoshoni, Ute,* and *Hupa,* and *Winnebago* is an RV. We think *Canarsie* and *Kikapoo* are funny. The Amerindians themselves have too often decided to take the advice of an early French destroyer of Amerindian culture and "forget what is past for their own preservation."

As for the rest of us, we called them Savages before we reduced them to so few we could think of them as Noble Savages, and it's disastrous to give a person a bad name. Consider *Adolph Hitler Clark,* not exactly the dictator's name but as close his foolish parents could get to it naming a boy after his Uncle Adolph, thinking "Hitler would be good for a middle name." By age 16 the boy had been in and out of police custody for eight years and at 17 he was charged with murder in Florida. A bad name leads to bad things.

First prejudice takes away people's names or gives them dehumanizing ones (*gook, slope, nigger, kike, squaw*); then we destroy people because "they are not human." It took the Spanish quite a big debate to decide whether the Central and South American Indians were, in fact, human beings. Meanwhile, the *conquistadores* crushed, largely obliterated, a civilization more advanced than their own.

What we did not eliminate or replace in Amerindian names we generally mangled. We tried numerous spellings (*Quintticook, Quinatucqet, Quenticutt* among them) before settling on *Connecticut*. We wiped out most of the Amerindian names of that state (except for the rivers, always less "ownable" than land) and made *Norwalk* out of *Naramuke* (point of land, I think). *Housatonic, Quinnipac, Hammonasset* remaining show us that our problem was more with power than with polysyllables.

One does not have to look far to see names that have been bent out of shape. *Kalamazoo* (Michigan) looks alright to us as it stands but is said to come from *ke-ke-kala-kala-mazoo* (where the water boils in the pot). *Fall River* (Massachusetts) is a mistranslation of *quequeteant* (falling water). *Cheesequake* (New Jersey) used to be *chauquisitt* (upland). Elsewhere *kelikonikan* became *Calico,* and *chickahauk* became *Kitty Hawk,* and in upstate New York you can see *Taconic* and *Taghanic* signs side by side. God knows what *Wheeling* (West Virginia) was once called. The many variations of the Mohawk's word *Ontario* (nice river) sometimes appear to be totally different words. *Toronto* is pretty close to *teronto* (sea of logs) and *Niagara* to *niakara* (spills into), but where Amerindian names, so-called, still exist, they very often would be more accurately described as "roughly based on the Amerindian." Some are unfathomable.

Take *Acadia,* for instance. Pierre de Gast gave that name in 1604 to a section of what are now the Canadian provinces of Nova Scotia and New Brunswick. It came from the Micmacs' *akade* (which simply means "place," a suffix often used to suggest that something there was abundant). From that Canadian name we got our Cajuns (Acadians) of Louisiana, much displaced.

Our ignorance of the native languages produced some hilarious results. We kept *Chicago* (which suggests "stinking," maybe as with wild onions). We named *Texas* when we misunderstood natives who were asked about the name of the place and kept repeating their word for "hello!" We named *Tampa* (Florida) unaware that the natives were saying *itimpi* (near it). It's like the case of the Australians who asked the aborigines, "What is the name of that animal?" The reply was *Kangaroo* ("I don't know").

Often we did not catch the whole word, or we shortened it. That's how we acquired in our American vocabulary *racoon* (*raughriughoun*), *possum* (*askupononq*), and *squash* (*isoquontersquash*). We did get *teepee* and *quahog* right but fell down on *seganku* (skunk) and *toaroebe* (terrapin). Where placenames became famous (*Okeefenoke, Chattanooga, Chattahoochie, Ho-Ho-Kus, Sippiwisset, Squibnocket, Chappaquiddick*), the strangeness more or less wore off. Where they did not become really common (*Kushakbolutka, Chickiechockie, Lake Pongokwayhaymock, Itchepuckesassa River*), they continue to sound strange to us. In some instances we lost the poetry of the names: *Canadaigua* (chosen spot), *Onteroa* (land in the sky), and *Naugatuck,* now considered a suitably ridiculous name to raise laughs in a sitcom. We called it *Bowlegs* (Oklahoma) for the seminole chief Bolek, who resisted being forcibly removed from Florida to that godforsaken "land of the red men," which is approximately what *Oklahoma* means.

Once Amerindians became less of a threat to our taking of their land, we started to like better such names as *Kawanishoning, Namescesepong,* and *Popmentang* in Pennsylvania. In Hampton Beach there is, or was, a hotel named *Quoquinnapassoauogog House.* During the last century's nostalgic infatuation with a romanticized Indian, the normal cultural process was sometimes reversed and Amerindian names were given even to places that had no Amerindian connections. Some placenames that sound Amerindian are not. *Savage* (Montana) is named for a white engineer of that surname. *Broken Bow* (Nebraska) was so named because two boys found a broken bow there, but it may well not have been an Indian's, and *Broken Bow* (Oklahoma) was borrowed from Nebraska. When we did take real Amerindian placenames, we did not always choose the best or get them right. Why is *Wyoming* not stressed on the first syllable (as it is in Thomas Campbell's *Gertrude of Wyoming,* 1899), and wouldn't it have been wiser to have chosen as the state name *Cheyenne,* also under consideration when the state was named?

Sentimental attachments and honest intentions did not invariably produce authenticity. Look at what the local-yokel accent in Maine did, not only with French (*Seal Trap* from *Ciel Troppe, Devil's Head* from *d'Orville, Sock's Island* from *Jacques*) but with the difficult Abnaki names. *Haymock* was once *Pongokwahemook* (woodpecker place), *Abol Mountain* was *Aboljackarnegassic* (devoid of trees), and *Hog Island* had quahogs. Also, personal names were fouled up. *Delano* became *Dilnow, Baring* became *Barrows,* and someone who lost a mitten would be known as *Milton.* So surely it is not surprising to learn that in Maine the place where there was no fish ("no nothing," in fact) was called *Knownothing,* and *Savade Pond* was just "surveyed." The Maine speech which is capable of commemorating Mr. Whited in *Whitehead Lake* and Sir Robert Mansell in *Manset* was just as capable of rendering the Abnakis' *quaquajo* (boundary mountain) as *Quaggy Joe* and the Amerindian for "island rocks" as *Ragged Ass* (subsequently cleaned up to *Raggertask,* now merely *Ragged Island*).

This is not to pick on Down East people of Maine. On Cape Cod *L'Hommedieu* is called "Lumadoo." Foreigners fall all over *Arkansas* and the British seem incapable of pronouncing *Chicago* correctly. *Seattle* was so garbled in transmission that its origin is concealed. We paid the Dwamish chief Tshehalalicht 1700 good American dollars for the use of his name. Later he worried that he had sold his soul with that bargain, but then realized we had so misspelled it that he did not have to worry. Such manglings were common. George R. Stewart in *Names on the Land* said that *Winneppesaukee* could be found in 132 different spellings.

What we did with Amerindian placenames we also perpetrated on their personal names, creating *Roman Nose* and *Slave Indians,* etc. Great chiefs we demoted to *Sagamore John* (Nipmuck), *Willie Boy* (Piute), and *Old Charlie* (Tsali of the Cheyennes). We made jokes about *Dragging Canoe* and *Running Water* (with three sons: *Hot, Cold,* and *Luke*) and then we went on to create the Atlanta Braves and the baseball team's mascot, *Noc-a-homa.* Some Indians like Gabriel Dumont and Louis Riel were Métis and might have had the noble names of the Indian heritage, not French ones, names of sober impressiveness, like *Lone Wolf* of the Kiowa and *Red Deer* (known to history as *Crispus Attucks* and now claimed by the blacks, the first man to fall in our American Revolution).

Crispus Attucks was, in fact, both Indian and black. In fact, a third of all American blacks have some Indian blood, though black soldiers also fought in the Indian wars for the republic. The 9th and 10th Cavalry regiments and 24th and 25th Infantry regiments in the West were black, winning 14 Medals of Honor in the Indian wars. Part Amerindian likewise are a great many white Americans, from almost any state but Kentucky. Kentucky was sacred territory, only visited by Amerindians, practically never home to them. Many Americans may be honoring one of their own ancestors when they praise Red Cloud of the Dakotas, Joseph Brant of the Mohawks, Pontiac of the Ottawas. The history of Massachusetts involves many sachems, sagamores, and other chiefs as well as more humble ancestors of modern-day residents. Their names are remembered in *Abrams Creek* (Abram Quarry, d. 1854, the last Indian at that site), *Chick-atawbut Hill* (his name meant "house afire"), *Hyannis* (from Qyanough or Yanno), *Nahant* and *Nahanton* (possibly from the chief Nahantum), and *Quanapowitt* (brother of the sachem the colonists nicknamed "Runnymarsh" and from whom they purchased land in Wakefield in 1641). Many more Amerindians are recalled by title in placenames involving *Sachem, Sagamore,* and, in Florida, *Mecanopy* (leading chief), their individual names having been lost.

Though we put some of their names and titles on geographical features, Amerindians themselves would not impose their personal names on nature: John Konkapot would not have named a brook and a river after himself, as we named them for him in Massachusetts. The names the Indians gave to places— like the world's longest placenames, bestowed by the Maori—were really more descriptions than distinct names. In one of their many tongues *assabet* was used for any stream that "turns black" (with mud), *catacoonam[a]ug* for any "great long fishing-place," *cochichewick* for any "dashing stream" or "place of the great cascade," *cohasset* for any "fishing cove," *housatonic* for anything at all "beyond the mountain," *mantan* for any island, *mattapan* for any resting place or portage halt, *neponset* ("he walks in his sleep") for any falls easily navigated in canoes.

The American aborigines, speaking any one of hundreds of languages, whether living in the Arctic wastes or anywhere else, right down to the tip of South America, seem to have universally regarded themselves as the humble creations of Manitou (the Great Spirit) or Wakan Tanaka (Unknowable Great One) or *Mangas Colorados* of the Apaches or whatever other creator they worshipped. They thought of themselves as part of creation, not masters of it. Even Osceola (Black Drink) or Tecumseh (who declared war on the US in 1790, later providing Gen. Sherman's bellicose middle name) or the fierce Winnebagos or the proud Delawares would not have been bold enough to put a name on nature as if they owned it. The land to them was sacred. We took it, even that of the Delawares, who had been promised their land would become our fourteenth state (and we made them wait until 1937 before we would even recognize them as a tribal unit). We named it. We said it was ours. They said the land was no man's, that it was a loan to mankind, who was only passing through.

There are many engrossing books on Amerindian names. Readers may wish to begin with popular books such as D'Arcy McNikle's *They Were Here First* (1949) or John Rydjord's *Indian Place-Names* (1968). The journal *Names* in Volume 15 has a special issue devoted to Amerindian names and much information in other issues. For more specific guidance and some leading scholarly works on the subject, I have concluded this section with a select bibliography. I am grateful to the expert Virgil J. Vogel for his suggestions about what to include in it.

His own works are models of scholarship and almost everything on Amerindian culture is inspiring. The late, great Joseph Campbell was launched for life on the serious study of comparative religion, iconography, and mythology after reading a single book, as a young boy, on the American Indian. If you pick up a primer like *The American Heritage Book of Indians* (written by William Brandon in 1961, reprinted with a brief foreword by President Kennedy in which he says that our treatment of the Indian was "a national disgrace"— though I cannot recall him doing much about it), you will be captivated. In these few pages here on Amerindian names I hope to have stirred your interest. I shall return to Amerindian placenames briefly in the next section, but there is not enough room in this basic account to do more than hit a few highlights. I regret having to omit much, not least the evocative power of these names, their poetic, almost magical, power, which Allen Walker Read and other sensitive placenames scholars have been quick to note. Think what a Milton could have done with the incantatory polysyllables of a name like *Susquehanna!*

Amerindian names constitute the earliest stratum of American names, the most elusive, the greatest challenge to the linguists and others who will contribute to *The Place Name Survey of the United States.* They are ours in a sense in which no later placenames ever can be.

Here are a handful of important, representative books on this vast subject to suggest range and richness:

Beauchamp, W. M. *Indian Names in New York* (1893)

Becker, Donald William. *Indian Place-Names in New Jersey* (1964)

Carter, Rebecca M. "Some Facts and Fancies about Mississippi Indian Place-Names" (unpublished master's thesis, University of Mississippi, 1963)

Donehoo, George P. *Indian Villages and Place Names in Pennsylvania* (1928, 1977)

Dunlap, A. K. and C. A. Weslager. *Indian Place Names in Delaware* (1950)

Ekstrom, Fannie H. *Indian Place-Names of the Penobscot Valley and the Maine Coast* (1941)

Holmer, Nils M. *Indian Place Names in North America* (1948)

Huden, John C. *Indian Place Names of New England* (1962)

Kelton, Dwight H. *Indian Names of Places Near the Great Lakes* (1883)

Kenny, Hamill. *The Origin and Meaning of the Indian Place Names of Maryland* (1961)

Pentland, David H. and H. Christopher Wolfart. *Bibliography of Algonquian Linguistics* (1983, containing some items on names of one of the principal Amerindian language groups)

Read, William Alexander. *Indian Place-Names in Alabama* (1937)

————. *Florida Place-Names of Indian Origin and Seminole Personal Names* (1934)

————. *Louisiana Place-Names of Indian Origin* (1927)

Ruttenber, E. M. *Footprints of the Red Man: Indian Geographical Names* (1906)

Sanchez, Nellie v. d. Grift. *Spanish and Indian Place-Names of California* (revised 1922)

Schoolcraft, Henry Rowe. *Information Respecting . . . the Indian Tribes of the United States* (6 vols., 1851-1856)

Swanton, John R. *The Indian Tribes of North America* (1968, names of tribes and places *passim*)

Tooker, William Wallace. *The Indian Place-Names on Long Island and Islands Adjacent* (1962)

Vogel, Virgil J. *Indian Place Names in Illinois* (1963)

————. *Iowa Place Names of Indian Origin* (1983)

————. *Indian Names in Michigan* (1986)

13. American Placenames from A to Z

Y ou can study the names of the magnificent mountains and rivers of this
great country or just the street names of your hometown (consider
Robert Steven Grumet's specialized *Native American Place Names in New
York City*). With such a range of placename possibilities and such an abundance of material, even in our own backyards, our local communities, it is no
wonder that scholars and hobbyists alike have turned what often has begun as
a casual interest into a consuming and lifelong pursuit. In this section I try to
suggest something of the wide variety of American placename topics and the
diversity and appeal in them. Often our placenames were thoughtfully given,
hotly debated, yet equally famous ones were also originally bestowed in careless or quirky ways as our territories, towns and neighborhoods were settled.

As we saw in the last section, the Amerindians gave some beautiful names to
this part of the planet well before white man arrived here. The earliest European visitors and colonists corrupted or erased many of those but also contributed their share of charming additions, such as *Hispaniola* and *Lachine*.
The newcomers arrived with optimism; soon they were documenting disap-
pointments with *Deception Bay, Want Water, Malheur River, Dead Man's
Gulch*. They could be romantic or hardnosed in their choice of names. One
chronicler noted that the western pioneers, finding that water was often scarce,
created *Stinking Water Branch, Dead Horse Fork, Cutthroat Gulch, Damnation
Creek*. "Perhaps the old trailsmen and prospectors figured settlers would be
slower to build along a river named Calamity," he opined. Or perhaps the
namers were realists.

Whatever their motives, where men went, they named. M. M. Martin
(1972) concentrated on collecting money names: *Bank, Cash, Coin, Cost,
Deposit* (I suspect this meant mineral deposit and does not belong in this list),
*Dime, Dinero, Dividend, Dollarville, Exchange, Hard Money, Lucre, Midas,
Money, Nickle* (the mineral?), *Penny, Profit, Rich, Ruble, Speculator, Tax,
Teller, Tightwad,* and so on. You could make a list of placenames under prac-
tically any rubric.

Rather than assail you now with organized lists, let me offer a medley of my favorite placenames. In Texas you can find *Big Tussle, Buck Naked, Jot 'em Down,* and (Fred Tarpley's candidate for the ugliest Texas placename) *Saspamco* (San Antonio Sewage Pipe and Manufacturing Company was responsible). *Tranquility* lasted only a year (1902) in Missouri; now it's a name on the moon. Gone are *Number Four* (New York), *Ninety Six* (South Carolina), and a lot more number names. Flown are *Fly* (Virginia) and *Boring* (Tennessee and Oregon). I hope we still boast *Mud* (West Virginia) and *Mud Butte* (a beaut from South Dakota). I know we still have *King of Prussia* (Pennsylvania), which took its name from an inn sign on which the German proprietor had put up a picture of Frederick the Great. Many are the hyped, chamber-of-commerce booster names such as *Frostproof* (Florida). Some towns were named for items on the shelves in the general store where the namers met to select a post office designation. *Titusville* (Florida) would not have been chosen had Clark Rice beaten Henry T. Titus in the domino game that decided this important issue. Mining localities in California, according to *Put's Golden Songster* (1858), included *Puke Ravine, Loafer's Retreat, Ground Hog's Glory, Hell's Delight, Bogus Thunder, Gouge Eye, Guano Hill, Gospel Gulch, Coon Hollow, Rough and Ready, Poodletown, One Eye, Seven-by-Nine Valley,* and of course *Poker Flat.* Horace Kephart's *Our Southern Highlanders* (1913) identified in Appalachia such places as *Naked Place, Mad Sheep Mountain, Broken Leg, Raw Dough, Burnt Pone, Sandy Mush, Vengeance, Four Killer,* and *Disputanta.* A "puke" and a "loafer" were easterners of sorts (as a *Paddy* was an Irishman and a *Hoosier* was from Indiana, a *Sucker* from Illinois) and "pone" was cornpone.

Every name enthusiast has his favorite state. I like Arkansas, where the last company town was named *Bauxite.* Or Kentucky, where at one time or another you could find *Hell's Half Acre, Cobblers Knobs, Fearsville, Viper, Lovely, Bug Hollow, Possum Scratch School, Rabbit Hash, Pippa Passes* (from Robert Browning), *Poverty, Relief,* and *Monkeys Eyebrow* (the US naming officials preferring to do away with apostrophes, which I cannot approve: how can they cope with *Coeur d'Elene*?). Charles Manning of Kentucky's Department of Public Information helpfully explained *Monkeys Eyebrow* by saying that grass growing on a sand ridge of the Ohio River looked like a monkey's eyebrow. Among Indiana gems are *Leisure* (named for the Leisure family, of course), *Hamlet* (for John Hamlet, 1863), and *Whisky Run Township* (honoring an Indian named Ouiska). I like to mention these Hoosier howlers just to remind you that in placename study you must take nothing at face value and (as one of my students put it) seldom even then.

Tell someone of an odd explanation of a name, or an odd name (say Minnesota's *Tweet*) and he may top you with names from his own state, individually or in pairs, as with Oklahoma's *Romulus* and *Remus, Alpha* and *Omega, Long* and *Short.* North Carolina claims the first *Washington* (1776); today there are many. *George* (Washington) was named by one Charlie Brown and dedicated on 4 July, 1957. What Charlie Brown had in mind is pretty clear. Other names may be deceiving. Stewart imagined *Wisdom* (Kentucky) to be a simple commendatory name. Unwise not to have investigated: it was named for the superintendent of local schools, Henry Wisdom.

Two places in Colorado, *Rifle* and *Powderhorn,* were named for creeks and *Gunsight* (Texas) for a mountain. *Farr West* (Utah) was west of Farr's Fort. Maybe more logically, *Maudlove* (Texas) was named in honor of a Mr. O'Connor's wife. Whether *Suee* (Tennessee) is from a pig-calling cry or a girl named Sue (less likely), I do not know but some day may find out, the good Lord willin' an' the creeks don't rise.

One source of puzzling placenames is the old custom of naming the town for the post office, the post office having been named for the postmaster (or postmistress). Hence Kansas has or had *Hamburgh* (W. B. Hamm), *Eve* (Eve Davis), *Lund* (Hans Westlund), *Von* (B. S. von Schriltz), *Conroton* (Charles Conro), and *Oemoore* (O. E. Moore).

Other odd origins come from a desire for "a good safe name" (so they took the name off the safe in the post office), misread or mistaken names on the applications to the postal authorities, and sheer damned determination, such as that of Ed Scheffen: told he'd find no silver in Arizona, just a tombstone, he found silver, named his claim *Tombstone,* and it became the name of a city. *Hungry Horse* (Montana) goes back to some horses lost and found in the severe winter of 1900-1901, but I'm not certain of the origin of *Hungry Horse* in Missouri or *Wild Horse* in Oklahoma (the latter may be for an animal or for an Indian). I do know the *Horseheads* (New York) derives from some animals found dead in 1789, while *Stretch yer Neck* (West Virginia, like its *Shabby Room* and *Get In Run*) has nothing to do with horses at all.

Such placenames prove truth is stranger than fiction. In a children's book I found a place named *Hard Times* (there are real ones) and in a Superman movie there was *Smallville* (they had to go to Canada to film a town "small" enough), but reality wins with Georgia's *Tear Britches Ridge, Turniptown, Possum Trot, Turkey Trot, Too Nigh, Hunger, Trouble,* and one of several US *Lickskillets.* There's another *Lickskillet* (which means the same as *Hard Times*) in Missouri, which also has *Shakerag, Jerktail, Tanglefoot, Flip, Acid, Buzzard's Roost, Runts Corner,* and *Toad-a-Loop.* Mrs. Beverly Phillips recalled naming, as a little girl, *Seldom Seen Hollow* in Missouri's Barry County, but there are some others of the name (as in West Virginia). Not very far from the Missouri one is *Adams Grave* and *Swashing Creek* and some local Joachim appears in *Yocum Branch* and *Yoakums Hill.*

In California you have one of the shortest nicknames (*L.A.* for what the airlines call *LAX*) for one of the longest US placenames and a great many inscrutable name changes (*Willmoore* to *Long Beach* is a simple one, from commemoration to commercialization). Texas seems to pop up over and over in any discussion of US placenames: collectors like *Swiss Alp* and *Flatonia, Pep,*

Plum, Next, Earth, Wink, Veribest, and more. Illinois has towns named *Kansas, Ohio, Oregon, Tennessee, Vermont, Virginia,* and *Wyoming,* and indeed half our states use the names of other states for their localities. In some cases, the locality was named before the state: the first *Wyoming* was in the east.

In Louisiana you can find not only famous street names (*Desire* and *Bourbon* are known everywhere) but also town names such as *Ada* (named for a mule), *Darley* (named for a horse), and *Bunkie* (named for a pet monkey), *Frogmore* (not from Prince Albert and Queen Victoria's burial place in England but from—more frogs), *Bayou Grisgris* (for voodoo), *Slabtown* (today *Ringgold,* but the buildings used to be cruder), *Peggys Island* (according to George R. Thomas not from a woman but from a peg-legged riverboat captain), *Ponchatula* (Choctaw for "falling hair"), and *Waterproof* (which Mary M. Hedrich, postmistress there some years back, explained had to be relocated three times because of high water).

There is *Clever* (Missouri) and there are dumb names from all over, from *Fireworks* (Illinois) to the pair of *Love* and *Loveless* in Arkansas. People cling to colorful names. They take a pride in the unusual; it brings them attention. "West Virginia: State with Funny Names" is the headline of an article in the 5 July 1975 *West Virginia Hillbilly.* (It takes a light approach and advertizes as "A Weakly Publication.") Can it be that Tennessee wins the "funny name" competition hands down with *Toad Suck, Bucksnort, Giltedge, Miser Station, Needmore, Defeated, Spot, Oral, Skullbone, Finger, Dollar, Greenback, Ducktown, Readyville, Owl City, Duplex, Factory, Wetmore, Weakly, Topsy, Chic, Christmasville, Chalk Level, Frog Jump,* and *Ozone?* (There's an *Ozone Park* in Queens, New York, so the last does not sound properly weird to me, and in fact "funny" depends a great deal on what you are used to, for strangers in New York howl with delight at signs directing them to *Queens Midtown Tunnel.*) The Volunteer State's names are anything but dull. There's a *Dull,* too.

Imitation of peculiar names carried this sort of thing all across the country and helped to define just what a place could be called. *Altoona* (Pennsylvania) may get a laugh; it was intended to honor Altona, a German seaport. A name that could have been "funny" wasn't: people wanted to name the town after the royal governor, whose name was *Belcher,* but he prudently suggested "the Prince of Orange," Britain's William III, and so we have a couple of dozen places across the country named for that first *Princeton.* Someone from Princeton (New Jersey) named Princeton (Illinois) and someone went west to name Princeton (Kansas). I think you get the idea. Maybe if it had been *Belcher* this clue to movements of people might never have existed, or maybe they would have improved it to *Bellechere* or something, as *Pittsburg* (Kansas) followed *Pittsburgh* (Pennsylvania).

However fanciful people may get with town names and spelling, naming a county is regarded as a more serious business. Most US counties (some of which are called parishes, as you know) are named for famous men, chiefly US presidents, with Washington, Jefferson, Jackson, and Madison leading the list, and lackluster Millard Fillmore getting three. There are more than 40 counties with names of French origin, about 50 with names of Spanish origin, and predictably more than 180 derived from Amerindian languages. We named some counties, as you now know Indians would never have done, for Amerindian men and even a few for Amerindian women. The most boastful county name is probably *Nonsuch* (Kentucky). The prettiest county name? That's a matter of taste.

One aspect of American placenames that those of us who are trying to devise guidelines for a US placename survey continue to struggle with is the vexed question of pronunciation. Are we all to pronounce *New York, Baltimore, Philadelphia,* or (say) *Fayette* (from Lafayette and in combinations such as *Fayetteville* and *Fayette County*) like the natives? President Kennedy called *Cuba* (there's one in New York State, too) "Cuber." Some people omit *R*s. "I say *tomayto* and you say *tomahto.*" How do you say *Illinois, La Jolla, New Orleans, Missouri?* Do you put the stress on the last syllable of *Tennessee* or the first? We are a country of many dialects and of millions of recent immigrants who cannot yet be said to speak any American dialect, unless you want to set up special categories such as "Grocery Korean" and "Cardless Hispanic." Are placenames to be pronounced in some Received Standard—we may ask: received by whom?—or set by the locals, who may wish to have "Noo" for *New,* the accent on the second syllable in *Albany* (but not in New York State), the stress on the first in some places named *Berlin,* and giggle at the outsider who pronounces the final *E* in *Rio Grande, Villa Grande, Del Norte.* Texans know instantly you're from "furrin parts" if you say the *X* in *Bexar,* but I know parts of the country where the *X* in *Texas* is silent. Our placenames come from so many different languages, who is to make the American rules for their pronunciation even if we somehow get a Standard American way of speaking? *Cairo* (Illinois) is "Cayro," *Russia* (Ohio) is "Rooshee," and nobody seems quite sure whether it's "Los" or "Las" with *Vegas* (though a few people realize the mountains called *Floridas* ought not to be pronounced with the stress on the middle syllable and that *El Mesa* is wrong). I am constantly surprised to hear television announcers get things wrong and this has been going on since before Ben Grauer (on radio and in old newsreels) put the hard *g* in *Los Angeles.* President Kennedy is said to have lost votes because he pronounced *Spokane* "Spoke-AYNE." I can't bring myself to say "Fill-UFF-ya" or "DEE-troyt" or other careless but established names in a country where a lot of people say "sowf" and "norf" or "no'uth" and "wayest."

I know we're not supposed to say *Frisco,* though that goes back a century or more and the name to me seems not unfriendly, but how to choose between "San Fruncisco" and "San Francisco?" I know many *R*-less people who give you "San Funcisco." In a country where a supposedly authoritative dictionary offers you five different pronunciations for *junta,* where are we to turn? Suppose you have never met a native of *Igo* (California) or *Orono* (Maine). What do you say? The authorities, I suppose, are the locals. You record what they say. Then the rest of the US will say it as *we* please in *our* local accents.

John F. Goff has written of pronunciations "unique to Georgians" (1978) and Claude H. Neuffer collected some 400 *Correct Mispronunciations of South Carolina Names* (1982). Similar work could be done in all the other states. Some names are relatively safe from mangling. *Montana,* to my mind, is the least mispronounced and prettiest state name. The US Board on Geographical Names has no real guidance to offer on pronunciation, and if they did the locals would probably ignore them, as they ignore the ban on apostrophes in *Martha's Vineyard.* Our pluralist persuasions and deteriorating educational system stymie the effects of regulation and make difficult books such as Allen Wolk's *The Naming of America* (1978) and the lessons of lexicographers (who want to report, not legislate, in any case). All you can hope for is a local guide like A. Christensen's *Pronunciation Guide to Nebraska Place Names* (1953), Robert R. Monaghan's *Pronunciation Guide of Oregon Place Names* (1953, which McArthur could correct in some instances), and George M. Stokes' *Guide to the Pronunciation of Texas Towns* (1978). But are you willing to take the word of a person who says "fie dolluhz" or that of a "fly attennon on uh a-uh-playun" as to how to pronounce anything? That, as they say in California, is "no-oh gid" (no good) at all. I pronounce names from foreign languages in those languages as well as I can. I pronounce American words in my American dialect. When I am in a place, I pronounce its name as the locals do so long as it doesn't sound totally ridiculous to me and so long as the locals do not think I'm making fun of them. When I am not in the place I pronounce its name as it is usual for people to say it in my particular brand of American. When it comes to *The Place Name Survey,* in due course, I think all we can do is note how residents of Baltimore traditionally have said the name of their city and let them go down in history with that burden.

Pronunciation is often regarded as a very minor (or intractable) problem, so I have taken a little space to address it. There are many more names and issues I want to discuss; therefore, for the sake of organization I shall now turn to an alphabetical ordering for the remainder of this section and suggest, in a paragraph or so, under each letter, other items and angles of approach to acquaint you with a variety of placenames and their interest.

A – AMERICA, US, AND US

Did you ever stop to think that it is extraordinary that two continents should have been named for one minor navigator, Amerigo Vespucci (1454-1512), whose surname most people would be hard-pressed to dredge up? Vespucci was the one who decided that South America was not the Indies and that the Amerindians were not Asian (though had he suggested they were of Asiatic extraction originally, he'd have been even more perceptive).

Martin Waldseemüller (1470?-1522?), who sketched the world in two maps published in *Cosmographia introductio* in 1507, was the first cartographer to use *America,* derived from Vespucci's *Amerigo.* This has not, of course, been allowed to go unchallenged. The Nicaraguan paper *Progresso Latino* claimed that *Americano* was a Nicaraguan placename (meaning *"grande, elevado, prominente"*) and was applied to non-volcanic mountains in that area long before Vespucci's time. Not to be outdone, the British countered with Ted J. Rawlings' claim in 1973, as the city of Bristol sought publicity for its 600th anniversary, that America might well have been named for Richard Americ, High Sheriff of Bristol and a heavy financial backer of John Cabot's historic voyage to Newfoundland in the late fifteenth century.

In any case, we have North America, Central America, and South America, though our United States of America is named as if there were no united states of Mexico or Brazil; we infuriate Spanish speakers by calling ourselves Americans when they say we are only *nordeamericanos* and (considering Canada) not even all of those. Actually, we got started calling ourselves the United States of America when Canada was only provinces in British North America, and the name we used when we were dealing with the French government during our revolution just stuck, despite efforts by various people at various times to call the emerging nation by names such as *Columbia, Fre[e]donia,* and *Usona.* We are now firmly established as the United States of America (though some people are not sure whether that term is singular or plural) and we are Americans (not *Usonians* or something else). New Jersey and Virginia brought the name *United States* to the Constitutional Convention of 1787 and by now the Union seems secure—the *Confederate States of America* having lost whatever you want to call it (the *Civil War,* the *War Between the States,* the *War of Northern Aggression,* the *Late Unpleasantness,* etc.). The Mexicans call us *Estados Unidos* or *EEUU* and the Canadians call us *The States;* but God bless *America!*

B – THE BIBLE

The Bible has had, as everyone knows, an immense influence upon our literature; it also has profoundly affected our placenaming in America.

The Puritans, who left England to escape religious persecution and set up their own theocracy on these shores, brought with them few books but *the* book, the Bible. They used to stick their finger in it at random for bibliomancy (fortune telling) or to select a personal name. For placenames they read diligently, especially in their favorite part, the Old Testament. In the New Jerusalem they came up with *Providence, Bethel, Salem* and *New Salem* and other names which, despite their foreign connections, now sound essentially American: *Pisgah, Gilead, Canaan, Zion.*

Popular in the Massachusetts Colony, biblical names were taken up in Connecticut: *Lebanon* there was soon followed by *Hebron, Goshen, Bethlehem, Bethany,* etc. Now in a state whose name is aboriginal, Amerindian names are rare, and biblical names plentiful. The Nutmeg Staters even selected *Bozrah,* though Jeremiah prophesied (49:13) that "Bozrah shall become a desolation, a reproach, a waste and a curse."

As New Englanders spread out they disseminated biblical placenames and fashioned others, like *Philadelphia* ("brotherly love" or maybe more accurately "sisterly love": in any case it is in *Revelations*). They tended to call any place of supposed debauchery *Sodom.* Stewart says that it is from the Bible that we got our "strange custom" that "Mount should precede and Mountain should follow" (*Mount Pisgah, Mount Olive, Bald Mountain, Black Mountain*) but surely some influence was from the French with names like *Montréal, Mont St.-Michel, Lac Champlain, Lac des Bois.*

The native American religion founded by Joseph Smith, The Church of Jesus Christ of Latter-day Saints, has an addition to the Bible, their *Book of Mormon;* it likewise has provided American religious placenames. We shall touch on the Mormons under *M.*

C – CLASSICAL NAMES

Early settlers who read more than the Bible were familiar with Greek and Roman classics that had long been the cornerstones of western education. Literate eighteenth- and nineteenth-century Americans strewed classy classical names around as evidence of their erudition and in admiration for classical ideals, just as they built their Capitol (in what they nearly called *Rome*) and raised other impressive edifices in classical style. They were trying hard to connect the new republic with what Edgar Allan Poe was to call

> *The glory that was Greece,*
> *And the grandeur that was Rome.*

The capital became *Washington,* but Washington himself was compared to Cincinnatus. John Meares (1756?-1809) in a trading expedition to the northwest (described in his *Voyages Made in the Years 1788 and 1789 to the North West Coast of America*) showed the trend was to be widespread: he named a peak there *Mount Olympus.* There followed *Olympic Peninsula, Olympia* (Washington, another in Florida), and more, until the map of the expanding new nation was dotted with placenames that had been famous not only in Greece and Rome but throughout the rest of the classical world as well. Americans' knowledge of classics was limited. They knew only selected authors and works. Proudly, boastfully, what they knew they used.

Classical names especially blossomed in upstate New York in the last century (*Ithaca, Troy, Homer*) and soon they spread, with neoclassic architecture, south and west, everywhere there was a desire for high achievement and a reputation for refinement. To call the college town *Athens* was thought better than mere *College Station.* Across the country we acquired *Hannibal, Seneca, Cicero, Cincinnati, Eureka.* Some parts of the country favored and clung to home-grown labels, rough-hewn pioneer names, even when they became forbidding-sounding or trite from repetition. Alaska alone has about 60 *Bear Creeks* and maybe 50 *Moose Creeks*. But classical allusions continued to have a civilized cachet; they were attractive to raw towns seeking a reputation for culture. In Missouri we nearly had two places named *Excelsior*. Then the inhabitants of the second would-be *Excelsior,* learning of the first, decided they needed something distinctive, peculiar to themselves. So they called their town *Peculiar*.

That's why we see marriage announcements such as "Student from Greece Weds Lawyer from Rome" and "Oblong Man and Peculiar Girl to Wed."

D – DERIVATIONS

Name scholars must spend a lot of time on etymology, the study of word origins. They have to know a vast number of languages and (as we hinted in the section on Amerindian names) they may never learn enough to be able to fathom all our placenames.

Inuit and Indians from long before recorded history, vikings and Celtic explorers from very ancient times—these are just some of the sources of our odder, older names. The standard Amerindian names come from literally hundreds of languages. Then came the Spanish (many speaking Gallician dialect), the French (many speaking Breton dialect), the British, the Dutch. . . . We also have some Hungarian and Hottentot placenames here. Leslie Konnyu's *Hungarians in the USA* (1967) points, for instance, to the surname *Kossuth* (that of a Hungarian patriot who visited the US in the last century to much acclaim) as a county name (Iowa) and a town name (New York, Indiana, Pennsylvania, Mississippi). There used to be a *New Buda* (Iowa) and there's still a *Buda* in Illinois and Texas. Georgia used to have a *Budapest*.

The Irish scholar P. H. Reaney once wrote that there has been more nonsense written about placename etymology than about any other subject. I'd suggest theology or genealogy; however, you get his drift. Our names come from many languages and Americans are not famed as masters of many languages. I have no American acquaintances who can manage 70 languages, like my Swedish friend Erik Gunnemark, and he was astounded when I listed for him some 900 Amerindian languages for the latest edition of his superb *Geolinguistics Handbook,* confessing to him that no American would be able to help him with the majority of them and very few with any of them. Nonetheless, whenever there is a placename of doubtful origin, Amerindian or later, you can be certain someone will confidently step forward with an explanation that (as H. L. Mencken would say) is "simple, neat, and wrong."

Remember *Dime Box?* Some allege it got its name because early Texans around those parts dropped their letters at an unattended post office, with a dime for postage. That sounds like far too much postage for those days, but it makes a good story. Remember *Fly?* One town of that name was once *String-*

town (the houses all strung out in a line would be one guess) but citizens gathered to improve the civic image by changing the name, it is said, and one cried "Damn that fly!" That *Albany*/"all Benny" business is popularly said to be from support of a publican called Benny, and to hell with the Duke of Albany, that foreigner. Here's a tale they believe in Mississippi: according to Elizabeth Padgett, when *Garley* and *Ebenezer* in Marion County decided to merge their school districts they could not agree on the name for the new consolidated entity. One man argued they should "name the place Bunker Hill, since they had such a battle over it." *Bunker Hill* it became, compounding the error that placed Bunker Hill in Massachusetts in the history books as the site of a battle in the Revolution. Actually, the battle was on Breed's Hill.

Who'd a thought it? (There's a *Who'd-A-Thought-It* in Mississippi, too.) Lots more of this sort of thing is to be found in the works on colorful names of various states and in summaries such as Hannah Campbell's *Why Did They Name It . . . ?* (1964), Myron J. Quimby's *Scratch Ankle, USA . . .* (1969), and similar amusing books.

Good advice: don't be overly trusting about explanations of placenames. *Zionsville* may be from a Mr. Zion. The first thing to occur to you may be the last explanation to credit. Too much placename etymology is done without the actual inspection that makes the work of Robert M. Rennick of Kentucky so valuable or without the meticulous collection of evidence that characterizes the scholarship of Allen Walker Read (who meticulously dates citations) or Gerald L. Cohen (who digs deep), and the best geographers (who deal in facts, not guesswork).

E – ENGLISH INFLUENCE

Placenames constitute one of the principal, lasting legacies of the British presence in North America, both in the United States and Canada. A similar British presence is recalled in the Caribbean, in Belize (formerly British Honduras), and farther south.

In *Connecticut Onomastic Review,* one of many publications from regional names institutes in the US, I have written of the placenaming debt Connecticut owes to Old England. Thirty towns in Connecticut are named for Britons (the way *Pennsylvania* was named for William Penn's father—William had first wanted it called *New Wales,* then humbly declined to have it named after himself) and what we might call former Britons (Washington, Madison, Putnam). Sixty Connecticut placenames are labels transferred from British towns and cities, making the English tongue more significant there than the Amerindian languages whose names were all over the area when the colonists arrived. Naturally after the Revolution we soured on British imports and bestowed *Lisbon, Berlin, Canton,* and *Darien* in Connecticut, but by then the English names were firmly set, as in many other states. Massachusetts, for instance, has these county names: *Barnstable* (*Barnstaple* in Britain), *Berkshire, Bristol,*

Dukes, Essex, Franklin, Hampden, Hampshire, Middlesex, Norfolk, Plymouth, Suffolk, and *Worcester,* plus a single Amerindian name, *Nantucket.* New Hampshire places include such English cathedral-town names as *Durham, Exeter,* and *Peterborough.*

Many other parts of America were settled by people whose origins militated against them creating a New England here and yet some of them considered English names both suitable and elegant. Mississippians chose *Oxford* for the site of their state university and *Cambridge* turned up as far afield as Nebraska and Minnesota. Problems in geographical naming arose when English terms did not exist for American features such as *branch, bayou,* or *arroyo* or when Americans took liberties (as Francis Moore, visiting in Georgia in 1735, censoriously noticed) and insisted on calling a hill at Savannah a *bluff.* What could Englishmen make of our names such as *Graveyard Spit, Deadball Gulch, Woods Hole, Hedge Fence* (for a *rip* of broken water) or such New Hampshire placenames as *Dixville Notch* and *The Flume,* such features of a volcanic national park in the West as *Chaos Jumbles* and *Cinder Cone? Fort Nonsense* is gone; much nonsense is written by the unwary.

In placenames, as in some other aspects, Britain and America are, as George Bernard Shaw remarked, two nations separated by a common language.

F – FRENCH INFLUENCE

Voltaire said in *Candide* that Canada was just a waste of snow. One early French explorer, granted land in *Nouvelle France* by the French king instead of something nice back home, complained that he might as well have been given an estate in China. And the place is still called *Lachine.* On the other hand, the French were as interested as any other Europeans in the New World and established a New France here very early. French explorers and traders and missionaries and settlers roamed what was known of the continent, mapped much, claimed much, and created a lasting French heritage of placenames dating from the time of Jacques Cartier.

Cartier (1491-1557) and his intrepid sailors from St. Malô in Brittany discovered *Canada* (the local word for a collection of huts) and the great St. Lawrence River. He reached *Hochelaga,* which he renamed *Montréal* (royal mountain) on his voyage of 1536-1537. In 1541 he sailed up the Ottawa River in search of rich land some natives whom the French derided as Hurons had told him about, but he did not find the equivalent of the *eldorado* the Spanish so diligently sought elsewhere. He found much of interest, however, and he advised later expeditions. He inspired Cardinal Richelieu's Hundred Associates to back the settlement of part of the area in 1627.

That bold venture failed, but St. Malô sailors arrived in greater numbers thereafter and so mixed with the natives that halfbreeds were called by the equivalent of "St. Malôites." Some of those halfbreeds founded Chicago, Detroit, Peoria, and other settlements. They brought the French language and

French ways with them to a wide area. So did the famous Sieur de Maisonneuve, Samuel de Champlain (1567?-1635); he spent 30 years exploring Lower Canada and the Great Lakes region. So did Father Jacques Marquette, a Jesuit sent to study the languages of New France in 1666; he accompanied Louis Joliette on the brave expedition that Governor Frontenac sent to check out the rumors that there was a great river highway from the St. Lawrence to the Gulf of Mexico. So did countless other priests and adventurers, fur traders and military men so that by 1665, though the French then had only some 4,000 settlers in the New World—by comparison the British had 75,000—being both bold and tireless they put many of their names on the maps, discovered the "big river" (which is what *Mississippi* means), and opened up the continent.

You may not live in a former French area, such as Louisiana (named for the French king), but think of all the French placenames you know in the US. Moreover, French is one of the two official languages of Canada, and today it is being used to rewrite the history of Québec, threatening in fact to wipe English names off the map under the direction of what used to be called the Provincial Legislature and now is *L'Assemblée Nationale* not of *La Belle Province* but the *Gouvernement du Québec*. In Montréal (now spelled with an accent), *Mountain Street,* named for Bishop Jehosophat Mountain (an early principal of McGill University), has become *rue de da Montaigne,* the good bishop and educator becoming a non-person of history. Where the Francophones do not eliminate English names altogether, they tend to perpetrate names like *Baie de Campbells Bay. Quelle horreur!* That's as odd as a French accent on the native name *Quebec*. Though I suppose we must expect Francophones to spell Amerindian names in a French fashion, just as Anglophones have adapted them to English.

G – GHOST TOWNS

All over the Americas there are abandoned settlements, from formerly great ceremonial cities to dinky shanty towns. *Tulum* in Mexico is now little more than a name. When the *conquistadores* first laid eyes on it it was more splendid than their own Seville. In the jungles of Central and South America stand the ruins of other once vital religious and commercial centers. We have nothing comparable to them in the US but we still have much diminished if still inhabited gold- and silver-mining sites which once deserved to be called cities (*Silver City, Virginia City, Central City*). We have run down old mill and factory towns, deserted railroad connections and whistle stops, once booming oil towns, now all empty or virtually empty. Fields and canyons stand deserted, once busy havens for religious sects (*Burning Bush*) or outlaw gangs. The placenames are about all that is left, as with *Nineveh* and *Tyre* and *Troy*. One might almost call Mystic (Connecticut) or Williamsburg (Virginia) revived ghost towns; the name and reputation were the reasons for giving these places a "reconstruction." Other old sites are not worth reviving. Flagstaff (Maine) and many other towns now lie under water. Dudleytown (Connecticut) lies under the curse on the Dudley family.

Some of the surviving names are redolent of history; the past rings in *Last Chance, Hardscrabble, Roaring Camp, Timbuctoo, Rogue River Valley, Shining Mountains* (as Meriwether Lewis described the Rockies). Other names have been more or less forgotten as the new has risen on the grave of the old and the linguistic epitaphs are obliterated. What was Hollywood before someone's wife borrowed that name, a name the movies made world-famous? What former names has your own town had?

There's a lot of charm in Pierre Burton's *Klondike Fever* (1958), Dick King's *The Ghost Towns of Texas* (1953), and F. S. Blanchard's *The Ghost Towns of New England* (1960). Seek out these books and others like them. You'll not regret the effort. No doubt your own state has its tales of faded glory and its share of mere names that manage to keep something of the past alive.

H – HISPANIC INFLUENCE

Some of our oldest placenames here are from the Spanish, and when there was an attempt to replace one of those (*Canaveral*) with *Kennedy,* the residents rose up to defend it. Spanish, too, is the name of our most populous state (*California,* the state with the most placenames, over 100,000, many of them Spanish, of course) and Spanish is increasingly important in the fast-growing state of Florida, and elsewhere. Spanish are the names of many of the western part of the country's leading cities and most important geographical features.

As Leif Eriksson learned his lesson with *Iceland* and gave a more inviting name to *Greenland* and to *Vinland* (land of vines), so the early Spanish explorers hoped to gain more support from their sponsors back home by names that suggested rich finds in the Americas, public-relations labels that sold the product. Also useful were names that flattered patrons and backers. Missionaries scattered religious names, especially those of patron saints. The Spanish way of having a saint for every day in the church calendar made this an easy way of noting when a place was named, and of course big religious holidays were also to be commemorated. The Blessed Virgin was to be honored in many names, and so on. North and South America the pope had "given" to His Most Catholic Majesty of Spain. It was to be named by and for Catholics. Spanish explorers tended to wash out *Washoe* and substitute *Sangre de Cristo*. They saw the mountains as toothed like saws and called them the *Sierras*. But they sometimes kept the native names, which is why we say *Appalachians* now, and in some places, especially in Mesoamerica, they attached saints' names to the native names and used both, a linguistic *mestizismo*. Certain saints were overrepresented. Sometimes a saint's name like *San Miguél* would give way to another, which is what happened in the case of *San Diego*. Sometimes we retain only a part of the name they gave: they named it for the Blessed Virgin but we call it the "City of the Angels," *Los Angeles*. They called another place, right across the country, *Caso Hueso*. We call it *Key West* now.

So we have the Buena Vista and Mission districts of San Francisco. *Albuquerque* was the name of a Spanish dukedom. The Spanish names are still noted for some streets in New Orleans, where the Cabildo (the palace from which the Spanish once ruled the area) stands. The entire southwestern part of the country is dominated by Spanish names. We have states named *Colorado* and *Nevada*. We have Spanish names in parts of the country where most people now do not realize the Spanish once roamed.

Large parts of what is now the US once belonged to Mexico. Today Hispanics, a term used to include Chicanos, Puerto Ricans, refugees from Cuba and elsewhere in the Caribbean and Central and South America, etc., are in many instances reclaiming US territories for Spanish-speakers. In *Nueva York,* what was once the Lower East Side is now *Loisada*. The story goes that three Koreans who entered a Miami elevator, chatting in their native language, were told by the elevator operator (in Spanish): "You're in America now. Speak Spanish!"

Inevitably, a sort of second round of Spanish placenames, especially for streets and neighborhoods in urban areas, is to be expected. Do you know where *Little Havana* is? That its name is in English only shows that the transition remains incomplete. If you are an *Anglo*, do you know the meaning of *Las Vegas, Los Álamos, Escondito, Yerba Buena, Buena Vista?* Can you see what's wrong with *El Mesa?* Errors like that will be less likely in the future in many parts of this country. *Se habla español.*

I – INHABITANTS

One of the many onomastic interests of Allen Walker Read that proved the scope of his studies to the committee that awarded him the coveted Doctor of Literature degree from Oxford University was what the inhabitants of various places call themselves. *Tar Heels, Suckers, Corn Crackers,* and *Hard Cases* are still state designations. Do you know what states? Walt Whitman in *North Amercian Review* (1885) listed some I've not heard today: *Gun Flints* (Rhode Island), *Fly Up the Creeks* (Florida, I'd say *Crackers*), *Clam Catchers* (New Jersey); that is slang from the Civil War. Prof. Read discusses terms like *Bostonians* and *Bay Staters, Brooklynites, Philadelphians, Baltimoreans* (known by enemies as *Baltimorons*) and gets into the linguistics of *Texans, Texonians, Texicans, Texasites, Texiards, Texcanos*. What do you call a resident of Massachusetts or Connecticut? A resident of Nassau County is a *Nausaunian,* of Oregon an *Oregonian.*

Where do you have to live to be a *Southerner?* You really need an expert like Wilbur Zelinsky to pinpoint the *Deep South,* the *Mid-West,* the *Middle Border,* the *Northwest, Dixie,* the *Sun Belt, Frost Belt, Rust Belt, Snow Belt, Bible Belt.* What do you call people from each of those areas?

We sometimes seem to be a country with only one coast (the *Coast* is the West Coast) and it takes a little figuring to discover why, when referring to Maine earlier, I wrote *Down East*. Why don't we say *Coasters, Mainites, Oregoners?* We say *Floridian,* but what do you call someone from Palm Springs, Palm Beach, Taos, or Lihue? People from Halifax are *Haligonians;* from New Brunswick, *Herring Chokers.*

What do you call yourself or your neighbors? As Prof. Read has demonstrated, there are patterns, fashions, and useful social and linguistic information in these terms. That may not have occurred to you. Now you know.

J – JERSEY

We sometimes say *Jersey* instead of *New Jersey,* and there's a *Jersey City,* but one never says *York City,* always *New York* or *New York City.* (The subways in Brooklyn sometimes have signs "To the City," but Brooklyn is part of the city. *The City* is San Francisco, most people would say, and the New York tracks laid end to end would get you only to Detroit.)

Nicknames such as *Jersey* are not common for states but there are cities called *Vegas, L.A., Chi, San Berdoo.* No one seems to object to *Jersey* the way some people do to *Frisco.* Objections may arise when *Jersey* becomes *Joisey.* What other US places do you know that have their names and accents played with irreverently, and why do you think they are singled out for ridicule, like *Podunk?*

K – KAMUELA

The native language of Hawaii today survives almost exclusively in songs, folklore, and names, both personal and placenames (*Mauna Loa, Maui, Molokai, Oahu, Na Pali, Kaneohe*), plus *aloha, poi, lei, luau.* We are very unlikely to know the translation of Hawaiian placenames such as *Puaa Kaa* (rolling pigs).

Why this "K for *Kamuela"?* The Hawaiian language doesn't have a *C,* so Mr. Curtis was honored with *Kurtistown,* and language differences explain why Mr. Parker, he of the great land holdings, whose forename was Samuel, wound up with *Kamuela* named for him. It is rather fitting that English, so guilty of mangling other languages, should suffer occasionally at the hands of some other tongue, don't you think?

This *K* bit can serve to remind us of all the alterations that names suffer when they are taken from one language into another, despite the fact that names are unusually resistant to alteration in that kind of process and because of that often preserve important linguistic and historical information for us.

L – LISTS

Boring as they are by my own admission, lists are often the best way to communicate large amounts of information succinctly. I offer two lists here. One contains 50 US town and city names to give you the ABCs of where people "are coming from" when they name places. The second list (expanded from information from Kelsie B. Harder) offers 100 common US placenames and their derivations.

50 US Placenames Beginning with the Initials A, B, and C

AKRON (Ohio) — from Greek *akron* (highest point)

ALAMEDA (California) — from Spanish for a walk shaded by poplars

ALBUQUERQUE (New Mexico) — after the Duke of Albuquerque, viceroy of Mexico (1702-1711)

ALEXANDRIA (Virginia) — for the Alexander family (original white owners of the site), reinforced by ancient Alexandria (named for Alexander the Great)

ALLENTOWN (Pennsylvania) — for its founder, William Allen

ALTON (Illinois) — for Alton Easton, son of its founder

ALUM ROCK (California) — for a natural feature near mineral springs

ANCHORAGE (Alaska) — for the anchorage of early supply ships

ANNAPOLIS (Maryland) — for Britain's Queen Anne with the Greek *polis* (city)

ASHEVILLE (North Carolina) — for state governor Samuel Ashe (1725-1813) with the French *ville* (city)

ATLANTA (Georgia) — Western & Atlantic Railroad terminus

ATLANTIC CITY (New Jersey) — a resort city on the Atlantic Ocean

AUGUSTA (Maine) — for the feminine forename based on *Augustus*

AUSTIN (Texas) — for Texas pioneer Stephen F. Austin (1793-1836), founder of *San Felipe de Austin,* etc.

BABYLON (New York) — from the biblical city of great wealth and alleged great vice

BAKERSFIELD (California) — for Colonel T. Baker, early landowner

BALTIMORE (Maryland) — for George Calvert, Lord Baltimore (1580?-1620), founder of the colony

BANGOR (Maine) — from the British placename or the hymn tune that bears its name

BATH (Maine) — for the Roman spa in southwestern England

BATON ROUGE (Louisiana) — from French translation of Choctaw *itu-uma* (red pole), probably a boundary marker

BAYONNE (New Jersey) — from the French city that gave us the bayonet

BEAUMONT (Texas) — from a surname (originally French *beau mont,* "pretty mountain")

BERKELEY (California) — from Bishop George Berkeley (1685-1753), British philosopher and promoter of tar as a medicine

BEVERLY HILLS (California) — from Beverly Farms (Massachusetts)

BIG SUR — California region named for the river, like *Big Horn, Big Sioux, Big Sandy*

BIRMINGHAM (Alabama) — from the English iron and steel center

BISMARCK (North Dakota) — Missouri River crossing called *Camp Greeley, Camp Hancock,* and *Edwinton* before being named for the German chancellor in the hope of a German investment in the railroad in the area

BLOOMINGTON (Indiana) — from (probably) an abundance of flowers in the area

BOISE (Idaho) — from French *boisé* (wooded), a good example of pronunciation concealing origin

BOSSIER CITY (Louisiana) — from Pierre E. J. B. Bossier, nineteenth-century general

BOSTON (Massachusetts) — after the British town in Lincolnshire

BRIDGEPORT (Connecticut) — for the port with a bridge over the Poquonock River

BROCKTON (Massachusetts) — for Sir Isaac Brock (1769-1812), lieutenant-governor of Upper Canada and hero of the War of 1812

BRONX, THE (New York) — from Jonas Bronck, early Dutch settler (how many other places with *The* can you name?)

BROOK FARM (Massachusetts) — from a farm with a brook (nineteenth-century utopian commune near West Roxbury)

BROOKLINE (Massachusetts) — from the name of Judge Samuel Sewell's estate (which had a brook as one boundary)

BROOKLYN (New York) — from Dutch *breukelen* (broken land) and a village of that name near Utrecht (Brooklyn has a New Utrecht, a Utrecht Avenue, etc.)

BUFFALO (Wyoming) — seat of Johnson County and named for the bison

CALUMET (Michigan) — from the French for Amerindian word for "peace pipe"

CAMDEN (New Jersey) — for Charles Pratt, Earl of Camden (1714-1794)

CANTON (Ohio) — from a Boston suburb, itself named for trade with China

CAROLINA (Puerto Rico) — from the female forename and not from the US state named for the male forename (Latin *Carolus* for Britain's King Charles)

CARSON CITY (Nevada) — for Christopher "Kit" Carson (1809-1868), Indian scout, Indian administrator, brigadier general, etc. (built on the site of *Eagle Station*)

CEDAR RAPIDS (Iowa) — from the rapids of the Cedar River

CHATTANOOGA (Tennessee) — from an Amerindian name of uncertain meaning, uncertain language (Creek? Cherokee?)

CHEYENNE (Wyoming) — from Dakota for "speak intelligibly," that is to speak the language of the local people or the "allies" (*Dakota*) who moved to that area

CHIDLEY, CAPE (Labrador headland at the entrance to Hudson Strait) — named for a British place by John Davys (1550?-1605) who, after (with friends Adrian Gilbert and Dr. John Dee) outlining the Northwest Passage idea to Elizabeth I's councillor Sir Thomas Walsingham (1583), sought The Passage, discovered Davys Strait.

CHICOPEE (Massachusetts) — from Algonquian for "swift river"

CINCINNATI (Ohio) — from Washington being seen as the modern equivalent of the Roman hero Cincinnatus (5th cent. B.C.) who was called from the plough to become general and dictator, saved Rome from the Aequi and Volscians, voluntarily resigned his dictatorship (458 B.C.), and returned to his farm. (That he became dictator again in 439 B.C. to defeat the plebians we liked to forget here.) The Society of the Cincinnati (followers of Cincinnatus, as it were) was founded by officers of the Continental Army just before disbanding in 1783; they made Washington president of this fraternal, purportedly non-political, organization. After the organization (1790), the governor of the Northwest Territory (Arthur St. Clair) renamed Losantiville (founded 1788) Cincinnati

CONCORD (New Hampshire) — for an expression of hope for amity and harmony in the new town (an omen name)

100 Common US Placenames

ALBANY — for James, Duke of York and Albany (1633-1701, eventually James II of the United Kingdom). Occurs in New York, Wyoming, Georgia, Ohio, Minnesota, Indiana, Illinois, California, Kentucky, Maine, Missouri, New Hampshire, Oregon, Texas, Vermont, Mississippi, and Wisconsin, the New York capital being the source for most of the other Albanys

ARLINGTON — for the home of John Custis II or for Henry Bennet, first Earl of Arlington (1618-1685); later for the home of Robert E. Lee

ASHLAND — for the Kentucky home of Henry Clay, or for the presence of ash trees

AUBURN — for Auburn in Yorkshire (England), famous because of Oliver Goldsmith's poem, "The Deserted Village"

AURORA — for the Roman goddess of the dawn, with pleasant suggestions of the dawn of a new day, new beginnings

AU SABLE — French "sandy place," common in areas once colonized by the French

BALD — descriptive term, as in *Bald Mountain, Bald Knob,* and *Bald Hill*

BEAR — for the animal, in such names as *Bear Creek, Bear Mountain,* and *Bear Hill*

BEAVER — for the animal, used alone (for counties and towns) and in combinations such as *Beaver Brook*

BEDFORD — for the town in Bedfordshire (England), for John Russell, fourth Duke of Bedford (1710-1771), and for the army officer Thomas Bedford

BENTON — for Thomas Hart Benton (1782-1858), US senator

BLACK — descriptive name (sometimes translated from Amerindian use), as in *Black Lake, Black Mountain, Black Oak*

BLUE — descriptive term (sometimes translated from Amerindian use), as in *Blue Mesa, Blue Creek, Blue Island*

BOONE — for frontiersman Daniel Boone (1734-1820), killed at The Alamo

BRIDGE — descriptive term, as in *Bridge, Bridgeport, Bridgehampton, Bridge View*

BRISTOL — for Bristol (formerly in Gloucestershire and Somerset, now in the new county of Avon, England), whence many ships sailed for America

BROWN — descriptive term and also for the common surname

CACHE — French "hiding place," especially popular in Western states

CALHOUN — for John C. Calhoun (1782-1850), leading statesman

CARBON — for coal deposits beneath or nearby, also in combinations such as *Carbondale*

CARROLL — for Charles Carroll of Maryland (1737-1832), early patriot, and others of the surname, often as *Carrollton*

CEDAR — for the coniferous tree, as in *Cedar Falls, Cedar Breaks, Cedar Rapids*

CENTER — stressing a central position, as in *Center, Center City, Centerville*, and related *Central City*, etc. Also *Central Valley, Central Falls, Cordillera Central*

CHARLES — for Charles I or Charles II or Americans named Charles, also in *Charleston*, etc.

CHARLOTTE — for the queen of George III and others with this forename, also in *Charlottesville*, etc.

CHESTER — for Chester in Cheshire (England) and persons of this name

CLARK — for heroes such as George Rogers Clark, Abraham Clark, William Clark, and others, also in *Clarksville*, and other combinations

CLINTON — for DeWitt Clinton (1769-1828), important New York figure, and others of the surname

COLUMBIA — feminine form from *Columbus*, a name for the nation. "Columbia, the Gem of the Ocean" was once a popular song about America

COLUMBUS — for the Admiral of the Ocean Sea

CUMBERLAND — for the British county or William Augustus, Duke of Cumberland (1721-1765), scourge of the Scottish Highlands

DECATUR — for Stephen Decatur (1779-1820), US naval hero

DEVIL — featured in many names such as *Devils Bend, Devils Lake, Devils Postpile*, also in Spanish form as *Diablo: Mount Diablo, Diablo Canyon*, etc.

DOUGLAS — generally for Stephen A. Douglas (1813-1861), famous statesman and political debater, or from the forename

EAST — descriptive term (along with WEST, NORTH, SOUTH), usually in combinations, also as in *East Chicago, East Detroit, East St. Louis*

ELK — for the animal, often in combinations like *Elkton*

FAIR — descriptive term, used in combinations such as *Fairfield, Fairhope, Fair Lawn*, etc.

FAYETTE, LAFAYETTE, LA FAYETTE — for the Marquis de Lafayette, also combined as in *Fayetteville*

FRANKLIN — for Benjamin Franklin and others of this surname

FULTON — for Robert Fulton (1765-1815), inventor of the steamboat

GRAND — descriptive term (French "large"), used alone or in combinations such as *Grand Rapids, Grand Fork, Grand Junction, Grand Manan*

GREAT — descriptive term, used in combinations such as *Great Salt Lake, Great Falls, Great American Desert*, the *Great Divide, Great Bear Lake*

GREEN — for the color or for people of this surname, sometimes in the latter case *Greene* and in combinations, *Greeneville*

HAMILTON — for Alexander Hamilton or others of this surname

HANCOCK — for John Hancock or others of this surname

HARRISON — for two US presidents and others of this surname

HENRY — for Patrick Henry or others of this surname, or from this forename, or in combinations, *Cape Henry*, etc.

HIGH — descriptive term, generally in combinations such as *High Point, High Sierra*

HUMBOLDT — for (Heinrich) Alexander, Freiherr von Humboldt (1769-1859), German scientist

JACKSON — for President Andrew Jackson and others of this surname

JASPER — for Sgt. William Jasper (1750-1779), hero of battles at Fort Sullivan (1776) and Savannah (where he fell)

JEFFERSON — mostly for President Thomas Jefferson, but occasionally for others of this surname

JOHNSON — for two presidents and others of this surname

KING — the title and the surname, often in combinations such as *King City, King of Prussia, Kings Canyon, Kings Peak, Kings County*

KNOX — for General Henry Knox (1750-1806) and others of the surname, as *Knox, Fort Knox, Knoxville*, etc.

LA GRANGE — for the home of the Marquis de Lafayette

LAKE — descriptive term used both specifically (*Lake of the Ozarks, Silver Lake*) and generically (*Lakeland*, etc.)

LAWRENCE — for James Lawrence (1781-1813), naval hero of the War of 1812, and others of this surname or (less often) forename, and in combinations such as *Lawrenceville*

LEBANON — a biblical reference (the Connecticut town of this name was incorporated 1700)

LEE — for Robert E. Lee, hero of the Confederacy, and others of that surname

LEWIS — for Capt. Meriwether Lewis (1774-1809) of the Lewis and Clark expedition (1803-1806) and others of this surname, occasionally from the forename, alone or in combinations (*Lewisburg, Lewistown, Lewisville*)

LIBERTY — a patriotic name (*Atascosita* was changed to *Liberty* in Texas, *Bedloes Island* to *Liberty Island* for the site of The Statue of Liberty in New York)

LINCOLN — generally for President Abraham Lincoln

MADISON — generally for President James Madison

MARION — for Francis Marion (1732-1795), Revolutionary War hero, as well as others of this surname, a few of this forename

MIAMI — for an Amerindian tribe and (from another Amerindian family) an Amerindian placename

MIDDLE — descriptive term, as in *Middle Village, Middletown, Middlebury, Middlesboro, Middle West, Middle America*

MILL — for a mill or someone of this name, and in combination as in *Mill City, Mill Basin*, also *Mills*

MONROE — chiefly for President James Monroe

MONTGOMERY — for Richard Montgomery (1738-1775), general in the Revolution, or others of this surname, also *Montgomery City*

MORGAN — for Daniel Morgan (1736-1802), general in the Revolution, and others of this name, also *Morgantown, Morganfield, Morgan City*

MOUNT — used first in the name, while *Mountain* comes last: *Mount Pleasant, Mount St. Helen, Black Mountain*, except for *Mountain View*, etc.

MUD — descriptive term, as in *Mud Flats, Mudville, Muddy Boggy Creek*, etc.

NEW — descriptive term used chiefly in combinations such as *Newton, Newport, New Market, New Hampshire, New England, New Harmony, Newcomerstown, New Roads, New Rochelle, New Egypt, New Orleans, New Providence, New Prague, New Quebec, New Iberia, Newfoundland*

OAK — for the tree (associated with Royalists in the Civil War in Britain) and in combinations such as *Oak Grove, Oak Island, Oakland, Oak Ridge* and *Oakridge*

OLD — descriptive term as in *Old Orchard Beach, Old Westbury, Old Town,* etc.

ORANGE — for the citrus tree and its fruit or the royal house of The Netherlands (Orange Nassau), and in combinations such as *Orange County, Orangeburg, Orange City*

PERRY — for Oliver Hazard Perry (1785-1819), navel hero of the War of 1812, and for others of the name

PLAIN — descriptive term for a flat area, also *Plains* and *Prairie,* French term seen in *Prairie du Chien, Prairie du Sac,* and English combinations like *Prairie View*

PLEASANT — booster name or for a nice place in the opinion of the namers, *Pleasant View, Pleasantville, Seat Pleasant, Mount Pleasant*

PLYMOUTH — for Plymouth (England, from which the *Mayflower* sailed), transferred then from *Plymouth* (Massachusetts, the first permanent white settlement in New England)

RICHMOND — for Richmond in Surrey (England) or for the first and fourth dukes of Richmond or people surnamed *Richmond*

ROCK — descriptive term used in combinations such as *Rock Island, Little Rock, Rockville, Rockdale,* the *Rockies, Rock Hill, Rock River*

SAINT or SAINTE, SAN, ST., STE. — in combinations such as *St. Louis, Saint Petersburg* and Spanish combinations such as *San Blas, Santa Barbara,* etc., French *Sault Sainte Marie,* etc.

SAND — descriptive term in *Sand Creek,* etc., and as *Sands Point, Sandy Hook,* etc.

SHELBY — mostly for Isaac Shelby (1750-1826), hero of the Battle of King's Mountain, or others of the name, and as *Selbyville,* etc.

SILVER — for appearance and presence of the metal, as in *Silver Springs, Silver City, Silver Lake, Silverton,* etc.

SPRING — for a spring in the area, as in *Springfield, Spring Valley, Spring Lake,* and *Palm Springs,* the *Springs, Crystal Springs*

SUGAR — for sugar maples or sugar cane, as in *Sugar Land, Sugar Notch, Sugar Hill*

TRENTON — for William Trent, founder of the county seat of Mercer County (1719) and capital of New Jersey (1790), famous after the Battle of Trenton (1776), so that many other places were then given its name

UNION — usually for the union of the American states but for other kinds of union also, likewise *Union City, Union Gap, Unionville,* etc.

UPPER — directional name, also for a higher point, in combinations such as *Upperville, Upper Sandusky,* etc.

VERMILLION — probably from Amerindian but also "red" in French, also as *Vermilion, Vermillion-on-the-Lake,* etc.

WARREN — mostly for Joseph Warren (1741-1775), Revolutionary War hero who sent Paul Revere on his famous ride, also for others of this surname and even of the forename

WASHINGTON — for the first president and other Washingtons, also *Washington Court House, Washington-on-the-Brazos, Washingtonville, Mount Washington. Lake Washington,* etc.

WAYNE — mostly for "Mad Anthony" Wayne (1745-1796), of Revolutionary War fame, also *Waynesville, Waynesburg,* etc.

WEBSTER — mostly for statesman Daniel Webster (1782-1852), also *Webster Groves, Webster Springs, Webster City,* etc.

WHITE — descriptive term but also for local persons of this surname, *White Mountains, White River, Whitesboro, White Plains,* etc.

WOOD — descriptive term and for local persons of the surname, *Wood Lake, Lake of the Woods, Woodville, Woods Hole,* and in *Woodlawn, Woodmont,* etc.

YORK — for James, Duke of York and Albany (as with ALBANY) as *York, Yorkville, Yorktown, New York, Cape York Peninsula,* etc.

M – MORMONS

Mormons is a more polite term than we usually give the members of new religions (*Dunkards, Holy Rollers, Shakers, Quakers, Methodists*). The name comes from the *Book of Mormon,* written on golden plates in "Reformed Egyptian," discovered in upstate New York and translated by Joseph Smith, Mormons believe. So the angel Moroni gave Smith a new Church of Jesus Christ of Latter-day Saints (often *LDS*) and a name for their state in the valley of the Great Salt Lake, *Deseret.* As it turned out, *Deseret* was rejected; the state was named for the Ute Indians. The Mormons did succeed in putting on the land such religious placenames as *Moroni, Lehi, Nephi.* Because they regarded themselves as saints, *St. George* is named not for the dragon-killer but for George A. Smith. The *LDS* custom of addressing each other by forenames ("Brother George" for Mr. Smith, "Brother Brigham" for Mr. Young) gave them *Brigham City* (rather than *Youngstown*). The centrality of the Temple in their thinking is underscored by all the broad streets of Salt Lake City being numbered from there, North, South, East, and West. This naming system helps you to find the 2000 block on *East First South* easily. Not so easy are some of the town names. *Iosepha* (Utah) was named a century ago by a group of Hawaiian settlers in honor of Joseph Smith.

Mormons are an example of how a tightly-knit group, in this case a band of co-religionists, can use names to express their ideology, carve out their identity, distinguish themselves from others (whom the Mormons call *Gentiles,* even if they are Jews), memorialize their leaders, and in general serve their zealous needs, however parochial. I say "parochial" though the Mormons have *stakes,* not parishes.

N – NATIVE AMERICAN NAMES

You will have seen the entire section on Amerindian names earlier (in which I avoided the term *Native American,* for everyone born in the US is a "native American" in my opinion). Now I use it as an excuse to fit in some more information on Indian names, as promised.

Every state has some Amerindian names, some only a few, some many. Of nearly 800 Amerindian placenames still in use in *Massachusetts* ("at the big hill," referring to the Blue Hills near what the British named Boston) even the official records leave many unexplained. In states where Amerindian names are scarcer or in more obscure languages, knowledge of them is even less.

But they do exist, and out of all proportion to the red man's post-colonial demographic and political clout. Missouri has such nuggets as *Kawanishoning, Namescesepong, Oskohary,* and *Lapachpeton. Ontario* occurs in Canada and California, *Miami* in Ohio and Florida. Moreover, some places you hardly think of as such (*Peoria* and *Des Moines,* for example) bear Amerindian names, as do the majestic *Yosemite* (*Yosemity*) and *Mississippi* (*Messipi*).

When Stephen Vincent Benét wrote "Bury my heart at Wounded Knee," because of his love for American names, he may have been thinking of *Sioux Falls, Council Bluffs, Chickasaw, Oscalloosa, Keokuk, Shenandoah.* We are unlikely ever to honor the treaties we made and (to use a phrase from Benet's "The Devil and Daniel Webster") "give the country back to the Indians." Nonetheless, our past is not so long that we can afford to forget the native heritage that was so inextricably linked with ours. That still survives, however reduced, part of the heritage now of all Americans of all colors. It especially remains in resonant, evocative placenames.

We have made a little progress since Francis Walker, Commissioner for Indian Affairs, said in 1872 about US guardianship of the Amerindians: "There is no question of national dignity, be it remembered, involved in the treatment of savages by a civilized power. With wild men, as with beasts, the question whether in any given situation one shall fight, coax, or run, is a question of what is safest."

What is safest, if we are to be a "civilized power," is to have more respect for the red man, his culture, his names, than so far we have generally shown.

O – OUT-OF-PLACE NAMES

We have noted earlier in other contexts such "out-of-place" names as *Virginia City* (Colorado, named for a resident nicknamed for his native state) and *Wyoming* (Pennsylvania). One could add *Michigan City* (Indiana) and other such names. Out of nostalgia or out of simple interest in other places, the US placenamer has created our own *Paris, Berlin* or *London* over and over. A *Stockholm* is as natural as *Old Swedes Church* in some places. So is a *Spanish Town* or *Seville.* If Idaho can have a *Moscow* ("it used to be *Hog Tavern,* but the ladies changed it") why not a *Manhattan* in Kansas or a *Manhattan Beach* in Brooklyn or California?

What are the "out-of-place" places in your vicinity, and why were they so named?

P – PEOPLE

Many of our placenames commemorate people. Places have been named for heroes, for patrons, for wives, for local characters (*Virginia City* again). Both distinguished and undistinguished presidents have counties named after them. Other political figures, however obscure (such as *Major Deegan* of the New York expressway), have put their names on things or been the recipients of such memorials. It's *Robert Moses State Park* and *Jacob K. Javits Convention Center* (why?) and *Huey Long Bridge, Washington* for the capital and the state, *Lincoln* for the capital of Nebraska, just as one Amerindian is commemorated in *joe-pye weed* and another in *Jim Thorpe* (Pennsylvania).

It's probably better to have people asking why there is no holiday for Thomas Jefferson (when there's one for Martin Luther King, Jr.) or nothing named after So-and-So than to have them saying, "Who the hell was Major Deegan?" as they look at the map or travel the highway. But the desire to see one's name noticed drives people to try to get things named after themselves. They give a lot of money to colleges and universities to get their names cut in stone over the door to a building. There's a Lowell House at Harvard but none to commemorate President Hoare.

When people are (say) obscure politicos, full names are sometimes resorted to, but *Logan Martin Lake* (Alabama) or *William Springer Lake* or *Carl L. Estes Lake* doesn't help a lot. It would be unkind to list many geographical features, towns, etc., that have been named for people better forgotten or never really famous.

Names commemorating the obscure had best be those of *Prince Street* (Rochester, New York), named for a horse, or *Juneau* (Alaska), named for an eccentric prospector. *Selma* (Alabama) was named for a character in the faked antique poems of "Ossian" (actually written by James Macpherson, 1736-1796); now *Selma* has taken on a different connotation in American history. *Tenaya Lake* and *Tenaya Canyon* (both in the Yosemite region) were named for Ten-i-ya, a guide to Lafayette Houghton Bunnell's expedition of 1851. You can imagine that Mr. Bunnell was named for the French marquis who helped us in our Revolution and for whom scads of US places were named when he visited in America later in life. *The MacDowell Colony* in New Hampshire is named for Edward MacDowell, the composer, who is buried there. After various people we have named prizes, fellowships, foundations, much more, and "Old Virginny," town drunk of *Virginia City,* proves that you don't need to be rich and famous to attain onomastic immortality. He was, oddly but importantly, commemorated by the good citizens of that frontier boomtown, a town where the streets were boringly just *A, B,* and *C* but the saloons had names like *Crystal* and *Bucket of Blood.*

Q – QUOH-QUINNA-PASSA-KESSA-NA-NAG-NOG

Under this catchy rubric (now that I have your attention) I'd like to discuss how Americans are encouraged to watch their *P*s and *Q*s in placenaming by the century-old US Board on Geographical Names (USBGN).

Had I put this under *USBGN* you might well have skipped it. "Just another government office with initials to hide behind," you might say. Honestly, the work of the USBGN is important: the USBGN decides on the official names on the national map, taking into account the historical records and the preferences of current residents. If the locals have changed *Chemin Couvert* (covered road) into *Smackover,* or if they want to make their *Billy Goat Hill* into *Angora Heights,* or to bring *Nigger Pond* more into line with modern sensibilities, the USBGN will usually go along with them. They might as well, because when the official name does not suit the locals they almost always just ignore it. The USBGN, after all, is dedicated to straightening out US placenames for government efficiency, not set up to be an onomastic dictatorship.

There are similar government bodies in other countries. I have mentioned earlier Alan Rayburn, a leading figure in the Canadian Society for the Study of Names and past president of the American Name Society; until his recent retirement he was for years the executive secretary of the Canadian board. His counterpart in the US was another former ANS president, Donald J. Orth, recently succeeded by Roger L. Payne. Some governments are more strict or more lenient than ours; however, every country needs an authority to decide on official names for cartography, administration, etc.

In New Hampshire's Hillsboro County, the USBGN decided, it was "not Quoquinnapassakessananagnog, Quohquinapassakesssananannagog, Quoooqui-napassakessanannaqug, nor Quoh-quinna-passa-kessa-na-nag-nog," but simply *Beaver Brook.*

That's but one of thousands upon thousands of name decisions made by the USBGN since its start about a century ago. "Responsible by law for establishing and maintaining uniform name usage throughout the US government" and for "developing policies, principles, and procedures governing the spelling and application of geographical names on federal maps and [in] other publications," the USBGN rules on "name controversies, new names, and name changes." It can create uniformity in government usage; it really cannot impose regulation on the most informal or independent of our people, who will call things (but not officially) whatever they wish.

The US Geological Survey provides the USBGN with access to all the information on the nation's 7.5 minute quadrangle topographical maps. The USBGN likewise has a wealth of historical maps and documents in its long-established, well-endowed, carefully operated library. All told, the USBGN has to deal with more than 3 million working names, another million or more former names, and all the variants and ramifications of these. It has to make sure that when a name is used (without the geographical coordinates) there is no confusion; that when derogatory names become offensive they are replaced; that naming for persons (always safest and best when they are dead) is regulated; that the needs of all branches of government (especially the Interior and the military) are harmonized with local preferences and practices; and that cartographers and onomasts (to use for once Erik Gunnemark's term for "name student") and everyone else interested in American placenames have a central clearinghouse and a control mechanism.

So well has the USBGN done its work that many of its principles, its categories of definition (discussed under *Terms,* below), and its operating methods have been adopted or adapted by foreign governments. The US has set world standards for placenaming policies that balance the bureaucratic needs for consistency and uniformity with the need in a democratic and pluralistic society to show proper respect for local preferences and actual practices. The next objective is an international, worldwide agreement to adopt (and expand, if necessary, because national needs vary from country to country) some standard system like the one USBGN uses, to develop a method of handling toponyms around the globe according to some standardized format. The world needs such a standardized system because cartographic and onomastic sciences, like all other sciences, have supranational concerns that call for standard methods and standard terminology. In this, in time, the USBGN hopes to lead the way. If and when it does, it will be a major contribution of our country to the handling of placenames in all the languages and all the countries of the world.

R – RESTORATION OF NAMES

Today the minority peoples in the far north of Canada, where Henry Hudson and other European explorers (searching for the North West Passage) put on the map the names of themselves and other Europeans, are agitating to take political control of their territories and with it to reclaim their culture, eradicate the foreign names, and restore the old names given by the Dene (Amerindian) and Inuit peoples (the latter we called Eskimos, "raw meat eaters," until they became politically active enough to resist the label). These people realize that placenames make a big difference. Do you feel occupying or occupied, connected with your past or alienated from it, living "at home" or on land that is foreign to your race and your heritage?

The Inuit, and the "status Indians," and the Métis (of mixed French and Indian ancestry) have been accorded recognition and rights by the Canadian Constitution of 1982. Now they are demanding their own names on their own lands. A compact known as the Iqaluit Agreement has paved the way for the creation of two new political entities in Canada's North West Territories. They will bear the names *Denedeh* (for the Dene of the Western Arctic) and *Nunavut* ("Our Place" for the Inuit of the Eastern Arctic), and the English placenames there will change: *Frobisher Bay* is already *Iqaluit,* and we shall have to get used to *Mittimatalik (Pond Inlet), Kangirtugaapik (Clyde River), Sallig (Coral Harbour), Kuujjuaq (Fort Chimo), Kangiqcliniq (Rankin Inlet), Sanirajaq (Hall Beach), Ikalututiak (Cambridge Bay)* and *Qikirtrarajuak (Broughton Island).* An expert has been hired to change as many as 100,000 placenames (mostly, of course, of uninhabited places) back to the native names; there are more than 3 million placenames that could be changed. The Inuit would have *Eskimo Point* called *Arviat* (place of the whale) and they propose to make 1989 the year in which *Mackenzie River* (a great waterway which at 2,600 miles is second in length only in North America to the Mississippi) goes back to *De Cho* (Big River, which means the same as *Mississippi,* as you have read here earlier), which is what it was called when Mackenzie discovered it in 1789.

Although there are now only 64 settlements in this northern tier (half as large as the whole continental US), geographical features in this vast area number between 3 and 4 million. All or most of them, the natives say, ought to have native names, though *Hudson Bay* will probably stay on the map.

Inuit names have already replaced Danish ones on the map of what used to be called Greenland. In Canada's far north expect to scrap *Chesterfield Inlet* and welcome *Iqluligaajuk. Resolute Bay,* poetic and historic enough in its own right, will become *Kaujuitok* or "the place where the sun never rises." Just as *Godthåb* is now *Nuuk* and *Thule* is now *Oaanaag* to the 53,000 inhabitants of the world's largest island (*Kalaallit Nunaat,* formerly *Grønland*), European placenames, centuries old in many cases, will be replaced by even older ones, though not, one hopes, in the case of *Baffin Land,* where the name of William Baffin, discoverer of an island so vast it can almost be said to be a continent, is honored.

The Amerindian area of the Dene will see such changes as *Fort Norman* to *Tulít'a* and *Nahanni Butte* to *Thenaagoo.* In Québec the Frenchification of placenames since the 1960s has reflected a similar—Anglophone/Francophone—cultural struggle. The *Québecois* have settled many names in Labrador and surrounding areas in more French forms, sometimes replacing English placenames with French ones or rendering native names in French form. Now the move is on to make *George River* (1876) which became *Port-Nouveau-Québec* (1965) into *Kangiqsualujjuaq.* Similarly, thousands of other placenames will change: *Wakeham Bay* became *Maricourt* and now will be *Kangiqsujuag* (which people are already beginning to confuse with *Kangiqsualujjuaq*). Inuit and Amerindian names in French form will have to take their proper native spellings and appear in neither of the two official languages of Canada.

If the areas here were not so populous and were there not so many non-aboriginal toes to be stepped on, parts of such states as Maine and the Dakotas in the US would likely be under pressure to restore native names. Such name changes in the US, however, are as unlikely to come to pass as the US recognition of the Amerindian title to vast parts of this nation that our Indians claim under a number of treaties between their nations and the US. The descendants of aboriginal populations in the US are, if anything, trying to achieve compensation for their losses rather than restitution of their culture. They are pursuing an economic rather than a cultural remedy for the sins of the past. Nonetheless, the Canadian example may have its effect on aboriginal minorities the world over, as I discuss in an extensive article in *Geolinguistics* for 1988, and, for example, our Navaho nation is large and may become more politically powerful.

The Inuit, instead of warring, used to settle matters with drumming and chanting insulting names at each other until one side backed down without bloodshed. Their tradition recognizes the importance of names as our "sticks and stones will break my bones but names will never hurt me" fails to do.

S – STATE NAMES

A brief mention here of the names of US states will suffice, for I have already mentioned a number of these in the course of treating toponymic subjects. A good official treatment of state-name origins is John P. Harrington's *Our State Names* (Smithsonian Institution Publication 4205, 1955). A more popular treatment is Pauline Arnold and Percival White's *How We Named Our States* (1965). To learn of state-name origins is to become aware of our melting-pot history, because you will find Amerindian names such as *Massachusetts* and *Iowa,* Spanish names such as *Nevada* and *Florida,* French names such as *Vermont* and *Louisiana,* and one Dutch name (*Rhode Island* was a red island to the Dutch).

Rhode Island is probably our silliest state name, while *Arkansas* and *Illinois* create the most difficulty in pronunciation. I have already said I like *Montana* the best. Some of our states—those that are commonwealths, for instance—have much longer official names, and *Providence Plantations* is included in the official name of Rhode Island, referring to its capital area.

What states might have been called, and were not, is an interesting topic, but we have no space for that here. Nor can we notice all the state nicknames (I like *Sooners* best and deplore the booster designations such as the *Garden State* and *Land of Enchantment*), but you can easily find them all and may know those in your vicinity. What's the name of your state, and why? What did they think of calling it? What and why did they nickname it? So infrequently do we ask ourselves such questions that I have had New York students who know that *Brooklyn* is "broken land" but say they cannot fathom why the *Empire State Building* was so named.

T – TERMS IN PLACENAMING

Whether we call a geographical place a pond or a lake, a town or a city, often depends on our own capricious definition. The USBGN has to develop and assign official designations that take account of size, population, location, and geographical principles. The USBGN system is scientific, elaborate, and specific, as the following list of terms indicates. Apart from *area* (which is a miscellaneous category that lumps together geographical features not conveniently sorted in other categories, such as *badlands, delta, garden*), the USBGN carefully distinguishes among: *airport, arch, arroyo, basin, bay, beach, bend, bridge, canal, cape, cave, cemetery, channel, civil division* (borough, county, township, etc.), *cliff, crater, dam, falls, flat, forest, gap* (saddle, pass, etc.), *geyser* (originally a Nordic placename, by the way), *glacier, harbor, island, isthmus, lake, levee, park, plain* (grassland, plateau, etc.), *populated place* (hamlet, village, town, city, etc.), *range, rapids, ridge, sea, slope, spring, stream* (bayou, run, etc.), *swamp, trail, tunnel, valley,* and *wood.* I emphasize that this is just a partial rundown. I omitted, for instance, *creek* and *locale.* Locale you may think of as a vague or general term but the USBGN specifically defines that as a place at which there is or was human activity but which lacks residents.

This scientific taxonomy has, in my view, certain irregularities. The USBGN notices *church, cemetery,* etc., but not non-religious buildings and such, and the inclusion of (say) *airport* seems to suggest to me that (say) *mall* is missing.

What we need is for maps the world over to include the same kinds of features and for everyone to agree on the precise meanings of terms, though a *pond* in New England might be called something else if in another part of the country and many people have no clear idea of the difference between a *branch* and a *run.* We don't put stream water or run water, just branch water, in bourbon. In Canada they have *tickles* and other terms we lack.

U – UNITED STATES

Carl Sandburg said, "The United States *is,* not *are.* The Civil War was fought over a verb." That was eloquent but not definitive, as the question of whether *United States* is singular or plural was debated long before the Late Unpleasantness or War Between the States. It is still debated in some quarters, among grammarians and toponymists as well as unreconstructed advocates of states' rights.

These united states were clearly regarded as plural by our Founding Fathers, who put together a federation of independent states to form a union independent of Britain. The British also regarded these states as individual units (each dependent upon Britain, not each a separate republic) and even after we broke away from Britain continued to speak of us as such: the British attaché in Washington in 1805 declared that his ambassador and his ambassador's wife were "bored to death with these United States." The Union was threatened and preserved and at the end of the nineteenth century, when people were arguing about whether the term *United States* was singular or plural, Harry Thurston Peck from the Olympian (or at least Morningside) Heights of Columbia University declared that *United States* was "a noun in the singular number."

Fowler, the British usage expert, did not deign to notice the problem, but in 1957 Nicholson revised Fowler; she called *these United States* "archaic (or pompous)." The term, Bergen and Cornelia Evans later said, was "felt to be poetic and is to be avoided before a verb." More recently, American expert Allen Walker Read has discussed the problems (*Names* 22, 1974, and later) and is as authoritative on this as he is on the origin of the United States' most famous word, *OK*. Prof. Read says that "the final stage of becoming a proper noun would occur when *United States* drops the article." True, there are countries called The Lebanon, and we refer to the Sahara (redundantly the Sahara Desert, for *sahara* means "desert," and the Palace of the *Alhambra* is also redundant). "Students of usage," Prof. Read tells me, "will want to watch the name *United States* carefully. Its grammar has been in a fluid condition for a long time, and trends are deserving of study."

In fact, trends and the reasons for them are more revelatory, more interesting, than mere word origins. The best logophiles, like Prof. Read, date not only etymologies but also changes in meaning and usage. These experts are concerned with what words tell of human interaction as well as language coinage.

While we wait for *United States* to become a full-fledged proper noun in the singular, we can rejoice that the US is one very singular nation and we are citizens of it, we *United Statesians, Usonians, Columbards, Yanks, Yankees, Americans*. (We have been called many things in our time.) We can cheerfully ignore Randolph Churchill's suggestion that we make *United States* singular by amending the Constitution and changing "the name of the Flag to 'Star and Stripe'."

V – VULGARITY

Throughout this text I have spared the blushes of the maiden cheek (as Sir W. S. Gilbert would say) and omitted name examples that I thought might offend by their vulgarity, so here I shall touch on the subject very briefly.

There has always been some tension between, on the one hand, Americans' desire to be thought proper and, on the other hand, our prevailing image as a race of raw colonials, uncouth frontiersmen, and eventually brash, crass world leaders. The brawling and sometimes bawdy spirit came with the territory and its history. It was strengthened by successive waves of refugees we welcomed to these shores. We opened our arms to these "yearning masses," some of them colorful, some of them criminal, and we derived variety and vigor from immigrants fleeing everything from *pogroms* to the police. The poor and oppressed found shelter here; inevitably we picked up some of their "less than couth" ways of acting and speaking. America both had and imported its rough elements.

Albert H. Marckwardt in *American English* (1958) attributed our genteel and occasionally faux-genteel side to the religious beliefs of the Puritans; however, I happen to think he, like many another scholar, relied too much on the self-conscious writings of clergymen and the whitewashed expressions of the rest of the educated minority. New Englanders, in fact, though repressed somewhat by the strict Puritan theocracy, were on the whole not of genteel background. They came for the most part from the lower classes and partook of their strong language as well as their strong faith. As was true of many others among the Puritan faithful, their consciences were as often their accomplices as their guides, and when they reached the secular environment of the new frontier they often freely flouted the orthodoxy and the good manners of their masters.

Even the most insulated of Americans eventually rubbed up against the motley and unrefined elements of the new nation—toughened soldiers, grizzled trappers, "half-man and half-alligator" adventurers, crusty farmers, indelicate denizens of the wild. From these outspoken people, later fortified by those unwashed masses of immigrants, we learned to curse and tell off-color jokes in many languages. The point here is that a strain of vulgarity inescapably found its way into American placenames, like it or not.

If you doubt this, browsing in *The Gazetteer of the United States,* a sober government publication, will confirm what I say. In recent years there has been some movement for a cleanup campaign and some efforts to remove or cosmeticize such names. Enough survive to titillate even the uninhibited. The current governor of New York has decreed that all the embarrassing old names of this type must be expunged. Even if they come off all the official maps of his state and all the other states, they will have to live on in history.

I shall not embarrass you with rude examples but content myself with remarking that there are unintentional "rough" names attributable to the fact that (say) Canadian officials do not know Ukrainian and occasionally come up with something that outrages the Ukrainians in the Prairie Provinces, and that here in the US even a knowledge of French is sometimes lacking. Early French explorers called certain large, breast-shaped mountains in the US Rockies "big breasts." We still have the *Grand Tetons.* We have made the placename so "lexically opaque" that I once saw over a handsome grotto containing a sentimental statue of Our Lady, the Blessed Virgin, a slab of stone carved deeply with this inscription: *Nôtrè Dame des Grand Tetons.*

W – "WATER, WATER EVERYWHERE"

Our country has vast coastlines, great lakes, powerful and stately rivers. Florida had to name at least 30,000 lakes. In Michigan you are never more than a few minutes' drive to one of the state's thousands of lakes. Michigan also has 36,000 miles of streams, about 1,400 square miles of inland waters (you could fit Luxembourg into that area and have room left for Malta and more), and 38,459 square miles of the Great Lakes. In North America's approximately 8 million square miles, there are millions of square miles of water. We also have more man-made lakes than any other country in the world.

So we have needed hydronyms (water names) for features as magnificent as the Mississippi, the Ohio, the Columbia, and other great rivers (highways of exploration and trade, keys to the opening of the new land) and for features as dinky as a waterhole or wash.

Wash came from the prospectors. Other terms came from foreign languages, such as *río* (Spanish), *coulée* (French), *kill* (Dutch). We have the *Red River* and the *Rouge River* and the *Colorado,* all for "red." We have *Crick Creek* (locally pronounced "Creek Crick") and *White Oak Creek* (originally *Quiyoughcohanock*), *Grassy Gutter, Bull Run, Long Branch, Rio Grande, Lost River State Park, Jackson Hole, Palm Springs, Great Salt Lake, Harper's Ferry, Spirit Lake, Walden Pond, Halls Crossing, Pearl Harbor,* the prehistoric and long-gone *Lake Cochise,* and Amerindian names of totally unknown meaning such as *Allegheny* and *Monongahela* as well as many that explorers got the natives to translate for them. The French found that *Ohio* means the same as *Mississippi.* We usually leave French, Spanish, and other languages' diaoritical marks off US placenames: *Rio Grande,* not *Río Grande.* We "translate," too.

X – "X MARKS THE SPOT"

People used to put an *X* (originally they used a Christian cross) to attest to documents when they had no heraldic seal and could not sign their names. One early American, the story goes, grew so wealthy that he took to signing with three *X*s, feeling his dignity required a middle name. Similarly, people used to put an *X* on maps when they wanted to indicate a place that had no known name.

Today almost all places and features have a name, but not very many have names that begin with an *X.* How many can you think of? *Xenia* (Ohio), the floating islands in Mexico City's suburb of *Xochimilco,* some other Mexican placenames of pre-Conquest origin? How about the *Xingu,* a river in Brazil?

Y – Y, OH WHY?

Yantley, Yarbo, Yellow Pine, York, Youngblood are all Alabama place-names, not one of them as striking as *Yreka* (California). *Yentna* and *Yukon* are Alaskan rivers. *Yuma, Yucca,* and *Youngstown* are fairly well-known but, among those who enter mail contests, nowhere near as famous as *Young America* (Minnesota). *Yale* is a mountain in Colorado and a lake in Florida. *Yantic* is a Connecticut river. *Young Ham* is in Georgia. There's a *Yosemite* in Kentucky and another in California. *Yankee Fork* names part of Idaho's Salmon River. *Yorktown* appears in a number of states, even Iowa, to com-memorate the battle in Virginia that successfully ended our Revolution. There's a *York* in Alabama, Maine, Nebraska, Pennsylvania, and North Carolina, while *Yorkville* is a county seat in Illinois and a neighborhood on Manhattan's Upper East Side. *Yuba* is in Wisconsin and elsewhere. *Yazoo City,* made famous by a native son who is a writer, *Yellowstone* and *Yellow Knife* are three of my favorite American placenames. William Trogdon (writing as William Least Heat Moon, an Amerindian name) has a wonderful book on his journey around America by car, *Blue Highways* (1982); in it you can read of what the "rootless family [that] drives up from Ypsilanti" can see in what he nicknames the Thumbland ("On a map, lower Michigan looks like a mitten with the squatty peninsula between Saginaw Bay and Lake Huron forming the Thumb"). He also recounts that Texas had its Spanish missions and adds that "near one, Ysleta, men had cultivated the same plot every year since 1681."

You could do worse than drive all over America from one *Y* place to another, keeping your eyes open, asking *why*.

You'll be able to guess why Hawaii could be left off your itinerary in that case.

Z – "LAST BUT NOT LEAST"

Publicity seekers have vied to get their names last in the telephone books, manufacturing such names as *Walter Zzzyzo* (which appeared in an Austin, Texas, directory). It took more *Z*s to be last in San Francisco and I don't know why some enterprising bed and mattress company doesn't get into the yellow pages as *ZZZZZZ*. That would be a much better name than some of the dumb names for such retailers here in New York, where we have a *Kleinsleep*, which is pretty stupid in a town where at least some people know German. Poor old Mrs. Klein must have selected the name with the same steadfast vanity that prompted Mr. Zzzyzo to list himself the way he did.

Placenames do not involve the search for personal fame (or notoriety) in the same way, and they do not seem to have striven so mightily for the distinction of a *Z* name. *Zion* from the Bible found its way to Arkansas, Illinois, Maryland, South Carolina, and other states. There is a *Zion National Park* due to the Mormons in Utah. There's that *Zionville* named for Henry Zion you heard about earlier. There are *Zarembo Island* (Alaska), *Zinc* (Arkansas and elsewhere because of mining) and *Zincville* (Oklahoma), *Zanesville* (Illinois and Ohio), several places named *Zurich,* and a mountain named *Zircle* (Colorado). There are *Zook* (Kansas), *Zwolle* (Louisiana), *Zilwaukee* (Michigan), *Zumbrota* (Minnesota), *Zama* (Mississippi), *Zalma* (Missouri), *Zeona* (South Dakota), *Zona* (West Virginia), *Zumwalt* (Oregon), *Zelienople* (Pennsylvania), *Zapata* (Texas), *Zachow* (Wisconsin), *Zuni* (New Mexico and Virginia), and *Zeeland* (North Dakota).

Perhaps half a dozen Americans have the surname *Z,* but so far as I know, there's no place that's simply *Z.* That is, not yet. In the world of placenames, stranger things have happened.

14. Placenames Around the Globe

I cannot pretend to do justice in one section here to a subject that George R. Stewart almost failed to cover adequately in his *Names on the Globe* and which few if any others have attempted to address in a single book. I must make a try at suggesting its nature and its fascination, though, so permit me to look first at our nearest neighbors and then mention a few places overseas that have names both kindred and exotic.

Placenaming in Canada has already entered this survey, because in Canada relatives of our own American Indians resided originally. Also, in Canada the French and the British transformed the placename map along with the cultural landscape, as they did in our country. The vikings and other early explorers left little onomastic evidence of their stay in Canada, but later colonizers produced placenames of which many are still in use. *Newfoundland* occurs in a letter dated 1502. *St. John's* in that province is said to have been founded on the Feast of St. John the Baptist (24 June) in 1497. Such names as *Labrador, Cape Breton, Cape Race, Sable Island,* and *Conception Bay* are almost as old. Early explorers, as we have seen, established such names as *Baffin Land* and *Montréal.* Later came the names of the missionaries and *coureurs des bois* and the colorful placenames of the pioneers: *Kicking Horse Pass, Cap de Vache-qui-Pisse* (cow who pisses), and *Push and Be Damned Rapids.* Venturers into the frozen north left such names as *Svartfeld Peninsula, Axel Heiberg Island, Hudson's Bay, Alert.*

Americans (and we use that term for the US inhabitants, though the Canadians resent us claiming a whole continent for ourselves and the Mexicans dismiss us as *nordeamericanos*) will be interested in the placenames Americans gave to Canada. Adolphus Greely contributed *Greely Fjord.* Elmer Ekblaw was responsible for *Elmerson Peninsula,* named for his son. In 1876 George Nares named the most northerly point of Canada *Cape Columbia,* for the US. Earlier, in 1861, I. I. Hayes had named the *United States Range* on Ellesmere Island. In the Canadian north you'll also find the namesakes of several US presidents:

Buchanan Bay, Lincoln Bay, Franklin Pierce Bay, though Pierce did not get included in the Presidential Range in his own state of New Hampshire, doubly unfortunate because DeWitt Clinton, who was never president, was included there. There's also a *Mount Grant* and in British Columbia a *Roosevelt Peak.* There's a *Washington* (Ontario), *Lincolnville* (Nova Scotia), and *Garfield* (Prince Edward Island). President Kennedy had a mountain named for him in the rush to Kennedyize everywhere just after his assassination, but the proposal to change *Sevogle* to *Mount Kennedy* in New Brunswick was rejected. For one thing, there's no mountain there. Fleeing to the Maritimes, the United Empire Loyalists long ago took some US placenames north with them. I live in Brooklyn (New York), so I'm especially pleased to see that *Brooklyn* occurs four times in Nova Scotia, once each in New Brunswick, Prince Edward Island, and Newfoundland, and (spelled differently) once in Ontario; all of these were imports from Brooklyn (New York).

At the annual meeting of ANS in San Francisco in 1975, Alan Rayburn noted the prevalence of US placenames in Canada (*Miami, New Denver,* an abandoned way station of the Klondike Gold Rush named *Little Chicago,* and *California Creek* and *Arizona Creek* in the Yukon). He commented that Canadians used to associate placenames from California, Ohio, Missouri, and Florida with "wealth and economic freedom" and sometimes borrowed such names "in derision because the places they described in Canada were poverty-stricken and forlorn."

We have noted earlier the Canadian political battle between Anglophones and Francophones. By dint of sheer numbers the English have prevailed throughout most of Canada, but Québec's motto is *"Je me souviens"* and they have indeed clung to their French tradition. Considering the extensive role of the French in the early days of Canada, they have until recent times (when many English placenames have given way to French ones) been underrepresented in placenames. The *Commision de Toponomie* in Québec has been working assiduously on that. In 1974 placenames of French origin constituted 64% of Québec's stock of names; today that figure is over 90%. French-Canadians have turned both *St. John* and *St. John's* into *St.-Jean.* In time the only placenames not in French in Québec may be the Inuit and Dene ones previously mentioned.

Québec's toponymic policy is rewriting history; however, at least it is clear-cut and consistent. In the past, name changing in Canada was haphazard. Successive explorers typically laid down one new set of placenames after another as they passed through territories. An established name, whether Amerindian, French, or English, might be altered as soon as a different language group moved in. Locals often wished to adopt a more "dignified" name than the rough-and-tumble French trappers had given or the English prospectors had adopted. Sometimes the new placenames combined or blended two names together to create a sort of bastard name.

World War I made *hamburger* into *Salisbury steak* and *sauerkraut* into *victory cabbage,* and *Kitchener* was substituted for *Berlin* (Ontario), *Briton Bay* for *German Bay.* World War II could not make *Swastika* (Ontario, adopted in 1906) into anything less German. The locals liked the name. *Wawa* (a Cree name for "wild goose") was defended when there was a move to substitute *Jamestown* (for Sir James Dunn, president of Algoma Steel). On the other hand, *La Rivière* (Manitoba) in 1963 succumbed to radio station CKY's advances and changed its name to *Seekaywye* (which outsiders sometimes imagine is Amerindian). This was in the same commercial spirit that caused a US town to adopt the name of a radio show, *Truth or Consequences* (New Mexico).

James Hector in 1858 named *Castle Mountain* but this was changed by order of the prime minister in 1946 to *Mount Eisenhower,* in honor of the supreme commander of the Allied Forces in World War II. Albertans were furious. They eventually (1974) succeeded in restoring *Castle Mountain;* only the most prominent peak is now *Eisenhower Peak.* Sir Winston Churchill in another finagle got *Grand Falls* changed to *Churchill Falls.* Premier Smallwood of Newfoundland had promised to give Churchill a placename in Labrador and following Churchill's death in 1965 Smallwood got the change through the provincial legislature (a trifle more democratically than Canadian Prime Minister William Lyon Mackenzie King had pulled the *Eisenhower* deal). Historic *Hamilton River* also became *Churchill River.*

All told there are over 350,000 official names on the more than 3.85 million square miles of Canada. By comparison, the United Kingdom occupies less than 100,000 square miles. According to an overview by Rayburn, English (Anglo, Celtic, American) names constitute 71% of the Canadian placenames now, French 21% (rapidly increasing), Amerindian 7%, all others 1%. Some of the most prominent places have retained their Amerindian names: *Quebec* (without the accent, Algonquian for "narrow passage"), *Ontario* (Wyandotte name for the nation we call the Senecas), *Manitoba* (Cree for "strait of the Spirit"), *Saskatchewan* (Cree for "swift-flowing river"), *Yukon* (Kutchin for "big river"), *Winnipeg, Saskatoon, Ketchikan, Missinaibi, Toronto,* etc. After the Treaty of Paris (1763), at the conclusion of the French and Indian Wars, the British wanted to change *Toronto* to *York, Niagara* to *Newark,* and so on, but for the most part resisted the temptation to replace the old names. To their credit, the British placed the capital of the Dominion of Canada at Ottawa and made that a famous name. Now no longer a Dominion, Canada may have some trouble, as we have seen, regarding dominion over the names in the north. More Amerindian and Inuit names are to be expected on Canadian maps. Suburban development near Toronto has brought names such as *Mississauga* to the fore and this is another way Amerindian names are gaining prominence.

There are many wonderful names and stories in William B. Hamilton's *The Macmillan Book of Canadian Place Names* (1978) and in more specialized studies; to name but two authors, André Lapierre on French names in Ontario (1983) and E. A. Seary on the placenames (1971) and family names (1977) of Newfoundland.

Canadian curiosities abound and I am grateful to Alan Rayburn for telling me that *Port Mouton* was named (1604) by a Frenchman for a spot where a sheep jumped off his ship. I knew that *St. Helen's Island* (I suppose that is only in French these days) was named not for the mother of the Emperor Constantine (she who found the True Cross) but for the wife of the founder of Montréal. Cleaning things up a little, let me mention in the Yukon *Snafu Creek* and *Tarfu Creek;* roughly "Situation Normal, All Fouled Up" and "Things Are Really Fouled Up." Portuguese placenames are conspicuous in Newfoundland (though the names are now in English): *Cabo Raso* (*Cape Race*), *Cabo de la Spera* (intended to suggest "hope," or "waiting," now *Cape Spear*), *Cabo de Bona Ventura* (now *Bonaventure*), etc. A vivid example of how mapmakers themselves can get on the map is the case of Sir William Edmond Logan (1798-1875), founder of Canada's geological survey and of Precambrian geology. He headed the Canadian survey from 1843 to 1869 and has had 10 different features named for him, including the highest peak in Canada (which is in the Yukon). *Mount Peters* (Alberta) honors F. H. Peters; he died in 1982 at the age of 100 while still serving as surveyor-general, a position he assumed in the 1920s.

If we skip down to our southern neighbor, Mexico (which we usually spell that way in English, though it's *México* in Spanish), once again we find a vast geographical area with a complex history of diverse cultures and consequently various strata of placenames. In *Names* 24 I wrote at length of the merging and mingling of native Aztec and other pre-Columbian names with those the Spanish gave after the conquest of Mexico. Aztec placenames are among the most beautiful of aboriginal names. *Teotihuacán* was one of the greatest cities of the world in its heyday. *Tzintzuntzan* imitated the sound of the hummingbird. *Mazatlán* was "place of the deer." *Coyoacán* was "place of the coyotes." *Popocatepetl* was "smoking mountain," a volcano which has not erupted since 1802.

The *conquistadores* put Spanish names on all they could, beginning with their landing at the place they called *Vera Cruz* (because that day was the Feast of the True Cross); the cross was their key to the door behind which lay great riches, their justification for conquest as well as their protection. The placenames they heard they could not understand, so they named places in Spanish and for what they saw: *Fresnillo* (little ash tree), *El Álamo* (cottonwood tree), *Minas Viejas* (old mines), *Capulines* (grasshoppers), *Puerto Lengua de Vaca* (Port Cow's Tongue, from its shape). They also expressed their feelings (*Esperanza* is "hope") and created what look like occasion names but may have something to do with the lay of the land (*Los Anteojos* is "eyeglasses," but it can never be said too often that great errors are made in placename studies conducted in libraries and not on site). They brought names from the Old Country, names from the Spanish language and Spanish history reflecting the long Moorish occupation (*Guadalupe* and *Guadalajara* contain the Arabic for "water"). Some of the missionaries—the soldiers were men of action, not of words—made valiant attempts to learn something of the native languages, but there were so many languages and conquest meant destroying culture, so they determined they would make Spanish the language of all Mexico. At least 40 native languages are still spoken in Mexico and 10% of the Mexican population even today speaks no Spanish at all. Nonetheless, Spanish is the basic language of the placenames and of all the united states of Mexico. Spanish-speakers imposed it.

In the Plaza de Los Tres Culturas in Mexico City now stand the ruins of an Aztec temple, a Franciscan church of the old Colonial period, and a modern building of the new Mexico. The plaza symbolizes for me the three main layers of culture and of names there. Names and name changes record the turbulent history of this great country. *Nueva Italia* (1873) proves an Italian settlement there. *La Guta de Xtacumbril-Xunán* combines Spanish and older tongues in "The Cave of the Hidden Women," and with it goes a story. The state of Jalisco used to be *Nueva Gallicia,* telling us where many of the poor but ambitious early explorers and conquerors came from; before they arrived it was *Chimahuacán.* Xicótopec became *Villas Juarez* officially; those who live there take little notice of the new name. Anti-clericalism replaced many of the early names of Spanish conquest: *Santa Clara del Cobre* (there was copper there) became *Villa Escalante. Santa Clara* spoke of devotion to the sister of St. Francis of Assisi and reminds us of the friars who accompanied the expeditions; *del Cobre* tells of Don Vasco de Quiroga, an enlightened ecclesiastic who taught people in each village a separate and useful trade, in this case the working of copper, still carried on there. Each village was given its own costume, too, because easy identification of the Indians, who all looked alike to the Spanish, was useful in many ways, especially to keeping them in the literal sense in their place. When the Spanish found *Huizache* they made it *El Huizache* and today the natives jokingly call it *San Juan sín Agua,* for precious water is scarce. Knowing Spanish is essential, but corrupted words can mislead the proud but incautious scholar: *Tijuana* is nobody's aunt Jane but from *teehuana* (city of the sea).

Mexico was only a part of the vast Spanish vice-royalty in the Americas. Spanish conquest extended throughout Central and South America. Spanish names are all over the Americas. On the road between *Río Hondo* and *Quiriga,* a Mayan site I wanted to see in Guatemala, I came upon a town named *Delicias y Jones,* my reaction being echoed in the name of the very next town, *Jesús María!* They named *El Salvador* from Our Savior. *Honduras* means "depths." *Costa Rica* was a "rich coast," but when they were not thinking about wealth they were thinking about religion; the names reflect this everywhere. It was a religious as well as a political decision to eradicate the pagan names, though many pre-Christian ones still exist, alone or in significant combination.

I do not have space here to expatiate on Mexican placenames, but if you are interested you can see what I do with them in the 50-page article on the "clash of cultures" they reflect. It's in *Names,* as I said. I regret only that my typewriter has no Spanish diacritical marks and that, when the editor was finished with it, I was in Europe and did not have the opportunity to proofread. So many of the accents have been put on wrong! I hope the names turn out right in the present book, but in so packed a treatment errors may creep in. (If you find some, write and tell me.)

In Latin America, with the exception of Belize (where British connections produced *Middlesex, Roaring Creek,* and *Monkey River*) the Spanish names are derived from religion, flora and fauna, political heroes, and similar ordinary sources. Wayne H. Finke has been reporting on them country by country and plans a comprehensive book on the subject, which will be welcome.

Often the Spanish spelling disguises the fact that aboriginal languages are reflected in the names. For example, in Puerto Rico some municipalities are named for local chiefs: *Arecibo* (1616 for Aracibo), *Bayamón* (1772 for Bayamon), *Caguas* (1775 for Caguax), *Canóvana* (for Canoba), *Cayey* and *Coamo* for chieftains of those names (as are *Guayama, Maricao,* and *Yauco*), *Guánica* for Huanicoy, *Guanyabo* for Guanay, *Hormigueros* for Horomico, *Humacao* for Macao, *Mayagüez* (from the river named 1760 after Mayagua), *Morovís* (1818 for Morovis), *Naguabo* for Daguao, and *Utado* (1739 for Otoao). *Barros* (mud) was changed to *Orocovís* to honor Orocobix, chief of Hatibonico. There are also some other aboriginal names such as *Aibonito* (from *Jatibonico,* "large place"), *Camuy* (sun), *Ceiba* (silk cotton tree), *Ciales* (stone), *Corozál* (Spanish suffix on the word for "spiny palm"), *Gurabo* and *Las Marías* (for other kinds of trees), *Manatí* (a kind of grass) and *Maunabo* (a kind of plant), *Yaabucoa* (a water fowl), and *Toa Alta* and *Toa Baja* (for high and low "mammas").

Most of the Puerto Rican names, however, are Spanish, of course, and include those of Queen Isabella, the explorer Juan Ponce de León, *Trujillo* (for a Spanish city in Cáceres), and the names of saints such as *San Juan.*

In Paraguay, a little over 30% of similar names are from Guarani, about 10% are descriptive (like *Bahía Negra*), and about 28% each are from religion (like *Ascunción*) or from historical figures (like *Coronel Bogado* or *Coronel Quevedo*). The municipalities of Panama are about 34% descriptive (like *El Valle*), about 32% indigenous (like *Panamá*), 17% religious (like *Santiago*), and there are five names of flora or fauna (like *Las Palmas*) and three historical references (*Almirante, Balboa, Colón*).

The percentages vary, as you would expect, from country to country but religion (especially the names of saints, on whose feast days places may have been named) and other religious names, historical, descriptive, and topographical categories predominate. The 113 municipality names of Bolivia are typical: 22% the names of saints (even *Todos Santos*), 22% other religious references (like *El Carmén*), 14% topographic (like *Lagunillas*), 14% descriptive (like *Villa Bella*), and strongly historical: 26% of the names are like *Puerto Suarez, Puerto Sucre, Puerto Siles, Puerto Heath,* etc. There is oddly only one name from flora: *El Reboré.*

One of the oldest Spanish names of what is now the continental United States is also found in Puerto Rico: *Florida* (flowery). The Puerto Ricans also have some straightforward names. One of the municipalities is "mess" or "confusion": *Añasco.*

I have written a little about Puerto Rico because it is of special interest to US readers. I wish I had space for a general survey of Latin American placenames. I do not. So those of you who have not had the opportunity to hear Prof. Finke's individual presentations at the scholarly conventions where much good research is reported will have to wait for his book to be published.

Let us now turn to the placenames of Britain, the majority of which, one might think, will not sound as strange to American ears as those involving Guarani and other exotic Latin American languages. However, British placenames go back centuries before the Christian era and full understanding of them requires a thorough acquaintance with pre-Celtic languages, Celtic, Welsh, Gaelic, Scandinavian tongues, Old English, Norman French, and Modern English, as well as Latin and more. To illustrate the problem some names of British counties can serve as indicative of the variety. Many of those involve the names of ancient rivers (*Aberdeenshire, Ayrshire, Cambridgeshire, Inverness-shire, Lancashire, Monmouthshire, Nairnshire, Northumberland, Wiltshire,* and the new county names *Avon, Clwyd, Humberside, Merseyside,* and two rivers together, *Tyne and Wear*). *Ayr* (running water) and *Avon* (river) are simple. Other United Kingdom county names involve fords (*Bedfordshire, Herefordshire, Oxfordshire, Staffordshire*) or other water (for instance, *Moray* "territory by the sea" or *Kent* "coastal area" or *Renfrewshire* "flowing brook"). All these emphasize the importance of water transportation in early settlement. Other county names involve personal names of very shadowy people or names of ancient tribes (*Anglesey, Angus, Argyll, Armagh, Breconshire, Caithness, Cardiganshire, Clackmannanshire, Cornwall, Cumberland, Devon, Dunbarton, East Lothian* and *West Lothian* and *Midlothian, Fermanagh, Fife, Glamorgan,* the second part of *Huntingdon and Peterborough, Kircudbrightshire, Leicestershire, Merionethshire, Montgomeryshire, Nottinghamshire, Roxburghshire, Rutland, Shetland, Shropshire, Tyrone, Worcestershire, Yorkshire,* and new *Cumbria,* maybe more). Who was Owen of *Tyrone* or Snot of *Nottinghamshire?* Compared to these, *Norfolk* and *Suffolk* and *Sussex* and *Middlesex* and (formerly) the kingdom of *Wessex* are easy. *Berkshire* is "hilly" and *Orkney* is "islands of the whale" and *Somerset* is where summer camp was and *Denbighshire* was a "little fort" and *Down* a "fort" and *Cheshire* a Roman *castra* (fort). And that does not even cover all the UK county names, which can be as obvious as *Flintshire* and as inexplicable as

Stirlingshire or *Greater Manchester*. At Manchester there was a Roman town, as at *Londinium*, but who knows what its name, *Mancunium*, meant?

Where languages are misunderstood or not understood at all in the naming systems, one can look for redundancies. In Britain there is *Torpenhow Hill* ("hill-hill-hill" if you know the languages) and *Bredon on the Hill* in Leicestershire (where Welsh *bre* and Old English *dun* both mean "hill") and there are many more strange names that go unnoticed unless you know enough languages to see why (say) *Pendel Hill* in Lancashire or *Avon River* are odd. If you know languages, you can walk through Chelsea in London and know there was once a bridge at *Pont Street* and a stream at *Bourne* (formerly *Westbourne*) but no holy convenience at *St. Loo*. Even if you don't know anything more than English you can go beyond eccentric names—Herb Caen of San Francisco returned from Britain exulting over discovering *Little Peaover, North Pidling, Burnham-on-the-Crouch, Great Snoring, Pett Bottom,* and he missed Leslie Dunkling's favorite, *Ugley*. You can find the fascinating history behind *Rotten Row* (maybe from *route de roi*), *Nether Wallop, Swinehead, Nasty, Foul Hole, Muck, Greedyguts, Bury St. Edmunds, Watling Street* ("street" here means "Roman road") and *Elephant and Castle* (corrupted from a pub name: *Infanta de Castille*). *Threehalfpenny Wood* comes from a man found drowned near West Wickham (Kent) "about 1800 with three halfpence in his pocket." Just think: philanthropists have paid millions to get things named after them— one of them displaced the *Trinity* and put his name on *Duke University*—and this beggar was commemorated for three ha'pence. And he died still holding onto it, bequeathing it to no one.

In a country where you can manage the language, names can add a great deal of interest to your travel. I had to go to *Mumbles* and visit the grave of Mr. Bowdler of *bowdlerize*. I noted that the church which holds only 30 people is ample for *Buckler's Hard*. I discovered why *Dorset* (which took its name from a Roman town called *Durnovaria* or "Fist Play" because there was a gladiatorial arena there) has two *Tollers* (*Toller Fratrum* and *Toller Porcorum,* involving monks and pigs). I holed up at *Mousehole* (locally pronounced "muzzle"). I adore the eccentricity of Britain: the Theatre Royal, Drury Lane, is in Catherine Street. The Bayswater Underground is in Queensway. Guess where you enter the Queensway station on the Underground. That's right: Bayswater Road. I liked the crazy signs: the Fleet Air Arm Museum (Yeovilton, Somerset) had a refreshment stand "Closed for Lunch." A barber in Kensal Green advertized "Haircuts While You Wait." Signs in Welsh and English, or Gaelic and English, along the roads send accident rates soaring: people run into things while trying to read "the hard part."

But most of all I like the way the British deal with names. Personal names like *Cholmondeley* ("Chumley") and *Menzies* ("Mengiss") and placenames like *Fowey* ("Foy"), *Worcestershire* ("Woostisher"), and *Hawick* ("Hoik"). I like the way that two places called *Fixton* changed their names because neither wanted to be *Little Fixton* and how tradition holds onto names like *The Crawls* and tells an old story. Lady Mary, the dying wife of Sir Roger de Tichborne (who would have been Lady Tichborne most likely, but don't spoil the story of Lady Mary), asked him on her deathbed to give land to the church for the poor. Not very concerned about her soul's rest, Sir Roger told her she could have for the poor all the land she could get out of bed and walk around, carrying a torch. In those ancient days people used to measure land by how much a hide would cover, how much one could plough in one day, how much one could walk around in a given time, etc. Well, that dying day in A.D. 1150 she made a tremendous, final effort and, they say, got 23 acres from the tightwad for the poor. At the end of her exertion she was crawling. So the place is still called *The Crawls*. With a piece of folklore this charming, who would want to check the historical accuracy? Not the British.

Resisting the temptation to get into the placenames of Scotland, Wales, Cornwall, the Isle of Man, Northern Ireland, etc., for contrast let us look at those of the Basques, who live in the Pyrenees. Their ancient and very strange language is mysterious to all but 600,000 Basques in Spain, 100,000 in France, and a few scattered elsewhere (including the US, where they came as shepherds). At least Finnish is a bit like Hungarian if resembling no other European language, but Basque is like nothing at all. Yet while for British placenames you may have to consult Addison's *Understanding British Place-Names* or McClure's *British Placenames in Their Historical Setting* or Nicolaisen's *Place Names of Scotland* and many other books, I can give you the essence of Basque placenames in a jiffy. They are quite simple, if you know just one obscure language. Basque placenames are basically related to height (or the lack of it) and other geography, new and old things, but not unknown tribes or heroes, just trees and other simple things in nature. (*Ashley* in Basque would be *Lizarraga*.) You can figure out a great many Basque placenames with these few facts: *aga* and *equi* (place of), *barri* or *berri* (new), *be* (below) and *garay* (on high), *buro* (boundary). Familiar Basque placenames and personal names are *Bilbao, Guérnica* (house of the beautiful peak), *Unamuno* (hill of asphodels), *Guevara* (flat area), *Guitérrez* (little burned), *Echegaray* (house on a hill), and *Goya* (higher up).

Every country has its own system or systems for placenames, few as simple as the Basques'. Italy oddly has a lot of derogatory names: *Canile* (kennel), *Porcile* (pig sty), *Puzzolia* (Stinktown). Perhaps the Italians who named those were thinking like the Chinese that if you give a place a bad name the gods will not get jealous. Another way the Chinese try to work magic with names is shown in the case of the Manchu emperor who changed *Wuting* (never still) to *Yungting* (always still) in the hope of preventing the continued flooding of that river; it didn't work. Oriental names are a world apart in every way, but you could try Ch'en Cheng-Hsiang's *Place-Names of Taiwan* (1960) or Kani Kagami's *Japanese Place-Names* (1964) for starters.

There are curiosities in every country's placenames, but I cannot go into many here. For the long and the short of it, let's just notice placename length. Among the world's shortest names is *Å* ("river," found in Norway, Sweden, and Denmark), *O* in Japan, *Y* in France. There are places called *Au* in Germany and in Switzerland (which also has *Gy, Lu,* and *Ob*). There's an *Ii* in Finland, *Al* and *Bo* in Norway, and of course you have heard of the biblical *Ur* of Chaldea. In British Columbia, there's an island with a glottal stop: *K'i.*

For toponymic toppers the jawbreaker is the name of a hill in Southern Hawke's Bay, New Zealand: *Taumatawhakatangihangakoauauotamateaturipu-kakapikimaungahoronukupokaiwhenuakitanatahu.* I think I have the spelling correct and I know it means "the hill where the flute was played by Tamatea, circumnavigator of lands, for his lady love." Officially they make do with a mere 57 letters (omitting letters 37 to 64 in an effort to simplify). *Krungtep Mahanakhon* (*Bangkok* to us) is just part of an official name than can run over 170 letters in some transcriptions. More familiar to name buffs in the West is the Welsh *Llanfairpwllgwyngyllogogerychwyrndrobbwllantysiliogogogoch.* Yes, they did put all that on the railway station sign and it means, translated word by word, "Church Mary a hollow white hazel near to the whirlpool Church saint's name cave red." Some authorities say it's a fake, created by a local tailor as an attention-getter. Americans, not to be outdone, counter with (spellings vary!) *Chargoggagoggmanchauggagogggchabungungaamuagogg.* That is alleged to be Amerindian "you fish on your side, I fish on my side, nobody fishes in the middle." Near Webster (Massachusetts), it also bears the name *Lake Webster* and is known by the locals as the *Lake,* although it is a pond· It has also been called *Chabanakongkomuk* (boundary lake). Such specialists as Huden (1962) tend to pooh-pooh these alleged Amerindian sesquipedalianisms. I do not know of any US placename that is verifiably longer than *Drimtaidhvrick-hillichatten,* which is on the Isle of Man—at least not one-word ones. Do you? Manitoba has a lake called *Pekwachnamaykoskwaskwaypinwanik,* probably the Canadian winner.

In several countries you can go to *Hell.* In Dublin (Eire), near the law courts, that was the old name of *Christ Church Lane.* Or you can get a lot of information out of the names of countries. *Norge* (Norway) is "the northern way." The Finns call Finland *Suomi.* Siam is now called *Thailand* (though we still have Siamese cats, Siamese connections, Siamese twins), where *tai* means "free." *Mongolia* tells you its people are "brave ones," *Nigeria* speaks of "flowing water," and both *Australia* and *Vietnam* are "southern." *Italia* was the home of the Vitali tribe. *Portugal* had a "warm harbor." *Hibernia,* the old name of Ireland (now *Eire* and *Northern Ireland*), was "wintry." The official English translations of country names can be show-stoppers: *Tibetan Autonomous Region of the People's Republic of China, Hashemite Kingdom of Jordan, Socialist People's Lybian Arab Jamahirrya,* and so on. There was a brave attempt at *Names of the Countries of the World in 20 Languages,* and if you won't quibble about the Cyrillic letters used to spell it in Russian and Bulgarian I can tell you that only *Angola* came out the same in all those 20 languages. (The world has over 5,000 languages now in use.) The book was rendered pretty useless pretty soon by name changes. Adrian Room is the expert on the subject of name changes and has recorded the thousands of them worldwide, from country names to those of towns and villages, that have taken place since 1900.

You are probably aware of the extensive Russian name changes that produced *Leningrad, Gorky, Stalingrad* and thousands more, as well as of the fact that practically no one can name all the countries in Africa right now, let alone give the meanings of most of them (*Ethiopia* tells you its inhabitants were "sunburned"). Continents and countries older than ours are better candidates for a long discussion of placename changes, but for US examples we can cite Cambridge (Massachusetts), once appropriately *Newtowne;* it has had a string of names. The island where the Statue of Liberty is (its official name, by the way, is *Liberty Enlightening the World*) has been *Minisais, Love, Kennedy, Corporation, Great Oyster, Fort Wood, Bedloe's Island,* and is now (as you have heard) *Liberty Island.* Up in Maine, Portland was *Machigonne, Indigreat, Elbow, The Neck, Casco,* and *Falmouth* before it got its present name in 1786. Names such as *Cambridge* and *Portland* have had their present form for quite a long while, by US standards and compared to an otherwise not very notable suburb of Chicago that has had the names *Babcock's Grove* (1833), *Du Page Center* (1834), *Stacy's Corners* (1835), *Newton's Station* (1849), *Danby* (1851), *Prospect Park* (1882), and *Glen Ellen* (1889). I suggest that to celebrate the centenary of that last name they change the name to *Chameleon. Glen Ellen* has a phoney sound to it anyway.

This section is intended to touch briefly on foreign countries' names, but to stay with US name changes a bit longer, as easier to grasp, maybe more relevant to us, consider that *Atlanta* has also been among other things a railroad *Terminus* and *Marthasville. Waterloo* is now called *Austin* (Texas). *Jernigan* has been promoted to *Orlando* (Florida). *Chicken Bristle* (Kentucky) changed its name to *Savoyard.*

In New York City, as elsewhere, real-estate developers have seen the commercial value of named neighborhoods and created between *Greenwich Village* and *Chinatown* other neighborhood names: *SoHo* (south of Houston Street), *NoHo* (north of that), *Tribeca* (triangle below Canal Street), etc. *Chelsea* and other up-and-coming areas have also received names, sometimes old ones that had long gone unused. In Brooklyn, next to *Brooklyn Heights* sprang up *Boreum Hill, Cobble Hill, Carroll Gardens* and other gentrification names. Forgotten names are returning: I live in *Fiske Terrace,* an enclave in *Midwood,* though nearby *Flatbush* has long been a common Brooklyn name. *Welfare Island* has become a moated bourgeois outpost in the East River as *Roosevelt Island,* in the same kind of move that is replacing *Hell's Kitchen* with *Clinton.*

In fashionable Westchester County, *Turkey Hole Rivulet* became *Tuckahoe Creek*. Leslie A. Dunkling noted that in an Appalachian version of this search for cachet "they made a *Mountain* out of a *Mole Hill*."

Placename changes, as we have seen, occur for a lot of reasons, from change of ownership to change of tone. They are adopted to avert the stigma of a derogatory name or to get something more attractive, and so on. Citizens of *Weed* (California, named for a prominent family that was mentioned in connection with the notorious Patty Hearst, you may recall) considered changing the town name to *Shastina* (for nearby Mount Shasta), then rejected the new name as sounding too much like that of a soft drink. Politics turned *Saigon* into *Ho Chi Minh City,* change of population the Arabic *Ishbilîya* to *Seville,* and whether we should say *Falklands* or *Malvinas* is still in dispute, *Port Stanley* or *Puerto Rivero* being the most prominent town there. Chinese and Portuguese collaborated to create *Macao;* first *Ho Heng* was named for a goddess (*A-Ma*), then the suffix *-gao* was tacked on, then the name was corrupted to *Macau* and now it's *Macao*.

Do you remember what *Zimbabwe* and *Tanzania* used to be called?

The names in your atlas are constantly in flux, though in politically stable countries such as the US and the UK placename changing is not chaotic, chiefly cosmetic. As the world turns, so do its names. In English we sometimes cling with British bulldog tenacity to our old ways whatever happens. We mispronounce *Paris* (and the British used to render *Calais* as "Callous," etc.) and Anglicize *Milano* (the British used to pronounce *Milan* "Millen," whence *millinery*), say *Venice* (never *Venezia*) and even *Leghorn* for *Livorno*. When it was brought to Sir Winston Churchill's attention that *Persia* is now *Iran* (though we still have Persian cats, Persian rugs, Persian slippers) and that the natives do not call other cities *Munich* or *Geneva* and such, the old man, ever more likely to bluster the more wrong he was, huffily pronounced: "I do not consider that names that have been familiar for generations should be altered to suit the foreigners living in those parts." For him it would always be *Constantinople,* not *Istanbul*. Now there's a pompous, provincial approach: there are two kinds of placenaming systems, the Traditional British and the Ignorant Wogs.

I think we all ought to be more amused than instructed by the British insularity. I believe that we ought to take a less cavalier attitude toward what other people want to call their places, trying as best we can to keep up with pronunciation changes in names such as *Kenya* and keeping up with the world and its name changes, even when they are politically less than welcome or quite uncertain. *Uncertain* is a town in Texas.

Do you know that *Cupheag* became *Stratford* (making way for a Shakespeare Festival in Connecticut)? That Florida's *Milton* was once *Hard Scrabble?* That Colorado's *Blue Mountain* used to be *Skull Creek?* That *Midway* used to be *Brooks Island* (though it's actually two islands, *Sand* and *Eastern*)? That

Hoover Dam was *Boulder Dam* and *MacArthur Park* was *Westlake Park?* That Canada's *Mekatewis Island* was, before 1966, *Nigger Lake?* There's a move to change *Mount McKinley* back to *Denali* and there was an abortive attempt to change *West Virginia* to *Kennedy!* I approve only when changes get rid of the embarrassing (*Jap Valley, Nigger Mountain*). Now it is US government policy to alter *Jap* to *Japanese* and *Nigger* to *Negro;* some day *Negro* may have to be changed to *African-American.* I can understand that. I confess I am a little sorry to see *S.O.B. Creek* become *Sob Creek,* though I can also appreciate why locals wanted to ditch *Stinking Lake* for *Burford* or our friends in Belorussia wanted to emulate our changing *Puercos* (dirty) to *Pecos* and alter their *Zagyrryayze* (filthy place) to *Berezynyanka* (birches), *Pyany Les* (drunken forest) to *Sosnovaya* (pine), and *Yazvy* (ulcers) to *Vostochnaya* (eastern place).

I say let the new groups coming in preserve the old names and preserve some old trees when they bulldoze for the housing development, let some historic buildings and old names remain in place.

Whenever I hear some nice nellies trying to dump a crude pioneering name or Babbity boosters trying to trade in a used name on a new model, I think of this impassioned defense of an Amerindian name, *Arkansas.* Sure, foreigners have trouble pronouncing it, but we Americans should echo this sentiment:

> Change the name of Arkansas! Hell, no! stand back and give him room according to his strength. Blood's his natural drink! and the wails of the dying is music to his ears! Cast your eyes on the gentleman, and lay low and hold your breath, for he's 'bout to turn himself loose! He's the bloodiest son of a wild-cat that lives, who would change the name of Arkansas! Hold him down to earth, for he is a child of sin! Don't attempt to look at him with your naked eye, gentlemen; use smoked glass. The man who would change the name of Arkansaw, by gosh, would use the meridians of longitude and the parallels of latitude for a seine, and drag the Atlantic ocean for whales! He would scratch himself awake with the lightning, and purr himself to sleep with the thunder! When he's cold, he would "bile" the Gulf of Mexico and bathe in it! When he's hot, he would fan himself with an equinoctial storm! When he's thirsty, he would reach up and suck a cloud dry like a sponge! When he's hungry, famine follows in his wake! You may put your hand on the sun's face, and make it night on earth; bite a piece out of the moon, and hurry the seasons; shake yourself and rumble the mountains; but, sir, you will never change the name of Arkansaw!
>
> The man who would change the name of Arkansaw, would massacre isolated communities as a pastime. He would destroy nationalities as a serious business! He would use the boundless vastness of the Great American Desert for his private graveyard! He would attempt to extract sunshine from cucumbers! Hide the stars in a nail-keg, put the sky to soak in a gourd, hang the Arkansaw River on a

clothesline; unbuckle the belly-band of Time, and turn the sun and moon out to pasture; but you will never change the name of Arkansaw! The world will again pause and wonder at the audacity of the lop-eared, lantern-jawed, half-breed, half-born, whiskey-soaked hyena who has proposed to change the name of Arkansaw! He's just starting to climb the political bannister, and wants to knock the hayseed out of his hair, pull the splinters out of his feet, and push on and up to the governorship. *But change the name of Arkansaw, hell, no!*

Cassius M. Johnson is said to have delivered that impassioned speech, in the best "half-man, half-alligator" style of nineteenth-century oratory, in the Arkansas legislature. It, like *Arkansas* itself, is pure Americana. It rejoices, as did one "Socrates Hyacinth" in the *Overland Monthly* for August 1869, in American names. The journalist who called himself that listed *Last Chance, Righteous Ridge, Scratch Gravel, Pinchtown, Marrow Bones* and these Texas examples: "*Lick Skillet, Buck Snort, Nip and Tuck, Jimtown, Rake Pocket, Hog Eye, Fair Play, Seven League, Steal Easy, Possum Trot, Flat Heel, Frog Level, Short Pone, Gourd Neck, Shake Rag, Poverty Slant, Black Ankle, Jim Ned.*"

Many of those names are gone, and it's sad. Long live *Arkansas!* As another version of the speech has it:

Compare the lily of the valley to the gorgeous sunrise; the discordant croak of the bullfrog to the melodious tones of a nightingale; the classic strains of Mozart to the bray of a Mexican mule; the puny arm of a Peruvian prince to the muscles of a Roman gladiator—but never change the name of Arkansas. Hell, no!

Elsewhere in the world names are not merely corrupted or clipped (as Wangunk *Machimoodus,* "place of many noises," in Connecticut was reduced to *Moodus*) but in some places they are junked with colonial or other factors. In Africa, countries, empires, come and go. *Lake Albert* becomes *Lake Mobuto Sese Seko* and *Queens Road* becomes *Lumumba Avenue* and *Elizabeth National Park* becomes *Rwenzori.* Names of colonial times (*Rhodesia, Léopoldville, Dahomey*) vanish as nationalism asserts itself. Some of the new names are good. Some are historical: *Ghana* recalls an ancient kingdom, though not coextensive with the new country, and *Mali* was a province of that old country. Some are new: had they offered a bigger prize than the $38 some newspapers reported they might have got something better than *Tanzania.* Some people care less about the new name than they do about the fact that they do not want to recall the past. They want fresh names for new status. The rest of us are going to have to get used to the new names, even if for a while we have no idea where the *Central African Republic* is (or was) or what is meant by *Can Phumo, Tuvala, Phoenix Islands,* or whether *El Chichón* is a dust storm or a new South American country.

15. On the Street Where You Live

I t can be a street or an avenue (though that ought to be lined with trees). Or a boulevard (though that should be broad and perhaps have a median). Or a lane, an alley, a circle (the British like *circus*), a drive, an esplanade or promenade, a line, a mews (though that ought to have stables, or converted stables), a park or parade, a parkway, a passage, a place or a close, a road, a row, a square, a terrace, a crescent (which ought to be curved), a walk. . . . The names for streets (mostly residential) are varied. We also have freeways, throughways, tollways, turnpikes, ways; there are plenty of ways of naming roads. The New Jersey Turnpike is nicknamed *Cancer Alley*.

The Americans say they live on a certain street, the British that they live in a certain road. Wherever we live the names of "our" streets are dear to us, full of memories and associations. To the onomasticians, these are merely odonyms.

Street names amuse us. In 1974 the *Kansas City Star* noted that a certain corner in Ann Arbor (Michigan) had signs declaring *Nixon/Bluett*. They confuse us. Arequippa (Peru) amazed linguists who gathered there for a convention: it had five streets named *Luna Pizarro*. Caracas (Venezuela) has not named the streets, but popular corners have nicknames that translate as *Danger, Keep Your Eye Peeled, Take Off Your Pants*. London and some other big cities have a number of streets with a common name like *Park Avenue,* and in Japan (besides the trouble you may have finding street names) you have the problem that houses are numbered in a street in the order in which they are built, not the way Americans put odd numbers on one side and even numbers on the other. Some British streets are numbered up one side and down the other: number 20 may be opposite number 420.

To become a London taxidriver, one has to spend months going around the city on a bicycle, learning which streets are where and how they are numbered, change their names as they go along, and so on; it's called acquiring "the knowledge," and it's quite a feat to qualify.

William Penn here introduced in Philadelphia an easy system of naming which has been widely imitated: at the water was *Front Street* and the principal street was called (in the British fashion) *High Street* (soon changed by the merchants to *Market Street*), while others were named for trees (*Chestnut, Walnut, Pine,* etc.). As a simple Quaker, Penn disapproved of naming streets after people, but that became common, too.

Naming streets in alphabetical order, naming them after US presidents in chronological order, simply numbering them, all have been tried. In Manhattan the lower, older part of the island is a maze of named streets but then the avenues, north and south, are numbered and the streets, east and west, are numbered—Fifth Avenue is roughly in the middle and you start 1 East or 1 West on each street from that avenue. The second most popular US street name is *Park* (in New York City an avenue rather than a street). I suppose the most typical US street name is *Main Street.*

We have all kinds of street names except, perhaps, the revolutionary kind that involves the dates of uprisings (*Cinco de Mayo*). In New Paltz (New York) they claim that *The Street of the Huguenots* is the oldest named street in America, but surely this is open to debate. So is "the most famous street in America": is it *Wall Street* (the stock market) or *Broadway* (the theatre) or not in New York City at all but *Bourbon Street* (jazz) or *Hollywood Boulevard* or *Rodeo Drive* (expensive boutiques) or elsewhere? If it's in *L.A.* it may be the three-mile stretch between *La Brea* and *La Cienega* called *Melrose.* "Melrose is right up there with the great streets of Europe," Judy Davidson told Daniel B. Wood of the *Christian Science Monitor,* 8 July 1988. The president lives on a street in Washington, where the names of states are featured and the layout has you running around in circles. (The White House is at 1600 *Pennsylvania Avenue.*)

Slang has its *Easy Street*—the equivalent in a British music-hall song was *Golden Square*—and *Skid Row.* In Clinton (New York) there's a *Sodom Road* and a *Sodom Four Corners;* the crime there was selling whiskey in the days of Temperance. In Guadalajara, the *nordeamericanos* have nicknamed *Minerva Circle, Manoeuvre Circle,* because of traffic chaos. In New York City, 42nd Street is *The Deuce* and drugs made 72nd and Broadway notorious as *Needle Park,* both nicknames well-known enough to serve as titles of dramatic works, one a play, one a movie. *Boulevard St.-Laurent* in Montréal a generation ago used to be called *St. Lawrence Main,* though it was not exactly a main street then. Many towns and cities have nicknamed streets, just as they used to have nicknamed neighborhoods (often "on the wrong side of the tracks").

Street names tell us of features long lost (the *Barbican* in London, *Rampart Street* in New Orleans, *Canal Street* in New York) and can also serve modern convenience, provided that there is not too much repetition of names. *Eaton Place, Eaton Terrace, Eaton Square* tell Londoners that they are all in the same neighborhood, but they can confuse foreigners, as can *Holland Road* and *Holland Park Avenue* (miles apart). Austin (Texas) has *Barton Drive, Barton*

Hills Drive, Barton View Drive, Barton Boulevard, Barton Springs Road, etc., with *Barton Skyway* far away from the rest. Brooklyn was once a number of small communities and a number of attempts at pattern get all jumbled with *19 Street, 19 Avenue, East 19th Street* (which is nowhere near *19 Street* or, for that matter, near *Bay 19th Street,* etc.). Manhattan's grid sometimes goes haywire: *West 4th* meets supposedly parallel *West 10th* (not far from the Cherry Lane Theatre, which is on *Commerce Street,* not *Cherry Lane* nearby). Van Dyke (Michigan) has *Ford, Dodge, Packard, Cadillac,* etc. Seattle (Washington)'s streets north to south downtown come in pairs: *Jefferson-James, Cherry-Columbia, Marion-Madison, Spring-Seneca, University-Union, Pike-Pine,* but to remember the series the locals have had to invent the irreverent "JJesus CChrist MMade SSeattle UUnder PProtest."

Numbers and boring *A, B, C* are functional (except when taxidrivers mishear a letter of the alphabet) but anything else is likely to get some criticism. A town in Northern Rhodesia (as it then was) tried *Auden, Browning, Coleridge, Dryden, Emerson,* and so on, only to have the *Manchester Guardian* complain of the choice of writers.

Large cities such as *L.A.* need a lot of names and descend to craziness as bad as San José's *Technology.* Chicago tries patterns but has to have a lot of them. It honors foreign heroes (*Pulaski, Garibaldi, Grattan*) as well as American ones. It honors writers (*Dickens, Homer, Dante,* and a few American ones, such as *Hawthorne*). It celebrates blacks (*Edmaire, Dunbar, Hooker*) and a great many Amerindians: *Illinois, Ohio, Calumet, Mackinaw, Milwaukee, Pensacola, Leoti, Winnemac, Osceola,* and *Caldwell* (his Indian name was Sauganash and he was a Pottawattamie chief). Opa-Locka (Florida), which you may remember as the jumping-off place for the Bay of Pigs debacle, uses *The Arabian Nights* (*Salih Drive, Caliph Street, Alibaba Avenue*), and Santa Claus (Indiana), a name probably chosen when the inhabitants were too full of Yuletide cheer, has *Silver Bell Terrace, Sled Run, Donner Lake.* You may recall that *Donner* and *Blitzen,* whose names mean "Thunder" and "Lightning" in German, were two of St. Nick's reindeer in popular culture in the days before "Rudolph the Red-Nosed Reindeer" came along.

A good street-naming system was created by James Geddes, hired by the surveyor-general in 1798 to lay out a village for salt production (*Salinas*) in upstate New York. His street names were straight American (*Free Street, Canal Street, Center Street, Salt Street*). More recently the citizens have turned to the romance of explorers and Indians (*LeMoyne Street, Hiawatha Street*), and the city was renamed in the era of the classical fad as *Syracuse.* In Rochester, they got some classical names the locals cannot pronounce (*Scio* is one). Better suited to the area are names such as Geddes put between *Free* and *Canal: Wolf, Turtle, Bear* recall the Onondagas, and the locals can say them. Also, they aren't mistaken for each other, as *Great* and *State* can be, and they are not too fanciful. A Jacksonville (Florida) developer came up with a theme and perpetrated *Tinker Bell Lane, Tom Thumb Drive, Peter Pan Place.* . . . Grow up!

I like an occasional strange name. *Mott* is not what you'd expect for the main drag of New York's Chinatown; it's named for a butcher. *Union Square* there is named for the union of two streets, though New Yorkers think it has something to do with the Civil War. I rather like *Street Boulevard* (for baseball great "Gabby" Street) and *Oraton Street* (for an Amerindian chief) and I sought but could not find the one named for Pontius Pilate (Marshall Rigan reported it) in Fort Worth (Texas). I once read a whole paper at an international convention on the street names of the French Quarter in New Orleans. I hated to see Connecticut convert a *Skunk Lane* into *Buckingham Ridge Lane.* I hated to learn from Anna H. Smith that there were in 1971 "forty or so *First Avenues, Lanes, Roads* or *Streets* in Johannesburg." I didn't like the system in Cosmos (Minnesota): *Mars, Jupiter, Comet.* Or in Silverado (California): *Wila Way, Hidea Way, Thisa Way, Thata Way, Halfa Way, Bytha Way,* etc.

I see why they made *Incinerator Road* into *Burnham Drive;* I think that was clever. I think it was clever of London to have a *Gracechurch Street* made out of "Grass Church" (St. Benet's had a turf roof ages ago). I like Newcastle's *Dog Leap Stairs* and Glasgow's *Goosedubs* ("dubs" are what we'd call "ponds") and Paris' wonderful street names. I regret I have room for only a couple: *rue du Cherche-Midi* (looking for noon) and that of the "dry tree" where the gallows once stood, *rue de l'Arbre Sec.*

We need more imagination in American street names. We need more honesty: no *Deer Run,* where no deer has ever been seen, matching the fake Early American decor. We need fewer tasteless inventions: a University of Washington librarian thought *Mar Cheri* "combined Spanish and French." *Whispering Pines Boulevard* is not a boulevard and it's out in the Mohave Desert with the nearest pine tree more than 50 miles southwest of it. Joanne Rife found such idiocy rife and in the Santa Inez *Valley News* she commented:

> The honesty of the Indians started with a name like Canyon-With-Bad-Tempered-Sharp-Fanged-Rattlesnakes; continued through the tough frontiersman who named it Rattlesnake Canyon; and came to pieces when Best-Built Modern Homes Corp. named it Pleasant Hollow.

Still, who would buy a house in *Rattlesnake Canyon* or *Dry Gulch?* Names are image; image sells houses. Sorry, *homes.* So *Wino Gulch* inevitably becomes *Thunderbird Estates.* It's an age of inflation. If Monopoly players had not howled protest, Atlantic City would have gussied up *Baltic* as *Fairmont* and *Mediterranean* as *Melrose.* They are building a *Taj Mahal* in Atlantic City as I write.

Taj Mahal has nothing to do with Atlantic City and the names really ought to have some connection with the place, whether they be street names, mall names (in Minneapolis -*dale* signals "mall" and it may not be bad to establish such a local convention), hotel names, or tract housing names. Calgary (Alberta) stressed the Stampede era with *Crowchild* and *Calf Robe* but was on a better track with names of Canadian Pacific Railway pioneers (*Van Horne, Stephen, McIntyre, Drinkwater*) even if a lot of people did not realize why such names were selected.

I think that if you are going to get an architect to design the houses in your development you also ought to hire a names consultant for the overall name. The name sets the tone; it may be an important selling point. Get a professional to choose the various street names. If you want to be cheap or cute, let your wife or kids pick the names and design the logo, or go into the boutique business. Your "complex" is a place people will live, and have friends come to visit, their home address if they decide to buy or rent after an inspection. Pick the name with care and name the mall, if you have one, with equal care; it may well be your community's center and it can create or destroy prestige. I repeat: redesign (if necessary) to leave some established native trees—and some established native names, if there are any. Don't just plunk down *Executive Oaks* (low-brow white-collar) or put *Golf* or *Club* in it (to suggest "goof-off" or cliquey). Don't call it *Marina* or *del Mar* if there's no water in sight or *Heights* if the site is flat. Spend some time and money getting a good name for your venture because you are going to be spending plenty to advertize your choice. Some people will have to live with it, *Underground, Harbor Place,* or housing.

Everyone ought to pay some attention to street names and the local history. Look up the origins of the names in your locality in a book in the library. If there isn't one, write one or get local institutions to fund research as a matter of civic duty and community concern. If you teach school, or know anyone who does, arrange for grade-school kids and high-school students to learn about the names in their neighborhood. It will teach them a little local pride; it can introduce them to using the library or collecting oral history; and perhaps it can create a bridge between them and the oldtimers who, if asked considerately, are usually only too glad to hand on knowledge to the young generation. Street names have a very personal appeal and make an exciting research or term-paper assignment. They are intriguing, educational, not too difficult to learn about, and fun. Put them into the curriculum in your schools.

What street do you live on, and why is it called that? The blocks near me are *Foster Avenue* and *Glenwood Road* but when they got to my block Brooklynite wit and taste both failed. My street is *Avenue H* and then we have *I, J,* etc. Maybe I should move to *Sutton Place.* I'm not malleable enough for *Malibu.*

I wanted to choose one city and large neighborhood to illustrate the variety and attraction of street names and I decided to offend none in the US by singling out an American example and excluding all the others. I made a foreign choice, yet one where the language is more or less similar and the history more or less familiar to us (which, I regret to say, excluded Canadian and Australian possibilities). I chose London and the neighborhood of Chelsea and environs, now part of a "royal borough" (Queen Victoria was born in Kensington) named *Kensington and Chelsea*.

London is named for King Lud of legend (whence *Ludgate*) and the Romans knew it as *Londinium*. They crossed the Thames to attack it at *Chelsea*, scaring the hell out of its defenders with an elephant at *Battersea*, so the story goes. London has a vast variety of street names (*Downing Street, King's Road, Birdcage Walk, The Strand, Artillery Row, Park Lane, Oxford Circus, Leicester Square, St. Giles, High Street*, the obsolete *Tyburn Way*, the nicknamed *Petticoat Lane, Harley Street* synonymous with medical "consultants," *the East End* and *the West End, Mayfair*, and many, many more) and Chelsea has as interesting a history as any of London's subdivisions.

Both London and Chelsea are ancient and have some names which date back to ancient customs, some names corrupted by ignorance of foreign languages imposed by conquerors (as in Spain the Moors left *Alcazár* "the castle," *Cadíz* "fortified place," *Guadalajara* "river of stones"), some names battered by time.

Begin in London with *Adam and Eve Mews*, an alley behind great houses where the stables were, this one named for a pub sign. Or *The Mall*, which recalls a ball game that gave us the expression *pell mell*. *Fleet Street* and *High Holborn* recall vanished rivers. *The Strand* was once a beach. *The Embankment* was constructed along the Thames. A royal favorite, Jane Shore, died in a ditch at *Shoreditch*. *Regent Street* was commissioned by and named for George IV (more famous as Prince Regent for his incompetent father George III), and the park named for "Mary the Good" (or perhaps another *bourne* or river), *Marylebone*, was renamed *Regent's Park* for him. Carlton House (whence *Carlton House Terrace*) was torn down by George IV and he moved into a royal residence that had once belonged to a duke of Buckingham, now *Buckingham Palace*. That's the most famous address in London, unless you want to count 10 Downing Street or a fictional address, Sherlock Holmes' 221 B Baker Street.

These are pretty straightforward names. Not so *Addle Hill*; that's from King Athelstan (old English *adel* "noble"). London used to be walled; the gate open to all was *Aldgate*. When the clergy used to process outside St. Paul's they said the "Our Father" in *Paternoster Row*, the "Hail Mary" in *Ave Maria Lane*, the Creed in *Creed Lane*, and concluded prayers in *Amen Court*. Even *America Square* misleads some by antedating (1760) trouble in these colonies.

Under *B* in London we find a variety of origins. From the Roman *barbicana* (built where the Saxons had had a *burgh kennin* or watchtower) comes the *Barbican*, now a horror of brutalist cement architecture. From colorful pub signs in the days when few could read came alley names still existing such as *Bear Alley, Beehive Passage*, two *Bell Yards* (one from *The Bell* and one from *La Belle*), *Bird in Hand Court, Bull's Head Passage, Black Raven Alley, Black Swan Alley*. A famous sign on a coaching inn which saw nearly 30 coaches a day leave for the West Country at the height of the business was *The Bolt in Tun,* a rebus for the name of the abbot (Bolton) who restored the church of St. Bartholomew the Great around 1520. Now the inn is gone but there's a *Bolt Court* off *Fleet Street* (a name synonymous with newspaper production until recent times; now the bulk of that industry is on the *Isle of Dogs*). A lot of the *B* names have been battered: *Beech Street* (for Nicholas de la Beche), *Bevis Marks* (for the boundaries of the abbey of Bury St. Edmunds in Suffolk), *Birchin Lane* (Birchouer family), *Bush Lane* (Busches), etc.

A trifle eccentric? More like proud and independent. Londoners were so much so that the arrogance of London toward the pope's nuncios very early on led to Canterbury, not London, being designated the ecclesiastical capital of England. London naming has always been somewhat original. Its names have survived haphazardly (as William Hogarth's house stands today, a relic jammed up against a shoe-polish factory). Incongruity abounds, as in the names of the two best pubs for game pie I found some years back, named *The Lamb and Flag* (from the Christian symbol of *Agnus Dei* or "Lamb of God" with a banner) and *The Bucket of Blood* (once the site of gory bare-knuckle boxing matches).

In any discussion of London it is practically a law that Dr. Samuel Johnson must be quoted:

> Why, Sir, you find no man, at all intellectual, who is willing to leave London. No, Sir, when a man is tired of London, he is tired of life; for there is in London all that life can afford.

Without questioning that statement, or gushing like H. G. Wells in *The New Machiavelli* (1911) that "London is the most interesting, beautiful and wonderful city in the world . . . delicate in her incidental and multitudinous littleness and stupendous in her pregnant totality," we can say that London is a great place for any English speaker to learn 2,000 years of history in names. London also can teach one very basic rule about name origins: never jump to conclusions.

You've seen some reason for that already. Let's continue with examples: *Carey Lane* (Kirone family), *Carter Lane* (Stephen le Chatterer), *Coleman Street* (for the *kohl mund* or cabbage patch King Egbert gave to Bishop Alban about A.D. 800), *Cheapside* (Old English *ceap,* "sell" or "barter"), *Cripplegate* (*crepul,* "tunnel"). *Billiter Street* once housed beletzers (who cast bells) and *Trump Street* horn makers. There were budgers (dealers in lambskins) in *Budge Row* in the thirteenth century but never a Roman bath in *Roman Bath Street* (the first London turkish bath was built there in 1679). Nobody really knows where *Piccadilly* came from. We guess that *St. Mary Axe* (pronounced, as in the Gilbert & Sullivan song of J. Wellington Wells, "Simmery Axe") involves a relic of the martyrdom of St. Ursula (not St. Mary).

From the earliest historians onward, London names have attracted attention, though it is only about a century (actually 1896) since dictionaries of *London*

Street Names began to appear. They have attracted Cockney taxidrivers and Scandinavian philologists. Reference books are many, both popular and academic. Let me leave you to look up the taxidriver (Al Smith, *Dictionary of London Street Names,* 1970) or the philologist (Eilert Ekwall, *Street Names of the City of London,* 1954) or some other authority on The City. I turn here to the lore and linguistics (I think you'll prefer the stories) of a suburb, the *Chelsea* I used to live in and know a bit about.

The first thing I noticed about Chelsea's names was how many of the property owners who had their seats elsewhere transferred placenames to this "royal borough." From Yorkshire came names like *Barkston, Bramham, Collingham, Glenbow, Horbury,* and *Scampston* (from *Scampston Hall,* near Malton in the East Riding—or third—of Yorkshire, a country house.) From the West Country came names such as *Abbotsbury* and *Melbury* (both Dorset), *Rosemoor* (Devon), *Camelford* (Cornwall). Such names tell us who bought up this suburban London property, or where they came from, while datable placenames from far off battles *(Alma, Inkerman, Porto Bello)* position things in time. Some name changes have obscured this kind of thing: *Danube* used to be *Little Blenheim,* a reference to the great house the nation gave to the duke of Marlborough after he won a foreign field of that name. The mansion was *Blenheim Palace.*

The names and titles of nobles fill in more information. Descendants of one of Marlborough's close associates (William Cadogan, 1672-1726, created Baron Cadogan of Reading in 1716 and Baron Cadogan of Oakley, Viscount Caversham, and Earl Cadogan in 1718) gave us *Cadogan Square, Oakley Street, Caversham Street,* and even *Elystan Street* (because the Cadogans liked to trace their lineage from Elystan Glodrydd, founder of the fourth royal tribe of Wales). *Rosemoor Street* (already mentioned) came from a Devonshire residence of the Cadogans. The first earl's brother Charles (1685-1776) did not inherit the earldom but was given the barony of Oakley and married Elizabeth, one of the heiresses of Sir Hans Sloane (1660-1753), who had bought the manor of Chelsea (1712) and retired to it eventually (1741). And that gave us *Hans Place, Sloane Avenue, Sloane Square,* and in a way the yuppie *Sloane Rangers.* Sloane and Cadogan relatives account for *Ellis Street, Margaretta Terrace, Paulton's Square, Teaworth Square,* and more. Genealogy is the clue to a lot of the names, you see.

The estate of the earls of Warwick and Holland was connected to Sir Walter Cope; at one time or another he owned all the parts of Kensington and in 1605 he built a house named or nicknamed *Cope's Castle,* later called *Holland House.* His heirs in the family of William Edwardes (who sold Holland House to Henry Fox, later created Baron Holland) and the descendants of Baron Holland also strewed names around. When the fourth Baron Holland died (1859) the estate went to his widow. She left it to Henry Edward Fox-Stangeways, Earl of Ilchester (a distant cousin of her husband), along with

Melbury (Dorset), etc. So from the Holland estate came names such as *Holland Road, Holland Park, Holland Walk* (nicknamed *Whoring Walk* by London *gays* who *troll* or *cruise* as Americans say), *Ilchester Place, Melbury Road, Warwick Road, Cope Place, Edwardes Square, Marloes Road* and *Philbeach Gardens* (from Edwardes' holdings in Pembrokeshire, that "end land"), *Templeton Place* and *Trebovir Road* (also Pembrokeshire), and so on. Without this history, many of these names would appear inexplicably out of place.

Robert Gunter was a rich pastry cook; the people nicknamed his impressive mansion *Currant Jelly Hall*. His son became a baronet and got hold of the manor of the de Vere earls of Oxford, which resulted in the placename *Earl's Court*. Today that suggests Australians, once drawn there by cheap tourist accommodations; there are jokes about *Kangaroo Court* and "how does it feel to be the right way up?" is asked of those from Down Under. In the Earl's Court area we find *Gunter Grove, Tregunter Road, Bramham Gardens* (from the Yorkshire village near the Gunter country seat), *Barkston Gardens* (from a place one Gunter represented in Parliament), *Wharfedale Street* (Gunter's country house, *Wetherby Grange,* is in Yorkshire on the river Wharfe), a road nearby named for the house, etc.

Many more names derived from James Weller Ladbroke (*Ladbroke Grove,* etc.) and W. H. Jenkins, who took land for housing development on long lease from Ladbroke. (In Britain buying freeholds is possible but many owners grant only leaseholds, though sometimes for 99 or even 999 years, and certain peers, such as the duke of Westminster, are said only to rent, never to sell.) Jenkins in 1844 started to put in houses and streets and got *Denbigh Road* and more from his native Herefordshire. He also used a lot of Welsh placenames: *Chepstow Villas* and *Pembridge Gardens* are two of them. The St. Quintin family brought names from Yorkshire. The family of developer John Thurloe produced *Thurloe Street, Alexander Square* (for his godson John Alexander), and so on. Henry Smith, an alderman of London (d. 1627) left a great acreage to charity and his benefactions for various reasons put names on the land such as *Egerton Crescent, Evelyn Gardens, Lennox Gardens, Sumner Place.* John Phillimore, a clothier from Gloucestershire (the shire named for the Roman *Glevum,* "bright") had descendants who contributed some names as did Stephen Pitt, a friend of Phillimore's grandson. So did the Stanhope earls of Harrington (*Stanhope Gardens, Harrington Road*). Famous residents are commemorated in placenames or sometimes blue-and-white markers on the houses in which they lived. The list is impressive: St. (or Sir) Thomas More, the eighth duke of Argyll, Mary Astell, Aubrey de Vere (first lord of the manor of Kensington courtesy of William the Conqueror), William Bolton (of the *Boltons*), Sir Edmund Burton of the reign of Edward VI (I used to live a half a block off *Burton's Court,* which stands in front of the Royal Hospital, Chelsea), George Canning the politician, Thomas Carlyle the writer, the Cheyney family (lords of the manor of Chelsea from the Restoration of Charles II to the sale to Sir Hans Sloane in 1712), Viscount Cremorne, Sir John

Danvers, the notorious Sir Charles Dilke, the famous actress Dame Ellen Terry, not to mention Dante Gabriel Rossetti, Oscar Wilde, George Eliot, Mark Twain. . . .

Chelsea has its less distinguished names, too: *Blacklands, Redfield, Wright* and *Young* were builders. The borough has its fathomable names: *Norland* was land to the north. And its unfathomable ones, such as *Notting Hill Gate*. But some digging is required to discover that an important duke of Westminster (1825–1899) was born at Eaton Hall (Cheshire) and that's where we got fashionable *Eaton Square, Eaton Terrace, Eaton Mews,* etc. *Folly Mews* was named after a house in *Porto Bello Road* (now synonymous with antique markets) that was left long unfinished and declared by the locals to be a folly. *Wilsham Street* was named within living memory, but nobody knows why. I suggest people keep investigating. Answers do turn up. For instance, *Draycott Avenue* looked puzzling until one found Sir Francis Schuckburg (who leased *Blacklands House* in the last century). His wife's "maiden name" was *Draycott*.

Sometimes we are put off the track by nicknames. Take the case of *Don Saltero*, who used to haunt the coffeehouse of a fellow Irishman, equally eccentric. (The coffeehouse owner used to collect his rents himself, seemed never to spend a penny on his properties or himself, and left, when he died in 1852, half a million pounds to Queen Victoria, who cerainly did not need it.) The *Don* was really James Salter. He had been valet to Sir Hans Sloane (who originated in County Down). He had a little museum in a couple of cramped rooms and exhibited perhaps the oddest collection ever assembled, including "a necklace made of Job's tears" and "a piece of Queen Catherine's skin," perhaps castoffs from the magnificent collection Sir Hans left to the nation. In the *Weekly Journal* for 22 June 1725, *Don Saltero* or Mr. Salter burst into verse:

> *Through various employs I've past*
> *A scraper, Vertuos'-Projector,*
> *Tooth Drawer, Trimmer, and at last*
> *I'm now a Gimcrack Whim Collector.*

This is the Mr. Salter whom Admiral Sir John Munden cashiered for failing in his duty as a sailor (he was acquitted) and with characteristic irony dubbed *Don Saltero*. This is the same Mr. Salter whom Sir Richard Steele wrote about in the celebrated *Tatler* after visiting his rooms to see the "ten thousand gimcracks" that were crammed into them. This is a Mr. Salter who proves that in tracking down the local characters as one tracks down the origins and (more interesting to most people) the stories the locals tell about placenames and placenames, one comes across a lot of curiosities. One maybe becomes a kind of "gimcrack whim collector" oneself.

You could do worse than dabble in history and genealogy and fact and folklore. You don't have to visit each of the 55 streets of greater London named for the "Iron Duke" of Wellington (an unusually high number in a city where owners and developers fare better in getting streets named for them than heroes), though the British might not think that so strange. They might cheer you on, as they did the fellow who set out to have a beer in each and every pub in Britain (learning a lot about placenames and pub names in the process). They might encourage you if you are found to be searching for facts and fictions about American-connected names or distant relatives. But they'll also, in London and pretty much all over Britain, welcome the amateur historian who (as we might say) wants to know their country or city *by name*.

You don't have to "collect" names at all. Just keep your eyes open. You'll see things like *Of Alley,* created when a great duke's estate near The Strand was put up for sale. Five streets were put in, and someone wrote on the map *George, Villiers, Duke, Of, Buckingham.*

PART THREE

THINGS

There is everything in a name. A rose by any other name would smell as sweet, but would not cost half as much during the winter months.

—George Ade, *Fables in Slang*

16. Naming Patterns from Rock to Pets

To write about street names in London, we have seen, is to write about history and genealogy. To write all about the naming of things would be tantamount to writing the history of the world. We could explain where name brands come from (*Yuban* from "Yule Banquet"), where companies get strange names (*United Diversified; One Potato,* a restaurant in New York, and *1 Potato 2 Inc.* traded on the stock exchange as *SPUD*), how placenames create oddities (such as *Tightwad Bank* in Missouri), what the newest condom brands are in the US (*Rubber Check, Love Gasket, Birds 'n' Bees*), what businesses are named (*Emotional Outlet* for discount clothes; *Yellow Pages* for used books; *The Hanger Club* for a male stripjoint), how the Japanese get English tradenames all wrong and produce howlers (*Trim Pecker* trousers, *Nail Remover, Carap* candy, *Hand-Maid Queer Aids* for bandaids), what famous people called their horses (Lady Godiva *Aethenoth,* The Cid *Babieca,* Napoleon *Marengo,* Tom Paine *Button,* Alexander the Great *Bucephalos* or "Oxhead"), or what famous people called their pets (Hitler's dog was *Blondi,* FDR's was *Falla* and Nixon's *Chequers,* LBJ called his beagles *Him* and *Her,* Christopher Morley his cats *Will* and *Shall,* "because nobody can tell them apart," and Dorothy Parker called her parrot *Onan* from the Bible, because it "spilled its seed on the ground"). Call a goat *Earl Butz* after a politician. Call a Ferrari *Testarossa* for the "red heads" on the cylinder valves. Call a record store *Moby Discs* or an antique shop *The Den of Antiquity* or *Where Did You Get that At?* The world (as Robert Louis Stevenson remarked) is so full of a number of things. Here I shall look at a few things that interest me. I hope that they will interest you. We might just as easily talk of other kinds of things, other patterns of naming, sensible, foolish, astounding, merely interesting.

For example, take pop music groups. I've noticed their names are more than simply, understandably vivid. They fall into certain patterns. There are geographical references (*Chicago, Boston, Kansas*), and names suggesting "trips" used to be popular (*Jefferson Airplane, Grand Funk Railroad*), as did boasting

163

names (*The Supremes, The Miracles, The Marvellettes*). There were dada names chosen at random (*Strawberry Alarm Clock, Peanut Butter Conspiracy, The Joy of Cooking*) and strange names with obscure references (*The Grateful Dead, Iron Butterfly, Steppenwolf*). The old-fashioned *Four Freshmen* (or punning *Four Tops*) over the years gave way to *Led Zepplin, Cream, The Sex Pistols* until the punk rockers came up with truly outrageous names, both personal (*Johnny Rotten* and *Sid Vicious*) and for the bands (*Dead Kennedys*). You can trace the history of American youth from *The Beach Boys* and the surfers to sex and drugs and rock and roll, from the friendly name to the catchy one to the tricky one (*The Police*) to the unquotable one in the age of gobbing, slam dancing, and worse. *Fats Domino* was followed by *Chubby Checkers* and after many remarkable names we arrived at *Boy George, Sting, Billy Idol* and *Madonna*. The effort has always been to get noticed, generally not under one's real names (though we had *Simon and Garfunkel* and *Peter, Paul, and Mary* and many more) but under some stage moniker. The greatest performers and combos did not necessarily have show-stopping names (*Elvis* and *The Beatles*) but the less talent one had the more useful it was to have a name that could not be forgotten. At least one famous name, show-biz legend has it, came about accidentally. It was an era when much attention was given to group names. (*The Quarry Men* had been improved into *The Beatles,* for instance). The new group was told to think up a really outstanding name. They came back with something so obscenely "far out" that the agent's reaction was sheer incredulity: "The *who*?" So *The Who* was born, believe it or not. (Better not.)

The names of C & W (country and western) and some other kinds of pop music are folksy and less extreme, but in this field practically everything has been tried one way or another except the sort of anagrams that baffle most Americans in British crossword puzzles. Pop music likes to play with your heads, not so much with words.

I collected thousands of rock music names the way some people collect barbed wire: they are called "barbarians" and the names of barbed wire varieties include *Brink Twist, Split Diamond, Staple Barb, Arrow Plate, Watkins Lazy Plate, Scutt's Clip, Corsicana Clip,* and *Missouri Hump.* What you want to look for are patterns (and, if possible, the reasons for them): children's kites in Britain are named for birds, in Germany for dragons, in France for insects. Hurricanes used to get feminine names; now equal rights legislation has dictated that half of them be named for males. Some other time I'd like to tell you of the "taxi-nomy" of New York City cabs. Protecting themselves against lawsuits, owners like to form a new corporation for each taxi, so they need a great many names, and these are Life in the Big Apple in a nutshell, if you know how to interpret them.

You can't always figure things out, I found. US radio stations all are given initials beginning with *K* or *W*. I thought *WIND* would be for Chicago, the "Windy City," but the station broadcasts from Indiana. In New York subways I saw ads for *WJIT* in Spanish; it finally dawned on me that the station plays the *hits* for the Hispanic listeners. I've been interviewed on the subject of names (and also for my books on superstition, magic and witchcraft) on several hundred US radio stations. I always ask: what do your call letters mean? *KFRU* told me "Kind Friends Remember Us" and *WFIR* "We're First In Roanoke." Why did they choose the call letters of your hometown radio stations?

When we see a name it's natural to wonder where it came from, what it means. Codenames are intended to conceal information. Indulge me if I harp on codenames a bit here, but it's a pet peeve of mine (as a former air historian and a serving officer who learned firsthand that occasionally *military intelligence* is an oxymoron) that the armed services do not seem to have learned the rules of the game, and that can cost and has cost human lives and botched many operations. What do these codenames tell you: *Overlord, Torch, Ultra, Potus, Dasher, Sea Lion, Ghost?* Ideally, nothing. But in fact *Overlord* (the Allies' codename for World War II's D-Day operations) alerts you to something important and aggressive. *Ultra* (the British codename for the project designed to decipher high-level German communications during World War II) telegraphs "very important," a serious error. *Dasher* might be a codename for a person who rushes around busily; it was his protectors' name for President Carter. As soon as you figure out that *Potus* is a personal codename it does not take a genius to connect it with *President of the United States* (Kennedy at the time). If *Operation Sea Lion* and *Operation Neptune* convey "naval operations," whoever created them was giving aid and comfort to the enemy.

Never tell anything in a codename, unless it can be calculated to deceive effectively. The British in World War II codenamed a couple of spies *Mutt* and *Jeff*, stupidly risking that if the Germans learned of one they would perhaps guess the existence of the other or, if they found both names, would see the relationship. Worse, they were both male agents. *Operation Ranch Hand* was opaque enough for the "defoliation" of Vietnam. *Moose* (Move Out Of Saigon Expeditiously) was self-indulgently clever and unnecessarily, dangerously dumb. *Wacht am Rhine* was good insofar as it suggested surveillance (it was really a plan for attack)—but why a German phrase for a plan targeted on Germany? *Enigma* should never have been used for a decoding operation. G. Gordon Liddy of Watergate fame had some operations called *Diamond, Sapphire,* and *Ruby;* easy for those involved to remember, maybe, but too easy to interrelate: hear two and you know they are paired, three and you start looking for a whole set of gem names. Codenames should be short, unmistakable and impenetrable, ideally never recognized as such, never suggesting type of operation, location, time, or personnel involved. Diversion and disguise are needed. A good codename for a person is a non-personal name, and vice versa—but nothing *regularly.* If you must give a male a personal secret name, call him *Mary.* And no associates named *Jesus* and *Joseph,* for God's sake. But don't think you can be cute. If you use *Hawkins* for a man named Winter, we'll figure it out. I suspect you cannot—but intelligence may be super-intelligent, and persist until an answer is found. Don't let them suspect to start with!

You'll find my review of a book on codenames in *Names,* and mentioning that also gives me an opportunity to suggest that bibliographies and reviews in that journal and others (such as the British one, *Nomina,* and *Onomastica Canadiana*) can inform you about books on practically any aspect of names. Individual ones (*Tyrone Scour* for a cleanser, *Giant Runt* for a breed of chickens, *Molympic*'s grab at the closely-guarded *Olympic,* Sir Peter Scott's "monster hoax by Sir Peter S" anagram in the scientific name for the Loch Ness Monster, *Nessiteras rhombopteryx,* new personal or placenames, specific names for all kinds of things) may not be there. Important general discussions certainly will.

Back to our general discussion of the names of things, enlivened by particular examples. We were speaking of military codenames, like *Elephant Herd.* Let us add that the military does better with the names of weapon systems. In 1969 the US Army announced a policy for naming missiles: "Names should appeal to the imagination, without a sacrifice of dignity, and should suggest an aggressive spirit and confidence in the capabilities of the system. . . ." Understandably, they should be easy enough for military personnel to master and use daily. Other services favored such policies as well. Thus *Hellfire* for a *hel*icopter-*fire*d missile and *SAM* for *s*urface-to-*a*ir *m*issile. *TOW* was *t*ube-launched, *o*ptically-sighted, *w*ire-guided, and you know *ICBM* (*i*ntercontinental *b*allistic *m*issile, which you can see could have been *IBM*). In the current atmosphere of strong anti-nuclear sentiment and diplomatic *détente* (the use of a French word no American is quite sure of is significant), there has been a noticeable shift in the naming of such weapons from the hawkish *Titan* and *Minuteman* to the dovish and downsized: *Peacemaker* (a strange name for a weapon of war?) and *Midgetman.* Weapon names themselves are weapons in political struggles: journalism took on "Evil Emperor" Reagan in *Star Wars* and *SDI* (*S*trategic *D*efense *I*nitiative). Disarmament negotiations have created their own snappy lexicon: *SALT* (*S*trategic *A*rms *L*imitation *T*alks) and *START* (*St*rategic *A*rms *R*eduction *T*alks), both designed for the headlines and cozy familiarity. These short names are good both in their reduction of military jargon to initials ("optically-sighted" is the language of military personnel such as the adjutant who once informed me of a date of "beginning of cessation of duty") and in that they do not sacrifice real or precise meaning for a nifty acronym. The best of these terms achieve economy with felicity.

The navy will want equal time. It used to be said that warships were given feminine names "because it costs so much to keep them in paint and powder." Actually, anything that moves fast can be *she* in English, but *she* for ships has a more grisly origin: virgins used to be sacrificed to the gods of the sea and their heads, sometimes their whole bodies, were displayed on the prow to prove the gory tribute had been paid. Think of carved figureheads. Perhaps more interesting are ship names of the omen sort, which we got from the British (*Victory, Repulse, Dreadnought*). The Royal Navy distributes ship names rather more arbitrarily; the US names ships according to class, a different rubric for each type. Submarines have been named for fish and more recently for cities. When one was named for a city and not a fish an admiral explained, "Fish don't vote." When one was named for Corpus Christi (body of Christ, but also a city name), there was an uproar. Battleships are named for states (*Missouri* may be the most famous). Destroyers, frigates, carriers, and so on are variously named for famous sea battles, naval heroes, presidents and other political figures (preferably deceased, but exceptions have been made in recent years for nonagenarian House Armed Services Committee chairman Carl Vinson and retired admirals Hyman Rickover and Arleigh Burke—this can be dangerous, for in World War II there were 130 ships for each admiral serving and now there are two ships for every admiral).

Most of us are more familiar with pleasure craft, named in Britain and America with more wit and whimsy: *Sail La Vie, Forsail, Fred's Folly, Hob E., Sea-Esta,* and the policeman or lawyer's *Miss Demena,* reflecting on the whole some statement like, "I know this is an expensive extravagance but I love it, even if my wife hates it" (compare *Her Fur Coat*). Leslie A. Dunkling's always charming *Guinness Book of Names* has entertaining pleasure boat names and Don H. Kennedy did a whole book on *Ship Names* (1974). Years ago, Sidney Harris sighted (and cited) *At Ease* (belonging to an army officer), *Aftermath* (belonging to a high-school algebra teacher who sailed in the summer), and (in the Royal Navy tradition) *Impregnable* (belonging to a crafty obstetrician). "Collecting" such names is fun for young and old; there seems to be a need for a sense of humor if you are going to own a boat. Another aspect: the names tell us often that a boat is a great way to pick up women. *Sex-Sea* is a quotable example.

Many things are named more or less automatically for their creators or key people associated with the things. In medicine, for instance, a boost to research is the possibility of being remembered: *Salk vaccine, Down's syndrome, Karposi's sarcoma.* If the disease name is too hard for the public, it may become something like *Lou Gehrig's disease* or *Lyme disease,* substituting a more familiar name for a complicated technical or formal name. This can lead to insensitive jokes like "I have Parkinson's disease and he has mine," no laughing matter. In Congress, bills often bear sponsors' names: *Mann Act, McCarran Act, Gramm-Rudman.* That prompted Sen. William Sprong, Jr., of Virginia in the 1960s to joke that if he and Sen. Fong (Hawaii) and Sen. Long (Louisiana) were to introduce a bill to curb unscrupulous piracy of US pop music by Asian entrepreneurs, it might be the *Long-Fong-Sprong Hong Kong Song Bill.*

As the lure of such honors as titles stimulates people to serve society, so "putting your name on something" can benefit us all. Vanity, perhaps, but, as Bernard Mandeville argued centuries ago, "Public vice is private benefit." Seriously.

I take names very seriously and hesitate to treat them too lightly. I do believe, however, that amusing examples may sugarcoat the pill of instruction here, and throughout this book I have deliberately written in an informal, even a personal way. As a teacher I don't mind having to tempt you with tidbits to get you to swallow the main course. I appreciate the usefulness of the trivial. Trivia buffs relish the oddest names, even accidental ones resulting from "lexical opacity" of placenames (an important linguistic fact): *Peculiar United Methodist Church* or the *Gunpowder Friends Meeting* (of Sparks, Maryland, no less).

Purposely amusing names can be attention-getters in business and set a tone for those which do not want to take themselves too seriously. A. Ross Eckler, editor of the always fascinating *Word Ways,* has collected a large number of cute names of beauty salons; I have room for just one example, *Hair Apparent.* Clothes boutiques like to be cute: in the UK *Mother Wouldn't Like It* and in the US *Knit Wit.* A pet store might be *Fish and Cheeps,* a UK fish and chip shop near a nuclear facility is *Fission Chips.* More on word play in another section. Here, the results of a publicity stunt: when the Union Pacific Railroad held a contest for a new name for the train that was slated to transport San Francisco's garbage, entries included *Onion Pacific, El Crapitan, Odorient Express, Downwind Zephyr, Smells Fargo, the Excess Express,* and *Raw Trash Cannonball.* These are, as you realize, based upon the patterns of real railroad names known to the public already, and there are patterns in many other areas of naming, if you think about it. Making you think about such things is what the entertainment here is essentially about.

You may not be entirely aware of some naming systems, such as those for naming racehorses. Thoroughbred horses have impressive genealogies—they are all descended from a few Arab steeds of the eighteenth century, one of whom was named *Eclipse*—and their bloodlines offer an interesting onomasticon (collection of names) because it has been meticulously regulated and recorded. Workaday horses have names like pets (*Dobbin, Silver, Blaze*) and particular breeds can be named for places (*Clydesdale*) or people (*Morgan*), but authentic thoroughbreds have individually supervised and registered individual names.

Racehorses are not to be named for living people without the permission of those people (but who would refuse to have a racehorse, or a rose, named for them?). That is but one prohibition in an elaborate code promulgated by official breeding and racing bodies in order to avoid confusions and prevent mischief. The first Jockey Club was established for this purpose in England about 1750, the first US national club in 1893. Among other regulations, the US says the names of deceased horses can be reused after three years (it's one year in Britain) but a name used on turf or at stud cannot be repeated for 15 years, and the names of famous horses (like star sportsmen's numbers) are retired. No vulgar or obscene names are supposed to be used; some slip past (as with vanity license plates). No overt advertizing is permitted: the owner of the British horse *Mr. Volvo* had to change the name to *Mr. Vee* before the horse could compete in Olympic equestrian events (despite the fact that the Olympics are notorious for both patriotic and product promotion). Thoroughbred names tend to follow lineal patterns: *Native Dancer* out of *Polynesian, Shut Out* out of *Goose Egg,* and many "bold" offspring of *Bold Ruler.* A notable exception was the great Triple Crown winner *Secretariat,* whimsically named for Mrs. Elizabeth C. Ham, secretary to Christopher T. Chenery, founder of the stud farm which bred the colt. Well, it was better than *Hamfisted* or *Hamburger.* Mrs. Alfred G. Vanderbilt dubbed three of her expensive horses *Social Climber, Loser Weeper,* and *Crashing Bore*—possibly an autobiographical statement but certainly a self-fulfilling prophecy, for all three were aptly named flops. Prince Charles played polo once on *Christine Keeler* (a name notorious from a UK sex scandal), such indiscretion evidently permitted among devil-may-care polo ponies. A survey conducted at the close of the 1970s showed that the most popular name elements for racehorses were *Prince* (a component in the names of 275 active thoroughbreds) and *Princess* (125), *Mr.* (500) and *Miss* (800). Thoroughbred names appear to combine the boasting and humor of the names of other expensive hobbies (such as pleasure sailing, though yachts get fancier names than sailboats) with the attention-grabbing names of show business and the personal names we often give our pets when we have some scintilla of imagination and go beyond *Blackie, Brownie, Whitey,* where at least the diminutives express affection.

Probably no names in the world of things are as thoughtful or intimate, as affectionate and as psychologically revealing as the names we give our pets. We seem to think a name ought to fit a breed's nationality: *Fifi* for a French poodle, maybe *Manfred* rather than *Murray* for a Doberman. I called my Weimaraner *Wolfram von Eschenbach* (familiarly *Wolf,* a name he himself could pronounce) because he was not tan enough to be *Tannhäuser* but had to be German, just as my English sheepdog was *Randall* (house wolf in Anglo-Saxon). More often than not we give pets "people names," if playful or cute ones, regarding them as members of the family. (Psychiatrists are interested in where they appear in family photos.) We generally avoid unpopular names such as *Fred* and *Marmaduke;* only a klutzy dog would be *Harvey.* We prefer *Prince* to *Earl.* We give the name *Princess,* which makes it difficult for women with this forename or nickname. We also think animals are cute and give them cute names. *Adorabool* was a cairn terrier owned by Annabel Bool. *Ali Katz* was an alley cat that belonged to a Mr. Katz. Literary friends of mine called pets *Clarissa* and *Elvira.* I knew a puppy called (after Lord Olivier) *Sir Larry;* it "autographed" everything in sight. I knew cats called *Eenie, Meenie, Mynee,* and *Paderewski* (the last was "the peeingest"). I knew a Schnauzer called *Memo* ("put it down on paper") and I've heard someone's idea for "a large dog that doesn't get to go out of the apartment until walked late at night," *Niagara.* My own promiscuous mutt of years ago was *Lady Brett* (think of Lady Brett

Ashley in the Hemingway novel) and I then had a spaniel named *Wilmot* (his ears hung down like the huge full wig of John Wilmot, Earl of Rochester). The friends who convinced me to bestow on a Weimaraner the name I mentioned (*Wolf,* "a name you can yell in the park rather than a fancy one for the pedigree, a name the dog can pronounce himself"), had pets with similar names: *Ralph* and *Arfer* (as in Godfrey).

By the bye, should names of breeds be consistent as far as capitalization is concerned? Note I wrote *Doberman* and *Weimaraner* but I usually write *spaniel* and *collie.*

Since Latin disappeared, we don't hear *Rex* and *Fido* any more. Leash laws did away with *Rover.* Traditional names (*Spot, Lassie, Lady, Pyewacket, Tom,* etc.) cling but more common people names are forenames (seldom misspelled as with real if silly people like *Jhane, Traycie, Jere,* etc.) or even surnames (*Garfield* was named for the cartoonist's ancestor, a US president). Some animals also have nicknames, which show "personality." (Rom Harré in *Psychology Today* in 1980 said of people, "It may be better to be called Sewage than merely John".) The names are seldom as tin-eared as (say) Japanese product names (*Shot Television* and *Green Piles* lawn fertilizer—the "dirty word" expert Reinhold Aman of *Maledicta* has many more but I can't quote them here), or Czechoslovakian (*Polio* detergent), Chinese (*Pansy* men's underwear), Norwegian (*Blue Peter* sardines), etc., though pet names are chosen by name amateurs, not professional ad men. Famous names can be mispronounced for pets as are street names (like Chicago's *Goethe,* locally "Goth-ee"), especially Siamese ones (for Siamese cats). People name pets now with as much care as they name babies (for whom, sometimes, pets seem to be substitutes). People consult books like Jean Taggart's *Pet Names* and the more recent Carolyne Boyce Johnes' *Please Don't Call Me Fido.* No more simple names like "General" Custer's horse *Vic* or Calvin Coolidge's dog *Bessie* or simply *White Dog* (a present from Capt. John Smith to Pocohontas' father). No more *G. Boy* (J. Edgar Hoover), *Willie* (Gen. Patton's dog, played in the film by a miscast, British dog named *James*), *Elsie* (the first Borzoi in America), or *Duke* (John Wayne's dog, from which he got his own nickname). Now it's at least *Mike the Magic Cat* (which belonged to astrologer Jeane Dixon, though she was not the author of the book on dog horoscopes), *Brumus* (Robert Kennedy's pet Labrador), or Gen. Omar Bradley's poodle (that's right, poodle; that you are startled by his choice shows something more about our ideas about pets) named *Fifi* (named for a D-Day beachhead).

Many people take the occasion of naming a pet to make a joke. (Better then than when naming the baby!) If you try to compete, you are in a tough league. I'm not talking about the obvious *Llama Turner* and *Fernando Llama, Newt Rockne* and *Isaak Newton, Joseph Gerbils,* or *Himalaya* (the pet rooster who turned out to be a hen). Nor *Heinz* (a mongrel of "57 varieties") or *Jeff* (a mutt) or *Beau Tai* (the pretty Siamese cat), to note a more ordinary pet. I mean *Noam Chimpsky* (after the renowned linguist Noam Chomsky) for the chimpanzee they taught to communicate in sign language. I mean the cat named *Ben Franklin* (because "it went on the cover of the *Saturday Evening Post*") whose name had to be changed to *Ben Hur* when it had kittens (it had been a *her* all along). Sometimes pet names are brilliant. They can also be fun, and columnist Herb Caen invented a gopher named *Broke,* a crow named *Magnon,* a rabbit named *Transit,* a sparrow named *Agnew*—this was some years ago—and an aardvark named *A-Million-Miles-for-One-of-your-Smiles-My-Mammy.*

Enough of this monkey business. (What's your best shot at naming a pet monkey?) Now to other matters, like money business. A good name can make the difference between success and failure with a product. It can even *be* the product. Remember the *Pet Rock?*

17. Names in Business and the Business of Names

W e have already mentioned the names of some business operations and a few products. Now let's get a little deeper into names in an enterprise not usually viewed in commercial terms but very much a business enterprise: Academia. We have thousands of two-year and four-year colleges and universities (many of the latter with large professional and graduate schools) and other educational institutions all over America. Education is a multi-billion-dollar US business—and its prices have risen faster than inflation through the last decade. These organizations have huge "plants," several echelons of management, well-paid workers (many in secure or tenured positions), gigantic annual budgets. Above all, name recognition and image are a large part of their success. At some "name" institutions, student fees for tuition alone can reach $20,000 or more annually, and research grants bring the institutions millions. This is Big Business.

Much of our academic tradition in the US, including the importance attached to prestigious names, comes to us by way of Britain. British universities were first designated by placenames: the oxen ford over one river and the bridge over another river gave birth to *Oxford* and *Cambridge*. These two ancient citadels of learning (together commanding the prestige of *Oxbridge*) are collections of colleges whose names reflect religious connections (*Christ's, Jesus, Corpus Christi, All Souls, St. Edmund* [for a Scottish king]) or powerful secular patrons (*Queens* at Oxford, *King's* and *Queen's* at Cambridge, *Balliol, Brasenose* [from King Alfred's gift], etc.). Endowing educational institutions was both pious and practical, a ticket to reward in Heaven and fame on earth, two kinds of immortality. When the first college was established in America (1636), John Harvard contributed £800 and 400 books from his extraordinary library; they named the institution after him. Perhaps no one since has gained so much for so little outlay here. The fact that philanthropy could combine noble objectives with the desire to leave a man or woman's name behind them as a living memorial was not lost on our pragmatic people.

These days, every educational institution, large or small and public or private, is a business looking for support. An anonymous "director of development" (fund raiser) told Tom Buckley of the *New York Times* years ago just how gifts are handled. You target your donor, alumnus or alumna or someone previously totally unaffiliated. Then:

> After the gift has been agreed to and the technicalities ironed out, the president or the chairman of the trustees asks the donor if he has any objections to having this or that named for him. Naturally the old fellow says he doesn't or he isn't sure or that he really wants anonymity. The clincher is when we say we understand his reluctance, but that by letting us use his name he will encourage others to give.

And in the *New York Times* 5 March 1989: "Albert Nerken was not interested in having Cooper Union name a building in his honor—a customary reward for big donations [here 7 million]. But the trustees decided to name the college's engineering school for him." So the name goes on, college officials sometimes wishing that certain names were not so unattractive but fully aware that, whatever the vast endowments, money is always needed to maintain, let alone expand. Even if not imposing in themselves, the names of donors can add an element of distinction, and *Harvey Mudd College* sounds better than *Southwestern Tech*. Thus whole institutions, not merely libraries and gymnasia and such, are named. Some institutions have been named for people distinguished by their fame and not their donations (*William and Mary, Washington and Lee, Franklin and Marshall, Medgar Evers*) but philanthropy accounts for the honors to Eli Yale, Ezra Cornell, Peter Cooper, Leland Stanford (who named Stanford after his son), James Duke, Andrew Carnegie, Johns Hopkins, *et al.* Carnegie left the bulk of his immense estate to support libraries. One of the greatest givers of all (John D. Rockefeller) did not put his name on the University of Chicago, but in New York there is a *Rockefeller University*. When the names do go on, we get weird names on buildings at New York University and elsewhere and such awkward designations as *Little Management Education Institute* in Cambridge (Massachusetts) and *Brisk Rabbinical College* in Skokie (Illinois).

It might not be a bad idea if educational institutions with unfortunate (especially confusingly duplicated) names not derived from donors were to go out and find people willing to pay—these days some can give 10 or 20 million or more—for the privilege of putting their names on the colleges or universities. I would not like to dishonor the memory of St. Mary, St. John, or St. Joseph or the Trinity, but there are too many places already with these names. Find donors who have made a name for themselves in business and now want to have the name remembered in the business of education. When you do, I'd say to educational administrators, use the surname only: *Mary Hardin Baylor,*

Mary Holmes College, Michael J. Owens Technical College are not the best way to do it. Almost any personal name might be preferable to the characterless designations that serve as names for universities in such huge state systems as those of California, New York, and Wisconsin. Now a student may transfer from the University of California at Davis to the University of California at Santa Barbara (or Santa Cruz, etc.) or from the State University of New York at Binghamton to SUNY Stony Brook, or from the University of Wisconsin (by itself understood to be the Madison campus) to the University of Wisconsin-Green Bay. Foreigners think we have states they must have overlooked when they run across *Ball State, Slippery Rock State, Wayne State, Frostburg State.* Surely even public institutions could profit, both financially and aesthetically, from accepting new gifts and new names. A specific name attracts attention, evokes images and even associations, besides designating (though *SUNY Potsdam* or *University of Missouri-Rolla* at least tell you where they are). Even the names of college teams are important, as one can see from the great concern a little concern like Hollins College, for instance, recently took over the team name.

Now more traditional commercial names will be our subject. They create images and associations as well as naming brands. Originally there were no brands, just produce and products. Then someone realized he could sell *Sunlight* as well as generic bars of soap, so he printed a brand name on a wrapper, taught people to "ask for it by name," built goodwill and promised consistent quality and encouraged "brand identification." In time advertizing created "brand loyalty" and brand new merchandising techniques and expensive advertizing campaigns (after all, the consumer ultimately pays for them). The introduction of brand names into commerce created a whole new ballgame, a whole new name game.

Now millions are spent to try out possible brand names and millions more to establish and promote winners. This adds so much to the price of the item that a consumer move toward generic products has grown up, especially in pharmaceuticals (where the difference between the brand name and the generic can be well over 200%), but brand names are now part of American life and international trade. They are even more significant than company names (many of which, as we shall see, tell you little or nothing about the company), themselves carefully chosen. Before any business or organization of any kind spends a lot of money on logos, signs, or any other promotion of the name, it ought to spend plenty of time and money to get the best business name possible. A good name *means business.* It can often spell the difference between success and failure in the crowded marketplace.

The selection of a business name should depend as much upon common sense and the observance of certain basic naming principles as on costly market surveys and other advertizing experts' tools. Before there were any such things as marketing experts, George Eastman picked a name for his new camera, that name being short, punchy, and pronounceable in any language (well, almost any). It began with *K,* the first letter of Eastman's mother's "maiden name" but, more importantly, a letter Eastman thought had "strength." It had another sharp *K* at the end. It was *Kodak,* a brilliant choice. People like it. Some things they don't like. Writer Nelson Algren once advised us never to trust a company with *Honest* in its name. (When in the UK anyone starts a sentence with "I must be honest," expect them to be up to something else.) People don't like *Federal* very much either; lots of Americans are instinctively "agin the gum-mint," though *Federal Express* worked OK (and ought to have been the name of the US Postal Service, but there *Express* is unusual and you have to pay extra for it). Consumers have their own ideas about names. They expect *Philadelphia Cream Cheese* to come from Philadelphia, and are annoyed to learn it is from New Jersey. (Where does *London Fog* originate, do you suppose? Maryland.) *Jiffy* is fine for peanut butter but would be better for fast services of some kind. *Jiffy Funeral Home* is not appealing. My favorite name for a funeral parlor is one in Cuernavaca, Mexico, which they seem to have picked up from a movie without knowing any Latin; it's *Quo Vadis.* Pizza lovers expect a pizzeria to be called something like *Dino's* or you can rip that off with *Domino's,* but not *O'Brien's.* Right now in New York the name *Ray* is on many pizzerias and there's a fierce argument over who was the original Ray, just what you might expect in a town where we have restaurants with names like *Formerly Joe's.* Even *The Leaning Tower of Pizza,* I think, is a more effective name than *Original Ray's.*

Fashions and conventions change in business naming as they do in personal naming. Once popular names (*Acme, Ajax,* oddities like *Uneeda*) are now more or less out. *US* is currently more used than *American,* and I advise omitting the periods. Not long ago, personal names were favored in business but now they are increasingly confined to small operations (like pizzerias) and long-established cachet names, even ugly ones (*Gump's, Tiffany's*). We have *Cartier's, Harry's Hardware, Carter's Little Liver Pills* (or did the government make them change that one?). People used to be proud to put their names on their businesses: King Gillette also put his signature and his picture on every box of razor blades. Now personal names are on fashion and other "personal products"—that may be the chief difference between them and cheaper "imitations" —while big companies have names like *Spandex, Essmark, K-Mart,* and *Trilogy,* names which identify neither their products nor whoever is supposed to guarantee quality. What do they sell? The names deliberately don't say. Nebulous names like *General Services Corporation, General Products,* anything with *Technologies, Systems, Dynamics* in them, that's the ticket in these days of holding companies that hold other holding companies. Some few people think the more arcane the name, the more important some idiocy like *Unysis* must be.

Following that line of thinking, *Atlantic Richfield Company* changed its corporate name to *Arco,* and *CSX* (in "technology" and "energy" and a couple of other vague concerns) kept just the *C* from its origin in *Chessie,* or, to give it its full original name, the *Chesapeake & Ohio Railroad,* etc. When mergers and buyouts and other "restructuring" hit, it was best not to be tied to a too specific name. So *Radio Corporation of America* transcended its limitations with *RCA* and escaped from oldtime "radio" into "communications" and "information services," as did some former parts of "Ma Bell" (hiring me to explain the change to their employees, who at first were less than approving of *US West Communications* and the loss of the famous *Bell*). Today *US Steel* is impersonally *USX* in an attempt to scrap the rusty image and get a high-tech, mod "feel." When the Veterans' Administration became a cabinet post it cost just over $85 to change the name (mostly spent on signs) but when *Esso* became *Exxon*—notice the fad for sexy *X* in fabricated names—it cost hundreds of millions of dollars. Worth it? *Stanford Research Institute* was a name that boasted a good university connection; change it to *SRI International* and it sounds global. *United Aircraft* went bigger and better with *United Technologies.* When you might be in new markets overnight, the less committal your corporate name is the longer you can hold onto it. *TRW* is in over 90 businesses all at once and who knows what new ventures will interest it next, so don't change the name—just tip the letters *TRW* to the right to suggest forward thrust and stick to the initials. Don't explain what they stand for.

Business name changing has been going on since the beginning, at first generally with change of ownership (but prestigious law firms may continue to list partners long gone, and Arabs aren't going to change names such as *Harrods*), later for image. *Xerox* started out in the 1940s as *Haloid. IBM* (International Business Machines) began life as *Computer Tabulating and Recording Company.* What's unusual today is the rapid pace and proliferation of name changes; business is more volatile than ever. Overnight one can be in totally new business ventures or new adjuncts to one's regular activities, so the telephone company is *Nynex* (which sounds like a spray to keep the neighbors off your lawn) and atrocities like *Allegis* emerge. Even stable companies prepare for expansion: *US Rubber* changes to *Uniroyal* and can make anything.

Inevitably there are exceptions to the new rule, bucking of prevailing trends. Owners may still want the "strokes" of seeing their names or may try to keep the personal touch, even with a vast network of subsidiaries. They associate themselves strongly with their companies and products, trade on those connections, maybe appear in their own commercials boasting "I bought the company" or saying that they keep their eye on what they put their name on. So Victor Kiam and Frank Perdue become media personalities, Famous Amos peddles cookies, and (though *Jolly Time* is the oldest and best popcorn company) Orville Redenbacher puts his "sincere" and odd name on products and television. There will always be the newcomer who alters *Harcourt Brace & World* to *Harcourt Brace Jovanovich;* I think it would have been better for Mr. Jovanovich to have become Mr. World. You still have companies trading on Big Names (*Roy Rogers, Paul Newman*), capitalizing on real assets; however, fewer names of celebrities are bought these days: no one in his right mind would now rent the name of a movie bit-player like Arthur Treacher just because it "reads" as British and will suit fish and chips. Finally, there are always adventurous entrepreneurs who start out small with their own names, make it big, and keep their personal names on the business despite the growth of franchises. *McDonald's* was bought from brothers who sold their hamburger money-spinner to Ray Kroc (he was smart enough to avoid *Kroc* in the company name). Today the name, even the *Mc* prefix, is famous worldwide, a valuable asset. *Detroit Automobile Company* has long had the name of its founder, *Ford,* and now they have an innovation: "the quality goes in before the name goes on." Good. Names you never thought would appear on US autos are everywhere, including *Mitsubishi,* the "guys who gave you World War II in the Pacific," formerly famous for the Zero aircraft.

Japanese names have caught on, surprisingly. Cute names will do for smallish enterprises like coffeehouses (*Sacred Grounds, Hasbeans,* oddities like *Tenth Street Coffee House* on Seventh Street) or caterers for movie companies (*For Stars* is my favorite) or cleaning services (*Maid to Order, Jills of All Trades*). Decorators of the cheaper sort—the classy ones use personal "star decorator" names—can have names like *Room Service.* For pictures and framing, try *Off the Wall,* for boutique clothes *Hung on You.* A punkish leather shop might be *Hide and Chic* or *Male Hide* or *The Marquis de Suede.* Hot dogs are sold at *Franks for the Memory.* More subtle are *Iron Works* for a health food store or *Change of Hobbit* or *Murder Ink* for specialized bookshops. *Groomingdale's* is a ripoff for a pet care establishment and on Fire Island the *gays* appreciated a bucket-shop cheap flower stall called *Bloomin' Pails.* I liked *Tanks a Lot* for a place that sold aquariums and *Van Gogh* for a New York moving outfit (but that depends on mispronouncing the painter's name, not "Van Goch" but as "Van Go," as New Yorkers invariably do).

Cutesiness can reach extremes like *Goliath Bar* (a stone's throw in the old days from Jerusalem's *King David Hotel*) or be offensive. There are many examples, none to be seen here. In 1972 it was reported that an Italian state genetic engineering firm was going to be called *Genitalia;* they thought better of it. Despite all the money lavished on the selection of automobile names— always significant, as when cultural shifts replace *New Yorker* with *Malibu* or violent names are in vogue—there are foolish decisions made. They hired poet Marianne Moore to think up a new name for a Ford (she came up with a lot of bird names, suggesting grace and flight) and then executives called it *Edsel* for a scion of the Ford family. Chevrolet, at least one of whose cars ought to have been the *Fiasco,* called one automobile the *Nova.* Hispanics read this as *no va* (it doesn't go). These days, with international trade so important, you have to consider all the ramifications of any tradename in all possible languages. Austria's *Horny Phon* video recorder and Finland's mineral pills made of reindeer horn and called *Horn-Y* are not right for the US market. Similarly some of our tradenames are wrong for overseas.

A great tradename (provided that it is not in the public domain as a dictionary word or owned by some other company) will work wonders in the supermarket cereal section and everywhere else; it's more important than the name of the manufacturer to the consumers. The addict of (say) *Oreos* has a fondness for them that totally ignores whether the product is from General Foods, Pillsbury, Philip Morris, or a byproduct of the lumbering industry. Cigarette companies are under seige, have diversified into the food business and, for all I know or care, *Beatrice* (an example of a personal name that can cover a multitude of activities because non-specific) may now be involved in Arab and Mexican cartels to make *Oil of Olé*.

Brand names are arguably the most painstakingly chosen names of all in our society. Almost all names try to impress us or project an image or "make a statement." Brand names seek to go beyond that and manipulate us to spend our hard-earned cash. "Men are the constant dupes of names," wrote James Fenimore Cooper in *The American Democrat* (1838), perhaps anticipating General Semantics, "while their happiness and wellbeing mainly depend on things." Names and things are not the same. Semanticists Alfred Korzybski and S. I. Hayakawa and economist Stuart Chase demonstrated how people get confused about reality and how brand-conscious consumers mindlessly mix up names and things named. Brand names and the advertizing copy that accompanies them make strong appeals to youth, to masculine and feminine "roles," to basic drives such as hunger and thirst and sex and ambition, to the yen for novelty and excitement and "reward." "You deserve a break today." How do they know? Maybe you don't. Maybe you can't afford to be yuppie, "upscale," "exclusive," and all the rest. Maybe you have neither the taste nor the wherewithal for "quality" (by which they mean high quality and high price).

Madison Avenue *Mavens* work overtime (at high rates) on brand-name theories and strategies, positioning their products in the market (even battling for shelf space in the supermarket), trying to be noticed among the tens of thousands of items in your local "superette" (from the Latin for big and the French for small). At vast cost they tell advertizers that red sells better than green and that *Crest* and *Zest* rhyme with "best." They conduct market studies to see what the public likes, reminiscent of Robespierre's remark that "the people are in the street and I must see where they are going, for I am their leader." They conclude that the public likes *Brite, Rite,* and *Lite.* There must be something in it if they can sell you beer with more water in it as "light" or charge more for food containing fewer (they say "less") calories. Market research expensively informs advertizing boys' clients that *Carleton* has class and that *Montclair* makes people think of "coolness," fortunately not of New Jersey. Names also have not only to hit the right note but have to be singable, in jingles. Art advisers say we must avoid *g, f, y*; the descenders (bits below the line in lower case letters) are not as attractive as other letters from the graphic art and packaging point of view. All product naming *is* packaging. Packaging (as Andy Warhol showed us with Brillo boxes and Campbell's soup cans) *is* art.

Product naming is more of an art than a science. The "scientific principles" can be briefly stated in the expert advice of one of the many firms devoted to the creation of tradenames. Anspach, Grossman and Portugal's basic rule, for both product and company names, is simply this: "A name should be short, memorable, distinctive, and have no bad connotations or associations." Expert witnesses like myself have to be hired when, in the choice of a tradename, you step on someone else's legal rights or want to plead your own case for ownership of this valuable commodity of a good business name.

I keep saying, only partly because it promotes the consulting business, that before a company spends a lot of money promoting a tradename it ought to spend some on getting the right name in the first place. Bad names can be expensive to change. The rule with experts, from onomasticians to lawyers, is that it is always preferable to hire a couple of good ones at the start than a lot of them later on.

Lawyers are to tell you what you can get away with and what you can't. Name experts are to tell you that *All* and *Yes* will work for detergents, that you want it *All,* for in three little letters it says that your product will work at all temperatures, on all kinds of clothes, will get all the dirt out, works all by itself and is all you need for that "whiter, brighter wash" we have been told is the measure of success. *Total* will do for a cereal that gives you the total of all daily vitamin requirements (people who worry about the taste of cereals eat those that are mostly sugar). *Contac* is catchy and will work. Who cares if people don't realize it comes from "*cont*inuous *ac*tion"? Anheuser-Busch picked a winner almost inadvertently with *Budweiser.* When the boys in the bar took to calling it *Bud,* suggesting friendliness and camaraderie, the company found itself selling not just foam but fellowship. That company was less fortunate with *Natural Light,* no match for the more straightforward (and imaginatively promoted) *Miller Lite.* Americans really don't like the taste of beer much. That's why they drink it so cold. So making it "light" in flavor didn't bother them. Moreover, the "light" line in diet foods, though no one on a diet would drink beer at all, was popular with the public. Some other products have to stress the "hearty" taste. Not beer. We're having more than one. *Joe Sixpack* doesn't drink one, deeply satisfying beer.

Lite didn't really go against the grain. Some successful brand names do. *Easy-Off* I would have sold to the *Nair* (*no hair*) people; I would have come up with something else for an oven cleaner. I would have voted against *Dove Bar* in the executive conference: who wants to eat soap? I would have worried about *Toyota* (Mr. Toyoda's more auspicious version of his name, with a better number of strokes to write it in Japanese). Won't it suggest "toy auto" in the US? Apparently not. I wish I had thought of *Twinkies* or *Pooper-Scooper,* but I fear I would have come up with *Dog-Gone* or even *Doo-Whacka-Doo.*

There's too little in the cup to warrant *Lunch Bucket* for the heat-up snack; you're inviting complaint. *Opium* and *Poison* are just dumb enough to sell to people who think that the more a thing costs the more it's worth. *Obsession* is good; the ads are self-indulgent. Perfumes have their own rules. Call it *Charlie* (for Charles Revlon), call it *Cher,* but we no longer think France (*Evening in Paris*) is so romantic.

Products targeted for yuppies, dinks, others with plenty of "disposable income" have their own rules. Be sophisticated or obscure, not simple and direct, because you are selling sizzle not steak and indulgence rather than value for money. Pretentious is all you can say of the Swedish-named brand touted as "the Rolls-Royce of ice cream," *Frusen-Glädje* (made in Utica, New York, and it tastes like it). So "in" is anything Japanese that non-Japanese companies take Japanese names (*Atari* means "look out" in the game of *Go*), and Japanese cars are made in Kentucky but it would be death to put *American* on them. *Duz* and *Dash* "play well in Peoria" but are a bit corny for the big cities. There they fall for frauds like *Haagen-Daz* (another hopelessly middle-class ice cream dolled up in fake foreign finery) or like the supposed sincerity of *Ben and Jerry.* Watch what kind of people they put in the commercials: if you wouldn't be seen dead around them, you probably won't like the product they're peddling.

For all the studies, surveys, expertise, many a famous brand name has been arrived at by accident or last-minute improvisation. Armour & Co.'s deodorant soap started as *Nodor,* then *Skindew* and ended as *Dial,* allegedly because a desperate ad man glanced at the telephone (in another version, the clock) just before he had to face a conference with a better idea. Perhaps *Eureka* for the vacuum cleaner had a similar origin. *Fiesta* was unveiled only after Ford had passed over *Amigo, Bravo, Pony,* and *Bambi* for a sporty family "compact" (which sounds better than "midget car"). After *Dry-Wees, Winks, Tenders, Tads, Solos, Zephyrs* and more such tries, a manufacturer decided on *Pampers* (rivalling *L'Eggs* for the title of product with the most pieces sold). If you think *Doublemint, Captain Crunch,* and *Head 'n Shoulders* are a trifle inane, you ought to hear the names of the rejects. Unlimited advertizing budgets can accustom us to almost anything. A *good* name is cheaper.

Brand naming will always be part guessing, to some extent dependent on the vagaries of chance as well as the uncertainties of the marketplace. Will the Dodge *Demon* have a tendency to burst into flames or be hell on repairs? Will it offend the Fundamentalists (who saw demonic symbolism in a century-old Proctor & Gamble symbol)? Do *Kwik* and *Rite* sidestep verboten dictionary words or merely sound cheap? They may be right for Woolworth's but not for fancier stores. *Ayds,* well-known for decades, so far has not suffered from the AIDS crisis. Many Amerindians refuse to buy the *Apache* pickup truck; it has the name of their tribal enemies. *Irish Mist* passes in most contexts but *Mist* in German is "manure." Japanese *Black Nikka* scotch doesn't sell well in Harlem, and *Pschitt* sounds like a fizzy drink opening in France but fizzles here.

The surest formula for success will always be having a unique and compelling product to offer. The names of the following successful products did so well that the owners of the brand names lost them to the generic: into the dictionary went *aspirin, kleenex, xerox, coke* (for any cola drink), *dacron, nylon, linoleum, thermos, scotch tape, cellophane, zipper,* even *Jockey shorts.* Or they would be in the dictionary if lexicographers had the guts to honor the citations they have collected and did not back down under threat of suit. *Sanka* would be there except that the company stresses *Sanka Brand,* because we desperately need a dictionary word for "sans caffeine coffee." We already have the adjective, *decaffeinated.* A brand name can be lost as such if it becomes generic, like *Wedgwood,* or first was in the dictionary, like *hallmark,* though I have testified in court on both of these and the battles will continue as long as the money for lawyers doesn't run out, it seems. *Coke* is still "a registered trademark" and nobody at Xerox is pleased to have you "xerox a copy on the IBM machine"; both companies are understandably prepared to fight the loss of these valuable names, just as McDonald's will oppose you if you try a McAnything. But people do. Every time they do, it's another nail in the coffin of an exclusive tradename.

Jell-o (someone's wife thought it up) has been pretty well held onto by the trademark owners, but any gelatin dessert, cal or no-cal, we tend to call "jello," whatever the brand. The hyphen helps, as does an odd spelling. Mr. Hall might have kept *Hall-Mark* forever. Not *Hallmark,* which is in the dictionary and in the public domain, whatever a judge in Kansas City may think. Even *opry* (as in *Grand Ole Opry*) is in a (dialect) dictionary, a version of "opera." Anyone can use it.

Now 19 million Hispanics hear Spanish commercials on TV channels and 249 US radio stations every day and the Hispanic market here is $140 billion a year, roughly the size of the whole Mexican market. Spanish commercials (Pepsi has one featuring Chayenne, a Puerto Rican teen idol, and will have more) raise the question of tradenames in Spanish in the US. (But whose Spanish? Cuban? Mexican? Puerto Rican?) Separate ad campaigns in all kinds of Spanish is the answer, and that means experts in various aspects of Spanish culture and language.

If you don't know the language well, you wind up with "We Earn Our Wings Every Day," making Eastern Airlines ads in Spanish suggest people are going to die and become angels. It's said that "Coke Brings Good Things to Life" in Chinese communicated "Coke Brings Your Ancestors Back From the Dead." Another *classic* debacle.

For effective tradenames, as with the creation of any good names, you have to have a profound understanding of those tricky "bad connotations or associations." Language, as Edward Sapir said, is culture. Naming successfully means grasping every nuance of the culture or cultures involved. A great tradename is a marvelous marketing tool. It is also a complex work of art.

PART FOUR

NAMES, LANGUAGE, AND LITERATURE

How every fool can play upon the word!

—William Shakespeare, *The Merchant of Venice*

18. Word Play

People love to play with words, especially names. They delight in discovering there's a new cereal called *Wheatables,* that the new local shop has a "cute" name, that near the Ohio State campus a sign reads *Brazilia Gourmet Coffee and Hot Nuts.* The previous page in the newspaper that told me of that coffeehouse's name had a piece on "gut" college courses with unofficial names like *Rocks for Jocks* (geology at Princeton; "some of the Yale guts have somewhat more vulgar nicknames") and *McGut* ("Elements of Computing"). I have already mentioned nicknames (many of which play on personal or business names—remember *Monkey Ward?*). Does your kid make *Barf 'n Choke* out of *Burger King?* Did the recent presidential campaign create political jibes about *DuTaxes* and "Don't Beat around the Bush" in your area as well as play with the names of local politicians? Names are frequently the subject of word play, sometimes with severe personal pain or unwanted business loss. In this section we deal briefly with word play. We look at acronyms and anagrams creating names, and with play on names.

Acronyms, based on the initial letters of words in a string, are convenient, like *IBM.* They can be joked about (*IBM* in one film referred to the Mafia, "*I*talian *B*usiness *M*en"). *ICBM* (*i*ntercontinental *b*allistic *m*issile) was also taken to mean "*I* Cost Bloody Millions." *AFM* is said to be "*A*nything *F*or *M*oney," *FORD* was "*F*ix *O*r *R*epair *D*aily," *CIA* was taken, in the days when William Casey went from Wall Street to Washington, by some to mean "Casey's *I*nvesting *A*gain." Employees often have interpretations of the acronymic names of the companies which indicate their attitude: for one of the quotable ones let's turn again to *IBM* as "*I*'ve *B*een *M*oved." That complains of frequent transfers within the organization.

Short ways of referring to long names, acronyms (like *MIRV, AFL/CIO*) were first adopted as conveniences, despite the fact that some governmental and military acronyms were not only ugly and foolish (*CINCUS* for naval *C*ommander-*in*-*C*hief *US* was unfortunately pronounced "sink us") but hard to

185

say. Later people chose the acronym first and then fitted the words to it. *CORE* (*C*ommittee *o*f *R*acial *E*quality) was easily remembered and had good connotations. Then came *NOW* (*N*ational *O*rganization of *W*omen). Then came *WITCH* (*W*omen's *I*nternational *T*errorist *C*onspiracy from *H*ell, a radical feminist group like *SCUM,* the *S*ociety for *C*utting *U*p *M*en) and *MADD* (*M*others *A*gainst *D*riving *D*runk—or maybe it's *D*runk *D*rivers, it really doesn't matter a lot because the attitude is expressed). There are acronyms that practically nobody can "translate," like *DAYTOP* (*D*rug *A*ddicts *Y*ield *T*o *P*ersuasion) or that were never really meant to be "translated," such as *WAVES* (awkwardly, *W*omen *A*ccepted for *V*oluntary *E*mergency *S*ervice). In New York City we had *DOG* (*D*og *O*wners' *G*uild) squared off in a dirty fight against *SCOOP* (*S*top *C*rapping *O*n *O*ur *P*avements). *WHO* (*W*orld *H*ealth *O*rganization) and *UN* (formerly *UNO, U*nited *N*ations *O*rganization) and *NATO* are good acronyms, simple, direct, not torturing the meaning. Way out is Palm Beach (Florida)'s *R*edirected *U*nilateral and *M*ultifaceted *P*lans to *E*levate *L*ower *S*trata and *T*imid *I*ndividuals and to *L*iven and *T*rain *S*cared *K*ids *in* (something or other), *RUMPELSTILTSKIN.* As a rule, the military and education areas have the most foolish acronyms, I think. I like *SWAT* (*S*pecial *W*eapons *a*nd *T*actics, sometimes said to be *S*pecial *W*eapons *A*ssault *T*eam, which might be better) and from Watergate days *CREEP* (*C*ommittee to *R*e-*E*lect the *P*resident). I also like *CRAP* (*C*alorific *R*ecovery *A*nerobic *P*rocess, by which an Oklahoma company converted manure to methane) and *SWINE* (*S*tudents *W*ildly *I*ndignant about *N*early *E*verything).

I'd better substantiate my remark about the Defense Department (formerly the War Department, before "Peace is Our Profession" came along). The vast number of awkwardly named weapons systems, officials, commands, and operations gave us not only that "sink us" acronym for the commander of the US Fleet (singularly inappropriate after Pearl Harbor—an event known, by the way, by a placename) but also *SAC* (*S*trategic *A*ir *C*ommand), *MAC* (*Mili*tary *A*ir *C*ommand), *JUSMAG* (*J*oint *US M*ilitary *A*dvisory *G*roup), *CINCLANT* (*C*ommander-*in*-*C*hief, At*lan*tic), *DACOWITS* (*D*efense *A*dvisory *C*ommittee *on W*omen *in t*he *S*ervices, ignoring the general rule that only the more important initials are to be noticed), *MAAG* (*M*ilitary *A*ssistance *A*dvisory *G*roup), *MILREP* (parts of the words *Mil*itary *Rep*resentative), *SACEUR* (*S*upreme *A*llied *C*ommander, *Eur*ope), and thousands more, so that there had to be a vast *Dictionary of Acronyms.* For the most part acronyms serve a useful purpose in introducing economy into both spoken and written communication. However, when they are difficult to say at least half of their usefulness is in question. They also serve to hide the truth about "advisers" and "representatives" and such. When carried to the extreme, the practice serves only to create a jargon that baffles the outsiders and sometimes confuses the insiders, obscures, and introduces unconscionable complication. Military men are notorious for their poor education—the brightest of them, like Gen. Alexander Haig, not knowing ordinary words, consistently invented his own terminology—and this can be ludicrous, as when in 1969 a Major-General (whom I shall charitably leave nameless because he has now "faded away" like a good old soldier) told a special committee of Congress that "we have no way of knowing what the *PHILAC* does operationally because the monitoring devise is *COMUSMACV*." That even elicited laughter in the *SOB* (*Senate Office Building*).

"This officer" (as we used to have to say in RCAF written communications) at *AFHQ* in Ottawa invented my own *SIRBIDKW* and blamed every *SNAFU* on them that I could. Nobody ever questioned it or realized it was my abbreviation for *Someone Is Responsible But I Don't Know Who*. As one of the Air Historian's assistants I compiled a lexicon of RCAF, USAF, and RAF acronyms I had to know; it came to over 4,000 items, many of them incomprehensible in our "need to know" little world. The USAF acronyms, in my opinion, were the craziest of the three and at *NORAD* much of what was said made little sense to most people, as far as I could gather. Even when the acronyms at my request were "spelled out" I was often stymied.

It is only fair to say that non-military people create bad acronyms also. Sociologist E. Digby Boltzwell is credited with *WASP* (*White Anglo-Saxon Protestant*) in which the *W* is unnecessary (all Anglo-Saxons are white—and do not include, by the way, the Irish, the Scots, the Welsh, the Cornish, the Manxmen *et al.,* technically). Some official of the *NIH* (*National Institutes of Health*) coined a new name for a disease: *GRID* (*Gay-Related Immune Deficiency*). That had to be changed to *AIDS* when it became clear it was not just a "gay plague." Worst of all is the duplication of acronyms: how can Canadians, for instance, distinguish between *CPR* (*Cardio-Pulmonary Resuscitation*) and *CPR* (*Canadian Pacific Railway*)?

The most famous acronym now? I'm not sure, but how about *VCR* in the field of technology and *SWAK* in the field of letter-writing (*Sealed With A Kiss*) and the UK vulgar humor of *NORWICH* (based on the placename and spelling "knickers" with an *N* to make it work, it's *Nickers Off Ready When I Come Home*, a *randy* remark?).

There are placenames derived from acronyms: one is *Sasco* (Arizona), from *Southern Arizona Smelting Company*, which became a ghost town when the company pulled up stakes in 1921. Some people (wrongly) believe *Azusa* (California) is from "A to Z in the USA." We see punchy corporate names like *Amoco, Texaco, BP* (*British Petroleum*). Product names include *BVD* (*Bradley, Vorhees and Day*). Transportation names include *Amtrak* and *BART* (*Bay Area Rapid Transit*). Country names include *Pakistan* (a composite of *Punjab, Afghanistan, Kashmir, Sind, Baluchistan*). Slang expressions abound: think of *BYOB* (*Bring Your Own Bottle*) and *BMOC* (*Big Man on Campus*). We use acronyms from foreign languages, such as the French *RSVP* (*répondez s'il vous plaît,* "answer please"), and many words in our own language were originally mere acronyms, such as *radar* (*radio detecting and ranging*), *laser* (*l*ight *a*mplification by *s*timulated *e*mission of *r*adiation), and *scuba* (*self*-contained *u*nderwater *b*reathing *a*pparatus). We use initials to invent new fore-names, such as *Arjay*.

I once had a student named *Usmail*, which I at first thought was some Hispanic version of *Ishmael;* it transpired that he had been named for the only contact his family in a remote Puerto Rican village enjoyed with the outside world, the red-white-and-blue truck that came frequently and had painted on its side *US Mail*.

I still have not mentioned one of the most common and resourceful uses of initials in word play, a use that most of us chuckle at or grimace at every day. I am referring to automobile "vanity" license plates, a popular way in recent years of expressing individuality and of cheaply making "a statement," as one so *easily* does with T-shirts with messages. Since California introduced these plates in 1970 Americans have taken to them like a duck to orange sauce, for ego trips or just plain fun. We all have ones we remember. How about *PHLOP* (on an Edsel), *A1 N A2* (Lawrence Welk's plate), *U-2* (a New Jersey undertaker), *XMAS* (William Noel), *BUGSY* (Western Exterminator Company), *YB BALD* (hair replacement specialist), *SNAAB* (a proud Saab owner) and *FANCY VW* (a Porsche owner with a sense of humor about it)? Personal names are seen (*JAX JAG* on a Jaguar), personal boasts (Muhammad Ali's *ALI 3 WC,* reminding observers of his three world championships, forgetting that *WC* is toilet). I saw lightweight champ Darrin Van Horn drive off in *1 BOXER*. There are also personal jokes and *OOO BABY* (seen in *L.A.*).

To "keep it clean" California and later other states banned combinations of letters such as *ASS, BUM, JEW, MEX, SEX, KKK, BRA, FAG,* etc. The American Association of Motor Vehicle Administrators got together and published a long list (these days we say a "laundry list") of proscribed combinations, mostly obscenities but some religious and racial and other references as well. In Québec *FOU* is ill-advised and in some places other foreign-language ploys have been used to put one over on the censors. Arthur Berliner collected quite a few striking examples when he was living in Connecticut.

In my neighborhood there's *LIPSTICK* on a red car and some *gay,* Jewish, or other "in" jokes. One plate I'm dead against is *NONE*. A Las Vegas resident with that plate received a bill for $900 from the traffic violations office when all the tickets that police wrote up there for cars that had no plates at all—the officers scribbled "none" in the space on their forms for license numbers—were spewed from the computers in his name.

The clown who has *STOLEN* on his vehicle is courting trouble. The average Joe (or Jane) just wants his (or her) little joke, maybe some of the distinction and special ID that politicos and such get with low numbers and other favored plates. The Queen of England needs no license on her vehicles. Her sister Princess Margaret was once given as a present *HRH 1* by an admiring commoner. In Britain you can transfer your plates from one vehicle to another and there's a brisk market in accidentally "good" ones, accidental because you cannot in Britain order a special message for your license plate. Here in the US you can enliven your trips by keeping an eye open for amusing plates. It's an entertaining game for the kids who otherwise get bored on long journeys (if you don't mind explaining *RU 12* and *I M NOT* to them). For a catalogue of "vanity" plates see T. C. Murray's *The License Plate Book;* it has more than 1,000 examples and hints on "how to recognize the hidden messages."

These are not the only name games you can play. More difficult are backward word play and palindromes. James Thurber cited the "backward" tribe known as *Sesumarongi.* An entire straight-faced essay has been penned about the *Nacirema,* with their secret "shrine rooms" (for excretory functions) and their hero named *Notgnihsaw.* It's "Body Ritual among the Nacirema," by University of Michigan anthropologist Horace Miner. Look it up. Forenames include *Silopanna* (*Annapolis* reversed) and placenames include *Ukiah* (California, *haiku* reversed). There was a man named *Neblow Wolben* and in a vampire story we encounter Dracula masquerading as *Alucard. Retlaw* was the name of a corporation based on Walt(er) Disney's first name. There was a pleasure boat named *Topknits.* In the 1960s there was a hassle in Santa Ana (California) when someone sobered up enough to notice that the streetname *Initram* was in questionable taste. In 1976 the Derby Lane dog races in Florida were won by *Cilohocla.* In Texas the town named *Tesnus* turned *Sunset* around. *Rockwell Springs* became *Nedrow* in honor of some character named Worden. *Pekin* (Maryland) was changed to *Nikep.* A spate of publicity followed, which is what I suppose most such name changes are all about.

Now, palindromes: words (or sentences or numbers) that read the same backwards or forwards, like Adam's *Madam, I'm Adam* or Napoleon's *Able was I ere I saw Elba,* or the paean to Teddy Roosevelt (*A man, a plan, a canal: Panama*), not as beloved as the teddy bear (named for him). Word fun, "recreational linguistics" as A. Ross Eckler's ever-clever journal *Word Ways* puts it. Eckler has published a whole book of *Names and Games,* great fun for logophiles, as are the various works of Willard R. Espy, Laurence Urdang's nifty journal *Verbatim,* etc. Traditional, accidentally palindromic forenames (*Asa, Anna, Hannah*) have encouraged weirdos like Asa and Hannah Reynolds to name their children *Alila, Anna, Asa, Atta, Axa, Aziza, Iri, Numun,* and more. I trust the children have by now conferred and put those parents into custodial care. Cutesy names are for pets and pillowtalk, not to be inflicted on helpless offspring. That goes for backwards names and the personal equivalent of *Atteentee* (AT&T, a road in Springfield, Virginia) or music-biz pop names (*Whodini, Nayobe, Motley Crëw*) and off-the-wall names for pets (more in *The Cat Doctor's Book of Cat Names,* by Susan McDonough, DVM) and subdivision streets (at *Camelot* in Fairfax, Virginia, *Round Table Court* and *King Arthur Road;* at *Christmas Lake Village* in *Santa Claus,* Indiana, the three main streets named for The Magi: we made up *Balthazar, Melchior, Caspar* when the Bible didn't give their names and we thought names made the story more convincing). There are other kinds of whimsy (or worse).

Leave name games to the anagram experts like Andy Aaron who sees that *George Herbert Walker Bush* contains *Rob Greek, Slaughter Hebrew* while *Michael Stanley Dukakis* is otherwise *Sank Humiliated Lackeys* and *Vice-President Quayle* is both *Evidently Epic Square* and *Nice Depravity Sequel.* I would add that *Canada* was once said to contain Spanish *Aca nada* (nothing there) and that I disapproved of religious fanatics seeing *Ronald Wilson Reagan* as the Anti-Christ (the letters of each name produce 666, the Mark of the Beast in *Revelations*), but I do see in *Ronald Wilson Reagan* the possibility of *Age, war and sin roll on.*

Would you like to play more word games? Try Odd Couples, *Tom* and *Diana Sawyer* or *Harrison* and *Gerald Ford.* Or create imposing names by putting together real names with common elements. What Southern college would not admit *Thomas Jefferson Davis?* How about *Arlene Francis Scott Key Fitzgerald Kennedy?* Or *Debra Harry S Truman Capote?* Some players don't bother about spelling and will accept the likes of *Diana Meryl Streep* or *Loretta Switt Rosie O'Grady.*

Title sequels: *The New Improved Testament, 1985, The Return of the Screw, Son of Son of Sam, The King and II, Jonathan Livingston Sequel.* Or musicals from classics: *Blood!* a (Bram New Musical of *Dracula*) and *Oedipus Rex* as *Life with Mother.* Plenty of word games appear in Mary Ann Madden's competitions in *New York* magazine. They involve such diversions as Fractured Names: child star/evangelist *Shirley Temple Macpherson* and the Spanish-language newspaper of Cannes, *Heraldo Riviera*, etc., etc., *und so weiter.*

19. Name Inflation: The Debasement of Language

I'm something of an expert on the debasement of language: I used to give as my "Merry England" speech (see Kingsley Amis' *Lucky Jim*) an after-dinner talk on "A Guided Tour of Gobbledygook." I got a lot of mileage out of it until it appeared in a couple of anthologies (*Classical Rhetoric for the Modern Student* and *A Question of Choice*) and I had to work up a new *schtick*. I wrote that about 30 years ago, and because I have spent the interim in academic and other circles where jargon and gobbledygook run rampant, I could hold forth on the subject practically endlessly. I shall confine myself to making this the briefest piece of all, just enough to make the point that onomastics concerns itself with more than the names of persons, places, and things; name study likewise gets into nomenclature, terminology, argot, euphemism, cant, the silliness of people who speak of *wellness* when they mean *health,* who breathe deeply while exercising and prattle about *aerobics,* who use words like *holistic* or can describe an invasion as an *incursion* or a crash in the stock market as a *downturn in the upswing* or your loss as someone else's *profit-taking.*

Educationalists babble about *overachievers* and *special education* and *remedial English* for those who have nothing to be remediated, not having learned *communication skills* in the first place, who now need *compensatory education* or *developmental education* or something to keep them from being educationally *underprivileged.* Bureaucrats waffle about *community-based programs, culturally-deprived environments* (also called *ghettos,* better called slums), *deinstitutionalization, infrastructures, a matrix of services, operationalizationalism, outreach, prioritization, proactive interreaction* (the product of *think-tanking* or maybe just *future planning*), and *viable scenarios of functional utilization within a feasible time-frame.* The "Intelligence Community" (which refers to the CIA as the Company) deals in *destabilization, disinformation, black bag jobs, terminations with extreme prejudice,* and the collection of facts, rumors and lies (*raw data*) by people (*humint*), communications sources (*comint*), electronic devices (*elint*) and signals (*sigint*), *covert activities,* etc.

191

CHAOS was their operation to find the Commies in the US anti-war movement, *Mongoose* their plan to assassinate Fidel Castro, *Mkultra* their research (begun 1953) into mind control via LSD, sensory deprivation, hypnosis, etc. The old garbage appears in the *New Age* with gurus and pseudoscientists of all persuasions, *assertiveness training, biorhythms, bioenergetics, est, do-in, macrobiotics, RET,* everything from acupuncture to *zone therapy.* The craziness of psychiatric terminology has given birth to a descriptive word of its own: *psychobabble.* Sociologists are too easy a target to be worth attacking, but we might note drug addicts are called *users,* illegal drugs are *non-decriminalized substances,* and the problem gets worse at least partly because those who are supposed to deal with it don't know what they themselves are saying or doing. You hear what I'm saying? I mean, you know what I mean, like? Right (if you will)!

Wine buffs (there's a fancy word for that—never use it) chat about "a pleasant little growth whose presumption will amuse you." The computer *hackers* have a language of their own, only dangerous when we start to regard people as machines with *input, output, overload, burn out,* and things that *turn them on.*

You think all this is mere nitpicking? You couldn't care less? ("I could care less" means the same thing now.) See the power of terminology: how many little *dolls* do you think manufacturers could have sold to *boys* had some genius not coined the term *action figures?* It's not simply that we can no longer understand legal documents without a lawyer (or IRS instructions even with the CPA trying to figure them out also). We've reached the point where you can't tell the difference between a janitor and a general—let's talk of the *superintendent* of West Point—and a carpenter might send you a bill for driving a nail specifying *on-site unit installation of interfibrous friction fastener.* At the same time your doctor who won't say *cancer* can hardly say anything else you can understand.

It's language inflation: every garbageman wants to be a *sanitary engineer.* It's euphemism: a *preemptive strike* means hitting them first. It's downright lies: *police action* (war), *freedom fighters* (insurgents), *contras* (rebel forces), and *glasnost* (which translates "public relations," not "openness"). It's polysyllablism and evasion: *impact assessment, privatization* in the UK and *income supplements* in the US to *recipients* who have no other income. Charity cases became *welfare cases,* then *welfare recipients,* and are now *welfare clients,* with *entitlements.* President Bush swears there will be no more taxes, but as you "read his lips" read also *revenue enhancement postures may have to be initiated.* How we'll do it is not *finalized* but if there is a chance to do it (*window of opportunity*), count on it, especially now that so many *senior citizens* and *terminal cases* have to have *extended care facilities* and even *dental health maintenance organizations* are ruinously expensive. Or do I *misspeak?* OK, all previous statements are *inoperative.* I misled (lied to) Congress, too. I get so confused with what the president remembers and doesn't remember and with

Watergate, Billygate, Irangate (I liked *Iranamok* better), *Abscam, Wright's Wrongs* in the House of Representatives. . . .

Politics and advertizing and other professions requiring a fair amount of lying inevitably debase the language, as George Orwell so brilliantly proved in "Politics and the English Language." William Safire notes that the Gettysburg Address today would allude not to the Civil War (War of Northern Aggression, if you prefer) but to a *recent period of uncertainty involving fairly high mobilization.* The contribution of politics to name slang (*gerrymander, Hooverville, Reaganomics*) is nothing compared to its vocabulary of debasement and deceit. Nobody expects advertizers or public relations flacks to be anything but economical with the truth. The rest of us need clear, honest words to work with.

Understand that I am not objecting to changes in the language. That is a healthy and inevitable thing. Nor do I balk at witty manipulations of the language; they yield us everything from puns to great poetry. The creation of a phrase (the *Great Society, voodoo economics*) can be very useful, as can even vulgar political jibes (*Don't step in Dukaka*). But when *tree* is replaced by *reforestation unit* and *death* becomes *negative patient care outcome* or "Nature's way of telling you to slow down," we have lost the vigor of *went west* or the pilots' old favorites *pranged, bought the farm, old Newton got him.* Then the "green language" of slang has given way to the grey language of euphemism, pusillanimity or pomposity. Terms and names in general must be kept sharp tools of thought. Inflation cheapens our language as surely as it does our money.

The consequences may be fatal to more than communication, for the mouthing of trendy neologisms may dull our minds to the reality of what we are saying or mean to say, which can have horrendous outcomes. In the words of Anthony Burgess, reviewing Judith S. Neaman and Carole E. Silver's *A Dictionary of Euphemisms* (1983):

> The people who make a fortune out of the instruments of death are to be called the Armament Community, which replaces the Munitions Interests strongly disliked by opponents of the Vietnam War. Total nuclear war has become an All Out Strategic Exchange. The strategy planners are Defence Intellectuals. A nuclear explosion is an Energetic Disassembly.

Remember *MAD* (*m*utual *a*ssured *d*estruction).

20. Names into Words

Another very brief entry, this one on a subject that the late, great Eric Partridge and others have devoted whole books to discussing: the people and places that got themselves into the dictionary. New words can be lively as well as deadening political and bureaucratic jargon, obscurantist and vulgarizing or strikingly useful, even if they come into the lexicon through the back door, as slang. Slang has a habit of substituting a euphemism or more convoluted term for a perfectly good word or phrase but often enriches us. *High hat* and *couch potato* are both neat and useful terms. *Crumblies* is new, cruel but powerful. *Duds,* centuries old, says something "clothes" cannot. With words derived from names, some words come from the name of the person who invented or is associated with the concept, others from the names of authors or their characters, some from placenames (*Watergate* was once merely an apartment building but later spawned many imitations, so that when a Congressman named Flood got into a sex scandal in Washington we conveniently had *Floodgate*).

The dictionary honors Captain Boycott, the Marquis de Sade (who was actually only a count, I think), Louis Braille, Rudolf Diesel. Maybe you've heard that sideburns were made famous by a Civil War general named Burnside or have actually been misled into believing that *hookers* came from a Gen. Hooker. But did you know that military men also gave us *cardigan* and *raglan* and another name (*Napoleon*) for a pastry the French call *mille feuilles?* Or that *grog* recalls a British admiral? The Norwegian traitor Vidkun Quisling proved that you don't have to be a Good Guy to get your name in the dictionary along with *silhouette, mesmerize,* and *guillotine* (the good doctor who invented the latter having designed it as a swifter, more merciful method than the ax). Sometimes in the process the meanings of the words undergo a sort of sea change: *derrick* is named for a London hangman himself rather than the tall gallows he introduced.

Some words have a long history in this line. Akedemos was a Greek who started a garden. Plato walked and taught in it, so a school became an *academy*. We have made words out of the names of mythological persons (*atlas*), biblical persons (*jezebel, doubting Thomas*), and literary characters (*shylock*). Research turns up the origins of *tawdry* (cheap trinkets were sold at medieval fairs of St. Audrey) and *dunce* (Duns Scotus was the brilliant St. Thomas Aquinas' theological opponent) and much more, including *all around Robin Hood's barn, Pyrrhic victory, higher than Gilderoy's kite, tighter than Kelsey's nuts, Hobson's choice, according to Hoyle*. We got *hamburger* from Hamburg (and then invented *cheeseburger,* etc.) but *sandwich* is a placename become a title become a word: John Montagu, fourth Earl of Sandwich, put his meat into slices of bread so he could snack without having to leave the gambling table for the dinner table.

We have *macadamized* roads thanks to John McAdam. We named *zeppelins* for the German Count Zeppelin. We got *saxophones* from Adolph Sax and *bloomers* from the nineteenth-century feminist Amelia Bloomer. Two engineers, Anton and John Klieg, developed *klieg* lights and one Dolby the *Dolby* sound system.

British policemen are known as *bobbies* and used to be called *peelers,* both words derived from the name of Sir Robert Peel, founder of the Metropolitan Police. That was an unusual case of both forename and surname being used and for the same thing. Examples could run on *ad infinitum* so let's have just three, all language terms: *bowdlerize* came from the English editor Thomas Bowdler (who in 1818 removed from Shakespeare's works anything he thought likely to be offensive), *spoonerism* is from an addle-tongued Oxford don named Spooner (who used to slip and say "queer old dean" when he meant "dear old queen"), and *malapropism* is for the sort of thing Mrs. Malaprop used to do in Richard Brinsley Sheridan's play *The Rivals* when she spoke of "an allegory on the banks of the Nile." Funny how the same sort of *mal àpropos* expression was not named after Shakespeare's Dogberry or other dramatic characters who got the same sort of laughs well before Sheridan. In America we have *Goldwynisms* such as "include me out" and "every Tom, Dick, and Harry is named Sebastian." Yogi Berra got a reputation but not a dictionary entry for statements like, "It ain't over till it's over."

It means a lot of linguistic archeology now if you want to unearth the originals of *the real McCoy, my name is Haines, tell it to Sweeney,* but I can quickly explain *John Hancock* (signature): that patriot affixed to the Declaration of Independence a very large signature so that King George could "read it without his spectacles." Or *Annie Oakley* (free admission pass). She was a star of the Wild West show, so great a shot she could shoot holes in playing cards thrown up into the air, so her name was used for free passes (punched, so that they could not be submitted for "refund") issued when showmen *papered the house.* Her name was once well-known; today it's practically forgotten (along with other theatre slang such as *do as Garrick did* and many others I wrote about in a piece on theatre slang in *Dramatics* years ago) because we now say *freebies* for such free tickets, and they are not customarily punched any more.

Any regular dictionary, or the *Dictionary of Slang and Unconventional English* or the *Dictionary of American Slang* or the British *Dictionary of Catch Phrases,* will have many words, current and obsolete, derived from real and fictional persons still famous or now obscure. We have no space to list all of them I have written about in *Pageant,* in *Word Ways,* and elsewhere.

I do want to notice briefly, however, placenames that have entered the dictionary as words. A short list would include *mecca, badminton, tuxedo, cantaloupe, waterloo, donnybrook,* and *bunk* and *bunkum* (both from a windbag Congressman from Buncombe County, North Carolina), as well as *Arizona tenor, Arkansas toothpick, go Hollywood, New York steak, Storeyville jazz, Beale Street blues,* etc. *Bedlam* is from the hospital for the insane in London of yore, St. Mary of Bethlehem. Notice how altered spellings may disguise origins.

Most people don't know that we got *dungarees* from Dhunga (India) and *jeans* from Genoa. In *Geolinguistics* I wrote extensively on words derived from placenames as evidence of ancient trade routes of textiles from France to England (*denim, corduroy, cambric,* etc.) and the "words with the place of origin stamped right on them" such as *cashmere, muslin, tangerine.* For terms such as *Texas leaguer* and *Bronx cheer* we know the geographical origin but usually not the circumstances which gave rise to the expression. We have *Balkanize, Finlandize,* and *Concord grapes* (from Massachusetts, not New Hampshire).

Words derived from names are featured in Ernest Weekley's *Words and Names* (1932), Bill Severn's *People Words* (1966), Eric Partridge's *Name into Word* (1970), and Willard R. Espy's *Thou Improper, Thou Uncommon Noun: An Etymology of Words That Once Were Names* (1978). See, too, James A. Ruffner's *Eponyms Dictionary* and Gerald L. Cohen's always lively but thoroughly scholarly journal *Comments on Etymology.* For that matter, thumb through *Webster's* (preferably not one of Webster's own dictionaries, in which you'll find *soup* as *soop*) and you'll be surprised and delighted at the number of people and places that have attached their names to things, not to mention terms like *Dickensian* and (they ought to be up to date) *Pinteresque.* Frank W. Tompa and the computers of the University of Waterloo (Ontario) searched the *New Oxford Dictionary* for me and turned up the following words from North American names: *acadialite, barnumize, boston* (but not *Boston coffee* and *Boston marriage*), *bowie-knife,* and so on down to *pocosin* or *poquosin* (from Algonquian "at the widening," now the name of a river in Virginia) and down the alphabet to *zunyite* (from the name of a mine in Colorado).

I wish I could establish *Ashleyize,* a verb meaning "to point out the bull - - - - in semi-literate, semi-meaningless statements that contain the word *meaningful* or the word *hopefully* misused." Also, I would hope (not "hopefully") that as *Bartlett's* means the book of quotations and *Robert's* the rules of order this book of mine might make it the *Ashley* of names and my humble self the *Hoyle* or authority on the rules of the name game.

21. Names in Literature

We have touched briefly on topics worth a whole book each; here is a topic worth a whole shelf of books, literary onomastics, the study of the way names function in fiction. European scholars have a headstart of centuries on their American counterparts in the study of placenames, but in literary onomastics we are among the world leaders in a study that goes all the way back to ancient Greece. As Elizabeth Rajec's bibliographies of *Literary Onomastics* make abundantly clear, names in literature, studied of course to some extent by all literary critics, are something of a specialty in the US.

As early as *Names* 11, a generation or so ago, Warren R. Maurer noted that "well-chosen character names" are "an integral part of a literary work of art." This generation of critics has studied them attentively. The case for American prominence in this field was stated by one of the leading US practitioners, W. F. H. Nicolaisen, a names scholar who (as we mentioned earlier) established an international reputation in placename study and then moved to names in literature, partly by way of names in folklore. In 1975 he reported in *Onoma* 19:

> If there is any aspect of the onomastic sciences which has made exceptionally noticeable advances in the United States over the last two decades, it is the field of *Literary Onomastics,* the study of names in literature. Like onomastics in its relationship to linguistics, its literary offspring started out in a handmaiden capacity serving, as Arthur F. Beringause put it in his introduction to the "Special Issue on Names in Literature" of *Names* (Vol. XVI, No. 4, December 1968), as "an indispensable aid in literary criticism." The fact that *Names,* after publishing a fair number of individual articles on this topic scattered throughout its volumes, should devote one of its rare special issues to this subject, alone speaks of the importance and status which literary onomastics has achieved in the United States and amongst the members of the American Name Society. That there has been, since 1973, an Annual Conference on Literary Ono-

mastics staged by the State University of New York at Brockport, resulting in a new journal *Literary Onomastics Studies,* further underlines this status. . . .

That CLO in upstate New York I have addressed on numerous occasions and my call for a broadening of the concept of literary onomastics (at a CLO banquet) appeared in the journal and in *Names in Literature,* a collection of articles on the subject edited by the leading spirits of the CLO, Grace Álvarez-Altman and Frederick M. Burelbach, already noted in an earlier section. For a German journal at Karl-Marx University (Leipzig) I reported on "Literary Onomastics in the United States: Its History and Its Future." There I stated that "by concerning itself with the author's strategies of communication, literary onomastics helps to stress the utilitarian aspect of literature in an age when meaning is a much-debated term and when some critics seem determined to put themselves out of business by arguing (or demonstrating) that nothing significant should or can be said these days about such old-fashioned things as the author's intent or the 'pot of message' of which H. G. Wells once wrote." In a keynote address to CLO I argued that "in watching authors use names effectively, we see points made clearly and subtly; we thrill at the mastery of technique as the poet is performing (as the American poet Ferlinghetti said) 'high above the heads of the audience' but with a dexterity critics can appreciate and (one hopes) explain." You'll note that in CLO and everywhere else names in literature are discussed I have always been at pains to make critics determine how the names *work,* not simply to list them or merely etymologize them, which was all too often the case in this field of criticism when I and my generation of critics came along. It reminded me of the (apocryphal?) story of the television reporter Mrs. Kennedy was showing with the cameras through the redecorated White House. "Would you point out some of the pictures to us?," he asked. "Certainly," replied Jackie. "There's a picture, and there's a picture, and there's another picture over there."

What names were supposed to do used to be a trifle clearer in fiction, back in the days of transparently *redende Namen* (significant names) which telegraphed the allegory or other points in didactic writing, clarified comic characters, gave greater dimension to representative tragic heroes, made the author's message unmistakeable in the era when people wrote as communication, not as therapy, and were anxious to express ideas even more than to express themselves. The audience could easily see that *Malvolio* meant evil and *Benvolio* meant good. They immediately apprehended who *Everyman* and *Sansjoy* were supposed to be, how *Fidelia* or *Sir Fopling Flutter* were to be judged and what they were up to. Ben Jonson in a serious comedy (set in Italy, the Elizabethans' idea of a corrupt society) brought together the crafty *Volpone* (fox), his clever servant *Mosca* (the fly that carried the contagion), the predators named for birds of prey: *Corbaccio* (crow), *Corvino* (raven), and *Voltore* (vulture), the animal names suggesting that those who stopped thinking (men think, and feel, and grow, and exist in the world of humans, animals, vegetables, and minerals) sank to the level of the beasts. Moreover, the names created something of the instructive tone of Aesop's fables. In his cautionary tale, Jonson also introduced visiting English people; one of them was *Sir Politic Would-be.* As Jonson attacked vice, changing from the tone of his earlier comedies in which he sported "with human follies, not with crimes," he followed Horace's advice to "teach delightfully," to amuse as you instruct. Personality and pattern were inevitably stressed. Names were made to score points.

Jonson's contemporary Shakespeare worked with found materials, mixing both historical and invented names (*Fortinbras* in *Hamlet* is "strong in arm"). Many of his character names are discussed in the special all-Shakespeare issue of *Names* I guest-edited in 1988, and there is my article on how to pronounce the names in Shakespeare, as well as bibliographies on all aspects of naming in Shakespeare.

The Restoration drama made much of names such as *Horner* for a randy rake, *Pinchwife, Millamant, Loveless.* In the eighteenth century, George Farquhar introduced a new kind of comedy but still, in *The Beaux' Stratagem,* called his two men on the make *Aimwell* and *Archer.* He also created *Lady Bountiful* and her daughter *Dorinda* (in whose name you see the French for "gold"). So common were such fictive names that some of them entered the dictionary. I've already mentioned *malapropism,* and could add *lothario* (the dashing lover), *boniface* (innkeeper), and more. The novels of the period presented *Mrs. Slipslop* and thousands more.

The nineteenth-century allegories of Hawthorne (in which *Young Goodman Brown* loses his wife, *Faith*) and the tales of Poe (in which the most unfortunate fellow walled up in "The Cask of Amontillado" is ironically *Fortunato*) continued the practice. In Britain Dickens used to collect strange names from the newspapers for use in fiction but always insisted that *Podsnap, Wardle, Pickwick, Mrs. Gamp, Uriah Heep, Scrooge* "fit" the characters exactly, nor was he above calling the boy who was "all of a twist" *Oliver Twist* or giving Mr. and Mrs. Bates a son (in those days to be called *Master Bates*). Dickens and other novelists believed character names could score points and had to sound right as well as read right. They spent a lot of time on them, if not the incredible amount of time Cervantes says his Don Quixote spent on choosing a name for his knightly steed, *Rosinante* ("formerly a nag," despite the name's romantic rumble).

Dickens and other novelists were very good, too, at fictive placenames. *Bleak House* may be the best, but in George Meredith's *The Ordeal of Richard Feverel,* for instance, the novelist has a rich family resident at *Raynham Abbey,* from whence they reign over the village below, *Lobourne.* Many readers find that once they become aware of these name devices the works take on fuller meaning for them. Consult Charles Passage's wonderful book on the character names in Dostoyevsky and you will see a lot that you have been missing, the

untranslatability of significant names obscuring much for us in foreign literature. When a woman is called *Sophia* (wisdom) it is probably not accidental.

The writers of our century have often spurned too-obvious names, thinking
them unsophisticated, heavy-handed, aware that they distance the reader from
the fiction and work against the desire for realism. The best writers are unwill-
ing to ignore such sharp weapons in the battle. We need look only so far as
Arthur Miller's *Willy Loman* (low man) or Tennessee Williams' more subtle
Blanche Du Bois and *Stella* in *A Streetcar Named Desire*. What a wonderful
title! Williams earlier had considered *Blanche's Chair in the Moon* and a title
connected to her name, *The Moth*. Rejected titles can tell us significant things
and are another important aspect of naming in literature. Williams had a soulful
heroine called *Alma,* an ambitious loser named *Chance Wayne,* and in *The
Glass Menagerie* changed his mother's name to *Amanda* to emphasize she is
"to be loved" and his sister Rose's name (in an original draft, still hinted at in
the talk of "blue roses") to *Laura,* the inspiration of the poet (from Petrarch).
He kept his own real name (*Tom*) for the narrator of the play; serendipitously
it also fits the fellow who tomcats around. I have written a long article in *Names*
on the more difficult-to-fathom character names in all the works of Edward
Albee: *Peter* works for someone who denies something thrice, *George* and
Martha recall the Washingtons, but the hardest names to explain are those
which have general cultural rather than specifically literary antecedents. Such
names make the placename scholars who like to be "scientific" and deal with
the name *qua* name uneasy; they fill those scholars with objections that this type
of linguistic literary criticism is merely "subjective." One has to study the
entire matrix of a name to understand all its resonances and associations—and
that goes for placenames (which are more than geographical designations) too.
Emerson noted that "every name was once a poem." The poetry of names
requires sensitivity as well as scholarship, art and science, for full
interpretation.

One of those little "poems" can be so effective that we take Sinclair Lewis'
Babbitt or Shakespeare's *Shylock* for the general vocabulary. Others appeal
mostly to the aficionados of obscurantism, puzzle-solvers. Characters' names in
Mark Helprin's *Winter's Tale* (1983) show what the analyst may be up
against: *Rev. Mootfowl, Pearly Soames, Rupert Binky, Daythril Moobcot,
Hardesty Marratta, Jesse Honey*. The critics found this "precious." Yes, it was
overdone: the newspapers in the novel were the *Evening Ghost* and the
Morning Whale. However, some readers find this sort of thing is fun. They
delve into the significance of *Pilgrim* in both John Bunyan and Kurt Vonne-
gut, Jr. They think *Mr. Zero* in Elmer Rice's *The Adding Machine* is too easy,
but it's no more obvious than *Regina* in both Ibsen and Lillian Hellman plays
or *Clay* in Bret Easton Ellis' *Less than Zero* (otherwise jam-packed with names
that require a profound knowledge of contemporary Californian sociology—
why *Blair* for a girl?). It may require special knowledge of language to appreciate *Nym* in Shakespeare's *Henry V*, where *Pistol* shoots off his mouth but his

sidekick Nym is a thief, his name from the Anglo-Saxon for "to steal." In Gay's
The Beggar's Opera, Peachum will "impeach 'em," turn the crooks in to the
police, and *Macheath* (son of the heath) is the highwayman who accosts people
on the lonely byways. Prudery may account in another place for critics saying
that *Lady Wishfort* "wishes strongly" (*fort* in French). In reality, sex is
rearing its head and she wishes for 't (*it* being sex, as with Clara Bow the *It Girl*
of the old movies). If you suggest that *Joe Christmas* in Faulkner's *Light in
August* is supposed to suggest the crucified *JC,* some critics will agree, some
not, just as some will see more than one meaning in the title (illumination in
August? giving birth in August?) and some will not. Why are a pair of gangsters in a Harold Pinter play called *Goldberg* and *McCann?* Even Pinter says
he doesn't know. Of course they had to be called something, but in a work of
art (as Coleridge said) there must be "a reason why it is thus, and not otherwise," intention, communication.

Modern art of all kinds is less direct. The very concept of Meaning is being
hotly debated. Certainty may be rarer, but that does not stop the critics from
arguing about Beckett's *Godot* or pointing out possible significance in the fact
that the character names are from a number of different languages, that *Lucky*
may be ironic or not, that repetitiveness in nicknames like *Didi* (French *dit, dit*
is "said, said") signals something which any interpretation has at least to take
into account somehow. There's no accident in the choice of the forename in
Thomas Mann's *The Confessions of Felix Krull, Confidence Man* or a mere
initial for a character in a Franz Kafka nightmare. Even namelessness can
make fictional points. In a García Lorca play (variously called *Bodas de
sangre, Bitter Oleander, Blood Wedding, The Marriage of Blood*) not giving a
character a name suggests to me both this dramatist's good points and his bad
ones, among them the compelling capturing of a more than local significance
and also the attempt to commit Literature with malice aforethought.

Are we reading too much into the works rather than out of them? You may
think so. It's only fair to confess that for years some critics have vehemently
argued that all this is presumptuous (reading writers' minds as well as their
writings) and subjective (reflecting our own ideas, rather than What Is There).
A lot of ink has been spilled in the debate. The art and the science of criticism
have had their extremists at both ends of the spectrum. The "scientists"
demand hard facts, and they would agree that *Sir Anthony Absolute* or *Candide*
are "readable." They would admit that *Sir Abraham Hazard* and to a lesser
extent *J. Alfred Prufrock* convey a creator's attitude toward his character. But
they balk at speculations about less obvious onomastic tricks. They will accept
the importance of the shift from *Gatz* to *Gatsby* in Fitzgerald's novel but when
it comes to (say) the preponderance of surnames as forenames in *Less than
Zero* they get uneasy as critics like myself start to regard the names not as mere
linguistic artifacts but as cultural artifacts. You have to know about every
aspect of our culture from arrivistes to assimilated Jews to understand what
Trent, Griffin, Walker signal when they are used as forenames. Also, *Spin,*

Derf, Kicker, Devo, Death as nicknames are full of information about *L.A.* in the novel that is *The Catcher in the Rye* of the eighties. What the placename "scientists" who dismiss literary onomastics as too subjective fail to see is that it has improved from mere etymologizing to studying names in fiction in all their contexts. Now it demands a broad and deep knowledge of the world outside the lab or the library. This many narrow linguists lack. Properly done, literary onomastic criticism can tell us much about art and society, and it is not to be dismissed just because occasional guesswork enters into it or because some conclusions may be less conclusive than others, more personal.

"With critic George Jean Nathan," I wrote in 1982, "I say to hell with impersonal criticism—the reality of impersonal criticism or scientific literary onomastics is unattainable anyway—for it is 'like an impersonal fist fight or an impersonal marriage, and as successful'."

I do not wish to draw you into the academic altercations between "scientific" and "impressionistic" students of names. I do want you to understand that authors take the naming of their characters seriously. Rightly so, because we have relevant testimony on this from authors themselves, from Cervantes to Michener, from Tom Wolfe of *Look Homeward, Angel* to Tom Wolfe of *The Bonfire of the Vanities* (which title is supposed to ring a bell and suggest Savonarola). Authors choose names, consciously or unconsciously, with a reason, some more or less carefully or deliberately than others. In some works the names of the characters (and the title, and placenames, and brand names, etc.) are more important than in others; but always, it stands to reason, art demands a reason, effect has a cause. Accept that and you have to accept the legitimacy of literary onomastic criticism. We critics (and readers) do the best we can with what we have, facts, intuitions, impressions. I think of Lichtenberg's observation that if a monkey looks into a mirror you cannot expect an angel to look out. In criticism as in creation, or computers, what you get out depends on what you can put in.

You don't have to become a literary critics, but if you are going to be a consumer of poetry, novels, plays, any literature, you will get more out of it if you play the name game with or on the author. You are fully entitled to react, or to research. You can add a lot to your appreciation of or analysis of every book you read, every play you see, every movie or television program you watch if you pay attention to fictive names. You will find there are "subtleties of the cultural matrix" or just that names contribute to plot, tone, and every other literary element. What you know about life will illuminate what you learn from literature, and *vice versa*.

Next time you run into a character called *Larry* or *Sidney* consider why he is not called (say) *Lance* or *Steve*. Why were those two funny girls *Laverne* and *Shirley*? What are the yuppie names of *thirtysomething*? These days you are not likely to encounter the equivalent of *Armageddon T. Thunderbird* or *Zeal-*

of-the-Land Busy or a *Chillingworth* or even a *Jefferson Hope*. But writers call the characters and places, etc., something. The question is *why that?*

You understand that *Stella* is the "star" that lowbrow *Stanley Kowalski* (Polish for *Smith*) worships. Why *Stanley?* Because his parents wanted to "Americanize" *Stanislaus* and the boy who bears the name, but *Stanley* is out of fashion and a might weak for a *macho* man (so maybe Mary McCarthy was on to something when she said Marlon Brando introduced "a new stereotype to the American theatre, the male impersonator" and Tennessee Williams was telling you something about himself, too).

Suddenly you see why it's *Ralph* and *Norton* more often than *Kramden* and *Ed* on *The Honeymooners,* and why the bus driver's wife is *Alice* (sit-by-the-fire) and not *Trixie.* Why *Neil* and *Brenda* for Long Island Jews in Roth's *Goodbye, Columbus?* Why *Hal* in *2001?* (Count back letters from *IBM.*) Why *Oscar Madison* for the slob and *Felix Unger* for the fastidious one in *The Odd Couple* (and why do these two Jewish actors not play people with "Jewish names"?)? Why *Lamont Cranston* and *Lois Lane* and *Rambo* and *Alexis Colby?* Soap-opera (daytime drama) characters used to be *Brett Fredericks* and *Ma Perkins,* etc. What are they called these days? Why?

Lydia Languish and *Mr. Murdstone* (hinting at "murder" and the hardness of stone in Dickens) are easy. Is *Christie Mahon* a Christlike man in Synge's *The Playboy of the Western World?* You can study name changes in fiction, even the rejected names, changed titles: Margaret Mitchell thought first of calling *Gone with the Wind, Tomorrow is Another Day.* Before he hit on *The Great Gatsby,* Fitzgerald played with *Trimalchio, Trimalchio in West Egg, On the Road to West Egg,* and *Red, White and Blue,* among other possibilities. You can see the humor in *The Flying Zucchinis* and *Gerry and the Atrics* on *The Muppets.* You can howl at Peter DeVries' pun names, like *Herbie Hind* and *Justin Case,* to cite but two. Surely you did not miss *Pussy Galore* in the James Bond movie or the comic names of *Doonesbury.* Names are always important, whether real ones or made up ones or real ones adapted for literary use. Fictional names carry connotations, what people used to call *vibes,* and not just in the sixties, for the Hon. Gwendolyn Fairfax speaks of "vibrations" of names in *The Importance of Being Earnest.* Names in fiction are chosen to suggest character, age, social position, and much more in the story. Don't ignore them, whether you are reading *The Iliad,* a medieval romance or a Harlequin romance. In school or college, names can be one good way to get into literary analysis and appreciation, to the same extent that placenames can teach history and geography.

In an interview in *Talking with Texans,* author Larry McMurtry showed that one doesn't have to be an old-schooler like Henry James or Dickens or Trollope or Melville or O'Neill to be concerned with character names. McMurtry confessed to being somewhat compulsive about getting just the right names. "If I spend time on anything," this celebrated writer said, "it's naming my characters and naming the places where they live. . . . You have to have the right names."

"Right" as in painting, maybe. "Right" to the conscious or the unconscious mind of the creator. When an admirer told Thomas Mann that the character name *Chauchat* was only a letter away from the French for "hot cat," the very deliberate writer replied, "I never thought of that, unless unconsciously." I have had writers read my criticism and tell me, "Now I see why I called him that." Mann may have been speaking with tongue in cheek, or my critical targets insincerely, but tell me: doesn't the instinctive, subconscious or unconscious factor figure prominently, along with the conscious deliberations, when we are putting names on anything, from babies to license plates? Not to admit that, I say, is to be "unscientific." I stand up for literary onomastic study in all cases and at all levels and I believe we must study the namers as well as the names, the constructs and the contexts, everything.

Speaking of "everything," one of the more neglected aspects of literary name study is folklore, what Tristram P. Coffin and Henning Cohen in *Collecting Folklore in America* (1970) call "literature flourishing in oral tradition," adding that even with that definition of folklore "some people may quibble." Since W. J. Thomas invented the word *folklore* in 1846 there have been many definitions of it. It certainly involves the non-verbal (arts, crafts, buildings, etc.) and the only partly verbal (songs, festivals, etc.); however, all aspects of it tend to have something to do with names. The field collectors and chairborne professors are merely the note-takers and theorizers; you and your grandmother may be the primary sources.

There's much to learn about names in old songs and ballads, the names given by the folk to things of common life, the names in children's games, in pop music, cartoon characters, and so on. It's a wonder that more teachers do not see the usefulness of asking students to research material they really know or care about, even if it is not High Culture, when students are set term papers. The way to keep students from tearing pages out of expensive library reference books is to send them out into the field to do original collecting. There would be less plagiarism and boredom, more enthusiasm and creativity, if they were asked to write about names in punk rock or comic books or the American love affair with automobiles, or sports. Start them with interviews with "living ancestors" and capture the reminiscences of the old folks before they leave us. What is already stashed in the library can come later, research better motivated. What is in the library will keep, barring the disintegration of paper.

Long ago the Greeks went around talking to people, who were more numerous and accessible than documents, and recorded (among other things) the folklore of placenames. Their enthusiasm was better than their etymology but they did come up with some perfectly fascinating, if often perfectly groundless, answers to why this or that place bore the name it did.

Today we have wonderful tales purporting to explain *Pissing Tree* (Virginia), *Sunday Rock* in the Adirondacks, *Busted by Thunder* (Kansas; the wagon that went West with a placard saying "Pike's Peak or Bust" returned with "Busted, by Thunder," it is said). You can find inspired guesses about *Grumble* (Cornwall), *Joe Batts Arm* (Newfoundland), and our own *Remote* (Oregon), *Booger Hole* (West Virginia), *Cle Elum* and *Pe Ell* (both Washington State), and the original names of *Swan River* (*Sweathouse River*), *Longview* (*Growlersburgh*), *Cedar Grove* (*Dog Walk*), and more. They got *Cocoa Beach* (Florida) and *Coffee* (Illinois), it is said, right off the grocery shelf, as it were. They reckoned as how *Marvin* (South Dakota) was a "good safe name." It was taken right off the safe in the general store where the namers met to decide the issue. Towns called *Egypt, Mesopotamia,* and *Cairo* (pronounced "KAY-ro" in Illinois) caused storekeeper Alexander McCune to say, "Here come the Arabians on their annual pilgrimage to Mecca," and the farmers called his town *Mecca.* Better than *Bastard Peak* (Wyoming), *Zap* (North Dakota), *Two Teats* (California), even *Okay* and *Goon Dip Mountain* in Arkansas. One *Mountain Lake* has no mountain and no lake.

Amerindian names led to wild stories. *Tidioute* (he looks far) is Munsee Wolf talk, but in Pennsylvania they tell of a hard-of-hearing gandy dancer on the railroad tracks asking, "Did he hoot?" *Wooden Money* was the nickname during the Depression of *Tenino* (Washington), the Amerindian name meaning "fork" or "junction" in Chinook, but it is alleged railroad men said "10-9-0."

The folk say *Savannah* (Georgia) derives from a drowning girl ("Save Anna!"), that *Ogonquit* (Maine) expressed exasperation with a rifle ("Oh, gun quit!"), that *Sheboygan* (Michigan) was the wail of a disappointed father ("She boy agin!"), and that many a "furrin" name is just an American expression, that *Pocotaglio* tells you how to make a porcupine hope: "Poke 'e tail, 'e go!" The same thing applies all over the world: in Australia they ask if *Katamatite* is from a drunk asking, "Kate, am I tight?" If you are ignorant of the language you don't see that, for instance, *Bayou Funny Creek* is from Choctaw *Bayuk* (river) and *fani* (squirrel) or that *Speaking Devil* is mangled Dutch, or that many a *Whisky* came from Choctaw *oski* (cane), that *Perth Amboy* is from *Embole* (point of land). You make up a story about a Scottish earl of Perth who arrived in New Jersey in a kilt only to be accosted by a native with, "Perth am girl?" "No," was the reply, "Perth am boy!"

Non-Amerindian names also have attracted "explanations." Gone are such post-office names as *Stareout, Nofog, Isolate, Mule,* and *Gladtidings* and with them the need for stories to explain them. Fortunately we still have *Laughing Pig* (Wyoming), *Taos* (New Mexico), *Helpmejack Creek* (Arkansas), *Ono* (Pennsylvania) and *Bread and Cheese Hollow* (where, the local historian in New York's Smithtown says, Richard "Bull" Smith used to eat his lunch). People who wanted to be ferried between *Faulkner* and *Perry,* used to "suck up booze until they swole up like toads" as they waited. Hence *Toad Suck* (Arkansas). *Deathball Creek* (Orgeon) is said to recall some frontiersman's biscuits. I do know that *Shawnee Town* (Arkansas) was changed to *Yelltown* because Archibald Yell paid $50 for the honor. I'm not sure *bum* comes from a shelter in Steyr (Austria) decorated with the painting of *Bummerl* (little dog), and I think every placename needs a cautious approach, even something simple like *Village* in the Northern Neck of Virginia (once upon a time *Union Village* because of its location on the border between two counties). I take with a grain of salt even expert Henry Schoolcraft's explanation of *Monguago* (Illinois, site of a battle in the ill-named War of 1812): from "Mo-gwan-go-nong," he says in his *Personal Memoirs*, "a man's name signifying dirty backsides." I constantly see unreliable explanations of placenames such as this from a Strout real-estate brochure in 1982:

> Rich in history and legend [saleable items, worth refurbishing, or installing], Huntingdon is the prosperous seat of Carroll County [Tennessee], about midway between Nashville and Memphis. . . . The Town was known as Huntsville until 1823, when the name was changed to set it apart from Huntsville, Alabama. Legend says that the [Chickasaw] Indians passing through it at the end of the hunting season and chanting, "Hunting done," gave it its name.

The Vicksburg (Mississippi) *Sunday Post* once asserted that *Graball* (Tallahatchie County) got its name because "some old guy ran a trade boat on the river and would allow customers to reach into a bag and pull out as many gifts as they could grab with one hand." That's about as credible as the explanation for *Shucktown* (Lauderdale County): a farmer, badgered for the return of a load of corn he had "borrowed," dumped a load of cornshuckings on the lender's land. Or *Helechawa* (Kentucky). It has been said to recall a bad road: "Hell each way." We make up weird names (*Dunrovin* for a cottage, *Hemaruka* in Saskatchewan from a CPR man's daughters *He*len, *Ma*rgaret, *Ru*th and *Ka*thleen, which is how an Ohio railroad man made *Helechawa* out of *Hele*n *Cha*se *Wa*ldrun). We make up weird stories, too. Can you blame us, or the Cornish who have such placenames as *Lower Drift, Catchall, Gloweth, Twelve Heads, Goonhaven, Black Head, Gummow's Shop, Probus, Crafthole, Boot, Rhude Cross, Broadwoodwidger, Zelah,* and the corrupted Cornish *Penny-Come-Quick?*

Names are interesting in that they tend to resist the natural corruption of words more than most other words, but they do get distorted. Thus *Brasenose* (a college at Oxford) was a *brasinium* (brew house) behind King Alfred's palace. *Achterstrasse* (back street) in Bonn (Germany) was once the *Acherstrasse* (road to Aachen). There are no snakes in Ireland (thanks to St. Patrick, the story goes), so *Adderville* (Donegal) is from *eader baille* (central town). People used to believe that *Antwerp* (at the wharf) was the place where Flemings cut off people's hands (*handt werpen*) and threw them into the water.

"Folklore does create place names," writes Nicolaisen authoritatively, "through the application of facets of popular belief and the localization of migratory legends," and I insist that these stories are to be included in the "literature" of literary onomastics. There were beech trees, never a beacon, at Beaconsfield; Blackheath in London was never black but bleak; *Blubber Lane* in Leicester (England) was the site of *The Blue Boar* pub. In the collected papers of the Names Institute I once published a long and, I think, worthy article called "If Your Wife Isn't Happy in *The Butcher's Arms* Maybe *The Feathers* Would Tickle Her Fancy," about pub names and linguistic corruption: *Bacchanals* to *Bag o' Nails, Catherine Wheel* to *Cat and Wheel, God Encompasses Us* to *Goat and Compasses* and *Caton Fidele* to *Cat and Fiddle* and *Infanta di Castille* to *Elephant and Castle.* The folk at work on English and other languages!

Farrar's *Origin of Language* says that when any corrupted word is regarded as "significant and in some sense appropriate it will stick." *The bitter end* was once *the end of the bitter,* a cable fastened to the ship's timbers or bitts. *Humble pie* was made of *umbles,* the innards. Today we have the "wrong" meaning of many words such as *carp, colonel, crabbed, farthingale, henchman, incentive, tribulation,* etc. We're the folks who made *flammable* out of *inflammable, Ozarks* out of *bois d'arc* and *Teddymore* (Mississippi) out of *tête de morte* (death's head, maybe a pirate's *Jolly Roger*). So there's a Walter not water in *Bridgewater* and they say there's a spook who shows a nightly candle in a shattered window at *Carrigogunnell Castle* (Ireland; *carraig-ó-gcoinneal* or "candle rock"), but it's just *carraig-ó-gCoinnell* (rock of the O'Connells). No rabbits but a king (*cyning*) once at *Coney Castle,* no tree but a tannery (*tcherrotterie*) at *The Cherry Tree* (Guernsey), once a Mr. Snooks at *Seven Oaks* in Kent, and the *Cromwell* in Ireland was a *crom-choill* (sloping wood), not the Lord Protector, Oliver. So without a lot of study you can get wrong all such "Newfie" names as *Horse Chops, Famish Gut, Fogo, Whale Gulch, Little Paradise, Goobish,* or Louisiana placenames such as *Advance, Retreat, Plain Dealing, Welcome, Wham, Bob Acres, Topsy, Hydropolis, Long Straw,* and *Zylks,* any one of which tempts one to tell a tale stranger than truth (such as that *Gasoline* in Texas was named for a real live gasoline engine, by God, that passed through back in "ought seven"). As a member of the Place Name Commission of the United States I am going to do my best to see that, while the geographers get the lay of the land right, the literary types get all the folk stories included in the records that we can. I treasure those stories; they are the authentic "barbaric yawp" which Whitman celebrated. I love the great little tales that Gerald L. Cohen digs up in Missouri and Robert M. Rennick finds like nuggets all over Kentucky.

Rennick rejects the story that *Ordinary* (Kentucky) resulted from the search for an "ordinary name"; he says it's from a tavern. He reports that Richard Radford, first postmaster of the place railroaders were calling *Daddy's Bag,* turned it around to make *Bagdad.* (Or you can have one of the "bag, Daddy" stories.) The postmaster at Vanceburg in the twenties liked to tell how *Crum* appeared in Lewis County. As the yarn goes, a well-stocked country store stood there until a twister blew the whole shebang away. Some time later, a local yokel reckoned there might be "a crumb of comfort there" anyway and opened another store in *Crum*. Rennick tells me that *Crum* was not an uncommon family name in northeast Kentucky. I ask you: do you want to spoil a good story with fact?

Believe what you like about *Dot Klish* (Arizona), *Tamalpais* (California), *Makapuu* (Hawaii), *Owyhee* (Nevada), *Nicodemus* (Kansas), *Ashuelot* (New Hampshire), *Pawtucket* (Rhode Island—is it "Pa took it"?) and all of these from Nebraska: *Funk, Rising City, Wahoo, Tryon,* and *Wynot*. Why not? The mind of the people is like mud, a poet once said, and from it rise strange and wonderful things. Cherish the wit and wisdom of the folk, even if it is not Great Literature.

One more bit of oral history. I shall try to be delicate as I present the tale of *Oronogo*. I feel pretty sure that it was named for the rich mines of *Orinoco*, but as Johnny Shrader told the tale to a great folk collector in Eureka Springs (Arkansas) in July of 1954, as Johnny himself had heard it near Joplin (Missouri) a good half-century earlier, it goes like this (thanks to Vance Randolph's collection of Ozark folktales, *Pissing in the Snow*, 1977):

> One time there was a bunch of Pukes lived over by Joplin, at a camp known as Minersville. The boys didn't have nothing but picks and shovels in them days, and maybe a windlass and a bucket. They just gophered around in prospect holes, because there wasn't no powder to speak of. . . .

Soon the storyteller turns his attention to "Old Lady Bradley," her boarding-house, and her waitress, name of Myrtle.

> Them overall boys was always a-following Myrtle around, but she never done no screwing unless they paid her first. A fellow named Taylor come down with the horn colic [modern: "got the hots"] one night, but he didn't have the two dollars. Taylor kept hollering how he'd have the money come Saturday night, but Myrtle just laughed, because she's heard that song before. "Catch me a gunnysack full of turkey fat," she says, "and we'll talk business." Taylor began to cry like a baby, but he didn't have no turkey-fat neither. "Bawling won't buy you nothing at the store," says Myrtle. "It's ore, or no go!"

There's your explanation, folks.

> The walls in that boardinghouse was just thin slabs, without no plaster. Everybody in the house could hear what Myrtle told Taylor, and them prospectors just laughed themselves sick. It was a kind of joke in all the saloons, and finally they had a meeting to change the name of the camp. Minersville don't sound very good

anyhow, but *ore-or-no-go* is kind of high toned. It all happened pretty near eighty years ago, but the name stuck. You can see Oronogo painted right on the post office window, any time you feel like driving up Main Street.

Literature is, these days, anything written down; "oral literature" is what is handed down by storytellers (which at least sometimes gets into print). The study of names in literature, in my view, means paying attention to both high culture and popular culture. There is something to be learned about us humans wherever names are seen or heard. Nothing human is alien to us.

To prove it, the next section deliberately goes out on a limb to discuss something arcane, indeed occult. It is about the names in magic and the magic in names, and it will be followed by a book-in-brief about telling fortunes with names. I predict you'll find it spellbinding.

PART FIVE

NAMES AND THE OCCULT

Read backwards: Anion, Lalle, Sabalos,
Sado, Poter, Aziel, Adonai Sado,
Vagoth Agra, Jod, Baphra!
Then cry: Komm! Komm!

—German formula for raising the Devil, quoted in
Leonard R. N. Ashley, *The Wonderful World of Magic and Witchcraft*

22. The Names in Magic and the Magic in Names

A t the outset of this section I should declare my special interest in superstition and the occult. I have authored books such as *The Wonderful
World of Superstition, Prophecy, and Luck* (1984, in Dutch 1986) and *The
Wonderful World of Magic and Witchcraft* (1986, in German 1988), combined
in one volume as *The Amazing World of Superstition, Prophecy, Luck, Magic
and Witchcraft* (1988). Their reception has proved that other people, too, are
interested in these things, both in America and abroad. I have also edited
papers of the Society for Psychical Research as *Phantasms of the Living* in
two volumes, and more. Dr. Samuel Johnson once said that "the most instructive work that could be written would be a History of Magik," and, although I
have not attempted that, I do see what Freud meant when he said that if he had
his life to live over he would have devoted it to the study of parapsychology.
I find the occult engrossing and the fact that it has so many followers utterly
fascinating, if a little disturbing. The subject may seem peripheral to this book;
however, it can serve to demonstrate better than some other topics that in
investigating almost anything one soon comes upon riveting names and the
power of names, that when you dig deeply into names you are getting close to
the essence, the very name of the game.

In the course of my researches into superstition (which leads people to
believe in something Out There) and magic (which offers a promise of being
able to do something about it), I have encountered much more than a few
strangely named groups (the *Ancient and Mystical Order of the Rosy Cross,*
the *Order of the Golden Dawn,* the *Minutemen of St. Germain*) as well as
oddly named individuals. There was Theophrastus Bombastus von Hohenheim,
who called himself *Phillipus Aureolus Paracelsus,* perhaps boasting he was
"beyond Celsus," who was a Greek physician second in fame only to Hippoc-
rates himself. There was Alphonse-Louis Constant, who translated his forenames into Hebrew and as *Eliphas Lévi* became the most notable ritual magi-
cian of the last century. (It was not difficult for me to beat his record for

attending such ceremonies, because in all his long life he was present at only three.) There was the prognosticator Michel de Nôstre-Dame—a peculiar choice of surname for a family of formerly Jewish physicians—whom I am sure you have heard of as *Nostradamus.* There were people who acquired extraordinary nicknames, such as Aleister Crowley, whose own mother joined others in calling him "the Beast." There were people who took odd names upon embracing magic (as others do when entering holy orders) and others who wrote under pseudonyms like *Paul Christian* and *Dion Fortune.* In the latter category was Pierre-Michel Vintras, who first called himself *Eugène Vintras* for reasons you would hardly credit and later took the name of an angel, *Strathaniel,* with bizarre results. One of Crowley's notorious disciples, Jack Parsons, rivaled his mentor in audacity: where Crowley liked to be regarded as "the Wickedest Man in the World" and "666" (as in *Revelations*), Parsons (d. 1952) changed his name to *Belarion Armilius al Dajjal Antichrist.* That would be difficult to surpass!

My studies introduced me to several Messiahs, including Mohammed Ahmed ibn Abdallah. He was *Madhi* whose prediction that he would meet his adversary "Chinese" Gordon face to face was fulfilled, after Gen. Gordon's death at Khartoum, when he was sent Gordon's head in a parcel. Another Messiah was the Englishwoman simply called Anne Lee. These were just two more of the strikingly-named persons who cropped up in my researches, researches which also offered to teach me how to confront demons like *Abaddon* (*Apollyon* in Greek), King of the Bottomless Pit; *Abraxas,* an entity who in the second century was thought to have a name in Greek equal to 365 and so was said to command legions of spirits (from his name we may get *Abracadabra*); the demons which in French bore my own forenames (*Léonard* and *Raymond*); and many more. Alphonse de Spina listed 10 species of these demonic creatures. St. Athanasius was convinced the atmosphere was filled with them. In the sixteenth century the learned Weir calculated that there were 44,435,556 of them, a more conservative estimate than de Spina's (who guessed 133,306,668). All have names, and when you have the name of one (they say) you have, in both senses of the word, his number.

The names of devils and demons and familiars are fun. The names of the Devil (*Satan, Lucifer, Old Nick, Mephistopheles, Robin Goodfellow,* many more) are significant. I have written about the names of the Devil from both the theological and linguistic points of view in *Literary Onomastic Studies* and elsewhere, suggesting that the names we give as we personify evil tell us a great deal about ourselves and our imagination. The names of God are the most powerful and most interesting names of all.

Here we come to a topic that may offend some readers. Especially if you are an Orthodox Jew, you may wish to skip the next page or so, for here I propose to reveal the secret name of God and you may believe that to read it will bring disaster upon you, if not the end of the world.

God in our Judao-Christian tradition is often said to be named *Jehovah*. That is not His name. It was rather His evasion: when asked for His name, he refused to reveal it, knowing full well that when you have anyone's name, even a divinity's, you have some part of him, some power over him. With a name, as with a nail clipping or a lock of hair, you have part of the self; with it you can work powerful magic. So when asked His name, God replied with the Hebrew *Yahweh* (our *Jehovah*), by which He simply asserted "I AM." That is all He wants you to know about Him, maybe all you ought to want to know.

In Hebrew studies you never see the name of God but simply *shemoth* (name substitutes): *Ehedeh, Iod, Tetragrammaton Elohim, El, Elohim Giber, Eloath Va-daath, El Adonai Tzaboath, Elohim Tzaboath, Shaddai. . . . El* is "God" (as in *Elizabeth, Nathaniel, Joel*) and *Elohim* is plural. All the archangels (whose names end in *-el*) were once minor deities (*Ralphael, Michael, Gabriel, Azrael,* and the rest) whom the One God conquered, as He did *Satan* (the Adversary), the Prince of Darkness who is also "the bearer of light," Latin *Lucifer.*

The four-letter (*tetragrammaton*) name with no vowels was really just the consonants for "I AM." That was not a name. From the period of the *mishnah* onward, The Name was a carefully guarded secret of the priests, uttered only in the Temple, behind the veil of the Holy of Holies where the Ark of the Covenant rested. It was to be pronounced solemnly only by the High Priest. The other priests did not get to hear it; when The Name was spoken the Levites drowned it out with loud singing lest it become known to them. Advanced students of the Cabala learned God's 12-letter name and His 42-letter name and His 72-letter name, and so did I, all but the long and absolutely explicit name that the High Priest spoke once, at *Yom Kippur,* the name that Talmudic scholars tell me "cannot be grasped." You had to be one of the inner circle to know The True Name of God, and maybe nobody knows it today, but it is not needed in any case until the Temple is reinstituted and the Cohens and the Levis and the Katzes return to their sacred duties. Meanwhile the name of God you need for magic I am going to be bold enough to write, dangerous as some people say that may be. If you do not wish to know it, stop reading now. If you do wish to know it, it is simply *Emeth.* To tell you more, or to explain how it is used to work magic, give life to a *golem,* work other wonders, is no part of this book. Indeed no printed instructions are valid; the *grimoire* (direction book for magic) must be handwritten and cannot be sold. So don't waste your money on instruction manuals in occult bookstores.

With The True Name of God, you have The Word, "the letters by which Heaven and Earth were created," as the Jews said. I think of it as comparable to the code of DNA, the instructions to "create life." Putting it into the breast of the sort of Frankenstein monster he built, Rabbi Loew, centuries ago in Prague, is said to have given life to the *golem,* created by cabalistic rites from inert matter. In an old horror film I saw this portrayed and the word on the life-giving parchment was *Aemaeth*. Close enough. I have never seen a real *golem*. I did see the grave of Rabbi Loew. But if the *golem* has existed and gone, just wait; because once created a *golem* is supposed to return every 33 years. If and when it does, flee. It is far too dangerous to meddle with. There is a name you can use to protect yourself against a *golem,* but I cannot find it anywhere. Maybe people will write in to me, as they did when first I published the name of God. In magic, names are protection and power both. In the beginning is the *word*.

The Talmud tells us that a man is said to have created life by reciting names. The *baal shem* (possessor of a name) has always been regarded as powerful, capable of creation and destruction, lord of what he can name (as Adam became, naming the animals). Say the name and the evil force is powerless (think of *Rumpelstiltskin* in a less frightening context) or can be commanded. *Exurgent mortui et ad me veniunt,* "the dead arise and come to me," as the necromancer says. Rabbinical scholars of the *ma'aseh bereshit* (act of creation) were stopped by their instructors before they could learn, as Christopher Marlowe's *Doctor Faustus* says, "more than heavenly power permits." Simon ben Azai got full occult knowledge. Like Faustus, he found it fatal. Simon ben Zoma went crazy; he never returned from what they called *pardess* (entering the orchard). Stay away from trouble. The Talmud says: don't even sleep in a house alone—it invites demons. One learned rabbi, named Akiva, seems to have mastered all the secrets, but don't you try it. You could die. Or, as Elisha ben Abuya warns, you could become a gnostic or something. Be warned.

Am I talking superstition or faith, magic or religion? The great expert Dr. Margaret Murray herself confessed that "so far it has been impossible to derive a theory which will decide where Magic ends and where Religion begins," and since then even Daniel Lawrence O'Keefe's profound *Stolen Lightning: A Social Theory of Magic* (1982) has failed to make the distinction absolutely clear. From magic, religion begins; into magic, religion deteriorates. My own religion, maybe yours, is full of magical acts, of which transubstantiation (*hoc est corpus* or "hocus-pocus") is but one. In Judaism and Islam, as far as this outsider can see, there is a lot that can be called magic. Thus, in discussing magic, which like religion has its names and formulae at the very heart of it, I hope I have not stepped on the toes of your religious beliefs. I do not mean to offend anyone or to make sacrilegious reference to miracles or the Mass or objects of power (a St. Christopher medal, a *mezzuzah,* a Hand of Fatima, even a Hand of Glory, magical amulets and talismans, and the like) by suggesting that one person's religion may seem to another to be superstition.

We refer to the religions of the ancients as mythology, assuming that we have true faith and they had mere superstition. The names the Greeks gave to occult forces made them as real to the Greeks as our God is to us. The name superstitions (or beliefs) of the past are still with us. The Roman omens, for instance. The capitol was built where they found a *caput* (human head). They drew messages from the flights of birds and the entrails of animals. And they had those omen names I mentioned earlier, like *Felix* and *Victor,* and always began the roll call before a battle with someone named *Victor.* Not to offend, again, my modern example will be taken from far afield: Vuk Stephanovitch Kradadjitch, the Serbian patriot, was named *Vuk* (wolf) to protect him from wolves, thought to eat infants (which belief we find only in our fairytales), just as you may have been given a saintly protector. I have earlier mentioned the omen names of ships (*Victory, Intrepid*) and could add the Chinese tractor brand *Feng Shou* (Abundant Harvest), though recently the Chinese increasingly have turned to names of propaganda rather than names of magical power, to names translating as *Move-Mountain, Self-Reliance, Toward the New, Benefit the Masses.* In Canton, I hear, *High-Class Street* became *People's Road* and *Happiness-Together Street* is now *Road of the Masses.* That names work their magic on people, if not on supernatural creatures, everyone recognizes.

As soon as I can devise a way of discussing our own name superstitions, without touching some raw nerves, I shall write a book on what I have found in those researches. Here I'll take a chance on your not being upset at my mentioning a few name practices that some will find irrational and others will defend as pious conventions.

Jews will understand that non-Jews think it superstitious that some Jews hold unusual beliefs about the rainbow or the color blue or make sure that salt is always on the table (as it was on the altar of the Temple) or that knives are removed by the grace after meals. Likewise, in some Jewish circles, parents will not name a baby after a living relative lest that diminish the life of the adult, there being only so much life in a name. It has not been unheard of for Jews now to change the name of a sick infant (perhaps to *Chaim,* "Life") to confuse the Angel of Death if he is sent to take the child. Judaism has a healthy respect for all names of power and a strong tradition of the power of names. So abiding is that that I have "non-religious" Jewish students who are told not to write the name of God (and don't know it anyway) who still insist on writing things like "the g-ds of the Greeks," the same cautious avoidance that traditionally led to the use not of a name but *Adonai* (Lord).

Jews may have a Hebrew name and also an "American" name with the same initial (*Irving* for *Isaac, Milton* for *Moise*). Is this superstition or convention? Numerology is unquestionably superstition in our eyes, whether ingrained in the Jewish Scriptures or the hobby of non-Jews, which I shall get into a bit later.

Followers of *Islam* (Surrender) also have a kind of numerology. Some believe that if one of the 99 names of Allah is written a certain (large) number of times on a piece of paper and carried on the person it will confer protection and power. The Arabic tradition says that odd numbers are luckier than even ones, which may explain *The Thousand and One Nights* as a title. Undoubtedly the belief in odd numbers is shared by other cultures. Ask anyone to choose a favorite number between 1 and 10; you'll get 3 or 7 more often than chance permits.

Was it pious or foolish for Roman Catholics (and some other Christians) to name babies after the saint(s) on whose day the children were born, giving the child the saint(s) as model(s) and protector(s)? Is it wise or foolish to believe that, in a state of grace, you are accompanied by a Guardian Angel? There's an old formula for finding out the name of your personal angel but I won't trouble you with it. In addition, I'll wager your priest won't give it to you and may even deny there is such a formula.

Angels and "ministers of grace" defend us. Do you know the name of the angel who wrestled with Jacob? It was *Sammael* (Venom of God). It is disconcerting that some ancient writers give the same name (or *Samael*) to the demon *Asmodeus,* the Angel of Death, the power that dethroned Solomon (who tried to control him with a magical ring, got the demon to build his Temple). Rabbinical tradition makes Asmodeus androgynous, but he/she was man enough to seduce Eve and (they say) father Cain. He also stood up to both Moses and St. Michael the Archangel. We know him by a Latin form of his (or her?) name. Are these supposed to be the names of real personages or poetic personifications of ideas? If *Mammon* and *Dives* can start as nouns and wind up as proper nouns, the names in the Scriptures have to be considered with care. If significant names such as *Adam* (Clay), *Isaac* (laughter), *Saul* (desire) occur, do they point to history or to fiction?

Some people have named (or learned the names of) devils and demons and tried to manipulate these creatures of fiction or history. Some people (such as the Inuit) will shuck a worn-out name in order to prolong life. Others may take a new name to mark a change in personality, entering a religious order or a coven. "Call me Mara," said Naomi, turning "bitter." I had a double first cousin who was a nun and it was not until she died that I learned the original name of *Mother St. Mary Fidelis.* Buddhist monks get a new name when they die. Some people have secret names. Fearing that if the name were known the voodoo practitioner or witchdoctor could work magic against their children, some African mothers whisper into the newborn's ear its secret name. When they grow up, the offspring *cannot* be forced to give their secret name, and you cannot "take" their souls (as you might steal the soul by taking a photograph, some believe). In places such as Tibet, some people do not know their "real" names. All their lives they wear around their necks little bags with their names inside them. If you think this is ridiculous, take off your scapular or "blessed" medal or your Hebrew letter or crucifix or Greek blue bead against vampires or Italian phallic symbol or whatever it is *you* may wear. In the bag a lama has put a piece of paper, on which he has written the individual's "true name," known only to that priest. I, who took my Tibetan prayer wheel apart to see what prayers I was twirling around, would be too curious to go through life wearing such a bag and not opening it. Wouldn't you? The Tibetans would not think of opening it, not until the person dies. Then another lama reads the name (so he can remember it in his prayers, as we remember the names of loved ones in ours, as the Church remembers the names of saints on their feast days, and so on) and promptly burns the paper (stymieing the demons who want to know the name so they can exert power over the deceased).

I have witnessed some of the marvels that Tibetan lamas can perform, from apparent self-evisceration to incredible feats of endurance, and I appreciate how Tibetans can believe in a world of demons and magic. I dare not say categorically that their system does not work. People who know far more than I ever will firmly believe that it does. One high-ranking lama once told me that the "beauty of the system is that even if the deceased is horribly tortured by demons he *cannot* reveal a 'real name' even he does not know."

You must admit there's a certain logic there. Maybe there's some logic behind our culture's old idea that a woman ought never to marry a man with the same surname as her own. Does it betray a fear of incest, of consanguinity unsuspected, or just the custom that a woman's status changes at marriage and her surname ought to reflect that? Others say that not changing her surname at marriage is unusual for a woman and that, clearly, she must therefore be an unusual woman, perhaps one with second sight or the power of prophecy, gifted like the seventh son of a seventh son (who ought to be named *Doctor,* old custom dictates).

Folklore records many ways in which people (usually girls) have attempted to discover whom they will marry. To find a future spouse's initial, you can peel an apple all in one long strip and then throw the strip over your left (that's *sinister*) shoulder; it should fall in such a way as to suggest the initial to you. Or there are various alphabet chants you can perform while going through some actions; the letter on which you fail is The One. In the olden days this could give you a headstart on embroidering initials on the linens in your dowry, I suppose, but a wise virgin, I should think, would wait until St. Agnes' Eve (or one of the other propitious occasions). Then, going through a rigamarole, she could actually *see* the person she was going to marry. On second thought, that might not provide his name!

Preparing another book (*Norden: The Folk Customs and Beliefs of Norway, Sweden, Denmark, Finland, Iceland, Greenland, The Faroes and The Lapps*) lately I have discovered many similar name superstitions and whom-shall-I-marry formulae in that part of the world, as well. All the *Abracadabra*—and just maybe that's not from *Abraxas* at all but from Hebrew *Abba* (Father), *Ben* (Son), *Ruach Acadash* (Holy Spirit, or Holy Ghost, if you like)—may make you laugh. Nonetheless, people have believed and believe today incredible things about magic and the magic in names. If you want to know more about that, start with Edward Cloud's classic *Magic in Names and Other Things* (1920, reprinted 1969).

23. Fortune Telling with Names

All magic is the search for power, and one power all people have yearned to have is the power to foretell the future. They have cast and read the *I Ching* or other objects (cleromancy). They have tried to guess what's coming by the fall of arrows (bellomancy). They have scanned the skies in astrology or with a mirror to reflect the moon (catoptromancy). They have watched how an ax quivers after it has been thrown into a tree trunk (axiomancy). They have studied the swing of a suspended object such as a ring (dactylomancy) or the behavior of horses (hippomancy) or fish (icthyomancy) or torches (lampadomancy) or water (lecanomancy) or meteors (meteoromancy) or other portents. They have listened to the hiss of molten lead (molybdomancy), the crackling of burning laurel branches (daphnomancy), the rumble of thunder (ceraunomancy), and other natural sounds. They have gazed intently into water or basalt mirrors or crystal balls. They have told fortunes with yarrow stalks or baked bones or pebbles or dice. They have dealt and read cards (cartomancy). They have pored over the entrails of sacrifices in augury. They have looked at the heads of animals (cephalomancy) or the bumps on the heads of people (phrenology). They have interpreted handwriting (graphology), though this and other pseudo-sciences have usually had more to do with trying to read personality than the future; however, character is fate. They have read the lines of the hands (chiromancy) to see not only what you were supposed to be and what you are but what you may yet be. They have gone into trances and other altered states of consciousness to practice metagnomy and mediumship and other occult arts. They have examined eggs (ooscopy) and human faces (physiognomy). They have employed fire in pyromancy, xylomancy, causimomancy. They have used incense (libanomancy) and even mice (myomancy). They have torn open sacrificial animals, and in one instance Gilles de Rais tore open hundreds of little boys. They have consulted wise men and prophets and books at random (bibliomancy, rhapsodomancy, stichomancy), fumbled in ashes (tephramancy) and soot (spodomancy). They have tried to interpret dreams (oneiromancy) and plumb the unconscious through such means as reading the Tarot. And, to end this long list of bizarre names, they have turned to onomancy or onomantia, the art of reading the future through names themselves.

Here we can freely discuss onomantia, or names foretelling, because it has nothing to do with the black arts of sciomancy (dealing with spirits) or necromancy (dealing with the dead) or other forbidden and black arts, which I meant only to allude to, not (I hope) in either an encouraging or intimidating fashion, in the section just prior to this one. Onomantia is connected with the less frightening but no less superstitious art of numerology, but it is less spooky and probably more common than sitting around in darkened rooms at séances, or organizing a group to run around in circles until they drop from exhaustion and examining how they have fallen (gyromancy), or just contemplating your fingernails (onychomancy). Numerology is an ancient pseudo-science become a modern fad which assigns (today most often ignorantly) a numerical value to each letter of a name to determine the bearer's personality and to project his or her destiny (assuming that is set). It resembles astrology, which right now seems to be more popular than religion. Today horoscopes run in thousands of otherwise sensible newspapers, people ask you your sign instead of just saying hello (I am tempted to tell them *Feces*), and world leaders (and their wives, like Nancy Reagan) are said not to be able to make a move without astrological advice. People more or less believe there are fire, water, earth, and air signs— it was Galen who first taught that everything is made of these Four Elements, from which came a psychosomatic theory of psychology based on the Four Humours, liquids ideally in balance in the body—and only 12 basic personalities, tied to the Zodiac, ruled by as many planets as were known when this idea first caught on. If challenged, most people say they do not take astrology seriously. But they keep sneaking a look at their horoscopes in the papers, buy astrological magazines, have horoscopes cast by computers or expensive astrologers, secretly believe, down deep, that "there's something in it." Well, yes, something—but not anything that can reasonably dictate whom you marry or when you should buy or sell stock or travel or keep your mouth shut when your mother-in-law makes a statement. The moon affects everyone's emotional life, especially women's, but it cannot dictate your Significant Other or exert planetary influence the way horoscopes say it can.

In a May 1988 issue of the Panama City daily, *Crítica,* reporter Chicho Donato cited two Aquarians, then President Reagan and General Manuél Noriega, as a 2 and a 7 respectively. A 7, he asserted, is tranquil, hardly ever losing his or her temper. So much for Noriega. Ronald Reagan he wrote,

is a two. Twos generate much deceit and hypocrisy. They are able to fake emotion even when they feel complete indifference. They deal in misinformation; they make offers and promise a lot but never keep their promises; they tend to be vain and foppish liars.

Later astrology entered US political headlines as well. Both my astrologer and numerologist friends (who, admittedly, tended to be Democrats) assured me that Governor Dukakis would win the presidential election in November 1988. They all had a 50-50 chance of being right, but they were wrong. It was better, I suppose, than reading *Ronald Wilson Reagan* as *666* (which I have explained to you). The Panamanian reporter ended with the forecast that August 1988 would be bad for both President Reagan and Vice-President Bush: the "partial eclipse on August 27," as well as the numbers, prefigured "serious problems" for them both. It is usually quite safe to predict "serious problems" for men in those positions, anyway. The numerologist who told me that John Tower would not be confirmed as Secretary of Defense was right, though the astrologers who may have advised President Bush and his party disagreed completely. Maybe a Tarot reading with a Falling Tower card turning up wrong could have told them.

Such silliness is not without effect, however, because untold millions of Americans (and others throughout the world) sincerely believe in astrology or numerology or both, ignorant as they are of Galen, Pythagoras, Cornelius Agrippa, Karl Jung, and others. My own reading as a Sagittarius with Scorpio rising tells me this is not the place to argue astrology. The time and place may, nonetheless, be propitious for me to talk about numerology and names.

Pythagoras was the one who stated that "the world is based upon the power of numbers." What he meant was that all relationships in the universe can be expressed in mathematical formulations. What he was taken to mean by pseudo-science was that numerology (deeply imbedded in the *kabalah* tradition and in other cultures) and similar occult "sciences" could reveal how our lives run. He would have been astonished to see people placing such faith in numerology that they changed their names (like singer Dionne Warwick) to increase their luck by altering the spelling. Ms. Warwick's career plummeted, she changed back, and popularity returned, she reports.

Over the centuries, the universal numbers (1 through 9) of Pythagoras—0 did not come in until the Arab mathematicians—have been built into an over-credulous method for turning a name number or a birth date, indeed any "vibratory" or powerful number, into a guide to personality and prognosis. Now vast numbers of otherwise sensible people really believe that the animal signs (whence *Zodiac*) rule, or can guide, their lives; others swear by the numbers.

Last year (1988) more Americans read the daily horoscopes than attended weekly church services, despite the fact that belief flourishes in God or at least in angels (a poll a few years back showed 54% of Americans were utterly convinced of the omnipresence of angels). We must note that astrology and numerology are absolutely forbidden by most major religions, but the faithful, in these days of Jews eating shrimp and pork in Chinese restaurants and Roman Catholic laity favoring birth control, abortion, etc., are, to put it politely, selective in their beliefs. They are not to be dictated to—except by the stars and the numbers.

Religion and numerology were closer together in the days of the cabalists. No one expects you to rush out and get Ginsberg's monumental *Kabbalah* of 1863 (reprinted) or ponderous tomes such as Scholem's *Major Trends in Jewish Mysticism* (1946), let alone more recent studies. Let's leave it at this: the cabalists had a way of translating letters into numbers.

They actually had several systems, but two will suffice for our purposes here. The first, the more recent and nowadays the more common of the two, is based on a simple arrangement of numbers and letters like this:

1	2	3	4	5	6	7	8	9
A	B	C	D	E	F	G	H	I
J	K	L	M	N	O	P	Q	R
S	T	U	V	W	X	Y	Z	

This uses all the Pythagorean numbers and works nicely for English or any other 26-letter alphabet. Don't worry about the Scandinavians and others. It may not be right but it is easy to remember. The older system, for reasons you wouldn't care to get into, violates English alphabetical order and omits 9 (which, as 3 times 3, is sacred, another superstition entirely). It goes like this:

1	2	3	4	5	6	7	8
A	B	C	D	E	U	O	F
I	K	G	M	H	V	Z	P
Q	R	L	T	N	W		
J		S		X			
Y							

There is, as I said, an explanation for this older system's arrangement, far more complicated but just as essentially practical as the seemingly random *QWERTYUIOP* on the top line of your typewriter. (That was adopted early so that salesmen could show how easy it was to use the machine by typing out *TYPEWRITER*.) The older system's arrangement you can just accept as a convention you do not fully understand, like the sleeve buttons on men's suits, or the way men's and women's jackets button on different sides. (OK, for the curious: so men can draw their swords more easily and women can cradle babies in their arms more easily. You read it here.) What you really need more than an explanation is a mnemonic aid, like *No Plan Like Yours to Study History Wisely* (which gives you the initials of all the reigning houses of Britain since 1066) or the strange sentences medical students confect to help them memorize lists in anatomy, etc. Unfortunately, nobody has come up with a viable mnemonic device in this case. Keep the diagram handy, or commit it to memory as is.

If you have been paying close attention, you will have noticed that the two systems I cite assign the same "values" to fewer than half the letters. Therefore they are likely to produce quite different results. Most people will use the "inferior," more modern, system because it is easier to find the letters that way. The would-be experts, of course, prefer the older, more difficult system; this helps to separate the sheep from the goats, always a major matter in magic. Make your choice: the benefit of simplicity or the challenge of doing things the hard way. Right there you have a character factor that will affect the outcome. The average person will probably try one system and if it does not yield a satisfying result will turn to the other. Whatever you like is fine with me.

If you are especially clever, you'll be saying to yourself: the Hebrews (like the Greeks) did not use arabic numerals (1, 2, 3, etc.) at all. Right. The ancients assigned numerical values to letters: *aleph* (the Hebrew equivalent of our *A*) served for 1, *beth* for 2, *gimel* for 3, and so on. So in a sense it was not numerology, but you get the idea. The Romans, being Italian, talked with their hands, and why not? It was a great idea to hold up fingers for I, II, III, make a V with thumb and palm for 5, cross hands to make an X for 10—their fingers suggested a mathematics with base 10—cup a hand as C for 100, etc. They also added letters to the alphabet such as *J* (though *I* could do similar work) and liked *X* (which the French name still says is "Greek *Y*"). These were swiftly incorporated into the Hebrew system of 8, the Romans likewise leaving out 9.

Explanations are supposed to simplify, this is getting more complicated. Simply take the point that both systems of numerology have long been in use and readily adjusted to changing circumstances and that both remain for numerologists to employ as they see fit.

Let us move on to finding what they call your "digital root." We can use the convenient modern system and my name for starters. Following the modern system, then, we get:

L.	R.	N.	ASHLEY
3	9	5	1 1 8 3 5 7

which adds up to 42. Using my full names we get:

LEONARD	RAYMOND	NELLIGAN	ASHLEY
3 5 6 5 1 9 4	9 1 7 4 6 5 4	5 5 3 3 9 7 1 5	1 1 8 3 5 7

which adds up to 132, which is the same as 42. Why? Because the rule is we call 42 $4+2=6$ and 132 $1+3+2=6$. My number in the long run, either way, is 6. Other names involve other numbers and, it is said, other "personalities," other fates. (A *Mike* is not a *Michael,* you see.) LEONARD ASHLEY produces first 58 then $5+8=13$ then $1+3=4$. He's a 4, not a 6. LEN ASHLEY is 38 then $3+8=11$ then $1+1=2$. He's a 2. So far I can be a 6 or a 4 or a 2. As I remarked some pages back, I don't like *Leonard* much and my close friends call me *Tim,* but as it happens the nickname doesn't change LEONARD ASHLEY at all because TIM ASHLEY comes out to 40 and $4+0=4$, just like LEONARD.

We'll ignore the magical aspects of *Leonard* (Inspector-General of Hell, the master worshipped at the witches' *sabbat*) and the (French) devil *Raymond* and *Ashley,* the ash tree in the field and Sacred Grove of the Druids. We'll stick with my "digital root," and I can have 6 or 4 or 2. The numerologists say that means only that the name I use indicates the personality I am then projecting, and the name a person uses to refer to me indicates the personality he or she perceives. Do you, for instance, sometimes feel like a *William,* sometimes like a *Bill,* seldom like the *Billy* of your youth? If you are *Margaret,* do some people call you *Marge* or *Peg* or *Peggy*? See what they mean?

You work out your "digital root" number(s) and with one of them chosen by you we can go on to find two more numbers said to be significant. First, we want your "heart number." For that, count up all the vowels. Those are *A, E, I, O, U,* and *Y* when it functions as does a vowel in a name like *Lynn,* but not when it does not, as in *Billy* or *Sally.* This will have to be reduced to a single digit; add up numbers until you produce it as we did in the "digital root" operation. This "heart number" that results is said to be the key to your innermost secrets, your deepest, even hidden, interests, needs, likes, dislikes, ambitions, dreams. Why *hidden* in connection with these vowels? I think it's because in the Hebrew tradition vowels are omitted in writing. Second, count up all the consonants for your "image number." Purists insist that *A* is to be regarded as a consonant here, because in Hebrew *aleph* is a "breathing" and not a vowel. You can count it or not. If you really believe the Hebrew ideas are better, this modern system is the wrong one for you anyway. After all, it's your fortune. The aim is to produce (as usual) a single digit; this one is the key to your outward personality. The "heart" is the secret you; the "image" is the public you, the one the world sees.

Now you have three important, personal numbers. Write them down secretly here (and let other people buy their own copies of my book):

DIGITAL ROOT _____

HEART NUMBER _____

IMAGE NUMBER _____

If you like you can add your "birth number." Let us say that you were born 1 September 1940. That's $1+9+1+9+4+0=24$ and $2+4=6$. Don't fret that everyone will know your age, because 3 January 1928 and many other dates all yield a 6. If your "digital root" is 6 and your "birth number" is also 6, numerologists will advise you to put special emphasis on 6 June each year. You may wish to bet on the sixth horse in the sixth race on that date. (I hope he doesn't come in sixth.) You may wish to bet on 6 in lotteries and such, move until you get one or more sixes in your address (alternatively, numbers that added up reduce to 6), and to try for sixes in your telephone or Social Security numbers and such. You can strive to stress sixes in taking important actions, and so on. I admit that this does work if you believe implicitly in it. It will give you confidence when you approach the job interview (or the sixth job interview, or the one at 666 Fifth Avenue). It can help you enter the audition or the sales presentation with confidence, etc. It also gives you a lot of "lucky" days such as 5 January, 4 February, 3 March, 2 April, even 3 December ($3+1+2=6$), and, one hopes, with all that an optimistic outlook on life. So superstition can deal in self-fulfilling prophecies.

With your personal number known, you can now read my summaries of what numerologists would tell you about what they like to call "personality clusters" or "profiles" that go along with the numbers 1 through 9. Here is the distillation of their "wisdom," the most erudite brief summary to be found anywhere.

1 *Aggression, ambition, action, arrogance.* These are some of the words that begin with the first letter of the alphabet. *ONE* is driving, determined, decisive, straightforward, but also single- even narrow-minded and one-tracked, looking out for Number One. *ONE* likes to be first to try new things but is more likely to take a chance than to take advice. *ONE* will bet it all on one shot, go it alone, and if counsel is sought you may suspect narcissism: *ONE* likes to have people concentrate on him or her. *ONE* wants to be the one in your life but is also shy of one-on-one relationships. Rather, *ONE* likes to be the common factor in a number of diverse relationships. You can snag *ONE* if you are ready to be an audience of one to *ONE*'s own principal concern, which is the undying love affair of *ONE* for *ONE* himself or herself. If you have one thing in common it will probably be that you and *ONE* agree that *ONE* is the Only One in The World. *ONE* is an independent but lonely number. *ONE* is self-sufficient. *ONE* is easily misjudged but misled only with difficulty. *ONE* stands alone, enjoys being first. All *ONE* really cares about is *ONE*. *ONE*'s idea of sharing is to call his son *Jr.* If an only child, a *ONE* is especially well educated, socially adept, sensitive to what others want, if not likely to give it to them.

2 *TWO* is even-handed, even-tempered, even ready to play second fiddle to be part of a pair. *TWO* is "feminine," which sexism defines as soft, sweet, passive, modest, shy, tidy, intuitive, helpful to the point of self-sacrifice at times, subordinate, self-conscious, self-effacing, a leaner and not a leader. *TWO* will not be the one to take control or to argue, unless too oppressed. *TWO* is too giving to be one-sided. *TWO* is conscientious, not contrary. *TWO* will try to see two sides to everything. *TWO* is a good diplomat, except that *TWO* feels two-faced when lying is demanded. *TWO* is a peace-maker, a compromiser, likes to bring two sides together but can complicate negotiations by favoring equality in every detail even when real equality is impossible or unnecessary. *TWO* can shilly-shally and vacillate and be of two minds, so *TWO* is an inefficient executive unless the work calls for continual fairness to all. *TWO* gets very disgruntled at the sight of any uneven scales. *TWO* can be two people: on occasion that much vaunted respect for equity and equal rights may be a mask for feelings of inadequacy or injustice. *TWO*'s equivocalness can make *TWO* seem duplicitous, alternately smiling and snaking, approving and disapproving, back-slapping and backstabbing. *TWO* already has read this and decided the description is unfair. *TWO* will flip-flop and, not to be too flip, more than often will flop. One *TWO* may like another *TWO* for his or her even-handedness but the relationship will be one of the most debatable (and debated), considered (and reconsidered), and generally anguished affairs imaginable. *TWO* relationships suffer from each partner waiting for the other to make the first move so that he or she can react and second-guess.

Odd but brilliant, bold and imaginative, versatile and energetic, sparkling and even scintillating, *THREE* is witty enough to smile now when I say that *THREE* in characteristic vanity has already begun to beam at these compliments. Also, *THREE* is erratic, unpredictable, and at times at odds with convention and expectation. *THREE* seeks praise but is not certain that others are reliable judges of what success really is. *THREE* rewards himself or herself with self-satisfaction while still thriving on recognition and encouragement. A lucky number, *THREE* can fail and still win commendations and often receives more applause than is warranted. If *THREE* should fail, *THREE* either does not realize it or takes it lightly. *THREE* sometimes succeeds without trying very hard (which is nice, for *THREE*) and does best when meticulous planning and patient execution are not required. *THREE* will go off in several directions at once and be frustrated by any necessity of choice, always looking for more than two alternatives, hating to commit. *THREE*, overanxious for approval, wants nonetheless to maintain independence, to run the show, set the standards, assess the results, to be judge, jury, and executioner. Give *THREE* responsibility and a free hand and occasionally he or she will be great—or will complain bitterly about lack of support and may go off in the wrong direction just to be different. *THREE* can be a bad boss, flighty, pushy, intermittently dictatorial, quick to condemn and slow to praise. *THREE* is a worse follower. To conduct with a *THREE* an ongoing relationship in the arts or business can be excruciating; to do so on the domestic front deserves a medal for heroism, and patience, beyond the call of duty. Every once in a while *THREE* will grin and admit all this is true. That can be totally disarming.

4 Four-square. Forthright. Maybe "four-eyed," behind the glasses of a scholar. *FOUR* is good at numbers (mathematician, engineer, accountant, if artistically gifted more likely to be a sculptor than a painter). *FOUR* is the most fundamental number and a *FOUR* person can be boring but never unreliable, or at least never unpredictable. The Four Elements and Four Humours we spoke of earlier were long thought to be the key to the universe and to human personality. There are four seasons, four cardinal points of the compass, four corners of the earth (round as it is). *FOUR* is likewise basic, regular, balanced, more centered than *THREE,* whose spark *FOUR* may lack. *FOUR* is down-to-earth, calm and industrious, maybe plodding, ready to get the job done by application rather than ingenuity. What time and patience can accomplish, *FOUR* will do. *FOUR* knows his or her limitations but is seldom jealous of brighter people, because *FOUR* thinks little of the arty, the flighty, and the fantastic. *FOUR* gone wrong is suspicious rather than devious, resentful of the "luck" of others they do not much respect, admiring talent but distrusting flair and genius. *FOUR* is not apt to do badly or to be outstanding except in fields where the long run and the bottom line are everything. Some experts say that *FOUR* is the number of poverty and defeat and depression. Others affirm that *FOUR* will avoid extremes and be happy with average success, avoiding dejection and exultation, getting along. The comparatively few *FOUR* people who make it big (chiefly by careful planning and dogged efforts and being in the right place at the right time) hold tightly the fruits of their hard-won success, clutching them with amazing tenacity, sometimes bitterly. The partner of a *FOUR* must be considerate, supportive, never interfering, absolutely never nagging. *FOUR* won't tolerate pushing for a moment and is likely to walk off without a word and never explain, never reappear, and (it must be added in all fairness) never regret.

5 Five adds one more (odd) element to *FOUR*. Thus a *FIVE* has all the solid qualities of a *FOUR* plus a touch of the bizarre, the restless, the volatile, maybe the unbalanced. *FIVE* will work hard but wants to brighten the workday with novelty, change, travel, risk (business speculation or even gambling), or adventure. *FIVE* can be unpredictable and, if challenged, may turn caustic, sarcastic, occasionally mean. *FIVE* can be insensitive and especially is unappreciative of the usefulness of stay-at-homes. *FIVE* thinks they must be missing all the fun of life. *FIVE* usually keeps all these observations to himself or (more often) herself, but that is for reasons of personal advantage, not out of fear of hurting anyone's feelings. A *FIVE* actually enjoys being "one up" on a *FOUR*. A *FIVE* can be an excellent salesperson and even when a bit negative or undisciplined can be driving and resourceful to the point where awed colleagues will excuse cynicism, competitiveness, and the fast pace a *FIVE* really enjoys setting. They can come to admire a *FIVE* without jealousy. *FIVE* is difficult to pin down and analyze sufficiently to be able to say what *FIVE* will do next. Check the older numerological system and you will see that the word *SEX* adds up to five. Hence by that system a *FIVE* will always be extremely ambitious, if not always as active as he or she would like you to believe, in that department of life. *FIVE* is not always a winner but will try repeatedly, undiscouraged. *FIVE* may turn to excess, debauchery, perversity and yet manage to get forgiven or famous. The number 5 turns up incredibly often in the lives of *FIVE* people; they count on it. *FIVE* is pleasant in his or her way; just don't expect them to be pleasant if you get in their way. A *FIVE* and a *FOUR* make a good if not always comfortable pair, supplying each other's deficiencies and not being at all dull. However, such an arrangement would be the idea of a *FOUR,* to start.

6 If you have read all of the above "profiles"—more likely you started by reading your own—you have seen many negative things. *SIX* is perfect. *SIX* has the evenness of *TWO* times the oddness of *THREE. SIX* means harmony and peace, dependability, social sense, domestic tranquility. *SIX* can be counted on to be loyal, always there for you, conscientious—and fiercely demanding of all these qualities in others, especially in lovers. *SIX* may be bland and ordinary for a while and then be galvanized into action by an idea or by anger. If taken advantage of, *SIX* gets furious. *SIX* can be wholesome to the point of priggishness and then, like a *THREE*, unexpectedly take a whole new tack, unreservedly, but never without conscious acceptance of the risk. *SIX,* not always as clever as *THREE,* may go farther in the long run and that without the ups and downs that beset a *FIVE,* more likely with the steady advance that is characteristic of a *FOUR.* But with more excitement. *SIX* is equipped to be resourceful in times of difficulty; pressure can reveal a surprising flair. *SIX* may be so taken for granted that promotion goes to more colorful people, but *SIX* must not be underestimated. Many experts single out *SIX* as a bundle of contradictions: generous and petty, methodical and fussy, smug and self-satisfied and suddenly (maybe outrageously) daring. The partner of a *SIX* may be chosen more for looks than for character but the *SIX* harbors a secret plan to mould him or her closer to the heart's desire; the partner may discover he or she has enrolled in a course rather than simply made a match! The partner of a *SIX* must be ready for feast or famine and sometimes the shock that sudden, unexpected success is more of a barrier to a happy, continued relationship than all the years of making do and getting by ever were.

7 We said that if you ask someone to choose a number between 1 and 10 they will most often choose 3 or 7. Say "lucky number" and it will very often be 7. *SEVEN* is lucky. *SEVEN* is a scholar, if only in the School of Life, maybe a mystic. *SEVEN* believes in the occult even if he or she feels they have no special "powers." *SEVEN,* though superstitious, is an intellectual, whether studying the Talmud or pumping gas, always ruminating. Reclusive and reserved, often more interested in ideas than in material comfort or worldly fame, *SEVEN* may be too dreamy to look for opportunities, too hesitant to grasp them when they come along. *SEVEN* can be extremely imaginative, except when it comes to seeing things from the other person's perspective. *SEVEN* will intuit an answer and get angry if pressed to explain it. But *SEVEN* will enjoy an argument more than a demand to sympathize or empathize. *SEVEN* hates to be disagreed with and absolutely detests being proved wrong. That leads to grudges for a *SEVEN*. *SEVEN* makes a fine teacher so long as he or she is honored as an authority. *SEVEN* will be too distant or disdainful, too proud or premptory to be a beloved teacher, to stoop to explanation; take it or leave it. *SEVEN* will withdraw if easy connections cannot be made with people—this they characteristically regard as the fault of others—and then *SEVEN* becomes haughty, aloof, superior; they invented "attitude" and work at perfecting it, unrelenting, unforgiving, antagonistic with little or no cause and snobbish without justification or humor. *SEVEN* is a useful if often unfeeling friend, always a bad enemy. Some say *ONE* and *SIX* add up to *SEVEN* having a much greater share of psychic powers than most people, and some *SEVEN* people do, while *SEVEN* also may exhibit more PMS than ESP. However, the ordinary *SEVEN* has too little faith or too much fear to embrace occult powers and in any case is seldom dedicated to the service of others. As a lover, *SEVEN* can be a party—but has to be catered to.

You must have guessed, if you have read straight through and are not just dropping in to see what an *EIGHT* is, that if *FOUR* is four-square and dependable, *EIGHT* is twice as much so, and twice as predictable. That guarantees *EIGHT* a good chance in all but the very most creative occupations, because determination usually counts for more in the marketplace than daring, and tenacity often triumphs over talent in the arts. What else could explain, say, the many performers we see on television? W. Somerset Maugham, master of the short story, once revealed that the art of the short story is to "stick to the point like grim death." An *EIGHT* has that philosophy. *EIGHT* can be tough as well as tenacious. Wherever brilliance or intuition are not requisites, *EIGHT* performs ably. Halved, the parts of 8 are equal; halved again, the parts are equal. This leads the numerologists to agree that whatever happens *EIGHT* will be equal to it and ready when necessary for a double dose of hard knocks or hard work. On the negative side, *EIGHT* is leary of razzle-dazzle and actively dislikes conspicuously bright people and all those who like to work for ovations. A female *EIGHT* is alleged to be capable of remarkably mean tactics to keep others from winning unfairly or by sheer cleverness or good fortune. *EIGHT* has strength of character and firm convictions unassailably held. Combine that with meanness and you have an ugly *EIGHT,* the more ugly if he or she knows the adversary is better equipped. *EIGHT* is too smart not to know his or her limitations, but confront an *EIGHT* with them and you have a dangerous foe on your hands. *EIGHT* will strive to work within bounds, but if *EIGHT* starts to lose, watch out for viciousness. Once in a while an *EIGHT* will kick over the traces and then you will have a determined eccentric, an indefatigable radical, perhaps a stern loner who (despite tension, alienation, self-doubt) will claw his or her way to astonishing heights. *EIGHT* losers are uncommon, but the few there are are uncommonly nasty. *EIGHT* winners are charming, a joy to have around. Don't cross them, ever.

Here we have 3 times 3, the Trinity trebled, the "sacred" primary number, the number of God Himself. That is why, as we noted, some numerologists don't use it in discussing mere mortals. *NINE* has versatility and vast potential (generally realized by them, not always realized in fact), a romantic and passionate nature (which can turn sour), an impulsive and occasionally heedless drive (often accompanied by super energy). *NINE* prefers the professions to business but can make lots of money in a profession or turn a business into a profession. *NINE* likes occupations in which innovation is rewarded and enthusiasm encouraged, not looked at askance, suspect. *NINE* can be paid in status instead of cash. The weaker side of this lies in the danger of getting all wrapped up in oneself—it is always said that a person wrapped up in himself makes a small package—and a *NINE* can readily lose touch with the great world. *NINE* loves to be creative, detests ugliness, and also (most unfortunately) people who are ugly or old or unlucky or unhappy. *NINE* can be cruel in contemptuous rejection of anything or anyone unpleasing to him or her. Especially her. Like Jonathan Swift (though he was not a *NINE*) a *NINE* can like Tom, Dick, and Harry as individuals and yet have an almost obsessively low opinion of mankind in general (whom Swift dismissed as "yahoos"). *NINE* can be so egocentric or secure that he or she does not deign to notice that his or her high ideals or grand schemes are irrelevant or inapplicable to the Average Joe. More damning, *NINE* can be ruthlessly ambitious, if often for a Good Cause. Power and fame can be dangerous drugs and *NINE*s are particularly addictive personalities more often than not. Two assassinated presidents, Lincoln and Kennedy, were *NINE*s, wonderful and highly controversial figures struck down in mid-careers that sharply divided public opinion, created murderous jealousies. After a *NINE* is "safely" dead, people feel more secure in glorifying them; a live *NINE* can be hard to handle. *NINE* demands a totally dedicated partner and seems to thrive on domestic friction created by that demand. If *NINE* cannot find a true worshipper, he or she may coerce or bribe a partner to give at least public evidence of devotion, for a *NINE* yearns for reputation and, like Mayor Ed Koch of New York City and others who may not be *NINE* at heart but can act like them, always asks, "How am I doin'?" Often they are doing superbly, but life is not easy for them.

I trust this is not too many pages on what some readers will undoubtedly think of as foolishness. I have attempted at least to be frank and to avoid the mindless, congratulatory, stroke-everyone approach of so many guru types, astrologers and numerologists and pop psychologists included, who stoop to please their customers. I hope you have found these "profiles" balanced, not too negative, and that they can serve as useful warnings of weaknesses as well as recognition of virtues. You may not like "your" number but, honestly, don't you think the estimates of your spouse or lover, friend or colleague are pretty close to accurate?

I conclude with two very special and rare kinds of people, the *ELEVEN* and the *TWENTY-TWO*. Some numerologists refuse to add the numbers together to produce the common *TWO* or *FOUR;* they may be as correct in this as they are in anything else. The world does have exceptional people.

11 A *NINE* may arouse enough opposition to cause assassination, but an *ELEVEN* may become a martyr. *ELEVEN* is a seer with a message for the world in religion or science or some other important field. *ELEVEN* can get so involved in the mission that he or she does not get the message that hatred is growing toward the message or (more likely) the messenger, or *ELEVEN* may be so dedicated as not to care, so concerned with the truth as not to face facts, so dedicated to the future as not to take heed of the dangers in the present. *ELEVEN* can sacrifice himself or herself or anybody else to The Cause. Convinced of the right, *ELEVEN* can endure being reviled or rejected and righteously run roughshod right over the sensibilities of other people. *ELEVEN* may have towering conceit or just otherworldliness; either may be concealed under a real or specious modesty, suspicious only in its exaggerated form. *ELEVEN* may sincerely believe that kowtowing to convention is beneath him or her and caving into restrictions is both undignified and counterproductive. *ELEVEN* has the invincible vanity of children and Churchills and sometimes the added callousness of a Picasso—all of which we may be willing to forget or forgive for the great gift of genius. *ELEVEN* may be a prodigy in one field and yet pontificate in another where he or she is not expert, like Einstein (though he had the sense to say that "politics is harder than physics"). Despite all, *ELEVEN* is a mover and shaker of the world, a giant if not always a friendly giant. *ELEVEN* may be driven by a full knowledge of greatness or by deep-seated but conquered frailties, sensed but repressed inadequacies, magically transmuting them (sublimating them really) into charismatic confidence and selfless service to the higher good. The feet of clay may be revealed to the few people close to the *ELEVEN,* which only make them love him or her more. Like Florence Nightingale, an *ELEVEN* can be a holy humanitarian and a holy terror, both at one and the same time, insufferable and indispensable. *ELEVEN* may earn the gratitude and awe of ordinary men and women and yet be lonely, with disciples instead of lovers. Most ordinary people, looking at an *ELEVEN,* would not trade their own less productive and more pedestrian existences for what they feel sure is the more painful travail of the preeminent. Do you want to be worshipped, or loved? However great you are, if you say "loved," you are probably a *TWO,* not an *ELEVEN,* though you may be gifted.

22 *ELEVEN* is great and *TWENTY-TWO* is twice as great. *TWENTY-TWO* lives a life of unalloyed success and revels in it, if only in the private conviction of later recognition. *TWENTY-TWO* can live with adulation and fame with no nagging insecurity, whether as a matchless entrepreneur (John D. Rockefeller) or as "the Napoleon of Crime," Sherlock Holmes' dreaded adversary, the brilliant but criminal Professor Moriarty. To play with words, maybe there was no police like Holmes, but there also was no master criminal like the Professor, and Moriarty did it all without drugs, shunning the limelight, devoting endless energy to clever if deplorable activities. *TWENTY-TWO,* for good or ill, is naturally rare. *TWENTY-TWO* flees from the glare of publicity in which *ELEVEN* basks. If you think you are a natural *TWENTY-TWO,* you are most likely to be a nutty *FOUR.* However, you could examine your life and see how many times 22 has been very significant to you (don't cheat, because if you are really a *TWENTY-TWO* that is beneath you). If the results are well beyond what Lady Bracknell might call the rules "that statistics have laid down for us," you may indeed be a *TWENTY-TWO.* If so, go out and do something utterly marvelous this week. Do something bigger and better next week. You are, in many ways, what you accomplish. Remember that an actor working in a restaurant is not an actor; he or she is a waiter. Actors act. *TWENTY-TWO* acts. If you are a *TWENTY-TWO* the world needs you, in some fields desperately.

So you see from what I have written here, drawing together the ideas of scores of numerologists, that your name and number are claimed to "tell you" a lot about yourself, who you are, who you can be. But I inherited my surname, I hear you object. True, but you also inherited your genes and much of your environment and consequently much of your fate. One might say that as you grew up you more or less changed the name you were given, or you might have done so and did not. If you made a big switch (*Frances Gumm* to *Judy Garland,* for instance) you cashed in your old identity and invested in a new one. The astrologers, who are up against modern man's distaste for anything that smacks of an attack on freedom and individuality, like to say: you are impelled even by the stars, not compelled. Your fate is at least somewhat in your own hands. If you don't like your name (and therefore your number), you can make changes. Your numerologist will be sure to tell you, I predict, that if you make changes you were fated to do so. Ricky Schroeder became *Rick.*

I think you have caught on to the fact that I am by no means trying to sell you numerology. My interest in the subject, as with magic and witchcraft, is largely academic and I have personal reservations about its legitimacy and efficacy. For one thing, now that you know the "best numbers," why can't we all get better ones than we have, maybe even join the rare ranks of *ELEVEN* and *TWENTY-TWO?* If the time and place we are born are so crucial that people pore over horoscopes, why don't we try to conceive new life or at least induce labor at the most propitious times, and why are not the airlines of the world overcrowded with pregnant women flying to the most propitious place to give birth? Why don't we all avoid conception except during the one best sign of the Zodiac? Most of all, nobody seems to want to tackle the question about how these "occult sciences" actually *work.* The last attempt at an explanation of how the planets impinge upon us that I can find was made by some kook in the Renaissance who actually asserted that we have tiny holes in our heads through which the Forces enter our bodies. Not very convincing. I have seen, however, no such bold attempt at explanation of *how* it all works from any astrologer or numerologist or palm reader. It is not enough to assert that this line in your hand "means" that. It is required to do more than to *say* it does so (or, more often, to copy from some old book that says it does so). How does it do so, if it does? Can I change my fate by extending my "life line" with a razor blade? Can I change my fate by changing my name?

What I believe is this: honest to God, your names do affect your life. Given the nature and prejudices of society, your surname can open some doors to you, close some others. You know that, and you know how it works. Your forenames in a sense write a script for your life, or impel if not compel. Your forenames and surname help to create the image you have of yourself, which unquestionably has something to do with what you become, and they also contribute to the idea and expectations other people have of you even before they meet you. Your nickname is not as arbitrary as it may seem nor need it have stuck if certain moves were made to remove it. It does in fact contain valuable information of what your peers thought or think about you. Your keeping it or rejecting it is significant. Your titles may bring prestige and power. No name is given entirely arbitrarily or borne without consequences. Even an alias or a pseudonym cannot be really arbitrary or without effect. To be polysyllabic about it, there are multitudinous and multifarious onomastic ramifications. In short, numerology may be superstition, but *your name counts.*

If you do not like your numerological "reading" here, I'm sorry. Remember that most people are not completely happy with their faces, either. My own advice is in the direction of rhinoplasty and the scrapping of *Edith* or changing *Millstein* to *Mills* or doing whatever else makes you happier than you are. If self-realization or self-improvement for you involves playing with numerology, by all means do it. Console yourself with the fact that many famous people have more or less changed their names and many serious people use astrological data all the time to trade on the stock exchanges and play politics. Who knows, maybe you were fated to read this book, work out your "digital number" and "heart number" and "image number," be dissatisfied with them, and improve them. Maybe the stars say that this very day would be a good time to change your name.

This has been a rather long section in a book where I have had to cut, cut, cut, but I think many people will find it to be a feature. I hope it helps you to "be Here now, and prepare for There." Finally we turn to something truly important as regards the fate of yourself and, at the time of life when most people take their most serious look at names, the names and "destinies" of your children.

Once again the distillation of innumerable books on a single topic, here is *what to name the baby*. I am already preparing a whole big book to follow this one, giving my research and opinions on thousands of individual forenames. Look for it. Meanwhile, the essence of it all can be briefly presented in the next, and last, section here.

PART SIX

WHAT TO NAME THE BABY

Creating a totally unique name for a child is traditional in many cultures. The Chinese have few "common" first names because each child is believed to be too special to be given a name many others have used before him.

—Sue Browder, *The New Age Baby Name Book*

24. A Dozen Tips for Giving a Child a Good Name

To end the survey of names and naming we come full circle. We come back to personal names. The end is also the high point, so we address the question of "what to name the baby," a question that has challenged families down through the ages and in all cultures but which is becoming something of an obsession now in our conservative but competitive society in which traditions are constantly up against the trends. Whenever I offer to discuss any and all aspects of naming on radio or television, questioners rapidly, sometimes exclusively, focus on concerns about forenames, whether I am talking to adults on a late-night call-in show or to children on *Nickleodeon* television. At some times in their lives parents are naturally supremely interested in the new arrival's name. The rest of the time they, and all of the time the rest of people, are concerned about their own names. Names are so personal.

Some cultures believe that a well-chosen name will bring prosperity or popularity or power. It can, others say, confound evil spirits, chart a successful course for a life. Whether they explain consequences in terms of the pseudo-science of superstition or the "soft science" of sociology, whether they study scriptures or statistics, whether they have elaborate rules to follow or a fairly free hand to invent, almost everywhere people are convinced that the choice of a baby's name is important, that a "good" one, a suitable and successful one, is worth serious consideration. By now you know that is my opinion. I believe that if corporations spend large sums before settling on a name for a product, then a baby (which represents to a family a financial and emotional investment that is incalculably large, comparatively) is worth taking time and care to name intelligently. It is the family's first truly significant gift to the infant after the gift of life itself.

That gift of a name, even in a world in which names change or can be altered, is a lifetime label that can profoundly affect the new life for its whole duration.

You fundamentally have to satisfy yourself, your spouse, your family, and the whole ethnic and wider community. Additionally, keep firmly in mind that ideally you must try to please the grownup of the next century who now is dependent on you for a sensible choice. That choice may be complicated by the demands of grandparents. They may like an overtly ethnic name or one they have come to think of as traditional, such as *Julius* among Jews or *George* among Greeks. Or names may be dictated by your religion (which may ask for a saint's name or a Mormon name, etc.). These supposedly unavoidable names may appear to create problems but you can get around these problems by bestowing one of them as a middle name. In the forenames but not first among them you also can put one of your own forenames if ego yearns for that. If you cannot tolerate a relative's name, demand for which is strong in your family, call the girl *Jamie* or the boy *Harlan* and tell the relatives that she or he has a variation of the name or the initial in honor of Uncle Hyman.

Strive to make your child "sole tenant of a name," however proud you are of your roots or your relatives. That advice comes from Martin Tupper, in whose lame verses there is still wise counsel:

> *He that is ambitious for his son, should give him untried names,*
> *For those that have served other men, haply may injure by their evils;*
> *Or otherwise may hinder by their glories; therefore set him by himself,*
> *To win for his individual name some clear specific purpose.*

Name is identity; everyone needs his or her own. Your family heritage, whatever it is, ought to be your child's proud possession, but make your child's name, ideally, his or her personal possession. Rather than boast the past, why not trust that he or she will be the first to make the family name truly distinguished? Experience suggests and research confirms that the individual who has been blessed with a well-chosen name tends to go through life better adjusted to family and more popular and successful with others, more secure and better able to take advantage of all potentials. Admittedly many other factors contribute to a person's success or failure, happiness or unhappiness. It would be wrong, however, not to realize that you hold in your hands one of the keys to his or her fate when the church or the state says to you: Name this child.

I don't want to say to you that children named *Mary* or seventh sons named *Doctor* will automatically acquire healing powers or second sight. I do not believe in such superstitions as, to quote one still alive in North Carolina, that a child named *Clay* will break a sad chain of infant mortality. I do not believe that a girl given a "very feminine" name will automatically better fit the stereotype of the "feminine" than one given a name like *Lee* or even *Barbara*, nor that a *Michael* is guaranteed fun and friends and a *Melvin* is going to be a loser. Nonetheless, to use a phrase you read in the last section, these names impel if they don't compel. Personal names do not lack a background or a context—even the newly-coined name is in the tradition of unique names, against the tradition of "accepted" names—and these can be evaluated. Out of research can come certain fundamental and sensible principles for naming your offspring (and in later life yourselves) which are to be ignored only at whatever cost the particular society wishes to exact. Every name decision has its effect. Every name rewards or costs the bearer, even if he or she is ready to pay the cost in pursuit of some perceived benefit in difference. Practically speaking, naming is decision. I want to help you to make the best decision possible, to find a name that will neither be too common (unless you are prepared for blending into the crowd) or too uncommon (unless you think saying no to convention is profitable). I want to educate you so that you can make a thoughtful choice. You need to know what is dated and what is trendy, what is currently regarded as admirable or trivial or pompous, what your society thinks of as too "frivolous" for a girl, too "weak" for a boy (because whatever you may think of the damage it does, society is striving to perpetuate its long-established sex roles along with other mores). Every year a couple of million babies are named right here in the US. Of course each and every parent wants to bestow, each and every child deserves, a name that will be a blessing rather than a burden.

I have consulted literally hundreds of books that purport to give useful advice on what to name the baby and from them and from my own researches and experience I offer you a dozen pointers for your consideration. I do not pretend that I can inform you of the best decision for you, only that I can help to make your decision more informed.

1. Don't limit your choices by slavishly deferring to family tradition. A woman, asked where she got her out-of-fashion hat, once said, "We don't get our hats; we *have* our hats." Some families have a strong tradition of personal names. Maybe you ought to take it seriously, maybe not. Generally speaking, instead of automatic names for your sons and (occasionally) daughters, instead of honoring a deceased relative or trying to please an influential or rich one, honor and please your newborn with a name not too loaded with ancestral baggage, stale or antiquated, but individual and fresh. Resist the temptation to name your children after yourselves; the surname will do its work. Perhaps *Jr.* or an aunt's name will not be a jinx, but there is usually no need to invite comparison or confusion. There's enough evidence that *Jr.* and such, barring exceptional cases, are more trouble than you may consider they are worth. Why take unnecessary chances?

2. Don't get cute. A name that may seem darling or clever for a cuddly infant or a toddler can become an embarrassment in later years. Nor should you name Brandy's new sister *Sherry,* nor make jokes like *Paige Turner.* Don't inflict

Kelly Kelly or *Sydney Sidney* and watch out for well-intentioned alliteration (though *Kris Kristofferson* has done well enough) or the likes of *Jack Jackson,* or tin-eared names like *Dwayne Spain,* maybe not even *Eldon Elder.* Avoid palindromes (*Otto, Ada, Ronnor*) and *Mary Christmas* and patterns of naming the children which deprive each of individuality for some pitiful joke.

Justin Tyme will do only for the cheap working name of a go-go dancer or male porn star. Leave it to gag writers to confect *Kitty Litter* and *Bertha Vanation* (from *Torch Song Trilogy*). "Fatty" Arbuckle, after his disgrace, returned to the movies as *Will B. Goode.* Elvis Presley's personal pilot went through life with *Milo High.* But your kid doesn't have to be called *Herb Gardiner* or *June Moon* or *Noël Powell* (pronounced "Pole" in England) or *May Dos Passos* or *Patience Scales* (the piano teacher). You can't please every kid: *Miswald Cenda Wrandvakist* went to court to change his name to *Linkolis Dislgrowels Wrangvaufgilmotkets.* But you can try to give a child a nice name.

Twins present special opportunities for naming, and for child abuse in naming. Because twins occur only once in more than 80 births, the lucky parents have been known to get carried way and to name *Jack* and *Jill, Paul* and *Paula, Heather* and *Jan.* I know parents who have proved that they can have their *Kate* and *Edith* too. The pet turtles in *Rocky* were called *Cuff* and *Link.* Cute! Cute is for some pets, for no people.

When the Wind family named their kids *North, East, South,* and *West,* they blew it.

Sometimes inadvertently parents make mistakes: *Peter Moss* will become *Pete Moss.* Use your wits to see to it that there is no conceivable way the name(s) you give will be hurt, or hurt the bearer.

3. Be wary of names that already have problems built into them. A lot of people thought *Dennis* was a fine name. Then came *Dennis the Menace.* I wouldn't use it any more, any more than I'd count on people having forgotten that "Dumb" often used to precede *Dora.* What happens is that a good name (*Elmer,* obviously a little hayseed but certainly strong at the time of the novel *Elmer Gantry*) hits the skids, the comedy writers notice this (creating *Elmer Fudd*) and the name is "finished." If you had the name first (presumably *Caspar Weinberger* is older than *Caspar,* the *Friendly Ghost*), too bad. By the time the blow strikes you may be too well-known by the name to change it, in which case get ready for jokes about "ghost-written speeches," etc., and brave it out. People may come to admire that. *Lionel* first had to worry about toy trains, then a *Charlie Brown* character called *Linus* and perhaps a racial suggestion from *Lionel Ritchie;* no wonder he's *Buck* now. *Buck* is usually a deliberately phoney name, as in *Buck Henry. Buck* (or *Bud,* etc.) clearly conceals the "real" name but makes light of doing so. You may have noticed that hardly anyone's called *Adolf* these days. Nor *Judas,* but Thomas Hardy and The Beatles both helped to make the name of the patron saint of lost causes, *Jude,* less of a lost cause itself.

No one can predict what history will bring to a name after you confer it. *James Earl Carter* was fine until *James Earl Ray* came along. I know a young woman who was happy with *Lee Bailey* until a certain lawyer gained prominence. "F— Lee Bailey," she says now. The least you can do is to do your best in the light of present knowledge and then, as Arnold Toynbee advised, hang on and hope.

4. Celebrated names do not always turn out to be cause for celebration. As it is usually not a great idea to name a baby after one of its great relatives, so it is seldom a wise move to name a baby after an illustrious person. The trend used to be more common (*George Washington Cable,* the brothers *Walt Whitman Rostow* and *Eugene Debs Rostow,* the near-miss *Ralph Waldo Ellison*). Why burden a child, as we have asked before, with someone else's identity? (Novelist Ellison's father had an answer: he wanted the boy to be a writer, like Ralph Waldo Emerson.) It's bad enough to be saddled with *William Wilberforce Wentworth, IV* (known to intimates as *Wobbly* because of his signature), but it is unfortunate to be given a stranger's name, one that may look incongruous (as when Socialist Debs' namesake grows up to be Arch-Conservative Rostow)! Moreover, some kinds of celebrity celebration (*Franklin Roosevelt Greer, Martin Luther King Junior Rodriguez, Tootsie Hoffman McClintock*) can date the grownup and provide perhaps unwanted clues to age or to such things as the parents' political opinions (*Hoby Thompson* is really *Ho Chi Minh Thompson,* as old as the early stages of the "conflict" or war in Vietnam). We seldom honor George Washington or Thomas Jefferson or the likes of Oliver Hazard Perry any more in the new names we bestow but we still have a bad habit of naming children for evanescent movie stars. That is where most of those women named *Gloria, Shirley, Linda,* and *Debbie* came from. We name for characters on daytime and nighttime soaps (we have already spoken of *Ashley, Alexis,* etc.) and even game shows (*Vanna*). There's not much guesswork involved in determining that someone named for Neil Armstrong was named in 1969, about the time of the moon landing. It is better than *Capsule* or *Module* or *Moon Unit* or such craziness, but still. . . . For girls, a datable name is worse, and will be just as bad into the next century unless agism disappears. I would not bank on society growing up and abandoning agism. In fact, I think the young are likely to turn against the old as this Republic staggers along, and when I get old enough to be a *senior citizen* I won't be surprised to be called a *senile citizen,* nor will I be alarmed (because we oldsters will have 75% of all the marbles, if not all our marbles personally, and money is protection and power).

The digression can help us put punch into this paragraph: name the old person as well as the young one—and ideally not for the even older.

5. Play the sex roles game. It might be wonderful if we, like some societies, jettisoned outmoded sexual stereotypes or at least did not encourage them with separate names for boys and girls, but to get along, go along: give boys and girls names society will accept in its masculine/feminine conventions. You don't have to go overboard with *Rocky, Brad, Bruno* (or *macho* names which to "outsiders" might appear to be feminine, like *Vinnie*). The kid might turn out to be wimpy, and then what? You certainly can sidestep *Reginald, Hubert, Percy,* and other names that were once *macho* but went from the warlords to the aristocracy to the ambitious lower middle class, where doting Mamas put the scions into little velvet suits with lace collars and gave them these fancy-schmancy names, or worse (*Algernon, Fauntleroy, Cadwallader, Murgatroyd*). Sure, the children may grow up and live them down. Sure, a father once named his son *Percy* so he would be tough: "Any boy named Percy is going to have to learn how to fight." Sure, you can overcome a name: Johnny Cash's song told the true story of Judge Sue K. Hicks of Madisonville (Tennessee), "a boy named Sue." Perhaps *Sue* even predisposed him to be a lawyer. But why handicap your child and then hope he will make *Venal, Delyte, Treat,* etc., acceptable? Not everyone can.

For girls, society wants you to avoid harsh-sounding names (*Hilda* and *Zelda*) and ditzy ones (*Dixie, Trixie, Bambi, Brandy*) and nicknames (*Taffy, Muffy, Corky*) and unfashionable flower names (*Pansy, Violet, Myrtle*) or coldly classical names (*Phoebe, Phyllis, Cassandra*) or just old-fashioned names (*Mildred, Maude, Matilda*) and even, among "better people" self-defined, the trashy-trendy (*Tiffany, Brittany, La Toya,* etc.). It also does not much approve of girls having boys' names (*Michael, Kyle, Glenn*) or, in most places, surnames as forenames (*Brooke, Blair, Peyton,* etc.). Society will defeat the move toward unisex names by dropping them for boys once it is clear that girls are being given them too (*Kelly, Robin, Murphy*). It may seem that society is more lenient as to what is acceptable as a girl's name than as a boy's. Reflection will show the opposite is true. The boy's forename, in fact, can reach for a wide variety of effects; the girl's name is almost always constrained to be "pretty" and very often "fashionable." If it were not for the convention that permits any surname as a male forename, it would be easy to say that there are many more first names for girls than for boys and that there is more variety but less seriousness exhibited in the naming of girls.

Keep in mind, however, that naming girls is more serious than naming boys. Realize that a female's forename is all she has that is hers in the name line as she goes through life. The male at least almost always retains his surname. The female changes her father's surname most often for her husband's. I say name girls with even more care than you take for boys, especially since we tend to put all our eggs in one basket and choose a single female forename, while boys often have several given names, often including the mother's "maiden name" as a middle name, to work with.

I see no reason why a girl ought not to be given as many names as a boy and, like him, use or not use them as she grows up. On top of that, a female name that permits of several established nicknames offers "more for your money" as you place your bets. Finally, *why* a diminutive?

6. Avoid sexually ambiguous names. This is worth a piece to itself although it has been said before in other connections. I know men named *Lee* and *Robin* and women nicknamed *Pat* and *Sam* (for *Samantha,* either from a movie or a TV series, I don't know which because I am not sure of her age). Despite this I still think sexually ambiguous names (*Leslie, Terry, Bobby*) are courting trouble.

In the film *Tron,* people are told, "You will each receive an identity disc," but society today does not always make them blue for boys and pink for girls. For some time now, America has been unisex in names as well as such things as certain clothes and hairstyles. In its 1959 edition, *Who's Who in American Women* (an unfortunate title in itself, when you think of it) made a notable gaffe in including male sports columnist *Shirley Povich. Shirley,* you know, was first a placename, then a surname, then a male forename, then a name in a Bronte novel for a girl who arrived when they wanted a boy, then the name of the cinema's darling (who was not, despite the joke to that effect, named for a synagogue in Shirley out on Long Island), then a much-given female forename, then old hat. Similar problems arise with placename-surname-male forename-female forename progressions such as *Beverly, Evelyn, Joyce.* Our observation that once a name is categorized as "feminine" it is no longer approved for males applies in all these cases, although I admit that this is not as true for Britain as it is for the US. Here confusions still arise from *Lynn, Kim, Randy* and some nicknames, especially preppie puppy names. Instead of a *Who's Who* we may in some circles need a *Who's What.*

For reasons having nothing to do with sexism, or the trends among yuppies, guppies (gay yuppies) *et al.,* I suggest steering clear of ambiguous names like *Dana, Courtney, Kerry,* even *Jamie.* I see what proud families are trying to do with surname-forenames for girls (*Byrd, MacKenzie,* even *Randolph*) but cannot applaud it. And I think female actors ("actresses" sounds sexist today) like *Michael Learned* and a descendant of Henry George who bears *George* as a forename but is female, and others, are giving some people the wrong idea (or, as our more inarticulate society puts it, "sending the wrong signal"). I think it foolish for Field Marshal Smuts' daughter to have been called *Louis* after her godfather (Louis Botha). I suggest that it is indicative of something unfortunate when my readers may not be able to guess the sex from such names of semi-celebrities as *Norris Church, Stockard Channing, Joey Heatherton, Sean Young, Morgan Fairchild, C. Z. Guest, Michael Strange,* and (as they say these days) "the list goes on."

Listen to what comedienne Joy (really Josephine) Behar says: "You have to be careful what you name your kids. You make them crazy." Could it be that calling the boy *Bonny* could make him grow up to be a *Bruce,* that unisex names actually precipitate sexual identity crises? What do you think?

Years ago one Bethany (dumb name except for a church!) wrote "Dear Abby" (smart woman!) and addressed the problem of men who get letters for (say) *Ms. Kelsie Harder* or women who get "male-oriented material" in the mail addressed to *Mr. Murphy O'Brien*. Bethany's *cri de coeur* was: don't "handicap a girl with a boy's name or a boy with a girl's name." It seems this lass with a dumb name had been baptized with an even dumber one for a little girl, *Peter*. She struggled with it until in her mid-teens she rebelled and changed it. "It's not fair," she wrote, adding (with a new twist on the automobile sales slogan of long ago), "Ask the person who owns one."

Please don't come and burn a bra on my lawn when you read this, but much as I can see the usefulness of *Ms.* and have been known to say *salesperson* (but resist *postperson,* etc.); much as I can understand why the Modern Language Association is trying to take sexism out of language (at the same time a sexist Affirmative Action for Women fills its conventions with Feminist Concerns and seems to want to replace Shakespeare with Alice Walker and *gender* for *genre* studies); nonetheless, I think ERA in this era should bring identifiable male names for males and identifiable female names for females. That women may take male names but males not women's names with impunity tells me there's something sexist at work right there.

7. Avoid hard-to-spell and "misspelled" names. Do you want your child to have to go through life spelling his or her name for people? That may help to make him or her an extrovert, but is perhaps even more likely to have a negative effect. People may in spite of all get it wrong, and you know how it makes you feel when people get your name wrong. You don't want your child to be regarded as illiterate ("can't spell their own name") or coming from backward parents. Thus, please, don't bestow a name like *Thom, Sheri, Diahanne, Shawn* or one of those startling show-biz confections (*Bever-Leigh, Jan'et, Tempestt, Stiv*) or teenage try-hard names (*Bobbye, Bretni, Kymber Lee,* etc.), or what some people are unkind enough to call "ghetto names" never before seen (by them) on land or sea and outraging whatever their ideas about othography may be. The farther a child will have to go to the top, the more a name that only friends in the know can spell correctly will hinder. People whose kids are born to the purple may be able to get way with difficult names and the unconventional. People who are ready to sacrifice anything to get their names up in lights may have the stamina to cope with *Barbra* (worse, *Barbera*) and such. Ordinary folks generally find extraordinary names more of a disadvantage than not, and names other folks resent as "misspelled" (actually we should think of them as brand new names) are handicaps. The handicapped—I believe "challenged" is the polite term this year, "crippled" can bring down wrath on anyone who dares to employ it—can and do succeed sometimes. We applaud their courage. I say don't ask for trouble and don't needlessly put your kid in an onomastic wheelchair and then say "Cope!"

Try the proposed new name on your friends and neighbors. If they cannot spell it the way you'd like, scrap it. Even if they can manage it, ask yourself if your child is never going to move out of the environment where people can spell it and like it. Better safe than sorry. How can one take a *Jheri* seriously? Not easily. Jeer at *Jere*.

8. Don't give too long a name. A baby is not to be regarded as a pizza on which you can put Everything. Most people need only one first name, one functioning middle name, and one last name. Only Royals need a string of forenames like *Albert Frederick Arthur George Andrew Patrick David* (to honor ancestors and patron saints of several countries). To name a person after another you need not repeat all of the other person's names: *Lyndon Smith* or *Johnson Smith* will do as well as *Lyndon Baines Johnson Smith*. Think of all those forms bureaucracy will present to your child for filling in "first name."

9. Beware of initial difficulties. Consider not only how the given names and the surname go together but also what initials they will have. Avoid *DOG, PIG, FAT, NUT, GAY,* and even *CIA* and *FBI* and *PCP*. Sir Arthur S. Sullivan hated his middle initial. Can you blame him? Just as you wouldn't call the boy *Dudley* for fear he'll be a *Dud*, don't call him (say) *Donald Ussher Davis,* either. There's nothing wrong with a spiffy monogram such as *SIR* or *TED* (especially for a *Theodore*), but don't strain for them. If you try for a special effect the result may not be so special. You cannot predict what may come along to render any particular set of initials fortunate or unfortunate. You can, however, make certain that as of the time of naming the initials of the names are not an invitation to mockery.

10. Avoid both the stale and the startling. Find a happy compromise between a trite name and one that tries too hard to be striking. Heed Alexander Pope's couplet:

> *Be not the first by whom the new is tried*
> *Nor yet the last to lay the old aside.*

If you've heard *Melissa* or *Jessica* too often lately, it is too late for you to give it as an unusual name. If you have never heard a name before and you find it in some book, ask yourself what the reason for its rarity may be. You don't want your child to be one of a dozen *Jennifer*s or *Jason*s in the kindergarten class; but, by the same token, it's hard for a child to be the only kid anyone has ever heard of with *Tima* or *Taura*. You may think your child is exceptional, but don't express that in terms of a strange name that attracts unwarranted and unwelcome attention, invites not just curiosity but ridicule, possibly labels the tot by association as an oddball. Where uncommon names are common, as among the Chinese or perhaps among the poorly educated here, a peculiar name is little problem. If you think the name you are giving is highly unusual where you are, avoid it. You want to raise a child, not eyebrows.

Seeking the unusual, perhaps you can revive a name that was popular in the US a century ago (*Emma, Alice, Florence,* or *Samuel, Warren, Clifford*). Or you may wish to adopt here a name currently more popular elsewhere in the English-speaking world (*Simon, Adam, Martin*). These names have a kind of refurbished freshness without sounding odd. Generally avoid "new" versions of older names such as *Shayla* (*Sheila*), *Renita* (*Renata*), *Terrance* (*Terence*), *Deshawn* (from *Séan*). Many people make fun of them.

Imagine a child calling for your kid, "Can _____ come out and play?" If it sounds crazy, drop the idea.

Very important is to be sure that when you reach for an unusual name you don't get the very same one that thousands of others with the same intention have found. You don't want to come up with a strange name that lots of other people have, because that way you lose on two counts, don't you? *Ashley* as a forename is bad; *Ashleigh* is worse; *Ash Lee* is worst.

11. Avoid trendy names. This is related to what I have just been saying. Soap-opera names (*Luke, Fallon,* etc.) and unusual names of actors (*Farrah, Dustin,* etc.) are the modern equivalents of the names once found in books and too much adopted in their day (*Rowena, Lorna, Ramona*). They are too trendy. It's time to retire *Jennifer,* and already late for *Jessica,* which recently dislodged it from the top of the list. But there is also too much use of *Nicole, Michelle, Stephanie,* the recent replacements for *Stacy, Tracy, Kimberly.* Go down the list a little, maybe to *Amy,* one of those names with a pleasant meaning. Always check the etymology of a name; some people may know it from reading the name books you and your spouse have been poring over. Etymology is no longer the main thing if indeed it ever was, but it needs to be considered along with everything else.

When in doubt, err on the side of conservatism. Pick the hardy perennial rather than the exotic bloom.

12. Consider how the name will sound and look in different situations. Try saying the name alone, in formal and informal sentences. Try whispering it lovingly. Think of how it will sound and look when said by a lover or publicly announced on ceremonial occasions. How will it look on a diploma or award certificate, in print, on a book cover, on a campaign poster, on an executive's stationery or office door?

Consider what others will do with it in distortions and nicknames. Be ingenious about this, because the kids in the playground will be very much so. Playground names can wound a child for life. Names that invite parody or disrespect can be very hard to live with.

"The real name of the little man was Harris," wrote Dickens in *The Old Curiosity Shop,* "but it had gradually merged into the less euphonious one of Trotters, which, with its prefatory adjective short, had been conferred upon him by reason of the small size of his legs." There's not much you can do to protect your loved one from that kind of naming, but you can defend him from having to come home from school to cry because *Dustin* has been unkindly turned into *Dustbin* or *Warren* has caused him to be known as *Rabbit.*

Apply these fundamental principles, thinking hard about the name's meaning and also about the associations it brings to mind, whether it is already established as a name or will elicit comment, how it fits with the surname and initials, whether it sounds good alone and in combination with other names, whether it duplicates or too closely approximates or just plays games with other names in the family, whether people will be able to spell it and pronounce it and accept it, and whether it will serve well as the name of an adult in any likely walk of life. A "good" name cannot guarantee a smooth passage for your son or daughter through the wide world. A well-chosen name, however, if luck is with you, can confer untold social and psychological benefits along the way.

Read all the name books you can get your hands on, remembering that (as Francis Bacon said) some books are only to be tasted, others to be digested. Most of these books will stress the word origin of the names or give you such information as "*Chandra* is the goddess of the moon in Hindu mythology." Always remember that the most important thing is not what the name is said to derive from but how it is taken by society, which says that *Ozwald* is "illiterate," *Elmo* is not as "lovable" as it once was, *Harvey* "a klutz," and so on.

Pay special attention not to Charlotte Yonge and other old name books or the encyclopedic volumes such as *The Oxford Dictionary of Christian Names* but to the recent compilations of baby names such as *Beyond Jennifer and Jason: An Enlightened Guide to Naming Your Baby* (1988) by Linda Rosenkrantz and Pamela Redmond Satran. If your taste runs to the avant-garde you can look at books such as Sue Browder's *The New Age Baby Name Book* in the 1987 edition. That purports to instruct you how to go about "choosing a name for the 21st century." Make lists of names that attract you. Narrow the list down to a few as a result of serious discussion. Then settle on one, or more, avoiding *Helene Elaine* and *Yvette Monette* and *Ellery Mallory* and such forename combinations.

Some books list as many as 6,000 names for the baby. I neither want to nor am able to give long lists here, but I can squeeze in 500 representative names you can mull over, including some I have warned against which may nevertheless appeal to your taste.

First, 125 old-fashioned girls' names, some few of which may be due for a comeback:

125 Old-Fashioned Girls' Names

Abigail	Clarissa	Florence	Lavinia	Muriel	Tamar
Adrienne	Constance	Frances	Letitia	Myra	Thelma
Agatha	Cynthia	Gabrielle	Lillian	Nicoletta	Tina
Agnes	Daphne	Genevieve	Lois	Noelle	Una
Alma	Delia	Gloria	Lola	Nora	Ursula
Amelia	Donna	Grace	Loretta	Odile	Valerie
Angelina	Dorothy	Gwyneth	Louisa	Patience	Velma
Anna	Edith	Harriet	Louise	Pauline	Venetia
Arabella	Eleanor	Hazel	Lucinda	Penelope	Vera
Beatrice	Eliza	Honoria	Lucy	Polly	Verity
Belle	Ella	Ida	Lydia	Priscilla	Veronica
Beryl	Eloise	Inez	Marcella	Regina	Victoria
Bessie	Elsie	Irene	Marian	Rhona	Viola
Betsy	Emma	Isabel	Marie	Rosalind	Virginia
Bettina	Emmaline	Joanne	Maud(e)	Rosamond	Wilma
Blanche	Enid	Johanna	Mavis	Sharon	Winifred
Bridget	Esther	Josephine	May	Sheila	Yvonne
Celia	Ethel	Julia	Miranda	Sophia	Zena
Charity	Eva	Juliet	Miriam	Sophie	Zenobia
Charlotte	Fern	Kitty	Moira	Stella	Zoë
Clara	Flora	Laurel	Molly	Tabitha	

Some of the old-fashioned girls' names (such as *Emily* and *Sara*) have already made a sort of comeback. Next, 125 girls' names, mostly of fairly recent vintage, that for one reason or another you probably ought to steer clear of. *Vicki,* for instance, has been described as "a name you'd see on a bracelet at Walgreen's." Just the process of deciding why all or almost all of these names won't do will teach you a lot about sensible name selection. Even if you don't like champagne, you can avoid wine coolers.

125 Girls' Names to Avoid Now

Adelaide	Candy	Ernestine	Imelda	Kiki	Melita
Andrea	Carrie	Fanny	Irma	Kim	Mellyn
Artemesia	Cheryl	Fiona	Jasmine	Lee	Merle
Ashley	Chloë	Gabby	Jemima	Lesbia	Missy
Audrey	Crystal	Gay	Jennifer	Lettice	Morgan
Avis	Dale	Gertrude	Jessica	Libra	Muffy
Babette	Dana	Gladys	Julie	Liza	Myfanwy
Bambi	Deirdra	Hayley	Kaity	Lola	Nellie
Belinda	Denyse	Heidi	Katrice	Luci	Nila
Bertha	Didi	Henrietta	Kay	Lynda	Nydra
Bonita	Edna	Hermione	Kelly	Lynn	Olga
Brenda	Elvira	Hilda	Kent	Mabel	Ophelia
Brittany	Enola	Ilene	Keziah	Matilda	Orchid

Oriel	Randi	Stacy	Tavia	Verna	Willie Mae
Orly	Rhoda	Stephanie	Tawana	Vicki	Wilma
Pansy	Robin	Sue Ellen	Tiffany	Violet	Yolanda
Poppy	Rula	Sybil	Toni	Virgo	Zilla
Prudence	Sadie	Tamika	Toya	Voneria	Zipporah
Queen(i)e	Sandi	Tammy	Tracy	Vonetta	Zita
Rae	Selma	Tanisha	Trisha	Wanda	Zsa Zsa
Ramona	Shannon	Tanya	Vanna	Wilhelmina	

Here are some old-fashioned boys' names. Most you will not want, but in these days when *Michael, David, Jason* are too common and *Matthew* is fading you might dare to bring one of these out of mothballs. See what you think. Most you won't like. Discussing why that is true may well help you to derive principles governing names you will like.

125 Old-Fashioned Boys' Names

Abraham	Carlos	Enoch	Herman	Lionel	Phineas
Aidan	Clement	Ernest	Hiram	Luke	Reginald
Albert	Clifford	Esmé	Homer	Malachy	Rex
Aldo	Conrad	Eugene	Horace	Manfred	Roland
Alfred	Cornelius	Ezra	Howard	Marion	Roy
Alva	Cyrus	Felix	Hubert	Matthias	Rupert
Alvin	Darcy	Ferdinand	Ira	Max	Seth
Ambrose	De Witt	Frank	Jasper	Mitchell	Sheridan
Amos	Dion	Frederick	Jeremiah	Montgomery	Stanley
Archibald	Duane	Gerard	Jerome	Morris	Thaddeus
Arnold	Duncan	Gershon	Jethro	Mortimer	Toby
Augustus	Dwight	Gilbert	Joachim	Moses	Tyrone
Basil	Earl	Godfrey	John	Nahum	Ulysses
Benjamin	Edgar	Graeme	Jonas	Nathan	Urban
Bertram	Edward	Gustav	King	Ned	Vernon
Blaise	Edwin	Guy	Lambert	Norman	Wallace
Boris	Elihu	Harold	Lemuel	Obadiah	Walter
Boyd	Elijah	Harvey	Leo	Oliver	Wilbur
Caleb	Elisha	Hector	Leopold	Oscar	Wilfred
Calvin	Ellis	Henry	Leroy	Oswald	Willard
Carleton	Emile	Herbert	Linus	Percival	

Finally, here are 125 other boys' names, a mix of old and contemporary but none too common, none too odd, perhaps therefore worth considering carefully. A *J* to replace *Jason?* Something better? Are we ready for a *K* trend? Many people think a *K* sounds "strong," but don't choose *Kyle, Kelly, Kerry, Kermit.*

What's in a Name?

125 Useful Boys' Names Not Too Over-Used

Aaron	Cameron	Eliot	Harry	Lewis	Ross
Adam	Carlos	Eric	Hilton	Liam	Russell
Adrian	Chad	Errol	Hugh	Lucas	Sebastian
Alan	Christian	Ethan	Ian	Luther	Shane
Alastair	Clark	Evan	Ivan	Lyle	Sheridan
Alexander	Clay	Fabian	Jackson	Malcolm	Simon
Amory	Clinton	Franco	Jared	Martin	Spencer
Angus	Colin	Franklin	Jarrett	Miles	Terence
Anthony	Conor	Gareth	Jeremy	Nathaniel	Timothy
Arthur	Corey	Gary	Joel	Nelson	Todd
Aubrey	Craig	Gavin	Jordan	Nicholas	Trevor
Barnaby	Curtis	Geoffrey	Joshua	Nigel	Troy
Bart	Damian	Giles	Julian	Norris	Valentine
Benedict	Damon	Glenn	Justin	Owen	Vincent
Bennett	Derek	Gordon	Karl	Patrick	Wade
Blair	Dermot	Graham	Keith	Perry	Warren
Bradley	Dirk	Grant	Kenneth	Philip	Wilson
Brendan	Donovan	Gregory	Kent	Quentin	Winston
Brett	Douglas	Hamilton	Kirk	Randall	Wyatt
Burt	Drew	Hardy	Lance	Randolph	Zachary
Byron	Edmund	Harlan	Lawrence	Raymond	

For charts of name popularity, see British expert Leslie A. Dunkling's *First Names First* and his *Guinness Book of Names*. The US has such experts as Cleveland Evans. Just to show you that all around the world names come into and go out of fashion, let me compare Norway in 1900 and 1980. In 1900 Norwegian boys were called *Olav, Ole, Johan, Karl, Hans, Kristian, Einar, Nils, Harald,* and *Peder.* Eighty years later the top boys' names were *Jan, Rune, Geir, Bjørn, Morten, Tomas, Jon, Lars, Frode,* and *Trond.* In 1900 Norwegian girls were most likely to get *Anna, Marie, Ingeborg, Olga, Marta, Borghild, Margit, Astrid, Jenny,* or *Gudrun.* In 1980 it was *Anne, Monika, Helge, Hilde, Nina, Anita, Linda, Marianne, Heidi,* and *Kristin.*

To see how names come and go here, compare the Top 10 where you are now with New York in 1948:

Boys		Girls	
John	Edward	Linda	Kathleen
James	Robert	Mary	Carol
Michael	Thomas	Barbara	Nancy
William	George	Patricia	Margaret
Richard	Louis	Susan	Diane

Today almost everywhere in the US *John* and *Mary* (*Mary* was just beginning to slip about 40 years ago) have dropped out of the Top 10. In fact, the New York Top 10 of 1948 for girls is completely replaced.

25. The Subjective Factor in Naming

C ritically important as, obviously, I consider a name to be, I cannot claim to have reduced any kind of name choice to hard and fast rules. Like literary onomastic interpretation, name choice in the first place cannot be a science, nor does it have that distinction on the basis of any repeatable experiments without exception. The same name can work out differently in different circumstances, defeating rigid expectations of omen names and numerology and all other purported predictors.

What we have here is the psychological, not the logical, but in psychology there are such things as self-fulfilling prophecies. Incontrovertibly, certain names, it can be demonstrated, put the bearers more than you might expect at the mercy of the biases and prejudices of the societies in which they live. These biases make a name "good" or "bad," "better" or "worse," most of the time.

For all the pointers I give you, for all the care you may take, choosing a name is ultimately not an exact science; it involves (as the Spanish say) "waves," and as we would say "vibrations," subjective judgments. However, a consensus has emerged over the years as to which names are desirable and which are not, an agreement no less real for its capacity for change. Aware of this, most parents will now avoid giving a child a name such as *Horace* or *Henrietta*. Most people have a vague sense of the "in" and "out" names at any given time, whether they have read reports such as Dunkling's or not. Those reports (based largely on newspaper announcements of births, which omit some classes of society) or, say, the results reported in Sewart's *American Given Names* (too limited to certain college alumni lists, perhaps thereby even more distorted), may or may not be totally reliable, but they surely can supplement what ordinary people ordinarily know. Most people pick up as it were by osmosis valuable information about historical trends. They likewise acquire, often without realizing how irrational these feelings can be, more or less unsupported but often strongly held opinions about the "feel" of this name or that.

People will tell you *Tammy* is less serious than *Barbara,* younger than *Gloria.* They think of a *Priscilla* as prim, *Lydia* as far less cultured than did the Greeks who invented the given name, *Stephen* more sophisticated than *Earl, Jeff* more likely to be a jock than *Howard, Marvin* more likely to be a nerd than *Michael, Jessica* to come from a lower class than *Elspeth* but to be less snooty than *Fiona.* A psychologist in Atlanta (Georgia) discovered that boys with his own first name (*Samuel*) were not as well respected in school as were *James, John, Craig, Gregory,* or *Richard.* His research showed that Atlanta kids assumed that *Curtis, Daryl,* and *Jerome* would be less intelligent than *Richard, Thomas,* and *Patrick.* Teachers, too, assumed that some names promised more intelligence than others. I find that a troublesome revelation in a world where expectations go a long way toward determining results. Call your kid *Bambi* or *Tabitha* (graceful as a gazelle) and you may be predisposing even the brightest teachers to think of her as sweet but sappy. Call your boy *Herman, Floyd, Jermaine, Tyrone, Oswaldo* and how do you think he will be perceived? By naming your daughter *Agnes* or *Mabel* you may not be condemning her to a life of spinsterhood but you certainly are not preparing her for blind dates in the way that you would if you called her *Kelly* or *Melissa.* Names in the past used often to be handed down like christening spoons in families. Today we all have more freedom. We must all be more responsible in our choices and weigh what "conventional wisdom" (often known to be misguided) has to say about various names.

No one has ever produced statistical evidence to prove that *Mabels* are generally homely or that *Homer* is not likely to get to first base. Some names, true, sound in such a way as to produce knee-jerk reactions (*Gertrude, Lulu, Zelda, Clyde, Claud, Cornelius,* quite apart from suggesting *Corny* and other nicknames). Literature and history have contributed the aura of a name like *Dora* or added "the Terrible" to every *Ivan.* But why *Wallace* and *Wanda* or *Sheldon* or *Leon* have the reputations they do is farther to seek. I have never seen any adequate explanation of why *Bruce* (selected as *macho* by cartoonists creating "Batman" Bruce Wayne and "The Hulk" Bruce Banner, the name now being an embarrassment) came to be tantamount to *gay.* It is easier to see how *Thelma* got to be synonymous with "frump" (as a fairly recent president's wife, known as *Pat,* but really a *Thelma,* seemed to understand). *Bertha* is "fat" because in World War I the huge cannon that Krupp (whose wife's name was said to be Bertha) manufactured to bombard Paris from 25 miles away was nicknamed *Big Bertha* by the Allies. *Bella* suggested "bellicose" before Bella Abzug came on the scene, though public personalities can do much to change the "color" of a name they bear. Recall what Humphrey Bogart did for *Humphrey* or President Eisenhower for *Ike,* at least for themselves. Some "loser" names have their bad qualities reinforced when sit-com writers use them: *Oscar, Sidney, Laverne, Archie, Ethel, Ralph.* Slang makes some ordinary names awkward: *Peter, Dick, Willie, John Thomas* (the latter in the UK mostly, along with a special meaning for *Roger, Charlie, Joey,* etc.), not to mention *Sheila* in Australia or *Mac* in Québec. How, even before "The Flint-stones," did *Fred* get its bouquet? It undoubtedly has one. The proof is in the fact that 7,000 Freds across the US have banded together for support and pro-tection in a Fred Society. There on TV with *Fred* went *Wilma* and *Barney.* Why? Hillbilly names (*Jethro, Earl, Jim Bob*) and dowdy names (*Maisie, Mil-dred, Mae*) and lots of other kinds of names have gone stale. The Brits would say they have "gone off."

George is a classic example of a name that is still around but much divested of former glory. George III did not help it for us (despite George Washington's contribution) nor George Pullman (who gave his forename to all Pullman porters). The fate of *George* was altered for the worse way back when a king of France said "Let George do it." The deterioration set in. The knight in shining armor combatting the dragon degenerated into the unsuccessful hus-band in *Hedda Gabler* and *Who's Afraid of Virginia Woolf?* In 1875 (we are told) *George* was sixth in the US name parade, seventh in 1900 and 1925, twenty-eighth in 1950, pretty much out of sight by 1980. It is possible that a president or other prominent person may give it a new lease on life outside the Greek community and the Russians who Americanize from *Georgi.* At the same time it is more likely to be used by writers of fiction in a negative way and continue to be the modern equivalent of *Caspar* (as in *Caspar Milquetoast*), wimpy. (*Caspar* produced *Jasper,* the villain of melodrama, not wimpy.)

This can convince people who never met a wimp named George. Note that you have reactions to *Louie, Al, Ricco, Egbert, Chico* though you may never have met anyone with these names. Some experts say we must blame television and the movies. Partly true, but that ignores the fact that these names are used as they are on the big and small screens just because they already are shorthand for stereotypes. Where did the stereotypes come from in the first place? Polls of children who have never met, sometimes never heard of, a *Sharon* or a *Mandy,* a *Giles* or a *Dominic,* still know exactly what the names "mean" to them, and they will tell you *Sally* is a social climber, *Lois* is a pushover but pretty, *Bernard* is a bookworm, *Mitzi* is a flake, *Richard* is better looking than *Hugh* but both are more handsome than any *Kenneth* or *Jamal* (both of which names are said to mean "handsome").

Rodney, Arnold, Ginger, Martha keep their general "feel" for us despite our personal experience of people with those names. So the Top 10 names in each category express preference and command respect. The names in an Atlanta survey, where students expressed approval of names not elsewhere so highly ranked, such as *Susan, Linda, Carol,* and *Cindy,* are interesting. These names that Atlanta liked then, it must be stressed, might not be scored as "smart" names in some other city or at the present time. After more than a quarter century of college teaching I can assure you that my personal experience has been that no *Carol* or *Cindy* ever impressed me as a prodigy. Very few named *Susan* and fewer named *Linda* were near the top of their classes.

Pursuing that line of thinking any further would serve little purpose and perhaps elicit hate mail. Blame Public Opinion; it has the last word on the meaning of names—*Philip* telegraphs not Greek "lover of horses" to us now but elegance, and he's taller and thinner than *Max*—and the reasons for that must be admitted to be most often rather obscure or completely inscrutable. The explanation lies in a complex tissue of historical and literary precedent, the sounds of the language, ideas of ethnic behavior and physical appearance, and more. It's at least as hard to explain as why red on the cover of a book or the label of any other product sells better, not just in China (where it signals "happiness" rather than "stop") but here.

Suppose we have names that society doesn't like. Must we defy criticism, must we play the script, are we tied to inevitable outcomes? No. We can give in and change our names, or we can improve *Harold* into either *Harry* or *Hal,* strengthen *Henry* into *Hank,* soften *Edith* into *Edie,* or insist on *Gene, Rod, Arnie, Fran, Mel, Abby,* etc. We can hide names (often middle names too fancy for daily use) under initials if we don't want to discard them altogether. Or we can take the stance that our names are not peculiar, just singular, however strange; that we are the only X you know and thereby claim distinction; that we can redefine what X means to you by the power of our personalities; that we can beat the odds and win the game, whether with syrupy *Ronald* or *Arnold* with muscles or shun-the-limelight *Geraldine* (which is not to say it still didn't turn out to be the name of one of the biggest losers in the history of US politics) or *Ollie* (where the image of skinny little Oliver Twist and big, fat Oliver Hardy and snotty Oliver of *Love Story* present not inconsiderable obstacles). In fact, as soon as an *Oliver* becomes an *Ollie* it's clear that his popularity is rising. It may be that there is no name, however wallflower, however wimpy, however lacking in cachet or loaded with cacophony, that someone cannot rescue.

Having such a name may crush some people while it spurs others to gallant action. With three "loser" names in a row, *Hubert Horatio Humphrey* for one example, some people get to the top. *Sidney Sheldon* combines two. Frankly, *Lee Harvey Oswald* was too much to beat. If you work hard enough, or if you live long enough, you may see *Clarence* and *Rosanna,* or some names similar, win out over *Jason* and *Jessica* or *John* (hanging in there despite slang meanings) and *Jane* (recovering lately from the Plain Jane syndrome).

I once concluded a book on military history by refusing to prognosticate. I wrote that if in writing history you guess right no one remembers and if you guess wrong no one will forget. I shall not conclude this book here by trying to tell you what names will be "in" even by the time it is published. Who could have predicted that *Sara, Max, Emma,* consigned to the reject heap years ago, would be rediscovered as treasures? Even if I were to say that, if in doubt, you should opt for (say) *James* and *Elizabeth* as good but not too common names, if enough of my readers took my advice that advice would turn out to be wrong.

I conclude with advising you only to name with care, name for life, name in the light of whatever illumination this modest book, so curt and frank and earnest (those are adjectives, not names), has been able to shed on the problems of all sorts of naming. I hope to have made you more aware of names in all walks of life, in personal affairs and in the world around you. I hope to have brought to you, insofar as a book of this size can do that, some appreciation of the inexhaustible complexity and charm of considering

what's in a name.